1 MONTH OF FREE READING

at
www.ForgottenBooks.com

By purchasing this book you are eligible for one month membership to ForgottenBooks.com, giving you unlimited access to our entire collection of over 1,000,000 titles via our web site and mobile apps.

To claim your free month visit:
www.forgottenbooks.com/free638614

* Offer is valid for 45 days from date of purchase. Terms and conditions apply.

ISBN 978-0-656-23971-9
PIBN 10638614

This book is a reproduction of an important historical work. Forgotten Books uses state-of-the-art technology to digitally reconstruct the work, preserving the original format whilst repairing imperfections present in the aged copy. In rare cases, an imperfection in the original, such as a blemish or missing page, may be replicated in our edition. We do, however, repair the vast majority of imperfections successfully; any imperfections that remain are intentionally left to preserve the state of such historical works.

Forgotten Books is a registered trademark of FB &c Ltd.
Copyright © 2018 FB &c Ltd.
FB &c Ltd, Dalton House, 60 Windsor Avenue, London, SW19 2RR.
Company number 08720141. Registered in England and Wales.

For support please visit www.forgottenbooks.com

THE ENGLISH FACTORIES
IN INDIA
1642–1645

A CALENDAR OF DOCUMENTS IN THE
INDIA OFFICE, WESTMINSTER

BY

WILLIAM FOSTER, C.I.E.

EDITOR OF 'LETTERS RECEIVED BY THE EAST INDIA COMPANY, 1615–17'
'THE EMBASSY OF SIR THOMAS ROE TO THE GREAT MOGUL', ETC.

PUBLISHED UNDER THE PATRONAGE OF HIS MAJESTY'S
SECRETARY OF STATE FOR INDIA IN COUNCIL

OXFORD
AT THE CLARENDON PRESS
1913

OXFORD UNIVERSITY PRESS
LONDON EDINBURGH GLASGOW NEW YORK
TORONTO MELBOURNE BOMBAY
HUMPHREY MILFORD M.A.
PUBLISHER TO THE UNIVERSITY

PREFACE

The documents here dealt with number one hundred and fifty-seven, and they are spread fairly evenly over the four years comprised in the present volume. Except for one letter on p. 183 (of slight importance), which comes from the *Egerton MSS.* at the British Museum, they are all drawn from the India Office archives. Neither the Public Record Office at home nor any of the Indian Record Offices has been able to contribute to the collection.

The period synchronizes roughly with the first phase of the Civil War in England, from the raising of the royal standard at Nottingham in August, 1642, to the battle of Naseby in June, 1645; and the consequent difficulty with which the East India Company's operations were carried on at home of course affected to some extent the proceedings of their servants in the East. Yet on the whole the embarrassment caused to the latter was smaller than might have been expected. Each year ships arrived from England, though with reduced cargoes, and each year one or more went back; and the most startling effect of the war on the Company's trade was the loss of the *John*, which in 1644 was betrayed to the royalists by her commander. In India itself the factors, though much hampered by debt and the lack of sufficient supplies from home, managed to keep going the trade with Mokha, Basrā, Gombroon, Achin,

Bantam, and other places; while in addition they dispatched ships from Surat to Macao and Manilla—the latter a pioneer venture which met with less success than it deserved. On the Coromandel Coast and in Bengal English commerce was making little headway; but this was largely due to the disturbed state of the Vijayanagar kingdom, now tottering to its fall.

The frontispiece consists of a map of the Malabar and Coromandel Coasts at this period, intended to supplement the map of Northern India given in the first volume of the present series (1618–21).

The index has been compiled by Mr. H. G. Bull, of the Record Department of the India Office.

INTRODUCTION

THE position of English commerce in the East at the beginning of 1642 went far to justify the pessimistic tone of most of the letters of that time here printed. From every factory came complaints of financial embarrassments. Alike at Bantam, Fort St. George, and Surat, the English merchants were deeply in debt, while the heavy interest—amounting in the case of Bantam to 4 or 5 per cent. per month (p. 34)—and current expenses were draining away what little cash they were able to procure. Both in the sale of their wares and in the purchase of Eastern products they had to face a formidable competition on the part of the Dutch, who were far better equipped both with goods and funds. The recent extension of the Company's sphere of action to Bengal, Sind, and Basrā had not produced results answering to the sanguine anticipations of the promoters. Sind, it is true, seems to have yielded a fair return both in indigo and calico; but Basrā had proved disappointing (p. 23), while Bengal had swallowed up large sums and returned little or nothing. Every letter to England implored a supply of money; but money the Company was finding it increasingly difficult to procure. The threatening aspect of public affairs at home had much to do with this; so had the competition of the group of interlopers known as Courteen's Association. An attempt to raise a Fourth Joint Stock in the spring of 1640 had failed miserably; and it was only with difficulty that in the autumn of the following year a sum of about 105,000*l.* (p. 41) was got together for the purpose of a (First) 'General Voyage', i.e. a venture for one year only. With this money the *Hopewell* was equipped and dispatched to the Coromandel Coast at the end of 1641, with a stock of over 17,000*l.*: the *Blessing* was sent to Bantam: and the *Crispiana* and *Aleppo Merchant* (the latter a hired vessel) to Surat with nearly 60,000*l.* (p. 61).

At the last-named settlement President Fremlen and his Council managed, with the help of a further loan from a wealthy Hindu merchant, Vīrjī Vōra, to fill the *London* with calico, sugar, cotton yarn, cinnamon, &c., and dispatched her to England at the close of January, 1642. A few days later the *Swan*, which had arrived from Bantam in the previous November, started on her return voyage to that port; and on her way she called at Goa to land two factors, who were to be stationed there to prevent the intrusion of Courteen's merchants. In the middle of February two pinnaces, the *Seahorse* and the *Prosperous*, left Swally for Gombroon, whence the *Prosperous* continued her voyage for Basrā; while a little later the *Supply* followed them to Persia with freight goods, arriving at Gombroon on March 19. Their calicoes were disposed of without difficulty and at a good profit, as the depredations of the Malabar pirates had deterred many of the Indian junks from venturing to that port; but the customs revenue (and consequently the English share of it) suffered in proportion (p. 32). In addition, the *Discovery* and a small pinnace named the *Francis* were dispeeded by the President and Council to the Red Sea, partly to trade, partly to guard the Indian junks against piratical attacks,[1] and partly to capture Malabar rovers. The *Francis* sailed on February 5, arrived at Mokha about a month later, left again for Gombroon on July 12, and finally reached Swally, in company with the *Seahorse* and *Prosperous*, at the end of October. The *Discovery* did not make a start until March 12, and consequently did not reach Mokha till April 13. The markets proved so bad that Wylde, the merchant in charge, decided to remain there to sell the goods at leisure. The vessel therefore sailed without him on August 22. She was much delayed by bad weather, with the result that she did not get to Swally until the last day of October. The English merchants were very glad to see her back, for sinister rumours were circulating in the Surat bazaars that, finding a large amount of treasure on board belonging to native merchants, the crew had carried her off to England (pp. 92, 144).

The Company's servants at Basrā wrote home in September an interesting letter (p. 57) describing their experiences of that city as a place of trade. They had been extremely well treated; but there

---

[1] The importance of the trade between Surat and Mokha is well shown by the fact, mentioned on p. 17, that the junks returning from the latter port in the autumn of 1641 brought upwards of 1,700,000 rials of eight.

INTRODUCTION

was small demand for their broadcloth or indeed for any other goods 'in these barren tymes'. They had, however, realized nearly 18,000*l.*, and were now about to return to India in the *Seahorse* and *Prosperous*. These two vessels reached Swally on October 29, and the former was then sent to examine the island of Salbet, off the coast of Kāthiāwār (p. 93).

The two ships from England, viz. the *Crispiana* and the *Aleppo Merchant*, anchored at Swally on September 21, 1642. On board the former was Edward Knipe, an old servant of the Company, who had returned to his allegiance after spending some time in the service of Courteen. He had now been engaged as a special factor for this voyage, and was to go back to England in whichever ship should be the last to leave. No time was lost at Surat in dispatching him with the *Aleppo Merchant* to Goa and Cochin, to sell broadcloth, lead, and coral, and to procure cinnamon, cardamoms, and pepper. He was also to fetch away from the former place the two factors (Pitt and Hill) who had been left there by the *Swan* early in the year. Knipe sailed on October 13, and ten days later his ship anchored in Goa Road, where he found a Dutch blockading squadron under Jan Dirksz. Galen. The latter was already much annoyed because Courteen's ship the *Hester* had slipped into Goa and sold sulphur to the Viceroy, while the *Swan*[1], which (as he alleged) had been permitted to go into the port under promise not to trade there, had nevertheless embarked a quantity of cinnamon. After some dispute, however, he permitted Knipe to send into Goa for the English factors and any merchandise they might have in hand. This done, the *Aleppo Merchant* sailed again on the last day of October, and after visiting Calicut and Ponnāni, anchored off Cochin on November 8. There Knipe sold most of his goods and obtained a quantity of cinnamon at cheap rates. Returning, he bought some pepper and cardamoms at Calicut, paid a pioneer visit to Basrūr (p. 109), and got back to Swally three days before Christmas.

The *Crispiana* and *Aleppo Merchant* left Swally on their homeward voyage about the middle of January, 1643, carrying a letter which contained, among other items of interest, the news that Shāh

[1] On her return voyage from Bantam to Surat. She reached the latter port on November 9, 1642 (p. 94).

Safī of Persia was dead and had been succeeded by a boy of ten, under the title of Shāh Abbās II (p. 83). At the end of the month the *Discovery* and *Supply* were dispatched to Gombroon, whence the former was to continue her voyage to Mokha while the latter returned to Surat. In the meantime the *Francis* was sent direct to the Red Sea in March, with a few freight goods and some stores for the *Discovery*. The *Seahorse* sailed for Gombroon and Basrā towards the end of the same month, and returned in November with an encouraging report. The *Francis* got back from Mokha in September, and the *Discovery* (by way of Cochin) at the beginning of November. John Wylde, the factor in charge, had died at Mokha in October, 1642, and thereupon some English goods, which Cranmer had been sent to sell at Jiddah, were seized and were only released on payment of a considerable sum. The Governor of Mokha promised to obtain restitution; but nothing resulted, and the English were forced to leave with their grievances unredressed (p. 161).

Knipe's success in selling coral, &c. on the Malabar Coast encouraged the President and Council at Surat to send a further quantity in that direction under the charge of Thurston and Pynn, who were landed at Cochin by the *Swan*, which sailed from Swally, bound for Bantam, on February 25, 1643. The factors found that the country was in a disturbed state, owing to wars between the Portuguese and a neighbouring Rājā; but they managed to secure a quantity of pepper, with which they returned to Surat in the *Discovery*.

In April, 1643, the Surat factors sent the *Supply* to Achin, laden chiefly with freight goods belonging to Indian merchants. The venture was not entirely successful, owing to the hold the Dutch had upon the trade; but the prospects appeared sufficiently encouraging to warrant a factory being established there under Maximilian Bowman. On her way back the *Supply* secured a quantity of cinnamon at Cochin, with which she returned to Swally in the middle of December.

In the autumn of 1642 the East India Company had succeeded in starting a Fourth Joint Stock, with a capital which was ultimately made up to 105,000*l.*; and had prepared for the East a fleet consisting of the *Dolphin*, *Hind*, and *Seaflower*—all for Surat—and the

INTRODUCTION

Hart for the Coast. In addition, the *Mary* was sent out to Bantam on account both of the First General Voyage and of the new Joint Stock. These ships sailed in the spring of 1643. The *Dolphin* and *Hind* reached Swally on September 18; while the *Seaflower*, which had called on her way at Mozambique and Bombay, did not arrive until ten days later. On November 10 the *Dolphin* was sent to Rājāpur and Goa, returning just before Christmas; and in the meantime the *Hind* made a voyage to Sind to fetch certain goods which were there awaiting shipment, while the *Seaflower* went to Gombroon for a like purpose. On her return she was dispatched to Bantam (April 20, 1644).

The pepper brought from Achin by the *Supply*, together with a quantity received by the *Expedition* from Bantam in November, and the usual investments in India itself, enabled the President and Council to dispeed the *Dolphin* and *Discovery* for England on January 29, 1644, with good cargoes. On the former vessel William Fremlen embarked, having made over his post as President to Francis Breton. The voyage proved a disastrous one. Want of water forced the two vessels to make for Mauritius, and on their way they encountered a fearful storm. The *Discovery* was never heard of again, and presumably went down with all hands.[1] The *Dolphin* narrowly escaped the same fate; but by cutting away her mainmast and bailing incessantly her crew managed to keep her afloat and get her to Mauritius (April 6). There they found the *Hopewell*, homeward bound from Bantam; she too had suffered much from the winds and waves, and the repair of the two ships, in which the Dutch settlers lent a helping hand, took until June 22, when they sailed in company for Madagascar and the Comoros. At the latter islands they were joined by the *Crispiana* from England; and, as it was judged unsafe for the *Dolphin* and *Hopewell* to attempt the voyage home in their crazy condition, all three sailed for Surat on August 17, and anchored there a month later. Fremlen had now to spend three months in India before making

---

[1] The loss thus occasioned was variously stated at 46,000*l.* (*Court Minutes*, 1644-49, p. 96), 30,000*l.* (*Ibid.*, p. 163), and about 52,000*l.* (Sambrooke's report on the East India trade, in *Home Miscellaneous*, vol. xl.). As the value of the cargoes of both vessels was only about 46,000*l.* (p. 159), the second figure (allowing for the ship and stores) seems nearest the mark.

a fresh attempt to reach his native land; and his anomalous position as ex-President raised some awkward questions at home as to the pay which he was entitled to draw for this period.

One of the latest events of Fremlen's administration was the dispatch of presents to Agra for the Emperor and his sons. A Dutch mission to court in 1642 had resulted in a favourable settlement of the question of the rating for customs purposes of goods exported by them. The calculation of exact values in such cases left an opening for extortion of which the officials were not slow to avail themselves; and it was an obvious advantage to have a definite scale laid down, based upon the actual cost of the goods, plus certain allowances supposed to represent the expense of getting them to the coast. Naturally, the English were eager to obtain a similar concession; and a change of Governors at Surat, which occurred in December, 1643, offered a suitable opportunity, as the late Governor, Jam Qulī Beg, was going to court and had promised his active assistance. Letters were therefore written to Shāh Jahān and his son Dārā Shikoh; and with these were sent handsome presents for both and for Prince Murād Bakhsh, the cost of which amounted to about 9,000 rupees, or rather over 1,000*l.* (p. 160). The actual negotiations were left to John Turner and the other factors at Agra, who were to enlist the help of Islām Khān, the then Wazīr. The results were eminently satisfactory. The presents produced a very favourable impression (p. 162), and the Emperor issued a *farmān* complying with the wishes of the English in the matter of the rating of their goods (p. 214). In addition he sent to the President a jewelled dagger (p. 230); while his son, Dārā Shikoh, forwarded a valuable jewel, and granted several *nishāns* to facilitate English trade in Sind (p. 215).

Breton's accession to the post of President was signalized by a decision to extend the area of English operations by dispatching two vessels to Macao and Manilla respectively. In the case of the former, the concurrence of the Viceroy of Goa was necessary, but this was readily forthcoming. The *Hind* was designated for the employment, and, warned by the fate of Courteen's *Bona Speranza* (p. xx), it was determined that no Portuguese goods should be carried, lest the Dutch should be given a pretext for interfering. Thurston was placed in charge of the venture, with three assistants

INTRODUCTION

(p. 165). The venture to Manilla was prompted by the hope of profiting by the rupture which had taken place between the Portuguese and the Spaniards, and the consequent cessation of the usual trade between the Philippines and Macao; and the instigator of the attempt was a Portuguese half-caste named De Brito, who had lived for some years at Manilla. The *Seahorse* was therefore fitted with a cargo, consisting largely of piece-goods, and Edward Pearce, Thomas Breton (brother of the President), and two other factors, accompanied by De Brito, were entrusted with the management of the enterprise. She sailed in the middle of February, 1644; and was followed by the *Hind* on April 26. The two met at Goa and proceeded on their voyage together, accompanied for part of the way by the *Supply*, which was bound for Achin. Soon after starting they overhauled a Malabar junk, but her crew baulked them of their prey by running the vessel ashore.

It had been intended to send a fresh consignment of goods to Mokha by the Dutch *Valkenburg*, which was preparing for a voyage to that port; and the proceeds were to be fetched away at the end of the season by the *Supply* and *Francis*, these vessels spending the interim in endeavouring to capture Malabar traders at the entrance of the Straits. But at the last moment the Dutch declined to accept any freight goods, as their ship had enough lading of her own; and the consignment was therefore put aboard an Indian junk, the *Salāmatī*, which sailed at the end of March, 1644. The result was anything but satisfactory; for, after battling for seventy days against contrary winds, the junk was forced to abandon the voyage and make for Gombroon, where she arrived on June 5. The goods on board were forwarded to Basrā for sale (p. 266).

At the end of March, likewise, the *Francis* and a small pinnace were dispatched to Basrā, carrying Robert Cranmer and two other Englishmen. They reached their destination on June 23. The place fully maintained its reputation of being a more profitable mart than either Mokha or Gombroon (p. 208); and when, in the middle of January, 1645, the factors returned in the *Francis* to Surat, they brought with them a handsome sum of money as the proceeds of the season's sales (p. 248).

Spiller, the head of the Tatta factory, spent the whole of the rainy season of 1644 in the upper districts of Sind, investigating the conditions of production and seeking for suitable places as centres for the purchase of indigo and calico. He reported that the latter was rapidly deteriorating in quality, owing to the great demand that had arisen for it of late years. As regards the former, he found that 'the people are so exceedingly opprest and kept so miserably poor that, notwithstanding the soil is fertile and propper and would produce large quantities of good indicoes, they have neither will nor means to manure and sow the ground'; and the competition of the local dyers for the small quantity produced (p. 203) made it unprofitable for the English to buy there during that season, though it was determined to make a renewed attempt the following year.

In England the Company, notwithstanding the general dislocation of trade produced by the Civil War, had succeeded in dispatching five ships to the East, viz. the *Endeavour* (a pinnace specially built for service in Indian waters) to the Coromandel Coast, the *William* and *Blessing* to Bantam, and the *Crispiana* and *John* to Surat. All these were the Company's own vessels, it having been found by experience that it was cheaper to build than to hire (p. 173). The three last-named left the Downs early in April, 1644, and proceeded for some time in company. Then the *Loyalty*, one of Courteen's ships, was encountered, bound for Mozambique and the Malabar Coast. The Company had arranged that the *John*, which, being a new ship, was an excellent sailer, should visit both places on her way to Surat, while the *Crispiana* was to go straight to the latter port; it was therefore agreed that, in order to anticipate the *Loyalty*, the *John* should leave the other two behind and make for Mozambique as rapidly as possible, rejoining the *Crispiana* at Johanna (one of the Comoro Islands). The separation took place on May 22. During the tedious weeks that followed there was much friction between the principal men on board the *John*. Mucknell, the master, was a man of violent temper and much addicted to drink; like most of the Company's sea commanders he had risen from the ranks, and he was inclined to be conceited and jealous of interference. Edward Knipe, the chief factor, soon aroused Mucknell's resentment by urging the other officers of the ship to remonstrate with him on his dissolute behaviour; and their relations were not improved when Knipe

INTRODUCTION xiii

dropped hints that he might be obliged to ask, on reaching India, that Mucknell should be deprived of his post. Henry Garry[1], the second factor, who had grievances of his own against Knipe, was accused afterwards of fomenting the discord between the other two by sympathizing with Mucknell; but this does not appear to have been a serious element in the quarrel. Mozambique was reached on August 11, and quitted ten days later. While there, Knipe arranged to provide passages for a Portuguese official, with his wife and a large suite; and this, though it brought some personal profit to the master, was magnified by him into a fresh grievance. The ship was now speeding towards Johanna, where the *Crispiana*—and possibly others of the Company's vessels—would be found; and Mucknell was manifestly ill at ease regarding Knipe's intentions towards him. The factors, on their side, suspected the master of scheming to miss the island; and they accordingly sent him a written order to put in there without fail—a step which roused him to fury, and confirmed him in his half-formed resolution of running away with the ship if the opportunity occurred. He afterwards boasted that he had intended to do this from the first. He had personally suffered at the hands of the Parliamentary Government (pp. 199, 262), and the idea of carrying over his fine new vessel to the royalist side was an attractive one. In his maudlin moments he may have dreamed of being knighted by the King (p. 265), and in any case he might count upon being handsomely rewarded for his daring action. But, vehement as he was, he was evidently somewhat irresolute in character; and in all probability he would not have ventured upon so risky a step had he not been goaded to it by his fear of losing his post as the result of Knipe's intended complaints. Even now, he put off all action for the present and obediently anchored his vessel at Johanna on August 25.

The fact that the *Crispiana* had already quitted the rendezvous favoured the carrying out of Mucknell's scheme, which he now proceeded to put in force. Craftily pretending to be desirous of a reconciliation with Knipe, he arranged for a dinner on shore, at which all the factors and those of the officers whom he mistrusted

---

[1] Remembered in Bombay history as having been in later years Governor of that island (for King Charles) when the transfer to the East India Company took place (*see* p. 245). His name is often written 'Gary'

were to be present, to celebrate a mutual forgiveness of all offences. Knipe and his associates fell easily into the trap. At the dinner (August 29) all was cordiality and friendliness; but immediately after Mucknell made an excuse to leave the company for a short time, and when the rest, tired of waiting for his return, made their way down to the shore to re-embark, they saw to their amazement that the ship was under sail. The master had slipped on board and harangued the crew, begging their assistance in averting his impending disgrace, and had then proceeded to announce his intention of carrying the ship back to England and handing her over to King Charles. The sailors were easily persuaded to agree, especially when promised a share in the money that was on board. The Portuguese passengers were therefore sent on shore, and the *John* sailed away.

Vivid narratives by eyewitnesses of these events will be found on pp. 196, 238, 261, 262, and we must leave to them all details of the homeward voyage. It must suffice here to record that the *John* reached the English coast in safety and was carried into Bristol, which was then being besieged by the Parliamentary forces. Her cargo, consisting chiefly of coral, was taken ashore, and being found intact when the city was stormed by Fairfax's troops, was to a great extent regained by the Company. The vessel herself was dispatched under Mucknell to prey upon Commonwealth shipping, and did considerable damage before her career was ended by shipwreck while endeavouring to evade some of the Parliament's cruisers. Mucknell himself, according to a letter from the Company to Surat in March, 1646, 'escaped to doe future misc[h]iefe, untill Gods hand or the gallowes make an end of him'; and this is the last glimpse we have of the disloyal commander of the *John*.

Meanwhile the *Crispiana*, as already related, had met the battered *Dolphin* and *Hopewell* at Johanna, and all three had proceeded to Surat, arriving September 18. A month later, the *Crispiana* sailed for Sind to fetch the goods provided there for England. The *Hopewell* was sent down the coast to Cochin, and on her return was sentenced to be broken up as past repair; while the *Dolphin* was refitted with a view to her speedy dispatch once more for England. She departed accordingly at the end of November, 1644, with Fremlen on board, and reached the Thames the following July.

Fremlen, it may be noted, did not long enjoy the fruits of his Indian service, for he died in March, 1646 (see *Court Minutes of the East India Company*, 1644-49, p. ix). Apparently he had not amassed a fortune, for Methwold, who acted as his executor, pressed the Company to pay full salary for Fremlen's last year in India, on the ground that, unless this were done, he could not discharge a legacy of 500*l.* to the Company's Hospital at Blackwall (*Ibid.*, p. 155). Probably Fremlen had sustained some loss by the disaster to the *Discovery* and the damage to the *Dolphin* in his first attempt to get to England; while another unlucky venture of his is related by Tavernier (*Les Six Voyages*, ed. 1676-77, vol. ii. p. 308). According to this story, Fremlen and Breton had combined with a Jew named 'Edouard Ferdinand'—doubtless the Duarte Fernandez Correa of the text—to purchase a large diamond, which was then entrusted to the Jew for sale when he went to Europe early in 1644 (*infra*, p. 159). On his arrival at Leghorn he was offered a sum of about 5,600*l.* for it, but this he refused as insufficient. He then took the stone to Venice to get it cut. This was successfully accomplished; but when the diamond was placed upon the wheel for polishing, it broke into nine pieces.

Early in January, 1645, the *Crispiana* in her turn set sail for England. In the letter she carried home (p. 227) Breton and his colleagues expressed their astonishment at the non-appearance of the *John*, concerning which they had only heard that she had been at Mozambique. Towards the end of the same month their apprehensions of disaster were verified by the appearance of Knipe and his associates, who, after remaining at Johanna until September 30, had then been taken off by Courteen's *Thomas and John*, bound for Kārwār on the Malabar Coast. Easterly winds, however, forced the vessel out of her course, with the result that she was obliged to put into Kishm, in Southern Arabia, for water and provisions. Proceeding along the coast, a Dutch ship was met with, which was making for Surat; and Knipe and his companions gladly accepted her captain's offer to carry them thither. Thanks to this friendly assistance, they at last reached their destination and reported to the President and Council the loss of their ship and their own subsequent sufferings.

Hardly knowing what to do with so highly-paid a merchant as

Knipe, the Surat Council determined to make him chief of the Agra factory; and an interesting account of his proceedings there will be found on p. 299. It will be noted that the operations of the English at this time extended over a considerable area, including Lucknow, though Agra remained their only permanent settlement in those parts.

The blow dealt to English interests in India by the defection of the *John* was a severe one (p. 249). Breton and his colleagues had been counting upon her money and goods not only for the partial discharge of their heavy debt, but for the provision of means for the many enterprises they had in hand. They were now besieged on all sides with demands for the payment of their obligations, and no fresh credit could be obtained. Fortunately, on March 4 the *Hind* and the *Seahorse* returned from the Far East; and when it became known that their voyages had proved 'reasonable prosperous', the clamour of the Company's creditors somewhat abated. The *Hind* had reached Macao on August 7, 1644, and found there Courteen's ship *William*. The factors received at first 'respective enterteinement' at the hands of the Portuguese authorities; but this friendliness did not extend to consideration in the matter of port dues, and the rapacity of the officials, combined with the stagnation of trade, due in part to a rebellion in China (p. 250), much reduced the profits on the voyage. The *Seahorse* had been hardly more successful in her pioneer voyage to Manilla. That city was found to be suffering likewise from poverty, and there was little or no market for the goods the English had brought; while the Spanish authorities, preoccupied with the war with Holland, were displeased to find that neither iron for guns nor saltpetre for gunpowder formed part of the vessel's lading. Further, a change of Governors was impending, and the arrival of the new chief had perforce to be awaited. Jealousy on the part of the local traders and indifference on the part of the authorities still further impeded the factors' efforts. Moreover, suspicions were not wanting that they were acting either as agents for the Portuguese or spies for the Dutch; while others averred that the ultimate object of the English was piracy. To allay these fears, Pearce and his companions decided to send back the *Seahorse* to Surat and themselves remain another year; and this was accordingly done, the Governor writing at the

INTRODUCTION

same time to urge that the next ship should bring a supply of iron and saltpetre. The long letter in which the factors related their experiences (p. 218) is of the greatest interest for its account of the state of affairs in the Philippines at this juncture.

The Surat factors were not willing of their own accord to run the risk of sending a ship past the Dutch fortress of Malacca laden with munitions of war for Manilla; but they wrote privately to the Company (p. 256), suggesting that, if a permit could be obtained from the Spanish King, a vessel should proceed thither direct from England by way of the Sunda Straits; or else that the Company should explicitly authorize such an attempt being made secretly from Surat. Meanwhile, the *Supply* (without any contraband of war) was dispatched from that port for the Philippines on April 29, 1645, with orders to touch at Achin, both going and returning, and to fetch away the factors and their goods from Manilla. It was just as well that this decision had been reached, for in the letters by the 1645 fleet the Company expressed grave disapproval of both the Macao and Manilla ventures and vetoed any further attempt of the kind from Surat (*O.C.* 1970).

Towards the close of March, 1645, the *Hind* and the *Francis* sailed in company for Mokha, whence the former was to return at once via Tuticorin, while the latter waited to bring back the factors at the close of the season. It had been intended that the *Francis* should from Mokha make a venture to Suakin—a project the Surat factors had for some time had in mind (pp. 213, 235, 252)—but this was found to be out of the question, in view of the lateness of her departure. Cranmer, with three assistants, was once more dispatched to Basrā in the *Seahorse* at the beginning of April, 1645, and reached their destination at the end of June. They found the port overcrowded with shipping and trade in poor condition. To make matters worse, on July 19 appeared two Dutch ships, foreshadowing severe competition at a place the English had hitherto had to themselves (p. 283). The newcomers arrogantly demanded special privileges; and although the Governor resolutely refused this claim, he was quite willing to place them on the same footing as other Europeans. With these terms they were forced to be content. They accordingly landed their goods; and, although their sales did not amount to much, they spoiled (it was complained) the market for the English (p. 283). One of their ships departed in mid-September; the other was accidentally burnt while preparing to follow. The English factors decided to remain until the following year; but on September 22 they dispatched to Surat the *Endeavour*, which had arrived on July 26 to replace the *Seahorse*, as the latter vessel was, in accordance with previous arrangements, to go to Tuticorin before returning to Surat. The *Endeavour* reached Swally on November 5; and the *Hind* and *Seahorse* got back to that port together just before Christmas.

In Persia at this time both the Dutch and the English were experiencing great difficulties in carrying on their trade, owing to the rapacity and insolence of the chief officials. The dwindling trade of the English—for silk was in no demand at home while civil war was raging (p. 170)—and their want of means were made the excuse for refusing their applications for the confirmation of the privileges they had enjoyed under the late King; while all sorts of ingenious devices were employed to defraud them of their proper share of the Gombroon customs (p. 208). To this treatment the factors, seeing no remedy, had to submit with what patience they could muster. The Hollanders, having more at stake, sought to assert themselves by threatening active reprisals, but this only led to their agent being beaten and for a time imprisoned at Ispahān (p. 170). The result was seen in the appearance (April, 1645) of a strong Dutch fleet at Gombroon, with an expeditionary force intended for the capture of Kishm and Ormus (pp. 255, 257, 268). Trade at the port had already been disorganized by a severe earthquake (p. 266), and the blockade instituted by the Hollanders brought it practically to a standstill. The reply received from Ispahān to their demands proving unsatisfactory, an attempt was made to storm the Persian fort on the island of Kishm (pp. 275, 277, 308). The Dutch were repulsed; but this proof of their warlike intentions so frightened the Persians that liberal promises of redressing all grievances were made, if they would send up representatives to the capital. Blocq, the commander of the fleet, thereupon repaired to Ispahān, but only to die soon after his arrival. Nevertheless, *farmāns* were obtained, granting practically all the Dutch demands (p. 307). A letter from the English factors at Ispahān in October, 1645, reported that their own negotiations

INTRODUCTION

with the King's principal minister had been cut short by his murder by certain high officials, who in their turn were executed by the order of the King (p. 296).

On September 25, 1645, three ships from England—the *Eagle, Falcon,* and *Lanneret*—anchored in Swally Hole. All three were new vessels, but only the first was to return for England, the other two being pinnaces intended for local traffic. They were straightway dispatched on coasting voyages; while the *Eagle* was prepared for her homeward journey, on which she set out at the beginning of 1646.

In the third volume of the present series (p. xxxiv) a table was given, showing the ships sent home from Surat each year for the period 1615-29. We can now continue the list for another sixteen years, premising that the cargoes often included silk from Persia or pepper from Bantam, the cost of which cannot be separated from that of the goods of Indian origin.

Year.	Ships sent home.	Approximate cost of cargoes.
1630	*Charles* (700 tons) and *Jonas* (800)	[valued in England at 170,000*l.*]
1631	*Discovery* (500) and *Reformation* (500)	
1632	*Blessing* (700)	[valued in England at 150,000*l.*]
1633	*James* (900)	
1634	*Mary* (800)	[valued in England at 58,000*l.*]
1635	*Jonas*	
1636	*Discovery*	
1637	*William* (700)	
1638	*Jonas*	
1639	*Mary* and *Swan* (300)	68,760*l.*
	Discovery	40,810*l.*
1640	*London* (800)	
	Crispiana (500)	59,450*l.*
1641	[None]	
1642	*London*	
1643	*Crispiana* and *Aleppo Merchant* (400)	58,770*l.*
1644	*Dolphin* (300) and *Discovery*	46,500*l.*
1645	*Crispiana*	

During the period here dealt with, Courteen's Association was still maintaining an active competition with the East India Company. In November, 1641, it dispatched three ships to the East, viz. the *Bona Speranza,* the *Henry Bonaventura,* and the *Hampton Merchant.* The last-named was driven back to Plymouth by a storm; and although she made a fresh start in February, 1642, she either gave up the voyage or was lost at sea, for we hear no more of her. Besides these three, which were designed for Sumatra, the *Loyalty*, *Unity*, and *Hester* were sent in the spring of 1642 to the western coast of India.[1] All these arrived in safety at Rājāpur and Kārwār (p. 62); and the *Hester* managed to procure some cinnamon at Goa. A quarrel which took place in the latter port between the *Hester* and the *Loyalty* is mentioned on p. 89. In November, 1642, Knipe found the former trading at Cochin; and on p. 109 he says that Courteen's factory at Bhatkal had been re-established. The *Henry Bonaventura* and the *Bona Speranza* reached Achin in April and July, 1642, respectively, and endeavoured, by giving a valuable present to the Queen, to obtain a grant of a monopoly of the pepper trade on the west coast of Sumatra. In this, however, they had been forestalled by the Dutch, and so they were obliged to content themselves with permission to buy return cargoes in Achin itself (*Batavia Dagh-Register*, 1641–42, p. 174). The *Henry Bonaventura* was laden with pepper and dispatched for England; but, meeting with a heavy storm on the way, was thrown upon the island of Mauritius and became a total wreck. Three of her crew were taken off by the Company's ship *Advice* in April, 1643. The *Bona Speranza* met a different fate. She proceeded to Goa, where, after the rupture of Boreel's negotiations with the Viceroy, she accepted a freight of Portuguese goods for Macao, on the assumption that the Dutch would not venture to attack a vessel wearing the English royal colours (as Courteen's ships were privileged to do). This hope proved deceptive; for in the Straits of Malacca she was met by two Dutch ships, and on her refusing to go with them to Malacca an action ensued, with the result that the English vessel was taken and her cargo confiscated (pp. 128, 129, 148).

Some time in 1643 Courteen dispatched to Achin a vessel called the *Little William*. In the middle of June she was wrecked on the African coast; but the crew managed to save a quantity of money she had on board, and after a hazardous voyage in their

---

[1] On p. 29 we find the Company declaring confidently that these would be the last ships sent out by Courteen, a Parliamentary Committee having ordered him to withdraw his factors and goods. The evidence on the latter point is inconclusive (see *Court Minutes*, 1640–43, pp. 242, 265); but if the order was ever issued, it was disregarded, as will be seen below.

INTRODUCTION xxi

longboat reached Madagascar at the end of August. In May, 1644, they were picked up by the Company's ship *Endeavour*, and carried to Madras, where, for want of means to convey it to any of Courteen's factories, the money was paid into the Company's treasury—an arrangement which led to long controversies both in England and India.

In January, 1644, we hear that two more of Courteen's ships— the *Planter* and the *William* (Captain Blackman)—had arrived in Indian waters, and that the former had returned to England with a cargo consisting chiefly of saltpetre (p. 148). The Association's factors were in difficulties at Goa, Rāybāg, and Achin for want of money, and Blackman was at a loss how to employ his ship with any prospect of profit. In April, however, armed with a licence from the Viceroy, he sailed for Macao, returning early in 1645 by way of Achin and Colombo (p. 254). At the latter place he found the new Viceroy, with whom he made an agreement to bring out in his next voyage a quantity of munitions of war, to be exchanged at Goa for cinnamon (p. 254). In July of that year he was met, homeward-bound, at St. Augustine's Bay by the Company's outgoing fleet (p. 312).

The ships designed for the East by the interlopers in 1644 were five in number, viz. the *Sun*, *Hester*, *James*, *Thomas and John*, and *Loyalty*. The primary purpose of the first three was to carry out a number of planters who were (in accordance with a scheme initiated by a certain Captain Bond) 'to erect a new commonwealth in Madagascar' (p. 176), a project which turned out a dismal failure.[1] The *Loyalty* arrived on the Malabar Coast in the autumn, and was dispatched to Gombroon with a small quantity of freight goods (p. 217). Both she and the *Thomas and John* found the Malabar factories heavily in debt, and as neither ship brought any means (p. 255) the prospect looked hopeless. From Gombroon the *Loyalty* went on to Basrā, arriving there early in August (p. 283), and departing again on October 11 (p. 299).

The intrusion of the interlopers' shipping into ports where the Company had long maintained factories was a clear infringement of the rights reserved to the latter in the grant of 1637 to Courteen's

---

[1] See *Court Minutes of the East India Company*, 1644-49, Introduction, p. vi; also my article in the *English Historical Review* for April, 1912.

Association [1], and naturally it aroused much indignation among the servants of the older body. At Gombroon the arrival of the *Loyalty* produced a protest from the factors there, to which an insolent reply was returned (p. 276); and when at Surat itself one of Courteen's ships, the *Hester*, appeared in September, 1645, flaunting the royal colours, the Company's factors, having three vessels at their disposal, determined on drastic action. Her commander was prevented from landing or embarking any goods and was forced to haul down his flag (p. 286). In July, 1645, we hear of another of Courteen's ships, the *James*, as being at Madagascar outward-bound (p. 312), and later she was met at Rājāpur (*O.C.* 1970). Of the general position of the interlopers the Surat factors wrote in January, 1646 (*O.C.* 1970) that 'they have scarcely credit enough to buy clothes to keep their bodies warme, although the climate requires not many.' The *Thomas and John* had started for England too late and had been forced to return to Goa, where she spent the rainy season and then resumed her homeward voyage. The *Sun* had gone to Persia with a cargo of logs from Madagascar; and another interloping vessel, the *Lioness*, under Captain Brookhaven, had reached Rājāpur from England, having visited Guinea —now a regular resort of Courteen's ships—on the way. The *Loyalty* was still in Indian waters seeking a cargo for England.

How prosperous the Hollanders were at this period is abundantly testified by the documents here calendared (cf. pp. 32, 217, 255). Not only in the Far East but in Arabia, Persia, and India itself, they easily outdistanced their English rivals, alike in the number of their ships and the extent of their resources. On p. 142 we find a complaint that at Surat the Indian merchants preferred to put their goods on board Dutch vessels rather than on English, 'findeing there much better accomodacion and noe less safety', with the result that the Hollanders had carried off all the freight goods then available. The fact that two of the vessels sent out to India by the English Company in 1643 were Dutch-built was a further 'discreditt to our nation, whilst this people (who know noe better) enquire whether England doth not affoard shipping of its owne, that it is enforced to seeke and buy them among strangers' (p. 141).

As there are many references in the present volume to the rela-

---

[1] See *Court Minutes of the East India Company*, 1635-39, p. 275.

tions between the Dutch and the Portuguese, a few notes on the subject may be found helpful. The treaty concluded at the Hague between Holland and Portugal in June, 1641,[1] provided for a cessation of hostilities during a period of ten years, each party retaining the territory which should be in its possession at the time of the publication of the peace. However, the Dutch authorities in the East were by no means willing to be stopped in their career of victory; and, when in the autumn of 1641 the Viceroy at Goa sent a special embassy to Batavia to beg for a truce pending the arrival of the ratified treaty from Europe, he was met with a refusal on the ground that formal instructions had not yet been received from Holland. A fresh fleet blockaded Goa during the cold weather of 1641-42; while in April, 1642, the Portuguese settlement of Negapatam, on the Coromandel Coast, was taken without resistance, but was ransomed for an immediate payment of 10,000 rials of eight and a promise of 40,000 more, an undertaking which was never carried out. In the autumn, however, the arrival of the necessary documents at Batavia left the Governor-General and his Council no option in the matter. Accordingly the truce was formally proclaimed there on October 7 (N.S.); and a fortnight later Pieter Boreel left for Malacca, Ceylon, India, &c., to notify the various authorities and to arrange matters with the Portuguese. Difficulties soon arose. In Ceylon the Dutch claimed the district immediately round Galle, in spite of the fact that it was actually in the occupation of the Portuguese, who had cooped up the Hollanders within the walls of the town. This demand being refused, Boreel left without proclaiming the peace, and sailed to Goa, where he arrived at the beginning of April, 1643 (N.S.). He was courteously received and treated with every consideration; but the Viceroy refused to give way on the points in dispute, and on the 27th Boreel re-embarked and hoisted the red flag, in token that hostilities would be resumed. The Dutch now actively prosecuted the war in all parts. The results were not entirely to their satisfaction. In May the Portuguese inflicted a defeat upon them near Galle in Ceylon; while in the following month the *Pauw*, returning richly laden from Persia, sought shelter from a storm in Marmagão (near Goa), under the impression that the war was over; whereupon the

[1] The text will be found in Biker's *Tratados* (vol. ii. p. 108).

Portuguese took possession of both ship and cargo, until such time as peace should be proclaimed.

In the autumn of 1643 a fresh fleet was dispatched from Batavia under Klaas Kornelisz. Blocq to blockade Goa, while another under François Caron was sent to prosecute the war in Ceylon. Landing at Galle, the Dutch marched to attack the Portuguese army, which was commanded by de Motta Galvão; but the latter had so skilfully chosen his position that Caron did not venture to assail him, and was forced to return to Galle. Colombo was next reconnoitred, with the result that it was pronounced too strong to be attacked with any prospect of success; and so the fleet passed on to Negombo, a fortress twenty miles to the northwards, which the Portuguese had retaken from the Dutch towards the close of 1640. Here Caron was more successful. The too confident Portuguese allowed the Hollanders to land, thinking then to overwhelm them; however, in the sharp conflict that followed the Dutch were victorious, and, entering the gate together with the fugitives, they quickly made themselves masters of the fortress (January 9, 1644 N.S.).[1] Caron now marched upon Colombo; but close to the city he found a river held so strongly by the enemy that further progress was impossible, and he was obliged to retrace his footsteps and content himself with diligently strengthening his new possession.[2] In March, 1644, he set out on his return voyage to Batavia.

In the meantime Blocq, from his station at the bar of Goa, negotiated in vain with the Viceroy for the surrender of the *Pauw* and her lading. He remained at his post till April, 1644, and then sailed for Batavia to report to the Governor-General. Advantage was taken of his departure to send an expedition to Ceylon, and in May Negombo was beleaguered. In July the Portuguese attempted to carry it by storm, but were beaten back with great loss; and in the following month they abandoned the siege. It was now decided at Batavia to depute Jan Maatzuiker, a member of the Council there and afterwards Governor-General (1653–78), to take up the negotiations at Goa; and with him went Blocq with a powerful

---

[1] *Lisbon Transcripts, Doc. Remett.*, book 48, f. 290; *Hague Transcripts*, series i. vol. xiii. no. 425; *Dagh-Register*, 1643–44, p. 230, &c.; Van Geer's *Opkomst van het Nederlandsch Gezag over Ceilon*, pt. i. p. 115.

[2] Caron's report in *Hague Transcripts*, series i. vol. xiv. no. 441.

INTRODUCTION

fleet. They reached their destination in September, 1644, and after some trouble an arrangement was reached on November 10 (N.S.)[1], by which Negombo and Galle were left in the hands of the Dutch, pending the conclusion of a fresh agreement between the two nations in Europe regarding Ceylon, and the *Pauw* was surrendered, with all her cargo; while on the other hand the Dutch agreed to pay 100,000 rials of eight in satisfaction for the ships they had seized at Goa and Malacca subsequent to the date on which the Hague treaty ought to have taken effect. Thus the long warfare between the Dutch and the Portuguese came at last to an end.

The cessation of hostilities between those two nations was viewed with some misgivings by the English merchants. The Portuguese no longer needed the aid of the latter in maintaining communications with Macao and other possessions; while, with Goa once more open to shipping from Lisbon, their competition in the sale of coral and other European goods in the Deccan was increasingly felt. A more serious outcome was that the cinnamon which the Portuguese, while the Dutch blockaded their ports, were quite willing to sell to the English, was no longer likely to be available. The new King of Portugal had in December, 1642, thrown open to his subjects the trade in all Indian commodities except cinnamon and other spices, which were reserved as a royal monopoly. In consequence the Viceroy was charged to do his best to prevent the sale of any to the English; and, although these orders were not put into execution immediately (p. 205), the Surat factors wrote in January, 1645, that it would be useless to send a ship to the Malabar Coast, ' being it is most certaine that neither pepper nor cinamon wilbe acquirable' (p. 231).

In acting thus, the Portuguese were of course entirely within their rights, and their proceedings caused no alteration in the cordial relations which had subsisted between Surat and Goa ever since the conclusion of the Accord by Methwold in January, 1635. At times, it is true, the English merchants grew a little tired of Portuguese punctiliousness in the matter of correspondence (pp. 16, 210); but the solid benefits resulting from the free intercourse of the two

---

[1] The text will be fonnd in Biker's *Tratados*, vol. ii. p. 138; Heeres's *Corpus Diplomaticum*, part i. p. 429; Baldaeus's *Malabar-Choromandel*, p. 92; &c. There is also a copy among the *Hague Transcripts* at the India Office (series i. vol. xiv. no. 445).

nations in India easily made up for incidental annoyances. In England attempts were not wanting to turn the truce into a more permanent arrangement. The treaty concluded with Portugal in 1642 (p. 30) provided that the Accord should remain in force, and that commissioners should be appointed on both sides to settle outstanding questions. The Company had already approached the Portuguese ambassador on the subject; but he had replied that he had no power to deal with the matter, at the same time assuring them that the truce would be 'inviolably kept' on the part of his fellow countrymen and promising that, should the latter desire to terminate the arrangement, two years' notice should be given in place of the six months previously stipulated (p. 30). At the beginning of 1643 the Portuguese Agent requested the Company to nominate commissioners in India to negotiate further; whereupon President Fremlen and four others of the chief factors at Surat were suggested. However, the Company's letters to King Charles at Oxford, asking for a royal commission for the purpose, remained unanswered; and since it seemed hopeless to obtain such a document 'in these distracted tymes', the Deputy-Governor (Methwold) and certain others were instructed to treat with the Portuguese Agent and induce him to write a letter to Goa explaining the position of affairs (*Court Minutes*, 1640–43, pp. 300, 371).

It now remains for us to deal with the events of this period on the eastern side of India. At the close of the last volume the English headquarters on that coast had just been fixed permanently in the new fort at Madraspatam by the Agent, Andrew Cogan. At Masulipatam Thomas Peniston was in charge; while at Balasore, in the Bay of Bengal, John Yard was supposed to be winding up affairs with a view to abandoning the trade in those parts, in obedience to the orders he had received to that effect. As a matter of fact, he did make a start for Masulipatam about the middle of January, 1642; but meeting with bad weather he returned to Balasore, and commerce in the 'Bay' went on as before.

Towards the end of January, 1642, the *Diamond*, though both small and leaky, was dispatched with a cargo of goods for Bantam, and got to that port with much difficulty in the middle of June. Some time before, the pinnace *Advice* had sailed for Gombroon, where she arrived on February 9, and left again on March 25,

INTRODUCTION xxvii

reaching Fort St. George on April 29 and Masulipatam a few days later. The next event of importance on the Coast recorded in these papers is the arrival at Fort St. George from England, on July 5, 1642, of the *Hopewell*, commanded by Andrew Trumball. Her cargo was under the charge of Francis Day, who had orders to use it solely for the purposes of the First General Voyage and not to allow any of the money to be absorbed in the payment of the debts of the Third Joint Stock; but, as was explained later (p. 113), this was found to be impossible, for no fresh investments could be negotiated until existing liabilities had been met, and it was therefore found expedient to employ part of the *Hopewell*'s capital in discharging the debts at Masulipatam. From that port the *Hopewell*, accompanied by the *Advice*, sailed in August for the Bay, where she spent two and a half months, leaving again on December 1. The *Advice* had been dispatched from Balasore on November 7 and got back to Madraspatam at Christmas. During the *Hopewell*'s stay the English factory at Hariharpur seems to have been closed (p. 126), partly on account of the silting-up of the mouth of the Pātuā[1], and Balasore thus became the only English station in Bengal (or rather Orissa). From the latter place Day wrote in November, deprecating its abandonment, and declaring that it was 'noe such dispisable place as is voted, it beinge an opulent kingdome and you haveinge bin already at great charges in gaininge the free custome of all sorts of goods'. The unwillingness of the factors to cease trading in the Bay, however unprofitable the results were to their employers, is to some extent explained by Trumball's revelations on p. 72 concerning the large amount of private trade on board the *Hopewell* belonging to Day and to the Masulipatam factors.

On p. 43 we have a vivid account of the stabbing of an English soldier at Madraspatam by a Portuguese, who was thereupon executed (August 13), much to the indignation of his fellow countrymen. We hear also about this time that the Nāyak to

[1] Walter Clavell in his account of Balasore (1676) says that it was found that 'the cloth of Harrapore (where our first factory was settled) was without much difficulty to be brought hither by land and, the river where our vessels usually had laine at being stop't up, it was noe easy matter to bring the cloth by sea, nor soe safe to have vessels ride before that place, as here in the roade of Ballasore' (*The Diaries of Streynsham Master*, vol. ii. p. 84).

whom Armagon belonged had been crushed between the Hindū and Muhammadan powers, now again at war. The Golconda army had overrun part of his territory, and the rest (including Armagon itself) had been occupied by a neighbouring Nāyak, to whom apparently the defence of the frontier had been entrusted by his uncle, Venkatapati, the King of Vijayanagar. At the beginning of October the King died, and after a short delay this nephew was elevated to the throne as Srī Ranga Rāyalu, though many of the other Nāyaks were opposed to his succession, and gave him a great deal of trouble.

On September 20, 1642, Cogan and his colleagues wrote to Bantam, enclosing a list of their debts and coolly admitting the falsity of their statement made eighteen months earlier that they had cleared off all liabilities. The Agent also intimated his intention of proceeding to Bantam in the *Advice* early in the new year, leaving Day to fill his place; this proposal, however, was resisted by Day and the other factors, and thereupon Cogan consented to remain. Another letter written at the same time to the Company mentions that the factory at Golconda had been withdrawn, leaving behind many irrecoverable debts; and it goes on to deny indignantly charges of extravagant expenditure, and to make a cogent defence of the policy of fortifying at Madraspatam. In point of fact the logic of events soon justified the action that had been taken by Day and Cogan; for, had not the English established themselves in a strong position before the Golconda troops overran the neighbouring country, the history of Fort St. George would probably never have been written.

The Fort was at this time 'better then half finished', and 'of such force, with the few wee have, that wee feare not what any can doe against us, espetially so long as wee have our Naique to our freind, or the sea open to furnish us with food' (p. 51). Of the private lives of the factors there, some curious details will be found on p. 76. A consultation held on December 29 records that 'a third bulwarke of turfe' had lately been raised, on which it was decided to mount four guns from the *Advice*. The cause assigned for taking this precaution is that the factors found 'the warrs and broyles increasing in this countrey, and now (by reason of our Great Naiques imprisonment) drawing nere to us' (p. 70).

INTRODUCTION

Damarla Venkatappa, under whose protection the English had settled at Madraspatam, was, it appears, violently opposed to the new ruler of Vijayanagar and, in order to secure his own position, opened negotiations with the Golconda invaders. Srī Ranga, detecting his treason, seized and imprisoned him, and stripped him of most of his territories (pp. 70, 80). Thereupon Damarla's brother levied troops to rescue him; and Srī Ranga, harassed on every side, was fain to pardon and reinstate his rebellious vassal.

The *Advice* was dispeeded from the Coast to Bantam at the beginning of January, 1643. On the arrival of the *Hopewell* at Fort St. George from Bengal towards the end of December, 1642, it was decided to send her on a voyage to Persia instead of to Bantam (as first intended) and on her return to dispatch her direct to England, for which purpose the Agent asked for a supply of pepper from Bantam. She sailed accordingly on December 30, reached Gombroon March 7, 1643, and got back to Madras on May 19. The proposal to send her home direct was not persisted in; and the factors afterwards explained that this was only contemplated in the event of her not returning in time to continue her voyage for Bantam (p. 114).

John Yard sailed from Balasore in the junk *Endeavour* on November 25, 1642, leaving Robert Hatch alone there. 'For ought wee can perceive', wrote the Madras factors (p. 78), 'by the relation of Mr. Day &c., Mr. John Yard hath but said the truth in all his letters concerning the fruitfulnes of Bengalla and the profitt that may be made to and from that place, if 'twere stocked as it ought'. This, however, was the difficulty, seeing how scarce money was on the Coast; and the Fort St. George factors could only leave it to the President and Council at Bantam either to order ' our absolute abandoninge those parts or furnish it as it ought to bee' (p. 78).

At some unascertained date a 'cowl' (*qaul*) had been obtained from the former King (Venkatapati) confirming the concessions made to the English at Madraspatam (p. 156)[1]; and it seems to

---

[1] Among the title-deeds handed over by Governor Gyfford to his successor in 1687 was 'one gold cowle plated from Yencraputty Raywolly' (*Madras Consultations* of July 30, 1687, quoted by Col. Love). This seems to have been the grant here referred to; and it may further be identified with 'the ancient phirmaund of this place granted by a Jentue king' which was lost at sea about 1693 (see my *Founding of Fort St. George*, p. 43).

have been found necessary, early in 1643, to send a present, through the Nāyak, to Srī Ranga Rāyalu, 'to have our priviledges confirmd' (p. 115). Nothing is said as to the result; but apparently no formal grant was obtained from the new monarch until Greenhill's mission in 1645, described later. At least this seems to be implied in the statement (p. 290) that the object of that mission was 'the reconfirmation of what was graunted unto Mr. Cogan by the great Nague under whose protection formerly wee liv'd.'

As we have seen, the *Hopewell* got back to Madras from Persia in May, 1643. Relations had long been strained between Day and Trumball, the master of the vessel; while the latter's peculiar methods of discipline had aroused much resentment among his subordinates. When, therefore, the Agent and his Council decided to send the *Hopewell* down the Coast to Tranquebar, a serious situation arose, for not only Day but many of the officers and crew refused to sail with Trumball. The latter afterwards alleged to the Company at home that he was the victim of a plot on the part of Day and the other factors, who resented his opposition to their private trade, and that the sailors were inveigled into bringing accusations against him, in order to supply a pretext for his removal. There is, however, evidence enough that his violence was strongly resented on board; while the fact that the Company, after investigating his charges against Day, re-employed the latter, suggests that Trumball failed to prove his case. To get over the immediate difficulty, Cogan and his Council suspended the master from his post, and sent the vessel to Tranquebar under the care of Day and the chief mate. On her return, in the middle of August, Trumball was permitted to resume charge, as the factors were unwilling to take the responsibility of ousting him altogether from a post to which he had been appointed by the Company. This decision, however, had perforce to be reconsidered. Day flatly declared that he would rather resign and proceed overland to Surat than venture upon a fresh voyage with Trumball; while those of the ship's company who had lodged complaints were equally unwilling to place themselves once more at the mercy of the enraged master. In this emergency Cogan, who was still anxious to get away from the Coast, suggested that Day should

INTRODUCTION

take his place as Agent, and that he himself should proceed to Bantam in command of the ship; and since no better way out of the difficulty could be found, the proposal was adopted. Day accordingly became Agent for the Coast, while Cogan departed for Masulipatam and Bantam in the *Hopewell* on August 28, 1643. From Bantam he sailed for England in December following. In a letter carried by the *Hopewell* the Madras factors wrote that the country was in the throes of civil war, 'one Nague against another, and most against the King'; but the latter, by means of a large present, had induced the King of Bījāpur to send an army to his assistance, and he was therefore likely to gain the upper hand (p. 115). They also announced the arrival of the *Advice*, which, in obedience to orders from home, had been dispatched from Bantam the previous spring on a voyage of discovery. She had missed the Cocos-Keeling Islands (one of the objects of her search); and although, after touching at Rodriguez and Mauritius, she reached Réunion, her officers failed to recognize in that island the one called 'the English Forest', of which they were in quest (p. 119). They were little more successful in their attempts to obtain negro slaves at the Comoros. From Fort St. George the *Advice* proceeded to the Bay, returning from thence towards the end of January, 1644.

On September 23, 1643, the *Hart* from England anchored in Madras Roads, bringing 10,000*l.* in specie and six chests of coral. With the bulk of her cargo she was sent on to Masulipatam, to discharge the most pressing of the Company's debts and to make an investment for Bantam. She quitted the former port on October 21, and reached Bantam in the middle of December.

The Bantam factors, writing in January, 1644, mention that Day had chosen William Netlam, who had just come out in the *Hart*, to proceed to Bengal and take charge of affairs there—an arrangement of which they strongly disapproved (p. 134).[1] Netlam duly repaired to Balasore (p. 207), and on p. 193 William Gurney is also mentioned as being there; but it would seem that Robert Hatch remained in charge at that place until he was relieved by

---

[1] In a list of factors printed on p. 132, Hatch and Travell are mentioned as the only factors in Bengal at this time; but the list was compiled at home, from such particulars as were available, and it seems improbable that Travell ever went thither (cf. pp. 120, 154).

Henry Olton, who arrived there in the *Endeavour* in the autumn of 1644.

A letter from Madras dated in January, 1644, and sent to Bantam by the *Advice*, is full not only of the usual lamentations of want of means but also of apprehensions of actual violence. Damarla, it appears, was once more in disgrace and, it would seem, in rebellion; and his place had been given to Malaya, a merchant who had grown wealthy through acting as the principal agent of the Dutch in their commercial transactions. Moved either by ambition or by a fear of being plundered himself should others get the upper hand, he was now taking an active part in support of Srī Ranga, and with the help of the Dutch was busily engaged in subduing the district which had been assigned to him. This brought him in collision with the English, for he demanded from them the surrender of their control over the revenues of the town of Madraspatam (p. 156). To such a claim the factors were determined never to yield; but they manifestly feared lest they should be attacked by Malaya, and they suspected—quite wrongly, it would seem—that the Dutch were at the bottom of the whole affair, their aim being 'to have the sole trade of the coast' (p. 154). However, a fresh turn in the unstable politics of Vijayanagar soon relieved them from their apprehensions. Malaya came in his turn under suspicion of treason and was dismissed from his new post.

A small vessel from England named the *Endeavour* (not to be confused with the junk of the same name which Yard had bought in Bengal) reached Fort St. George at the beginning of July, 1644, and was thence sent to Masulipatam. From the latter port she proceeded to Chicacole and Balasore. The money she had brought out sufficed to pay the debts at Madras; while on August 4 the *Swan* arrived from Bantam with a fair cargo and a new Agent in the person of Thomas Ivy. Writing in the following month to the Company by that vessel (then about to return, with Day on board, to Bantam), Ivy and his colleagues stated that up to that time Fort St. George had cost for building nearly 2,300*l.*, and 2,000*l.* more would be required to finish it. Three out of the four bastions had been completed[1]; but the fourth was yet lacking, as also the

---

[1] Cogan, when interrogated at home concerning the state of the building, declared that 'three bulwarcks and the tower (or house) in the midst is finished, and 34 peeces of

INTRODUCTION xxxiii

connecting walls and the necessary warehouses and lodging rooms. The garrison numbered fifty, at a cost of a little more than a pound a month each; and double that number would be needed when the Fort was finished. The factors were still unhappy, for, though they had now received the desired supply of money, they found that the Dutch had already secured all the calicoes worth buying. They had, however, made up a cargo for the *Swan*, consisting of some rather inferior piece-goods, indigo, and gunpowder. The neighbouring districts were in a disturbed state, owing to a fresh invasion by the troops of the King of Golconda. The commander of this army had summoned the Dutch at Pulicat to submit, and the English expected to be attacked in their turn; but they were relieved by the sudden appearance of a Hindu force, which completely routed the invaders (p. 193).

The *Endeavour* returned to Masulipatam from Bengal, bringing with her Robert Hatch, in November, 1644; and a month later she was dispatched to Persia and Surat. On January 6, 1645, the *Seaflower* arrived from Bantam and was sent on to Fort St. George for a return cargo. This procured, she started on her voyage back to Bantam on May 5. At the end of July the *Advice* reached Madras from that port, and was thereupon sent down the coast to Tegnapatam, where she embarked a large quantity of goods that had been prepared for her. With these she got back to Fort St. George on September 7, and was then dispatched to Masulipatam to complete her lading for Bantam.

A letter from Madras dated September 8, 1645, advised that a quarrel between the Dutch and Malaya, who was backed by the Vijayanagar monarch, had resulted in open warfare, and that consequently Pulicat was in a state of siege. The piece-goods in the hands of weavers employed by the Dutch had been seized upon by Malaya's soldiers, and the factors were much exercised over the question whether it would be safe to purchase these from the captors, as they were being urged to do. Their hesitation was increased by the threats of the Dutch to search all English ships and take out of them any cloth thus acquired; but they were somewhat en-

ordnance mounted er I came from thence, and some part of the materialls provided to goe on with the rest.' See *The Founding of Fort St. George*, p. 23, and *Court Minutes of the East India Company*, 1644-49, pp. 54-57.

couraged by the receipt, on October 1, of a letter from Srī Ranga, declaring that the seizures had been made by his authority and desiring them to complete the purchase (p. 285). At the same time he invited them to send a representative to his court; and as this seemed a fitting opportunity 'to have our old priviledges reconfirm'd, with the adition of a great many more', it was decided to depute thither the Second in Council, Henry Greenhill, with four other Englishmen as attendants.

No details have come down to us of Greenhill's proceedings at Vellore, but the grant that resulted, dated in November, 1645, is printed on p. 305. It followed much the same lines as the original concession from the Nāyak Damarla Venkatappa. The English were freed from all customs or duties at the port on their merchandise, and also from tolls on provisions brought from the inland districts; while their goods passing through the district of Punamallee were to pay, as before, only half the usual duties. The customs paid by other merchants were to be shared with the royal treasury. The town of Madraspatam and a piece of ground adjoining were made over to the English, and they were authorized to administer the 'government and justice' of the same. The concession regarding goods recovered from wrecks was renewed; and a promise was given that the settlement should be independent of the control of any of the neighbouring Nāyaks. Nothing was said regarding the right of mintage previously granted.

One interesting point about this grant is that the new settlement is therein designated Srīrangarayapatam—the term obviously applying only to the Fort and its surroundings, since Madraspatam is separately mentioned. As noted in the introduction to the previous volume (p. xlii), the new settlement had been previously known to the natives as Chennappapatam, after Damarla's father. The explanation seems to be that the King at this time bestowed his own name upon the town, as a mark of favour and in order to wipe out the memory of a family now in disgrace.[1] It is not surprising to find that this attempt to alter a well-established designation proved a failure; and to this day a form of the old name is still used by natives of Madras.

No vessel being available for dispatch to Bengal this season, the

[1] See the remarks on p. 32 of my *Founding of Fort St. George*.

Madras Council ordered Olton, whom they intended to make chief at Vīravāsaram, to take passage from Balasore to Masulipatam in a Dutch vessel, leaving Netlam in charge at the former place; and they intimated their intention of closing before long 'that unproffittable factorie', where there was 'litle or noe bussiness' (p. 293). Olton duly obeyed these directions and, after handing over the remaining cash to Netlam, proceeded to Fort St. George (*O.C.* 1981).

The present volume introduces us to Gabriel Boughton, the English surgeon whose professional skill is generally alleged to have been the means of obtaining for his nation important privileges in Bengal. The story, as given in Stewart's *History of Bengal* (p. 251), is that in 1636, the Emperor's daughter, Jahānārā, having been badly burnt owing to an accident, a message was sent to Surat desiring the assistance of a European surgeon; that Boughton, the surgeon of the *Hopewell*, was thereupon sent to court and was successful in effecting a cure; and that, upon being invited to name his reward, he magnanimously refused to accept anything for himself, but requested 'that his nation might have liberty to trade free of all duties to Bengal, and to establish factories in that country'. The narrative adds that, this privilege having been duly granted, Boughton proceeded to Pippli, and in 1638, an English ship happening to arrive in that port, he, in virtue of his grant, secured for her merchants complete exemption from customs duties; and that later on, by curing a favourite of Shāh Shujā, the Emperor's second son, who was then Governor of Bengal, he greatly increased his influence and was able to assist his countrymen to start factories at Balasore and Hugli, in addition to that at Pippli.

This account is demonstrably wrong in dates and in several other respects. The English never had a factory at Pippli; while that at Balasore owed nothing to Boughton's assistance. Moreover, as pointed out by Yule and others, the accident to the Princess occurred early in 1644, when the court was at Delhi; and not only would it have been impossible to procure a surgeon from Surat in time to be of any service, but we are expressly told, from an Indian source, that her recovery was due to a famous Lahore physician. The actual facts of Boughton's deputation are given on p. 229 of the present volume. Asālat Khān, a prominent official at court, had repeatedly asked for an English surgeon; and the arrival of the *Hopewell*, in September, 1644, enabled the President and Council to gratify his wishes. According to the memorandum referred to below, Boughton, her surgeon, had been at Madras (though no trace of his presence there can be found in the extant records) and had proceeded thence to Bantam in 1643, with the intention of going home. The vessel's failure to complete her voyage left him at Surat, we are told, penniless; and this would account for his readiness, there being no other opportunity of employment, to enter the service of Asālat Khān. It is not clear when he started to take up his new post; and the Surat factors make no further mention of him, as they certainly would have done had any important grant of privileges resulted from his mission. An interesting letter recently discovered (see the *Indian Antiquary* for May, 1912) shows, however, that he was with Asālat Khān at Balkh in 1646; and we shall hear something of him in later years from the other side of India. Meanwhile we may note that, on the death of his patron in 1647, Boughton seems to have proceeded to the court of Shāh Shujā, in Bengal. There, it is said, he cured a favourite member of the Prince's *haram*, with the result that he gained considerable influence with the Shāh and was able to afford useful help to his fellow countrymen when they were seeking to establish themselves at Hugli in 1651. Boughton himself died in 1652 or 1653.

The question of the source from which Stewart drew his version of the story is not without interest. Stewart's own reference is unintelligible; but the fact that much the same account, though in a briefer form, was given at an earlier date by Orme in his *Military Transactions* has enabled both to be traced to a document now preserved in vol. xxx (p. 35) of the *Fort St. George Factory Records* in the India Office.[1] This is a copy of a memorandum written in February, 1685, by some factor in Bengal, giving an account of the origin and progress of the English settlement in that province; and it evidently embodies the tradition then current of Boughton's share in procuring the necessary privileges. Its inaccuracies are therefore easily explained. We may further note that

[1] See an article by me in the *Indian Antiquary* for September, 1911, where this document is printed in full.

INTRODUCTION xxxvii

a rather earlier embodiment of the legend is to be found in Thomas Bowrey's *Geographical Account of the Countries round the Bay of Bengal*, 1669-79 (Hakluyt Society, 1905). In this no mention is made of the cure of the Princess Jahānārā, while Mīr Jumla is substituted for Shāh Shujā as Boughton's second patron.

Several references occur in the present instalment (pp. 9, 200, 232, 312) to the operations of the French in Madagascar and elsewhere; while on p. 134 there is an allusion to Tasman's discoveries in the South Seas. Among other points of interest, attention may be directed to the remarks on pp. 136 and 202 concerning the decline of indigo cultivation; also to the account given on the latter page of the practice of mixing that commodity with sand. On pp. 161 and 216 we find references to marine insurance at Surat. Dhanjī, the Company's broker at Agra, whose moving account of the death of John Drake was given in the last volume, was, we hear, dismissed in 1644 for negligence and disrespect, and 'chiefly for endeavouring to distroy Mr. Turner by sorcery' (p. 215). Finally, on p. 152 we have an interesting epilogue to the story of John Leachland and his Indian wife, showing the efforts made by the Surat Council to dispose respectably of the daughter who was the offspring of that ill-starred union.

THE ENGLISH FACTORIES IN INDIA

1642-45

JOHN ALLISON, COMMANDER OF THE *DISCOVERY*, AT GOMBROON TO THE PRESIDENT AND COUNCIL AT SURAT, JANUARY 12, 1642 (*O.C.* 1786).

Wrote last by the Dutch 'pram' [*see the previous volume*, p. 41]. On December 23 he took the ship over to Larak to procure ballast, returning the 28th. Found that Mr. Hall had arrived from Ispahān two days before. The whole cargo was put on shore in good condition, and the passengers were 'well content, loving, and courteous.' So also was the Sultān [i.e. the Governor] until a dispute arose between him and Mr. Wheeler as to the number of Englishmen to be allowed to watch at the custom-house. The result was that on January 4 those employed in this duty were attacked by about three hundred men, who killed one of them, seized the rest and carried them to the Sultān's door, where they were so unmercifully beaten that some died. 'Had it not bene for the Companies estate on shoare and the merchants lives theare resident, I would have heaved out all the ballast which I had formerly taken in and a runn the *Discovery* ashoare at three quarter flud before the towne (for its all soft oose), and then with Gods assistance I would not a doubted but to a beate theire durty brittle towne and castle about theire eares; and I hope to live to be employed about some such action or some other to be revenged on such unmercilesse dogs, who hath so barbarously and cruelly tortured and murthered these poore honest men.' The surgeon's mate[1], while on shore, had three arrows shot into him and died next morning. Thirteen men have been buried since they left Swally, and others are sick; the crew will therefore have to be reinforced before the ship goes to Mokha. An anchor and cable

---

[1] His name is given in *O.C.* 1783 as Daniel 'Wormeleiton'.

also needed. Fears there will be little freight forthcoming here. The Agent is daily expected. (*Copy.* 2½ *pp.*)

PRESIDENT FREMLEN, FRANCIS BRETON, AND JOHN WYLDE AT SWALLY MARINE TO THE COMPANY, JANUARY 27, 1642 (*O.C.* 1787).

On July 25 received overland from Masulipatam the Company's letters of November 13, 1640; and on September 27 the *London* and *Discovery* arrived with those dated March 26 and 27, 1641.[1] The *Crispiana* sailed from Swally on January 3, 1641, 'full and richly laden'. A letter left by her master at Johanna on February 3 was picked up there by William Bailey, master of the *Reformation*, on May 8, brought to Masulipatam on July 9, and received here on August 13. Enclose transcripts of her invoice and of the letter sent in her. Now answer the letter of November 13, 1640. Rejoiced to hear of the safe arrival of four ships and wish the *Jewel* had been among them. Fear that all hope of her safety must now be abandoned, especially as she was a slow and unsafe vessel. Similarly, the *Pearl*, *Comfort*, *Swan*, and *Expedition* were all bad sailers and much slower than the Dutch ships. Trust that in future the Company will buy or build vessels like the *Coaster* or *Caesar* and not 'such mishapen ill conditioned cole tubbs' as those mentioned. Are glad that the letters forwarded by way of Basrā arrived seasonably. Thank the Company for the men and stores now sent for their small shipping. Reprisals are made upon the Malabars at every opportunity. The *Seahorse* and *Francis*, in March last, soon after leaving Swally for Basrā, captured three Malabar vessels laden with coco-nuts, &c. Fourteen of the principal men were made prisoners, two of the vessels were burnt, and the rest of the Malabars were turned adrift in the third without sail or oars. They got to Surat, with the aid of one of the Mogul's junks, and there demanded justice from the Governor. He, however, 'having some few daies before bine beholding to us for undertaking convoy of his junck to Bussora (which then in company of your vessells voiaged) and bringing thence horses, for which hee covenanted to pay you five tomands fraught for each horse his servants bought and delivered us for transport hither, and a rupee for each abassee

[1] None of the letters mentioned is extant.

expended on such horses as should by your servants bee bought and brought hither for your accompt, became deafe to their clamors. And so, with a litle formall seeming displeasure for ceizing so neare this port merchants vessells bound to this port, this busines was overpast; and wee not troubled with giving passes to this theftuous nation untill Mirza Jam Cully Beague our new Governors coming, who by his continued importunity prevayled with us to graunt passes to nine only, and to promise safe conduct to them, if your vessells encountred them to the norwards of Damaon; but if to the s[outh]wards of that place, or elcewheare, they became obvious to your people, they might imploy their most of power and courage to chastize and surprize them. Unto this, though wee were in a manner inforced to submit, because the Governor pretending that the coast trending somewhat below Bullsar is his Kings and therfore ought properly so farr to protect such as would trade to his ports, yet wee consented with so much seeming unwillingnes that the Mallabars doe hardly credit us.' In point of fact the cargoes which the latter bring to Surat are of such small value that they are not worth troubling about. 'The best way to revenge you of them, and repaire your losses, is to waylay their vessels bound to Aden and Mocha.' The *Supply* was sent thither for that purpose, but arrived too late; however, the *Francis* goes to Mokha shortly and will, it is hoped, have better success, 'notwithstanding the maenaces Esquire Courtyns grand Captain Hall delivered in Mr. Prowds hearing that, if wee disturbed or surprized the Mallabars, hee or his subordinates would affoard like measure to the Guzuratt juncks whearever they encountred them. Nor may they hope other from such rash insolent fellowes, unlesse Your Worships can timely contrive to reduce or restraine their bravings; for in the heights of their jollities they know no master but the King, whose flag being advanced on theire ships topmasts gives their wisedomes cause of wonder how your shipmasters dare, being in sight therof, to keepe the English flag abroad.' Are glad that satisfaction has been recovered from Gosnoll for the missing bale of calicoes; and have warned other pursers that they are responsible for all goods included in their bills of lading. Will say no more about their controversy with the factors in Persia, though they are of opinion that good has resulted, as the factors have since shown much greater diligence. The orders to Agent Merry to return to India were forwarded to Gombroon by the *Discovery* on November 18. Owing to the large quantities of broadcloth brought out in private trade, the Company's consignment had to be sent to Persia for sale. Merry will on arrival be admitted to the Surat Council, as directed. Possibly he may be sent to Ahmadābād to replace Robinson, who has been recalled; but for the present George Tash will be left in charge of that factory. The English house at Gombroon is not the absolute property of the Company. A sum of 200 tūmāns was lent upon the security of the building, with the proviso that the English should occupy it rent-free for eight years; but, the owner dying not long after in debt to the King, his estate was seized and the house is now royal property. By giving a present, the Agent obtained a farmān allowing the English to enjoy the benefit of the former contract; yet unless another farmān be procured, granting them a longer period, they are likely to be turned out or made to pay rent for it. Consider it necessary to retain a factory at Ispahān, for otherwise the Persian officials may refuse to pay the English share of the customs; and besides the King will probably insist upon this, as also upon an annual present. Other news from Persia. Goods landed there by the Dutch. Narrate the purchase at Ahmadābād by Benjamin Robinson, without authority, of 670 bales of the previous year's indigo. This is of inferior quality; and, moreover, 'at opening the bales the indico was discovered to bee full of holes, which small wormes, bred from the juice of a trees barke mixed with indico at its making to give it the better coullor, had eaten not only through that but through all the indicoe made the passed yeare, as wee in the 218 bales returned from Gomroone, and many other merchants of this towne in divers parcells which they owned, have experimented; which though the indico looseth nothing of its owne substance, because the wormes feed only on the intermixture, yet some dust is therby caused and much losse in weight induced.' Altogether, the Company is likely to lose 2,426*l.* by Robinson's action; and to meet this he has only about 1,380*l.* in England and whatever is due to him as ten years' salary. He has been so much affected by the occurrence that they feared 'hee would have pitcht upon some desperate resolutions';

but he is now in a better frame of mind and willingly goes home in this ship 'to prostrate himself to your mercy.' They praise his abilities and express regret that this unfortunate incident should have spoilt his career.[1] This ship (the *London*) carries home 814 bales of Sarkhej indigo, part of which (being last year's growth and making) 'is the best and purest that ever Serquez vented; made so by the strict injunction and inforcement of the Ahmudabad Governor' [*see the previous volume*, p. 274]. Hope to send a large consignment of equal quality by the *Discovery*. Are glad to find that Biāna indigo is in good demand in England. They could have supplied a large quantity, had the Company sent the necessary means to purchase it; but as they have not been pleased to do this, the ship must be filled up with sugar and other low-priced commodities. The non-arrival of the large supplies of money expected 'hath now so much declined your credit that, after the proceed of the rials was paid out [or] rather ceized on by your Suratt creditors (as will in consultations held in October more plainely appeare), nothing was left to send to Ahmudabad to cleare your goods thence; where also, besides Benjamin Robinsons debt for his indico, Your Worships owed upwards of 10,000 *li.* sterling, and without monies it was impossible to bring them thence; insomuch that wee even despaired of sending home your ship *London* this yeare. In these necessitous and calamitous times, your greatest creditor, Virgee Voura, whose indeed requiry of his monies brought first your credit in question in Suratt, . . . undertooke our releife.' He unexpectedly offered a loan of 100,000 rupees, payable in Ahmadābād, and thus enabled them to provide a lading for the *London*. Their want of means has forced them to 'forbid continuance of cloth investments in all your factories, especially in Agra, which furnisheth most of the kinds of browne cloth wherof in Ahmudabad those dyed severall sortments requested at Bantam, Mocha, Persia, and Bussora are made; for which places the intended investments were inhibited also, and so must continue untill you are pleased to affoard us tooles to worke with.' Further, it has been found necessary to keep back for Mokha a certain quantity of indigo and

[1] The Company, after investigating the matter, fined Robinson 1,000*l.*, but re-engaged him and allowed him to pay by instalments the part of the fine not already covered by the amount due to him for wages (*Court Minutes*, 1640-43, pp. 305, 330, &c.).

calicoes, the proceeds of which will be applied to the reduction of their debt, or (if they can get further credit) to make an investment at Agra in goods for England. Urge a plentiful supply of money if the *Discovery* is to be sent home (as they hope) fully laden in November next. Have notified the Agra factors of the want of weight in the Biāna indigo. Regret the defects in the 'joories' from Sind. Now send 89 bales of calicoes from those parts, 75 being from 'Nussurpore[1]' and the rest from 'Durd[   ][2], a towne scituated higher up that great river of Indus.' Both are somewhat dearer than usual, but the general dearth of cotton wool last year throughout India has increased the price of yarn and consequently of calico in all places. Have ordered 20,000 pieces of Sind calico for next season, and hope to provide them at cheaper rates. Some broad 'Scinda joories' are now forwarded; also 59 bales of indigo from thence. 'Saltpeeter wee send none; nor should not have medled with sugar, if not to prevent dead fraught.' Part of that carried by this ship was bought at Ahmadābād; the rest is Bantam sugar, received by the *Swan*. Have put 146 bales of cotton yarn into the *London*. Could not procure any good dry ginger. A quantity of Nosārī calicoes forwarded. At Broach and Baroda Dutch competition and the dearness of cotton wool forced up the prices to an unreasonable figure; hence they bought but little. A considerable quantity of Agra calicoes sent. Of these the 'Dereabads' came partly 'whited' and partly 'browne', and the latter have since been bleached at Surat and the neighbouring factories. All of them were bought 'at Lucknoo and other townes beyond Agra, where they are made and whence they are carried to Agra for sale.' Twelve bales of 'Keyrabads' sent; they are both broader and longer than Broach baftas. Of 'Mercooles' they forward 52 bales; also a quantity of 'Eckburies, a larger and longer sort of Agra cloathing then the Mercoolees.' A great many of these were bought, but most were 'transformed in Ahmudabad into byrams, selaes, cassedees, large chints, and other sorts of sundry denominations requested at Bantam and Mocha specially.' Have also provided a quantity of Agra calicoes similar to narrow baftas. 'The cloth is very even and substantially made neare

---

[1] Nasarpur, not far from Hyderābād (Sind): see the 1634-36 volume, p. 128.
[2] Probably Dādū, in the Lārkāna District.

Agra, and there tearmed Guzzees, of uncertaine lengthes, some of 80, some 70, some more, some lesse (most above 40 coveds); sold there by the hundred coveds; of which in Ahmudabad cannikeenes of both sortes, ardeas, blew baftaes, and the like are made and sent to Mocha, Persia, Bussora, &c.' Some of these calicoes being found suitable for England, they have been bleached and are now forwarded. If approved at home, large quantities can be provided at cheaper rates than the Tatta or the Gujarāt cloth. Bornford and his assistants at Agra have saved the Company much money by buying such goods at first hand and sending them to Ahmadābād to be dyed, whereas formerly they were bought at the latter place at second or third hand. Want of money has, however, put a stop to their operations, and John Turner and Francis Hammersly have consequently been recalled to Agra from 'the out-townes.' Could not procure 'Guiney stuffes' in time for this ship, but will send some by the next. Forward some 'tapseels', part woven in Surat and part bought in Sind. Of Ahmadābād 'cloathing' they have laden some white 'dutties', some 'whited seriaes broad', some quilts, and some 'pintadoes'. Could not get any gum-lac from Agra or Ahmadābād, but have now bought a parcel in Surat; also some olibanum, aloes Socotrina, and myrrh. Vīrjī Vōra was for some time unable to fulfil his contract made with President Methwold to provide Deccan pepper, but he afterwards agreed to deliver the stipulated quantity at Calicut in October, 1641, if the English would fetch it from thence. The *London* was accordingly sent thither, with William Pitt and Thomas Hill on board; also John Wylde and George Oxenden, who were to be left at Goa on the way.[1] The ship sailed on October 25 and reached Calicut on November 11. On her arrival Vīrjī Vōra's servants declared that the pepper was at 'Punnone' [Ponnāni], to which place the *London* proceeded accordingly. There she was furnished with a small quantity of pepper, of bad quality, besides some cardamoms and turmeric; and, after embarking at Goa some arrack and cinnamon, she returned to Swally on December 27. The pepper was taken on shore, as being unfit to send for England; and 50 tons of Bantam pepper have been laden instead. They are very angry with Vīrjī Vōra for 'this peece of villany', but they can do nothing

[1] Cf. *Dagh-Register*, 1641-42, pp. 223, 235, 239.

to punish him until they are able to pay the money they owe him. Wylde and Oxenden were sent to Goa to congratulate the new Viceroy, settle certain accounts, and procure (if possible) some cinnamon. Their mission was 'so gratefull and so well accepted' that they obtained without difficulty a considerable quantity of cinnamon, which is now sent home. Moreover, 'besides the clearing those severall depending accompts with that state and its officers (whose debts you now receave in cinamon), wee come to know that the V[ice] Roy will bee yet further intreated to furnish you with greater quantities of that comoditie; and hath allready suspended subscription to a petition exhibited to him by Leonard Woodman [1], imploring license to setle a residence for his masters servants in Goa, untill hee had first consulted with your President and receaved his refusall of such favor.' It has accordingly been determined by consultation that the *Swan* on her way to Bantam shall land Pitt and Hill at Goa, 'not only to pay for part of the cinamon for which you are yet indebted to the Jesuits (who were the readiest and rendred themselves the ablest to serve you in these occasions), but to continue a residence there, so to prevent the Courtinians entrusion', purchase more cinnamon, and attend to other affairs affecting the Company. Cardamoms and turmeric sent home. Acknowledge that their borrowings have exceeded the limits fixed by the Company, but they could not otherwise have provided such large cargoes for England, Basrā, and elsewhere. By the *London* alone they return 6,955*l.* more than was sent out in her and the *Discovery*. Refer to their accounts, &c., for particulars. They had expected a much larger remittance and on the strength of this had involved themselves in engagements which could not be cancelled; but they hope to receive means before long which will set matters on a proper footing. Thank the Company for 'advizing so timely the unlawfull undertakings of the Deip and St. Malloes shipping, and in sending the *Discovery* to secure your owne and this countries vessells from their cruell rapinous clutches; whose purposes (the very day they became knowne unto us) we publisht to this townes Governor and inhabitants, and with them our resolves not to bee lyable to any damage that should by those French vessells accrew unto them; which we then assured them would bee early in the

[1] The agent for Courteen's Association.

Red Sea Streights, for (besides your advice of them) jointly with your letters wee received others from Agent Cogan &c., and with them copy of a commission given by Cardinall Richliew to one David Digger, captaine of the *Rose* of Diepe . . . who, arriving safely to the iland of St. Laurence, spawnd there and produced a demy pynnace, called the *Magdalen*, which was there set together, rig'd, fitted, and furnished with two minion cutts, oares, men, and what elce wanting; in which aequipage Mr. Bayly found and left them at Augustine Bay; whence (wee since come to know from the master of this pynnace) they set saile and shaped their course to the Red Sea Streights, where, meeting with overboisterous weather, they parted company;[1] when this pynnace, not daring to oppose those growne seas and being very poorely fitted with edible provisions, steered before the winde, which blowing towards the coast of India brought them in sight of your ships *London* and *Discovery* off Damaon, and afterwards on board the former; where her master and company desiring supply of victualls was denyed by Mr. Prowd, if they intended to spend them on board their owne vessell, yet offered to releive and receave them into the *London* if they could resolve to leave her, which could not in probability without hazard conveigh them to Europe. Necessity inforced their consent and retirement to the *London*. Their vessell being then adrift, Mr. Prowd &c. bought her for your use and behoofe at 30*l*. sterling (to bee paid in India), put 12 of your seamen into her, and brought her with him into Swally Hole; where, after she had made one voiage to Suratt with lead and corall, she was (being brought on ground to cleanse), by her masters negligence cheifly and by the weathers roughnes, bilged; yet her guns, anchors, masts, and rigging were all saved, and are estimated to be worth much more then you pay for the vessell and them together.' Of her original crew six were Scots and six Frenchmen. The former were added to the crew of the *Discovery*; the latter served on the *London* without pay until she returned from the Malabar Coast, when, finding three Dutch ships at Swally, they petitioned for leave to join them, 'unlesse

---

[1] Apparently the ship returned to Madagascar; for François Cauche (*Relations Veritables et Curieuses de l'Isle de Madagascar*, 1651, p. 24) chronicles the arrival there from the Red Sea of a Dieppe ship under one Digart, though the name of the vessel is given as the *Marguerite*.

they also might have wages for their service'. As the vessels were shorthanded Mr. Proud was permitted to enrol these Frenchmen and to apportion them wages. No news has been heard of any other French ship; 'so that it is thought those of St. Malloes were elcewhere disposed. For all the vessells belonging to this, Cambaiett, and Dio ports sent last yeare to Mocha are safe returned, with good advance on the merchandizes they carryd hence; and some of them redispeeded. Others also are preparing to follow, but are not suffered to lade untill both the great junkes belonging to this King are full; which also wee feare will somewhat decline that ample fraught wee hoped to have made on the *Discovery*.' Pepper is not particularly scarce 'in Decan or Mallabar', and yet it is said to be very dear. The Dutch at 'Rawbaag' [Rāybāg] declare that the 'Courtinians' are paying 27 pagodas per 'gunney' [sack: *see the previous volume*, p. 237]. 'Wee would not willingly pay so deare for their interruption in that trade, whilest the Dutch effect what you had recomended to William Pitts agitation with no charge to you.' Indeed, as pepper fetches only 16*d*. per lb. at home, it is a wonder that the trade is thought to be worth following. When the *London* passed by Rājāpur on December 13, Courteen's ship *William* was lying there ready to set sail for England, with a cargo of pepper, saltpetre, cinnamon, cardamoms, &c. The cinnamon is said to have been bought near Cochin from the 'Ceiloan caphila[1]'. Except for this commodity, her lading is not likely to produce much profit. 'If by such returnes a trade to India can subsist, wee shall thinke the better of yours, notwithstanding your continued complaints against it.' Hope seasonably to hear of the exclusion of Courteen's factors, 'notwithstanding his Woodmans this yeares investment with the title of Agent, confirmed by His Majesties commission, as in a pardon graunted by him to one of his masters servants, who, having absented himself and fearing punishment, retired to Goa and would not bee thence recalled untill the Agent sent him his pardon, signed, sealed and delivered, which for the rarenes of the stile and method wee have herewith inclosed to you. The *Paradox* and *William* arived very early, the former in July, the latter towards the fine of August. When the *London* and *Discovery* anchored in Augustine Bay, they found there Mr. Courtyns *William* and *Hester*, the one bound to

[1] The Portuguese fleet of small vessels bringing merchandise to Goa from Ceylon.

India, the other to England.' Refer to Mr. Proud for details. 'What fate attends the Choromandell actions wee cannot divine. New complaints we find yearly exhibited against it, and wee cannot but credit the reality of them. Would to God wee knew how to rectify and redresse them. Your affaires are now without all question more orderly, though for ought wee perceave litle more fortunately, then formerly managed; for though from thence wee receave accompts of your busines, yet they come clogged with such excessive expences and charges (wherof those of housekeeping are reasonable enough) that our Bantam freinds and ourselves seldome see the moiety of what Your Worships, they, and wee furnish.' At Bantam they have received little more than 20,000 pagodas out of the cargoes of the *Expedition, Hopewell,* and *Reformation,* which aggregated over 30,000*l.* sterling. From Surat Cogan and his colleagues have been furnished with 22,864 pagodas, and yet only 11,042 pagodas have been received in return. The last remittance of 14,000 pagodas the Coast factors were required to make good upon the arrival of means from England or Bantam; but this has not been done, and probably only four or five thousand pagodas' worth of goods may be expected in lieu thereof. The Bantam factors suspect those at Surat of endeavouring to secure goods from the Coast which should properly be sent to the former factory; and, although assured to the contrary, 'they take liberty to slight and deride us with most unbefitting language', as shown in the accompanying letter. Have forwarded to the Coast factors the Company's letters. 'They have lately replyed therto; which, together with the Agents particular, in answer to what hee stands accused touching consortship with Mr. Ivy in the matter of private trade,[1] goe jointly herewith enclosed. Wherein because hee pretends that the foundation of Fort St. George was laid by our order, wee must necessarily contradict and convince him from his owne letters, which it seemes have bine received also by Your Worships. If not, as last yeare, wee are againe ready to prove (what peradventure the first projector of it, Francis Day, being at home with you, will vouch) that they first pretended the Naigue promised to build a fort for us at his owne charge; which when advized us, wee wondred more at, then we trusted in, such without example kindnes; but then sundry pretences

[1] See the *Court Minutes of the East India Company,* 1640–43, p. 144.

being framed to make it appeare more probable, wee consented to suffer the Naigue doe what he pleased with and on his owne ground, since it could not then hurt [and] might somewhat have helped your affaires, if hee would have made good his promises. However, wee prescribed the most of caution, and urged (even in the same words) what Your Worships have bine pleased to say of it—that Armagon was not deserted with intent to raise out of its ruine a new charge unto you. But ere our letters arrived the worke was begun by Francis Day, and paid for from your cash; which when wee blamed in the Agent, and put him in mind of the Naigues specious promises, hee answered that hee had said as much to the Naigue, who (as well he might) derided him for thinking so much folly as that hee, without any obligation to, would build a fort for us. In a word, the fault was laid upon Mr. Daies misunderstanding the Naigue, and so the walls were raysed; which, rather then the worke should cease, Day offered we know not what contribution towards it. Now the greatest part of them are finished, and may happily stand to doe you good service, for without such defensible places your goods and servants among such treacherous people are in continuall hazard; the just feare wherof hath induced the Portugalls, Dutch, and Danes to frame unto themselves more safe habitations; and such questionlesse will be wanting unto you, although, considering the subsistance of your present affaires and the meane trade you drive on that coast, this Fort St. George is in its erection unseasonable, in its being over chargeable. However, hitherto we have heard a faire report of it. The worst is its over neare vicinity to the Portugalls of St. Thome; not in respect of any hurt they can doe the Fort, but because of the many idlers, both men and weomen, who fraequent the Fort so much that divers of the English souldiers are (as Mr. Cogan saith) married; which hee pretends must necessarily bee tolerated, or the hotshots will take liberty otherwise to coole themselves (strange tenents to bee received for truth). How forward the worke is wee desire you heare read from its founders letters; for more then there is done (if they will heare us) shall not bee added untill wee or they receave answer to what was therof writ by the *Crispiana*; although much inconvenience [and] some danger may attend this desistence from prosecuting the worke to perfection. In those parts abundance of good and good cheape cloth is said to bee procurable, and wee find the experiment therof in the large investments the Dutch yearly make therabouts; so that, if you could resolve to inlarge your trade, wee conceave by what wee have heard of it that the Fort is conveniently enough scited and may serve you to many good purposes; and therfore, since you have bine pleased to referr its maintenance or dissolution to our doome, we have seriously considered of it and at last resolved to let it stand till your next yeares battery; by which time also, becoming better acquainted with that people, wee shall better know how to determine it. Wee shall not need herein more to inlarge of your Coast factors actions, because their owne letters speakes the *Reformations* arrivall, carga[zoon], and dispeed to Bantam, the *Dyamond* and *Endeavors* dismission to the Bay Bengala, to pay debts and bring your factors thence (who have so often bine fruitlesly called thence), and such other their proceedings as merit your notice; of whose subordinacy wee are heartily weary, and could (if you were pleased to thinke it fittest for your service) even wish them againe submitted to Bantam, because our reprehensions (when wee apprehend their proceedings unreasonable or improvident), though presented to them in a mild modest dyalect, appeare so offensive and greivous that they are againe retorted uncivilly and unsatisfactorily, insomuch that wee are somewhat troubled to resolve how to deale with them. . . . With all other your subordinate inland factories wee agree well enough and are complyed with observantly, for, if wee conceive any reason to find fault with any misdoeings or neglects in them, they are readily rectified; but if wee blame these Coast factors overbreife expressions in their journalls (wherwith nor wee nor no men elce, wee thinke, can be satisfied), or if from such abstracts of accompts (rather then accompts themselves) wee cannot rightly apprehend their meanings, and therfore desire better information, as in our letter of the 30th June . . . wee receave taunting replies, as in their letter of the 3d September . . . and must quietly take them for current payment, unlesse wee should determine to bandy disputations ad infinitum. To avoid therfore future difference with them about such matters, wee have willingly, upon your intimation therof in your letter by ship *William*[1], willed them to account with Bantam, and in all other matters to demeane themselves towards us, as Your Worships in your said letter have bine pleased to direct

[1] Dispatched from England to Bantam in March, 1641.

them; which also is amplified and more particularly insinuated in our letter to them of the 18th October.' Thank the Company for increasing Edward Pearce's salary. 'The small guns, cordage, and surplusage of men now come on the *London* and *Discovery* have so well strengthned and fitted your trading vessells that even the *Francis*, being of somewhat lesse then 100 tons burthen, sayled by 30 men (wherof her commander, George Gilson, was one), confronted nine saile of Mallavar frigatts, chased them, and, if one houre of daylight had favoured her, had undoubtedly ruin'd some of them. These pynnaces are very usefull to your occasions and excuse a great charge of greater shipping. However, the *Francis* begins to grow old; the *Michaell* remaines at Bantam. The *Seahorse* is yet serviceable for five or six yeares or longer; so that on her and the *Supply* wee now cheifly depend. And they being not sufficient, wee are induced to bring to your remembrance our former requests [and] your promises of furnishing one or two from England, of the dimensions intimated by the *Crispiana*; for these wee have allready, excepting the *Supply*, are neither soe capacious, defensible, nor proffitable for you as others of 200 or 250 tonns would bee. And some such the ensueing yeare wee hope to heare of before the fine of August; when, being so well fitted as usually your ships come from England, [they] may safely ride before, or enter into, this river, and therby infinitely forward your returnes for England, as Mr. Courtyns *Paradox* did, and so enabled Mr. Woodman &c. to give the *William* so timely dispeed.' Have communicated to 'Joseph Pinto Pereiro' the Company's offer of a passage to England[1]; but he does not propose to leave India until he hears that Portugal is absolutely quiet. At the request of the Jesuits at Goa, 'who indeed have bine at all times as able as ready to assist in your affaires', a passage on the *London* has been granted to an aged member of their order, named Francisco Carvalho. Can say nothing fresh about John Drake's indigo, or about the missing bales. Have demanded back from 'the Banyan doctor' the interest formerly paid him[2]; but he alleges that he was an agent only and has passed on the money to the actual lenders, who refuse to return what they consider justly due to them. 'Wee find indeed how great trouble

[1] See the *Court Minutes of the East India Company*, 1640-43, p. 148.
[2] See the previous volume, p. 202.

befalls you in thus clearing your servants ingagements; but, if this were all, the disease were easily cured by the generall notice we have and shall from time to time exhibit to the lenders, that whosoever dieth or departeth hence insolvent, the Honourable Company shall not bee lyable to pay their debts, but [these?] shall bee continued a losse to the kind and free hearted lender. But besides the former, the stuffing your vessels with private trade, and debasing (by underselling) your commodities values, are much more nocent to you, and cannot (though then now, we beleive, private trade was never lesse practized[1]) bee totally remedied, notwithstanding the Presidents personall attendance on the Maryne all the time your vessels lade to the neighbouring ports, and imploying covert watches, wherby wee know some are terrified from, others prevented in, these unwarrantable practizes.' It is true that when the ships are lading for England, the President's other duties prevent him from watching in person; yet the factors in charge are specially warned to attend to this point, though 'by what you write of the great quantities of particular goods brought thence on the *London* and *Discovery*, they litle (it seemes) reguarded; for which wee can better greive then propound a remedy.' Tapī Dās is ready to repay the money he received on account of Skibbow's debt to Gopaljī, if Methwold declares that this ought to be done.[2] The *Discovery* will be sent to Mokha in February, 'to prevent the French pyrates theftuous practizes'. Fremlen thanks the Company for their many favours and 'tendreth his subscription to your imposition of officiating the place of President for five yeares continuance from the time he entred theron.' 'Your Worships rightly apprehend how litle the title of Captaine serves to the navigating and goverment of your shipps and men at sea, and how much cost and ceremony attends that denomination, and have therfore taken a necessary resolution to blow downe that buble.'[3] Commend Proud and Allison, the masters of the *London* and *Discovery*. The latter's diligence is shown by the amount of freight goods carried to Persia, which produced 39,560 mahmūdīs;

---

[1] From the particulars given in the Dutch records of the time it would seem that this statement was far from true, and that Fremlen was prominent in trading on his own account to the detriment of his employers (see the previous volume, p. 297, and *infra*, p. 31).
[2] See the *Court Minutes of the East India Company*, 1640-43, p. 148.
[3] In December, 1640, the Company resolved to style the commanders of their ships 'masters' and not 'captains' (*Court Minutes*, 1640-43, p. 119).

whereas in the previous cruise of the *Discovery*, when Minors was commander, room could only be found for 20,608½ mahmūdīs' worth of freight. It is hoped that her freight to Mokha will not come far short of 45,000 mahmūdīs. Praise William Broadbent, who has been master of the *Supply* since October 30, 1639, at 5*l.* per month, and recommend him for the command of a larger ship. Have communicated with Bantam regarding the deficiency in the weight of cloves. Send home their general books, pursers' books, and the accounts of the subordinate factories. Hitherto the latter have been balanced to the end of September; but this date has now been changed to May in the case of Masulipatam, Agra, and 'Scinda', and to August in the case of Ahmadābād, Broach, and Baroda; 'that so in the vacant times of raines, when wee have least to doe, wee may make the exacter and more timely audit of them', before transferring them to the general books. Thank the Company for the 'chirurgery chest' and the two pipes of Canary wine. Advise certain deficiencies in the former, with a note of articles included which are superfluous or can be more cheaply procured in India. Duarte Fernandez Correa has sent a chest of goods on the *London*, to be delivered to Mr. Methwold, to whom he has written as to its disposal. 'S[enho]r Duarte is abundantly usefull unto us, and with most of ready willingnes assists in the maintenance of our free and fraequent respondence with the Portugalls, who, having most of them litle elce to doe, spoile more paper with their frivolous common complements then is easily credible; and yet they must bee answered with most of punctuality; otherwise they thinke themselves slighted or dishonoured, [and] us discurteous or ignorant of that part of good manners.' Desire a constant supply of sailors for their small shipping, as those here are continually lessened by their 'debauchure'. The *Blessing* has been lying at Goa ever since Methwold left her there, as the Portuguese would not buy her, and she was not worth fetching away. A few months ago she was so leaky that she had to be hauled on shore; so when the *London* went thither the hull was broken up and some of the materials brought back to Surat. Since 'bounders to the Dutches insolence' cannot be procured, they must bear it as best they can. Goods supplied to Bantam. Complain of the taunting letters received from that Presidency. Explain that the *Supply* was dispatched thither with a cargo of piece-goods, but after eight days at sea was forced to return. Refute other allegations by the Bantam factors, and point out that they are now sending thither in the *Swan* a cargo far more valuable than that she brought from thence. Defend the orders they gave to the Coast factors to pay their debts before making an investment for Bantam. William Hurt[1] would have been appointed General Purser in place of John Wylde, but at his urgent request he has been permitted to return to England in the *London*. As Wylde is now bound for Mokha, his post has been given to Richard Fitch, who came out as purser of the *Crispiana* and has since served in the *Blessing* and the *Supply*. [John] Perkins, purser of the *Discovery*, died some days before that ship sailed for Persia, and has been succeeded by his mate, John Sims. Robert Heynes made purser of the *Supply* and Edward Kinnersley of the *Swan*. Benjamin Robinson returns in this ship; also Richard Fisher, who came from Bantam as purser in the *Swan*. William Jesson has been notified of the increased wages granted to him.[2] A favourable report of his diligence and honesty has been received from Agra. Have now answered all the points in the Company's letters, and will proceed to other matters, referring for details or omissions to Proud's narration or to the President's journal [*missing*]. As regards the goods &c. brought out by the ships, the rials were welcome, though not half as many as they needed. Out of the number $28\frac{1}{2}$ were 'wanting in tale' and $17\frac{1}{4}$ were false. Of the $6,482\frac{1}{2}$ 'rex dollors' 28 were found to be of copper and are consequently returned. The rest sold at 216 rupees 16 pice the hundred; while the rials of eight fetched as usual $212\frac{1}{4}$ rupees per hundred for the new and $215\frac{1}{4}$ rupees per hundred for the old ones. 'Some daies before your ships brought these, upwards of 1,700,000 r[ial]s were landed from the junkes returned from Mocha'; consequently it took 33 days to pass the Company's rials through the mint, and then all the rupees that resulted were paid to their creditors, 'who greedily expected much larger distribution.' Of the gold coins, the 20s. pieces fetched from 21 to 22 mahmūdīs each, and the Venetians [sequins] $9\frac{1}{8}$ and $9\frac{1}{4}$ mahmūdīs. At Goa these coins produced $44\frac{1}{8}$

---

[1] Purser of the *London*.
[2] See the *Court Minutes of the East India Company*, 1640-43, p. 154.

and 20⅛ 'tangoes' [*see the* 1634-36 *volume*, p. 160] respectively, while the rial of eight was valued at 11 'tangoes'. Earnestly beg for a larger remittance by the next ships to clear off their debts. The sale of the broadcloth was spoiled by the competition of that brought by the seamen as private trade. Unless this can be stopped at home, it will be useless to send so large a consignment in future. No effectual means for its suppression can be used here. Moreover, last year the Armenians brought overland from Persia very great quantities of broadcloth, and sold it at such low rates that Lahore and Agra are both 'cloyed'; while the demand at the latter place has been further reduced 'through the Kings continued absence from Agra, whither if the revolted Raja of Congura[1] and the expected coming of the Persian King upon Candahar would permit his repaire, it would questionlesse sell readily.' Bornford has now been instructed to barter the broadcloth for indigo or calicoes. Although broadcloth is not in demand, scarlet and green 'baies and perpetuanaes' would probably sell to profit. Disposal of the lead received. As regards the coral, Vīrjī Vōra, who is in great favour with the present Governor of Surat 'and consequently awing all other Banyan merchants to his observance', is treating for its purchase, but in so dilatory a fashion that they have resolved to send part to Goa to procure cinnamon, and part to Ahmadābād, unless he makes a good offer in the meantime. They desire in future a double quantity of 'the finest sort or di Grezio' and 20 chests of the third quality ['terraglia' *in the margin*], but none of 'the midle sort or ricaduti',[2] for which there is little demand. Enclose a list of prices of other goods suitable for this market. No sword blades should be sent, except perhaps a few from Germany; 'for, besides those the Moores tearme Alimony and Genoobee (which wee construe of Allmaine and Genoa[3]), none are requested.' The paper, quills, and ink have been received and distributed. Ink could be dispensed with, if the Company would send out some copperas; but a thousand quills are needed per annum. They were forced to procure a supply from Agra, but

---

[1] This refers to the unsuccessful revolt of Jagat Singh, son of Rājā Bāsū of the Himalayan district of Kāngra.
[2] For these terms see the 1630-33 volume, pp. 31, 129.
[3] This was no doubt correct. *Alamānī* is Hindūstānī for 'German'.

found them 'nothing comparable in goodnes nor so fit for use' as the English quills. The knives and scarlet cloth have been used as presents. Now pass to the movements of their shipping. The *Expedition* left Swally on January 27, 1641, reached Gombroon February 11, and departed again for India on March 11.[1] Details of her cargo. She was then dispatched to Bantam on April 22 and reached that port on August 10. On September 24 the *Francis* returned from Basrā. She had left Swally, in company with the *Seahorse*, on March 6 and, after touching at Gombroon, they arrived at their destination on May 20. The *Francis* sailed from thence on August 11 with $11,036\frac{1}{8}$ rials and six horses, and took in at Gombroon a quantity of indigo left there by the *Expedition* but found to be unsaleable. On October 13 she was dispatched from Swally in search of the *Seahorse*. They met near Jask, and returning called at 'Scinda' on November 25, took in some goods, and, sailing thence on December 14, anchored in company at Swally on the 23rd. The *Francis* will shortly be sent to Mokha and thence to Persia to meet the *Seahorse*, which is to go again to Basrā. They will then call at 'Scinda' to bring away the goods collected there for England, and may be expected at Swally next October. The *London* and *Discovery* arrived on September 27, 1641; and with them the *Supply* returned from the Red Sea. She had been dispatched thither on January 14, reached Gombroon on February 12, left again on February 23, and reached Aden on March 31. She then proceeded to 'the Bab', and between April 3 and May 1 overhauled 45 vessels bound for Mokha, all of which, however, proved to belong to 'our freinds' and were consequently allowed to proceed unmolested. The *Supply* next sailed for Masulipatam, but met with such bad weather that she was forced to take refuge at Socotra. In these circumstances it was decided to make for Gombroon, which was reached on August 16. After embarking some silk, she left again on September 1, and fell in with the *London* and *Discovery* on the 23rd. On October 13 she was sent to Damān for arrack and returned nine days later. Her next employment was to carry pepper and freight goods to Persia, and on this errand she departed December 10. During next rains she will be 'doubled', to fit her for further service. The

---

[1] She arrived at Swally on April 10 (*Dagh-Register*, 1640–41, p. 380).

Swan from Bantam anchored at Swally on November 13, bringing a very poor return for what had been sent thither. She had on board two Portuguese passengers with a large quantity of private goods, for the freight of which they alleged that they had given satisfaction at Bantam. Near Diu the *Swan* encountered sixteen Malabar frigates, but upon her showing a bold front they fled. She will be sent back to Bantam as soon as the *London* has departed. The *Seahorse* remained at Basrā until October 16, 'in expectation of better markets', and then sailed with 8,000 rials of eight and a horse, valued at 375 rupees, sent as a gift from the Bāshā to the President. On her way back she called at Gombroon, where she took in certain goods and money for Surat. She will shortly be dispeeded to Persia and Basrā. The factors at the latter place will be directed to send her at once back to Gombroon with the proceeds of any further sales they may have effected; there she will meet the *Supply*, which will be dispatched from Swally with a cargo including further goods for Basrā. The *Seahorse* will then take in the latter in exchange for her own lading, and will return to Basrā, where she will ' attend the bringing off the last remaines of monies, and with them the factors', unless the Company order their further stay. On her way back, she will call at Gombroon and 'Scinda' for any goods that may be ready. The *Diamond* sailed on January 27, 1641, in company with the *Expedition* and, after visiting 'Scinda', reached Gombroon on March 6. Thence she departed on March 26 for Masulipatam, with nine horses for the Company's account. Adverse winds forced her into Muskat to water; and later she was obliged to put into 'Matacalla' [Baticola] in Ceylon for the same purpose. Sailing thence on May 11, she anchored on the 16th 'before our new fort' [Fort St. George] and landed one of the horses. Four days later she was sent in search of the *John*, which was cast away at Armagon, but nothing could be recovered. The *Diamond* then departed on May 24 and reached Masulipatam on the 28th; 'from which port she is since sent to Bengala to trim and bring thence those factors, for whose clearing she and another vessell (bought needlesly by John Yard in the Bay, called the *Endeavor*) carried in goods and monies to the amount of pago[das] 3,193. 13. 4, and fraught goods and pass[engers] paying for their transp[ort] pag[odas] 681. 13. 6. These were re-expected in October or November last; and the *Dyamond* designed to carry to Bantam from the Coast such goods as could not be fitted to accompany the *Reformation.*' The *Prosperous*, which is the smallest of all their vessels (being little more than 30 tons), was for some time laid up in the river at Surat for want of men; but on the arrival of the *London* she was fitted up and sent with that vessel to the Malabar Coast. She has now been hired by 'our house sheraffe [i.e. shroff] Tappidas' for 5,000 mahmūdīs to voyage to Basrā and back, in company with the *Seahorse*. Arrival at Swally of three Dutch ships from Japan in March, 1641.[1] Their cargoes produced here nearly 600,000 rupees. They sailed on April 6 for Gombroon, where they arrived before the end of May, and were then sent back to Batavia. On April 8 the *Zealand* left Swally for Batavia, laden with indigo, calicoes, &c. Five days later the *Snoek* from Persia anchored at Swally, and was sent away fully laden on April 24. On October 24 the *Vliegende Hert* arrived, and confirmed the report of the capture of a Portuguese carrack before Goa;[2] 'wherin, though much treasure was not found for the Company, yet the saylors got good pillage.' 'The carracks self they intend to Battavia, and have removed her from Goa to Ceiloan, where they have a fleete of 10 or 12 great ships, with which it is thought they intend, together with the souldiers and other meanes in them, to assault and (if they can) surprize Columbo before the expected peace bee published; to treat and enquire wherof the V[ice] Roy hath on a Dutch vessell sent a gentleman of good quality[3] to the Battavian Generall, so desirous the Portugalls are even to beg peace, or a cessation of armes at least untill it come confirmed from Europe. Besides this carrack the Dutch have also neare unto Goa taken a Portugall vessell richly laden from Mozambique with elephants teeth and a great quantity of gold. And before Macao in China it is reported that they have

[1] See the previous volume, p. 298. The account there given of the voyage is repeated in the text.

[2] See the introduction to the previous volume, p. xxviii.

[3] Diego Mendez de Brito, with whom was associated Frei Gonçalo de São José. They carried to Batavia a letter from the Viceroy, requesting a truce pending the arrival from Europe of information that the peace had been confirmed. This was refused, and De Brito was sent back to Goa in a fleet dispatched under Jan Dirkz. Galen to commence a fresh blockade (*Hague Transcripts*, series i. vol. xii. no. 386; *Lisbon Transcripts, Doc. Remett.*, book 48, f. 115).

another fleete of six great and small ships, to forbid the Portugalls trade thence to Mannilia; wherby (as it is now happened) they have done them a very great deale of pleasure; otherwise, if they had, as accustomary, voiaged thither, the Spaniards upon this Lusitanian revolt would have ceized on all.' On November 5 the *Dolfijn* reached Swally from Batavia, bringing over 150 tons of pepper, which will be sent to Mokha on the *Vliegende Hert*. 'On this coast neare Dabull this *Dolphin* was assaulted by six Mallabar friggats, who continued the fight three houres and then, their captaine falling, they also fell off and left her [1]; who from Vingurla brings tydings that, the Portugalls having bought an offensive and defensive league of amity of the King of Beejapore for 100,000 pago[das], the Dutch were therupon excluded from Vingurla and other ports of that Kings dominions [2].' The *Dolfijn*, after thirteen days' stay at Swally, returned to Batavia with the surplus goods left behind by the *Snoek*. On December 25 the *Henriette Louise* and *Enkhuizen*, with a small pinnace [the *Klein Zutphen*] arrived from Batavia. They landed spices, coral, and 52,000 rials, and then departed for Persia on January 8. Another Dutch ship is expected from China richly laden. 'In a word, they flourish abund[an]tly, and are very fortunate in theire undertakings. So powerfull they are withall that, unlesse the hoped peace take off the edge of their indeavors, the Portugalls, being no better provided, cannot resist them. But they [i.e. the Portuguese] ... are abundantly comforted and contented with their new Kings inauguration; and were exceedingly busied in solemnizing so great happines when the carrack was surprized; which they seeme not to resent, because they pretend and avouch that both shipp and goods were insured by Dutch merchants, then late come to inhabit in Lisboa, from whom this losse will be undoubtedly recovered by their new King; whose commands were no sooner seen by the V[ice]Roy and Councell at Goa then obeyed, and generally received by the whole nation, who from him propound to themselves a generall reformation and repairation of their declining fortunes; to whom all the forts and citties alongst this coast, as low as Goa, send by your ship *London* their submissive yet congratula-

---

[1] See the *Dagh-Register*, 1641–42, p. 189.
[2] A copy of this treaty (concluded June 4 (N.S.) 1641) is given in *Hague Transcripts*, series i. vol. xii. no. 385. It is printed in the *Dagh-Register* for 1641–42, p. 208.'

tory letters.' Request that these may be duly delivered, as also the other Portuguese letters accompanying them. 'The Danes drive a poore feint trade, not worth mentioning. We thinke that of Esquire Courtyn is litle better conditioned.' Grieve to report 'the fayling of those pregnant hopes wee had enterteyned of ample and proffitable returnes from Bussora; where this yeare, in reguard of warrs twixt the Great Turkes ministers and the Bashaw, the waies have bine so dangerous that very few merchants strangers (as accustomary in great caphilaes) have resorted thither; wherby it is come to passe that few of your goods have bine sold, and those also put off at meane proffit; and wee, who expected thence upwards of 80,000 rials, have not received 20,000 rials. However, those differences being reconciled and the Bashawes peace bought with a valid present, better times are certainly expected, and we hope to share in them. However, untill your goodes allready there are sold, wee are resolved not to send others thither, but have diverted those primarily intended to Bussora to Mocha, where the passed yeare the markets were good and [it] is hoped will bec so the ensuing season.' The *Discovery* and *Francis* will be sent thither under John Wylde, assisted by George Oxenden [1], Robert Cranmer, and perhaps another factor. These all proceed on the *Francis*; while William Fursman, if sufficiently recovered from his present sickness, may follow on the *Discovery*. Of the Englishmen taken prisoners by the Malabars, some have escaped, and thirteen have been ransomed for 1,210 rials. No factors have died during the past twelve months, and only three other Englishmen, who were 'forediseased' on board the ships. 'Towards the fine of September, Mazel Mulkes covenanted time of governing this country and farming this custome house and mint expiring, Jam Cullibeag, assisted with the former Dewon and one Mirza Arub [2], purposely designed to the custome house busines, entred on this goverment; whose face is now quite changed, for, wheras before dispatch of all busines depended solely on Mazel Mulks direction, because hee being obliged to pay the King three yeares 72 lacks of m[ahmūdī]s for provenue of this adjacent country, mint, and custome

[1] He had gone home in 1639 (see the preceding volume, p. 117), and had been re-engaged by the Company in January, 1641 (*Court Minutes*, 1640-43, p. 137).
[2] Mīrzā Arab. On this change of administration see the introduction to the previous volume, p. xxvi.

house, not any of the Kings ministers intermedled. But hee, it seemes, promised more then hee could performe by 31 laacks or 3,100,000 m[ahmūdī]s, which hee yet owes the King, and is therfore called to court to cleare acco[unt]s, which it is knowne hee cannot doe. And therfore this his fayling induced the King to thinke on some more provident course, and at last determined to confer the superintendence and goverment of all on Mirza Jam Cullibeage, on whose knowledg of this country and approved fidelity hee much confides. Yet because hee is alltogether unlearned [1], the aforenamed persons are adjoyned to his assistance, and a certaine exhibition allowed all of them yearly from the King; unto whose accompt whatever this country, mint, and custome howse produceth is brought. So that, though with somewhat more trouble and retardance then accustomary, in respect of procury of their mutuall dependent assents to the dispatch of busines, by which only all affaires are agitated, yet in what concernes the custome howse dispatches, wee and all other merchants rejoice exceedingly in Mazel Mulks displacing. For he, having this, Baroach, and Cambaiett ports under his goverment, exacted most unreasonable and unjust customes, because merchants, having brought downe their goods from the inland countries, must of necessity fall into his merciless clutches, if they at all intend either from Cambaiett or Suratt to imbarque them. Besides, his long continuance in these imployments had armed him with so much experience that merchants suffered much therby, as by his other oppressive dealings. These that now officiate this place want all these meanes to greive merchants, and (for ought wee yet perceave) will to doe it, if those meanes were extant. For whilest this custome howse only is under their goverment, merchants have liberty, though peradventure not so much conveniency, to ship off their goods from Baroach and Cambaiett, which both are yet Mazel Mulks; who, to hinder this and improve that port of Cambaiet, hath publisht resolved releasment of halfe customes to such strangers merchants as will repaire thither, and forbidden exportation by land from Cambaiett of all such goods as are there either made or cured, that soe those

---

[1] The Dutch records say that he could neither read nor write. They add that he was now sixty years of age, and that his allowance from the Emperor was 40,000 'R⁰' [rupees?] per annum. The date of the transfer of the post is given as October $\frac{4}{14}$ (*Dagh-Register*, 1641-42, p. 188).

at least may not only advance his sea customes but impleat a great junck built here by him at conclusion of his goverment; which also, ere hee left this place, hee dispeeded (though litle more then halfe built) to Goga, whence this yeare she voiageth to Mocha. Thus by Mazel Mulkes happy removall your goods, as well in Baroach as this custome howse, passe much cheaper then in his time; whom wee hope (though he flatters himself with a suddaine returnall) never more to see established in this goverment. Towards the fine of October certaine tydings came that Asaph Caun, besides howses, house moveables, catle, and jewells, dyed possessed of 17 crores of rup[ee]s, each crore importing 100 lacks, and each lack 100,000 rup[ee]s; all which this King, pretending to be his heire by marriage of his daughter, hath ceized.'[1] Long beads sent for barter at Madagascar. Enclose a list [*missing*] of Englishmen captured by the Malabars, and of the amounts paid for their release. Two of these, John Moss and Richard Husband, were taken in a vessel belonging to Duarte Fernandez Correa, who has since paid the amount of Moss's ransom, Husband having previously made his escape and reached Surat. The sums paid in other cases have been charged to the account of the men who are now going home, 'that so Your Worships . . . may either levy it from their wages or mercifully remit it.' Some private trade received by the *London* and *Discovery*, directed to two men that are dead and to one that has gone home, will be sold and brought to account. Enclose a list of Perkins' effects; these will be disposed of and the result advised. Accounts sent of the estates of three deceased factors, viz. Robert Adams, Edward Abbot, and Samuel Pauncefote. Similar statements regarding John Willoughby's and Francis Honywood's effects are awaited from Persia. Thus much was written before leaving Surat on January 25. On reaching Swally they found that part of the goods advised above could not be embarked in the *London* for want of room. By taking out some of the cinnamon they have found space for some of the cotton yarn; but a quantity of indigo, piecegoods, turmeric, &c. must necessarily be left behind.[2] A bale of cinnamon and a box of seed pearls sent home in the *London* by

---

[1] See the introduction to the preceding volume, p. xxvii.
[2] A short account of the final cargo of the *London* is given at p. 191 of the *Dagh-Register*, 1641-42.

Lewis Roberts, formerly boatswain's mate in the *Blessing*, who is now living at Goa under the name of Lewis Ribeiro Soarez and has rendered various services to the Company. Agent Merry has also forwarded a chest of rhubarb, concerning which he has written to the Company. Enclose a list [*missing*] of factors, &c., in India, Persia, and Basrā. Bornford from Agra, Wylde from Surat, Adler from Persia, and Thurston from Basrā have announced their determination to go home by the next ships; and therefore some able men will be needed to supply their places. William Fursman, whose covenanted time expired last March, wished this year to visit England, but he has been persuaded to remain. Recommend his re-engagement for three years from the expiration of his covenants at 50*l*. per annum. Hope 'to fit all things for clozure of your Third Joint Stock' by the time of the departure of the *Discovery* in November next, 'provided you please to send meanes, not only to pay for lading, but those 317,967 rupees wee are now indebted more then all you can depend on in India can sattisfy,' as shown in the enclosed account [*missing*] of 'quick stock' in this country. Earnestly entreat an ample supply of money for this purpose. *PS*.—Forward a small box of letters from the Dutch 'Comandore' here, directed to the Netherlands Company. (45 *pp. Received August* 24, 1642.)

THE EAST INDIA COMPANY TO [THE PRESIDENT AND COUNCIL AT SURAT], MARCH 24, 1642 (*Factory Records, Miscellaneous*, vol. xii. p. 59).

Wrote last on November 29 by the *Hopewell*, which was detained by contrary winds and did not quit the Downs until January 4. Trust that she met with better weather than was encountered by the fleet dispatched by Courteen. This sailed in November and consisted of three ships, 'vizt. the *Bonsperance, Bonaventure,* and *Hampton Merchant,* of burthen betweene 2 and 300 tonns apeece', carrying 16,553 rials of eight, iron, steel, lead, broadcloth, cotton wool, &c., in addition to the lead, coral, and money dispatched in the *Paradox*, which sailed 'about September[1] last'. These three ships, after reaching the latitude of Southern Spain, were dispersed by violent winds, and the *Hampton Merchant* was forced to return

[1] Apparently 'February' 1641, is meant (see *Court Minutes*, 1640-43, p. 146).

THE ENGLISH FACTORIES 27

to Plymouth, where she remained until the end of February before she could make a fresh start. Courteen's ship *Hester*, which left Cannanore on March 15 [1641], reached Plymouth on December 11, bringing pepper, indigo, cinnamon, saltpetre, gum-lac, and turmeric. The sale of these commodities has interfered much with 'our marketts', especially in the case of the indigo. Plans for the General Voyage. Instructions given for the investment of the stock sent out in the *Hopewell*, and for the disposal of the vessel in the meantime. To Bantam they have sent a ship of 250 tons, called the *Blessing*, with a cargo amounting to 16,064*l*. 3*s*. 1*d*. She was dispatched on January 14, but contrary winds detained her in the Downs till February 19, and they are rather afraid that she will lose her voyage in consequence. On reaching Bantam she is to be sent to Surat to fetch a lading of Indian commodities. On February 14 they received by way of Aleppo the Surat letter of March 4, 1641, one from Persia of September 15, 1640, and two from Basrā of June 14 and August 24, 1641, with copy of the 'articles agreed betweene our people and the Bashaw and Shawbander for trade in those parts'.[1] Now reply to the first of these. Approve generally the disposal of their shipping. Measures to be taken as regards the fraud imputed to the broker at Gombroon. Merry has complained of the deputation of Wylde from Surat to Persia as being an affront; but as Merry and the Surat factors are now (in all probability) 'meaniall[2] associates', the Company trust that harmony has been re-established. Dispatch of the *Expedition* from Surat to Bantam, to be returned with a lading of pepper. Commend the renewal of the attempt to establish trade at Basrā. Relate the skirmish between the *Seahorse* and *Francis* and the Malabar fleet. Hope that the prisoners have been exchanged for the Englishmen still in the hands of the Malabars. The factors at Basrā write that the Bāshā has offered them a piece of ground near the custom-house for a factory, but in reply they have been forbidden to build any dwelling-houses or warehouses. 'For the trade in that port of Bussora wee find noe extreordinary encoragement; and you know that *aury sacra fames* is that which makes difficult adventures and

---

[1] None of these documents is extant.
[2] This word had not yet acquired a contemptuous sense. All that is implied is that the two men were now forming part of the same household.

hard undertakeings be attempted where there is but hope of gaine. There marketts likewise were not very quick; for from their first arrivall the 20th May unto the date of their latter letters of 24 August they had not put any quantity of there carga[zoon] away, and for the gaines arrising they have byn from 36 to 50 per cent. upon some of the comodities.' The money received there had been sent to Surat on the *Francis*, while the *Seahorse* was to follow in the middle of October, the factors remaining (if necessary) until the following season. Hope that the latter vessel will arrive in good time, as it is desirable that the shipping for England should leave Surat rather in the middle than at the end of December. As for the Hollanders' 'insolent carriage towards our pinnace *Michaell*, wee must with patience beare such affronts as yet, since they have the better end of the staffe'. The Malabar vessel captured by the *Michael* was of little value, and was sunk after the rice and the crew of twenty men had been taken out of her. Desire to learn how Merry left matters in Persia; whether his departure is resented at court; and what has been done about securing the moiety of the Gombroon customs. Have now prepared for India the *Crispiana*, under the charge of Thomas Steevens, on account of the General Voyage; and have also chartered upon freight the *Aleppo Merchant*, commanded by John Millet, master and part owner[1]. List of the goods laden on these two ships, including 200,000 rials of eight (invoiced at 5s. each). In preparing return cargoes, special care should be taken that the calicoes are not damaged in the process of bleaching. Edward Knipe entertained as factor for the voyage at 200*l.* per annum. During his stay at Surat he is to be 'an assistant unto you in Counsell'; and he is to return on the last of the two vessels to leave India. Anthony Panton sent as minister, on a salary of 50*l.* and a gratuity of 10*l.* The *Hester* brought a letter from John Brightwell, sometime master of the *Hope*, and also one from Thomas[2] Moss of that ship, relating their cruel usage at the hands of the Malabars in a place called 'Burgare' on that coast; means should be sought of exchanging or ransoming these or any other English captives. One chest of 'chirurgerie' and another of drugs and medicines sent. Millet has been permitted to carry out five

[1] For a copy of the charter-party see p. 8 of Knipe's letter-book.
[2] This should be 'John'; cf. p. 25, and *Court Minutes*, 1640–43, pp. 232, 273.

tons, and bring back ten tons, of goods in private trade, provided that the commodities thus carried are not those the Company trade in; desire therefore that lists of his goods, both outwards and homewards, be forwarded to them. Robert Tindall, who went out in the *Blessing* in 1634, 'hath here a troblesome woman to his wife, who is continually peticioning for his wages and clamoring because he comes not home'; he should therefore be returned by the first ship. As in past years some of the masters have grumbled at the taking of wine from their vessels for use ashore, a pipe of Canary is now sent for the Surat factory. Breton is to succeed Fremlen as President at a salary of 350*l.*; and Merry, who for the present must rank as third, will then become second. The shipping of the General Voyage is to be used, if necessary, by the Joint Stock, in return for the assistance to be afforded by the latter to the former. Knipe may be retained on shore for a time if his services are required, but he is in any case to return with the present ships. If the *Aleppo Merchant* cannot be sent back at once, she may be employed on freight to Gombroon and then to the Red Sea. Now understand from Courteen that his three ships already mentioned are bound for Achin and the West Coast of Sumatra; and that he is also dispatching three others for India, viz. the *Unity*, under Gervase Russell, the *Loyalty*, under John Durson, and the *Hester*, under Robert Hogg. Cargoes of these vessels. They 'are consigned directly for the Coast of Mallabarr, unto their factories of Rajapore and Carwarr, or what other residences they have in those parts. And as you see these have a small carga[zoon] for 700 tonns of shipping, as they are accounted, soe is it now ordered here by a Committee of Parliament that these shipps must be the last which Mr. Courteene shall sett out for India to bring home what factores and goodes he shall have in those parts; but if any remaines shalbe left in those parts after the coming away of these shipps, they are to be by his direction brought unto our factories and wee are to bring them home for the same fraight which wee pay unto others.' Henry Robinson has been permitted to send on the *Aleppo Merchant* a parcel of coral, the proceeds of which are to be invested in 'such toyes and household provizions' as he has named, excluding all goods usually imported by the Company. Search to be made at Surat for the articles concluded with the Khān of Shirāz about the capture of Ormus [*see the* *previous volume*, p. 306]. Presume that fewer factors are now required; if so, the surplus may be sent home. Cannot say anything certain about next year's shipping; 'yet are wee noe waie doubtfull but that there wilbe stock and meanes found, sufficient at the least to furnish and sett forth a shipp of 300 tonns, if not more.' To provide the necessary cargo, the President and Council are desired to borrow at interest to the amount of 20,000*l.* and invest the same in indigo and calicoes. They are of course acquainted at Surat with the particulars of the truce concluded by Methwold with the then Viceroy of Goa; 'which pacification is now growing towards its conclusion, yet is there noe appearance of any breach, but a freindly shew of a further continuance. Nottwithstanding, the Portugall Ambassador here resident have bynn mooved by us for the settling of a firme peace betwixt us and them; to which proposition of ours the Ambassador replies that he hath noe commission to treate and conclude the peace in India, but promiseth that whatsoever was agreed heretofore between us and the Conde de Linharees shalbe inviolably kept; and, if any breach should happen betweene the nations, there shalbe twoe yeares time given to withdraw the goodes and merchandizes of the one nation from out of the power of the other; and when a treaty shalbe taken in hand, it shalbe referred for its perfecting unto some commissioners on both parts with you in India'.[1] It would not perhaps be wise to trust too much to the 'large expressions' of the Portuguese, and the factors are advised to be friendly but wary in intercourse with them. Two letters from the Portuguese Ambassador, addressed to the Viceroy at Goa, are forwarded herewith for transmission. Explain that in speaking of the ships belonging to the General Voyage being used by the Joint Stock, they did not mean that any such employment was to be allowed to hinder the return of those vessels to England, but merely that if one were obliged to remain for another year it might be so utilised. (*Copy.* 17¾ *pp.*)

[1] A treaty between England and Portugal was ratified at York on May 22, 1642. By clause xii it was agreed that the truce concluded at Goa in 1635 should be continued, and that commissioners should be appointed on either side to settle outstanding differences (see *Court Minutes,* 1640-43, p. xix, &c.; also *Lisbon Transcripts, Doc. Remett.*, book 48, f. 114).

THOMAS MERRY, WILLIAM HALL, AND THOMAS WHEELER AT GOMBROON TO THE COMPANY, APRIL 16, 1642 (*O.C.* 1783).

... Account of the attack on the English at the custom-house [see p. 1]. ... The *London*, which left Swally on January 20 [sic], doubtless carried home intelligence of the return of the *Seahorse* and *Francis* from Basrā, and of the dispatch of the *Discovery* and *Supply* to Persia at the beginning of this monsoon. The *Discovery* reached Gombroon in December, and left again on February 1. The *Supply* arrived about the end of December with pepper and freight goods, and sailed for Surat on January 13. The pinnace *Advice*, from the Coast of Coromandel, came in on February 9, and departed on March 25. The *Seahorse* and *Prosperous* anchored here on March 14.[1] The former was under orders to proceed to Basrā and bring thence to Gombroon 'that factories cash' for transhipment on the *Supply*; but as her speedy discharge was prevented by bad weather, they sent the *Prosperous* to Basrā instead. Her return is hourly expected. The *Supply* came in on March 19, and is now awaiting the arrival of the *Prosperous*. Merry will take his passage in her for Surat. 'Freight goods wee are forbidden to take for her reladeing to Surratt (by reason of some trouble which the President &c. are come into about goods stollen out of the freights of shipp *Discovery* this yeare) unles for some well knowne men.' Trust that hereafter the Company's ships will be employed in carrying its own goods, which will be more profitable than taking freights, especially considering the expense incurred by being forced to pay pretended losses. Narrate a recent instance in which it was found that the goods had never been put on board the ship, but had been stolen in the boat on the way. The broadcloth brought by the *Discovery* was sold at a very small profit; but the Coast goods yielded about 30 per cent. 'towards charges and interest', though dearly bought

[1] The Dutch *Dagh-Register* for 1641-42 (p. 195) says that these two vessels sailed from Swally on February $\frac{17}{27}$, accompanied by the *William*, belonging to the President (see the previous volume of the present series, p. 297). Their lading, which included a quantity of private trade, consisted of piece-goods, indigo, cotton yarn, Indian steel, pepper, &c. The *Supply* followed eight days later with freight goods.

It will be noticed that the English factors, in writing to their employers, say nothing about the *William*, for obvious reasons.

and badly chosen. The piece-goods, &c., from Surat also produced a good return. Disposal of the proceeds. . . . A farmān has been obtained at Ispahān, directing the Shāhbandar to pay at Gombroon the English share of the customs. 'What their amount may bee wee yet knowe not, but cannot hope they will exceede 350 or 400 tomands att most, soe much hath hee stolen out of the small quantity of goods this yeare arived; there being noe more jounckes come hither this yeare then 14 from all places, whereas in former yeares there hath come to this port 50, 60, and sometimes more. The Mallavars doe soe infest the Indian seas that many are fearefull to adventure forth. Of Hollands shipps there have arived this yeare four from Batavia: their *Hendretta Louis*, *Enchuson*, and *Klein Zutphen* first, and after them their *Ackerslote*. One more they expect from Surratt, arrived there from China. They have this yeare cleared all their debt in Persia, and boasteth of 15,000 tomands overplus (though wee creditt it not), by sale of theise ships cargazoones and their ould remaines.' Enclose particulars of the lading of the Dutch vessels. . . . (*Extracts only.* 4½ *pp*. Received December 8.)

THE VOYAGE OF THE *HOPEWELL* FROM ENGLAND TO THE COROMANDEL COAST (*Marine Records*, vol. lxv. p. 1).[1]

1641, *December* 31. Quitted the Downs. 1642, *January* 2. Lost sight of the Lizard. *February* 8. Anchored at Bonavista [one of the Cape Verd Islands]. *February* 11. Sailed again. *May* 16. Reached St. Augustine's. *May* 21. Departed. *May* 30. Anchored at Johanna. *June* 1. Sailed. *June* 26. Saw the coast of Ceylon. *July* 4. Saw 'Madrassapatam'. *July* 5. Anchored in the roads. *July* 19. Sailed. *July* 24. Reached Masulipatam. *August* 6. Sailed for the Bay of Bengal, accompanied by the *Advice*. *August* 14. Reached their destination. *December* 1. Sailed from Balasore. *December* 8. Anchored at Masulipatam. (25¼ *pp*.)

---

[1] Apparently a copy, made at a somewhat later date. The record is a very meagre one, and the name of the writer is not given; but, as the voyage from Madras to Tranquebar is omitted, it may be Trumball's own record. The writer mentions that this was his second voyage in the *Hopewell*.

For the Company's instructions to Trumball at his departure see *Court Minutes of the East India Company*, 1640–43, p. 214.

ANDREW COGAN AND HENRY GREENHILL AT FORT ST. GEORGE TO THE PRESIDENT AND COUNCIL AT BANTAM, JULY 17, 1642 (*O.C.* 1789).

Having just heard that a Dutch ship is leaving Pulicat to-morrow morning for Batavia, they write a few lines to announce the arrival here on July 5 of Francis Day in the *Hopewell* from England, with money and goods belonging to the First General Voyage. The Company had ordered that no part of this should be used in paying off the debts of the Third Joint Stock, but that all should be invested for England, Persia, and Bantam; nevertheless, it was decided by consultation to pay the debts at Masulipatam, and two days ago the *Advice* was sent thither with money for that purpose and to commence an investment. A Dutch ship which reached Pulicat on July 1 reported that on June 1, when she left Batavia, the *Diamond* had not arrived at Bantam; since then, however, the pilot of a Portuguese ship, which anchored here on the 13th, has told them that on June 2 he saw in the Straits of Sunda a ship and a pinnace which they believe to have been the Danish *Golden Sun* and the *Diamond*. To-morrow the *Hopewell* will be dispeeded for Masulipatam. (*Copy.* 1 *p. Received October* 28.)

PRESIDENT AARON BAKER AND COUNCIL AT BANTAM TO THE PRESIDENT AND COUNCIL AT SURAT, JULY 25, 1642[1] (*O.C.* 1790).

Answer first their letter of November 11 and 17, and in so doing will, for the sake of peace, pass over the 'bitter, nipping invectives interlarded' therein. Can see no reason for giving them credit in the Bantam books for money due to them from the Coast; this is a matter they must settle with the Coast factors. Object to the instructions given to the latter from Surat 'to transport the generall charges of that place for the yeares past to our acco[unt].' Such a course is unreasonable, considering that the Coast 'is subordinate and accomptible to Suratt'. Any charges directly arising from the provision of goods for Bantam may of course be added (as usual) to the invoice; but they cannot consent to be charged with the

[1] Sent in the *Swan*.

expenses of the ships, the building of a fort, the maintenance of its garrison, and Yard's 'exhorbitancies in the Bay of Bengala'. As regards the cargoes of the *Hopewell* and the *Reformation*, these have been charged to the Coast by Bantam, as is the right course. Now answer the letter brought by the *Swan*, dated February 1. That vessel left Swally on the 5th and Goa on the 21st of that month, and after a tedious passage reached Bantam on June 9. It must be a great advantage at Surat to be able to borrow money, when necessary, at 1 or 1¼ per cent. per month; here it would be requisite to pay 4 or 5 per cent. It was to avoid this excessive interest that last year, being in great need of money, they took up 6,000 rials from the Portuguese who embarked in the *Swan*, and gave them bills on Surat for the amount. Regret to be unable at present to clear accounts with that Presidency. The commodities demanded from Surat are of such small value and yet so bulky that the biggest ship available here could not carry enough to discharge the debt; while, as for money, they have none to send. Entreat their forbearance accordingly. 'And whilest your minds is busied in these precogitations, remember a little likewise that we have helpt you off with 26,000 rials worth of goods, sent us by the *Michael*, the most part whereof was—you know what [1]; and this, we conceive, will (if duly weighed) prove a good motive to prevail with your patience for a short forbearance. We are forced now to plead with you like the poor debtor in the Gospell that was endebted to his fellow servant one hundred pence: Have patience with us and we wil pay you al. But were our masters in England once again resolved to prosecute their Indian trade (which yet, as it seemes, hangs in suspence), a yearly supply of 15 or 20,000*l*. sterling would be very necessary to be sent out to Suratt for our acco[unt], to furnish us with severall sortments of cloth for these parts; and then, if this course were followed, we should hardly come behind-hand in acco[un]t with you. But as the case now stands, we know not in this particular what to forecast or project otherwise. We see they desire to have all that possibly they can home, and send little or nothing out; which makes us to suppose their trade is even at a period.' Deny that the lead sent to Surat in the *Swan* was

---

[1] 'Private trade' is obviously intended. The resentment of the Surat factors at this implication will be seen from their letter to the Company of January 17, 1643 (p. 85).

overrated. Cannot explain the deficiency found therein. As the price of sugar at Surat is now abated, they send only a small quantity and will forward no more in future. 'We heartely commisserate the poor and deplorable estate of the Companies affaires in Suratt. With us, we assure you, till it pleased God to arrive us the *Swan* from your parts and the *Diamond* from the Coast, the case was in many degrees worse then can be supposed with you; being here driven to that extremity that private men were fain to lend the Company their monies to mainteyne the table and defray other petty expences. And yet we kept our griefes to our selves and set the best outside upon all things that possibly we could; that so the world might take the lesse notice of it.' Acknowledge the courtesy done them by the remittance of the 10,000 pagodas from Surat to the Coast, but understand that a good part of that amount has now been sent back in goods on the *Advice*, and that the rest will shortly be repaid. Declare that they know nothing of the goods taken by the Portuguese in the *Swan* beyond those advised in their letter; and deny having received any presents ('as loaves[1] of gold and we know not what') in lieu of freight money. Consider that the Surat factors ought, in the circumstances, to have forced the Portuguese to pay freight on the whole. At the same time, it must be admitted that the service which the latter did the Company in furnishing this factory with money when it was utterly destitute, might well have excused the remission of freight on a moderate amount of goods. As John Jeffreys [purser of the *Swan*] appears to have assisted the Portuguese to ship part of the excess goods, he should be made to pay the freight thereon. Provisioning of the *Swan*. Censure Cogan for 'sending our pynnace *Advice* for Persia and returning us your *Diamond* in her room . . . without your requiry and contrary to our expresse order.' The result has been that, owing to the leakiness of the *Diamond*, the goods she brought from the Coast have been damaged to the extent of 1,000*l*. Errors in the *Swan's* invoice. Remarks on her cargo. Will follow their advice as to the packing of tortoise-shells. Send a quantity of 'damar' [resin], as it is in demand at Surat. 'From Perack and the parts near thereunto adjoyning it is (as we suppose) that the Dutch procure the tinn which in such ample quantities (you

[1] See a note on p. 33 of the 1634–36 volume.

say) they bring yearly to Suratt. Their tutinggle [1] they bring from Tiwan [Taiwan, i.e. Formosa]; but what they pay for either we are altogither ignorant. It will not concerne us much to enquire into these comodities, being, we are sure, they are seldome or never to be procured in those petty places hereabouts where we have either trade or correspondence.' Anthony Ramsay will be duly credited with the goods received on his account. The five Jesuits that came in the *Swan* proceeded to Batavia, where they embarked in a small Portuguese vessel for Macao. Padre Andreas Xavier was unable to repay here the thirty rials lent him in Surat; his bill is therefore returned in order that the money may be recovered from the 'Padre Provincial'. Anchors sent as desired. Know not when they will be able to forward to the Coast 'those eleven pieces of ordnance for your Fort St. George which you consigned them by the *Swan*.' The Surat letter of April 4, received from the Dutch on June 14, requires no special answer. Now proceed to relate the course of events in these parts. Movements of shippings. Want of money at Bantam. The *Diamond* left 'Madrazpatam' on January 27, called at 'Porta Nova' for some longcloth, and then on February 12 was forced by contrary winds and want of ballast to put into 'Tricombar' [Tranquebar]. She sailed thence on February 23 in company with the Danish *Golden Sun*, and after a tedious and dangerous voyage both reached Bantam on June 16. On the way they lost company, and the *Diamond* was obliged to call at the island of Engano for water—a risky proceeding, as the crew consisted only of 'eight Englishmen and a boy, besides a few blacks'; and in addition they were beholden to the Danes for all kinds of stores. Blame the Coast factors for sending away the vessel so badly furnished. Great damage to the cargo by leakage. It is true that the *Diamond* was lately 'new planked in the Bay of Bengala'; but the work was badly done and she will never be other than 'a leaky old rotten toole'. After patching her up, she was sent to Jambi. Negotiations between Ralph Cartwright and the Sultan of Mataran, at whose request a number of Javanese were permitted to embark in the *Reformation* for Bantam, intending to go in an English ship to Surat and so to Mecca. On her way

---

[1] Spelt 'tutinagle' in another part of the same letter. It is of course the 'tutenague' of commerce, on which see *Hobson-Jobson*, s.v.

to this place, however, the *Reformation* and a junk in her company (belonging to the English) were stopped by a Dutch squadron, the junk seized and the ship fired upon, one man being killed and three or four wounded. The Dutch attempted to take the Javanese out of the *Reformation*, but they resisted and were all slain save one who had hidden himself. No doubt this outrage was committed to bring the English into disrepute with the Javanese and ruin their trade. The *Expedition* was disappointed of cloves at Macassar, owing to the action of the Dutch. Cannot detain the *Swan* any longer; but hope to send the *Diamond* after her to Surat in October with a further supply of goods, calling at 'Madrazpatam' on her way. A Persian horse wanted for the Queen of Jambi. Scarlet cloth presented to Francisco de Souza de Castro. The silk 'puttolaes' received in the *Expedition* were invoiced by 'tannes [1]', without mentioning the number of pieces and the length of each; and on opening the bales and sorting the contents, they found nearly two 'tannes' wanting. Request definite details in future; also that no more 'puttolaes' be sent at present, but some other piece-goods instead. If any 'Mallabars' be captured, thirty or forty 'good lusty young fellows' should be sent to Bantam as servants. 'Two old persons of that nation (or rather Maldevaes, as we suppose), being formerly taken by the *Michael* and by reason of their age unfit for the Companies service, we have here released and sent them for Suratt upon this ship'; also a third, 'named Bickoo' [Bhikkhū], who has served 12 or 14 years, having been captured by the *Blessing* on the Malabar Coast. The twenty 'Guzeratt laskars' who came on the *Expedition* are returned in the present ship; 'unto whome, during her stay here, we have given the same allowance that our own people have, being one rial of eight and 60 lb. of rice each man per month, with which they have seemed very well pleased.' Advances made to them on account of wages. One of the Surat 'washers' here has been allowed to return, 'being a quarrelsome old knave'; another is desired in his place, together with 'three or four baskets of good Suratt soap'. Pitch and tar sent in lieu of 'dammer'. The Danes desire to return to Europe this year, but their *Golden Sun* is in such a bad state that this is unlikely. A brick factory, which is

---

[1] Hind. *thān*, the piece or roll. Valentyn (pt. iv. sec. ii. p. 147) says that a *tanni* is 28 'bastas' (i.e. *hāth*) or cubits.

being built here, is said to be intended for them. Proceedings of the Dutch. Two more Surat letters (April 20 and 28) just received. Thomas Whatmore has gone to Jambi as master of the *Diamond*, but will be sent to Surat, as desired, in October next. Explain that they could not spare the *Reformation* for the present voyage; and besides the *Swan* is quite large enough to carry all the goods available. *P.S.*—Enclose some letters from Batavia for the Dutch 'comandore' in Surat. A fleet of nine or ten ships is about to be dispatched from Batavia to Goa; 'so that as yet, it seemes, they are not agreed for an absolute peace here in India.' News of a small English ship spoken by the Hollanders on their way out; probably she is bound for the Coast. (*Copy.* 18 *pp*.)

ANDREW COGAN, HENRY GREENHILL, AND JOHN BROWN AT FORT ST. GEORGE TO THE PRESIDENT AND COUNCIL AT BANTAM, SEPTEMBER 20, 1642 (*O.C.* 1791).[1]

Reply to theirs of March 26 (received May 19) and July 18 (received August 30). Admit the 'many disasters and losses' that have befallen the Company on this Coast; but trust that in time 'all will be made good with interest'. Cogan confesses that 'it was a most ridiculous scarecrow that frighted him from Porta Nova, thereby to possess the Dutch with the cloath provided by us'; however, it is easy to be wise after the event. Such orders have been given to Day, who has been sent into the Bay, that they do not doubt that Yard will leave those parts. On his arrival here, 'many things are to be objected against him', and so it will not be convenient to send him on at once in that ship to Bantam. Cogan requests an order for his own repair to the latter place, 'for with a new Agent he hopes of new and better success in our maisters affairs.' An Arab horse will be bought and forwarded for presentation to the Queen of Jambi. Agree in wishing that the *Reformation*'s cargo had been tenfold more than it was. 'The reason why the Coast is no better stockt is because (as is said in most of our masters letters) wee and our predecessors have consumed so much of their estate sent hither that now they even feare to send more.' Note what is said as to the little esteem at Bantam of the 'redd Armous earth' [*see the* 1624–29 *volume*, p. 188]. Here 'no man

[1] A second copy will be found among the *O.C. Duplicates.*

will carry it away to have it of gift; and that which was sent coold with as little labour have byn cast ashore as put on boord the *Reformation*, but that Mr. Bayly woold needs have 8 or 10 chests, being he was confident it woold turne to a good acco[un]t in England.' Were induced to believe this 'because it was told us that from Surrat one of the Companies commanders did carry home about 10 tonns and made infinite profit of it.' The price put upon it was a mere guess. Suggest that the chests be emptied into the sea rather than returned hither. Answer several minor points. Gunpowder could not be supplied for want of casks. ' Nevertheless wee are accostomed to great gunns, &c., yet the very mention of gunns or a foarte in any letter even scares us, for wee are very sencible how ridiculous wee have made ourselves by doeing what is done, and lye at our masters mercies for all. You will know ere wee can whether the Company intend to give over the Coast trade or noe; and so accordingly wee know you will dispose of the ordnance' [*see* p. 36]. Cannot provide better cloth than that sent in the *Reformation*, unless they have a stock of money beforehand. 'If wee bespeake any sorts of paintings of sutch lengths, breadths, and worke, it is necessarie wee give monies in hand; and under four or five months time no man will undertake to deliver a bale.' The wheat and butter desired will be provided at Masulipatam. Comment on the ingratitude of the Portuguese, who pretend 'on the least occasion' that the truce is being broken. Any future consignment of indigo will be put into baskets; but there was no time to do this with what was embarked in the *Reformation*. Regret to hear of the straits to which the President and Council have been reduced for money; however, things cannot continue long on this footing, for either the Company will remedy the want or give over the trade altogether. As regards the 66,436 rials of eight said to be due from the Coast to Bantam they will answer later. The armour and buff coat brought out in the *William* were intended for the King of Golconda, who has often inquired for them; beg their early transmission to the Coast. Enclose an exact statement of their indebtedness. The total may appear great, but on examination 'it will appeare no more then needs must; for wee profess to God not to have spent a pice in any vaineglorious way, for wee have long since given over all the Coast vanities (as it is mentioned to the Company). Tis truth wee advised you from Maddaraspatan the 27th of March, 1640 [*sic.* 1641 ?], that wee were cleere out of debt; but wee then knew the contrary, and so it will appeare by our bookes of accompt; for wee did still but robb Peter to pay Paule—take upp of one to pay another, to maineteine our credits. And the reason that moved us to write so was the President &c. of Surrat had given us order to lay the burthen of our debts on them, and before wee coold get monies to charge on them to the full amounts of our debts they contradicted theire order againe, and commanded us peremtorily that, whatever shoold be sent from Bantam or England, with it first to imburse them with what wee had charged on that Presidency, then pay our debts, and the remainder invest for Bantam, for (say they) wee see no reason why Surrat shoold pay Bantam debts, &c.; and fearing that this might deterre you from sending ought hither (being advised so much), wee writt you as wee did.' In reply to the demand 'to know what warrant and order wee had from Surrat to biuld the new foart of Maddaraspatan', they refer to what is said in the enclosed letter to the Company. Will certainly not agree to 'the sending any factor or factors by the way of Surrat'. Enclose Richard Hudson's account. Apparently the Dutch are not free from losses; 'nor cann the Dane[s] much bragg of theire ritch voyages', for it is said that the goods they carried from the Coast to Bantam last year produced not more than 50 per cent. profit, while those sent from this place, bad as they were, are believed to have made 100 per cent. at least. Fear that the *Jonas* is lost, and that this will much dishearten the Company. 'Such a trade doe they drive that the losse of one shippe appeares more to them then ten to the Dutch.' Were grieved to learn, from the Bantam letter of July 18, of the tedious passage of the *Diamond*, but believe that the *Golden Sun* took just as long. It is strange that the former should prove so leaky, 'for she had almost as much spent uppon her in the Bay as woold have built a new vessell of her burthen.' They will no doubt be censured for not having sent the *Advice* to Bantam instead of her. As a matter of fact, they had intended to do this, and to dispatch the *Diamond* to Persia; but the latter was detained so long in the Bay that it was deemed advisable to let the *Advice* go to Gombroon in her place. Moreover, the *Advice*'s rudder was so defective that on her return she was obliged to proceed to the Bay to have it put right; so, had she been sent to Bantam, she might never have reached that port. In any case, the freight earned by her to and from Persia, amounting to 824*l.*, would have been lost, 'for no man woold have laden a pice of goods on the *Dyamond*, for feare of the Mallavars.' A copy of the Bantam letter has been forwarded to Surat. 'The Company hath taken a resolution to set a period to the Third Joynt Stock and in the interim, so that the trade may not fall to the ground, some of the cheife adventurers have undertaken a Generall Voyage. . . . Part of what they underwrite (the totall being 105,000*l.* starling) they have sent hither uppon the shippe *Hopewell*, it being 17,290*l.* 14*s.* 9*d.*' She arrived here on July 6, with her crew all 'well and lusty'. The Company had forbidden the money to be used to pay debts; but their creditors were so clamorous that they were forced to satisfy them. Still, they do not doubt that, when the time comes to make an investment for England, they will be able to borrow the same amount at a cheaper rate of interest. Propose to turn over to the General Voyage the goods on hand for the Third Joint Stock. Cannot send the *Advice* to Bantam until some time in January. On her Cogan intends to take his passage, 'for by the postscript of the Companies letter wee doe gather that Mr. Day is the man appoynted to succeed; and yourselves know that it is very necessary . . . that Andrew Cogan continue on yeare at Bantam, to purge himself of what may be objected against him, and then his time will be more then expired with the Company.' Although they have been forced to pay their debts at Masulipatam, they cannot get a pice of what is due to them: 'nor are wee ever like to get ought unless wee force it from them. If therefore you please to enorder it, after our investment is made, wee may ceaze uppon theire juncks at Massilupatam. It is our opinion that, if wee doe doe so, wee shall be paid (elce not); and our privilidges with the Kinge no way impared, for the Kinge hath often enordered the payment of what is due to us, and knows not the contrary but that all is paid.' Enclose an account of what has passed in those parts since the *Reformation* sailed. *PS.*—The Masulipatam books are sent herewith, as received from thence. (*Copy.* 6 *pp. Received by Dutch conveyance October* 28.)

EVENTS ON THE COAST OF COROMANDEL, JANUARY—
SEPTEMBER, 1642 (*O.C.* 1791A).[1]

'The 9th January, the Danes being satisfied in their demands[2], they released the jouncke, and wee had libertie to lade our goods; which the 12th was compleated and she dispeded to us[3]; where the 20th she arrived, and [the] 25th [haveinge laden what wee had to lade, &c.] wee dispeded hir for Porta Nova; where shee tooke in as much goods as filld her upp. Hir whole cargazoone amo[unted] to 13,365 pa[godas] 26 fa[nams] 5 ca[sh]; and from thence she was dispeded the 5th February, but it seems it was the 16 of June ere she arrived at Bantam—a most taedious passage [the like seldome heard off]. And now wee returne againe to Bengalla, wher the *Dyamond* left Mr. John Yard with his *Endeavour*; who it seemes could not be made readie untill the 15 of January; when then he sett sayle to come for Messilupitam, but meeting variable winds and foule weather was forced, after the expence of a month, to retourn againe, having in that time lost some of his [her] anchors and almost all her sails; and yet (which is strange to us) the Dutch, that set saile ten days after them, gained Messilupatam and Pullicat [but twas towards the latter end of March].' On March 1 Greenhill was dispatched to Masulipatam to perfect the accounts, Rogers having made many errors; he returned May 9. The pinnace *Advice* arrived on April 29 from Gombroon, whence she had started on March 26. She brought back the lead which had been sent on her; also some rosewater, raisins, almonds, pistachios, and hazel nuts. For the freight goods on board a sum of 17,895 shāhīs had been received at Gombroon. On May 3 she proceeded to Masulipatam to land her passengers and freight goods; this done, she sailed again on the 17th, and reached Fort St. George on June 3, bringing a few piece-goods, &c. On July 6 arrived the *Hopewell* from England, with Trumball as master and Day as merchant. Nine days later

---

[1] Enclosed in the previous letter. It is repeated (in substance) as part of *O.C.* 1792, and again under *O.C.* 1799; also (under 1791) among the *O.C. Duplicates*. From these versions some additions have been made (within brackets).
[2] See the former part of this narrative (p. 314 of the last volume), where it is stated that the Danes had seized a junk belonging to the Sar-i-Khail, and that in consequence the Governor of Masulipatam had prevented the English from lading the *Diamond*.
[3] At Fort St. George.

THE ENGLISH FACTORIES 43

the *Advice* was sent to Masulipatam with money to pay debts and commence an investment for Bantam. She had orders next to proceed to the Bay, ' where and nowhere elce on the Coast 'twas held by the mariners she coold be hawled on ground to amend the defects of her rudder.' She reached Masulipatam on July 19. There on the 24th she was joined by the *Hopewell*, which had left Fort St. George on the 21st; and both sailed for the Bay on August 5 [6th *in the other versions*]. The *Advice* carried a small freight, producing 78 pagodas 5 fanams, equivalent to 156 pieces of eight 40 pence[1]. ' The 11th of August three Portugall soldiers belonging to the armada (11 small frigotts sent for the releife of St. Thoma[2] with 270 soldiers) came to our towne and in a base arack house fell to drincking with a Dane, and at length together by the ears. In fine the three Portugalls with their rapiers made uppon him and wounded him in seven places. Notice of which being given us, wee sent two soldiers to part them; who no sooner entred within the yard and commanded them to desist but on of the three aforesaid soldiers, by name Anthony Myrando, ran the one of our two solders into the right pappe, that instantly he dyed without speaking one word.[3] So soone as they perceived what they had done they all three fledd; but within lesse then half an hower were all thre taken. And being truly informed which was the homicide, wee kept him and suffered the others to departe for St. Thoma; from whence wee received many letters to release him, for that he was a phydalgo [Port. *fidalgo*, a man of birth]; but what thorough our Naique[s] importunitie, togither with our owne people, wee cold not repreive him till advized to Surrat,[4] but were even forced to execute him the 13th ditto [in] the morning; and because he pretended to be a gentleman

---

[1] The rial of eight being taken at 5*s.* and the pagoda at 10*s.*

[2] The Dutch had contemplated an attack upon San Thomé, but abandoned the idea upon finding that it had been reinforced (*Hague Transcripts*, series i. vol. xiii. no. 407; *Lisbon Transcripts, Doc. Remett.*, book 48, f. 117).

[3] His name is given in the other versions as James Jaques.

[4] *O.C.* 1792 enlarges this passage as follows: ' The homicide wee kept prisoner untill wee had acquainted our Naique, butt lett the other [two?] goe. Thereuppon the Naique instantly sent 4 or 500 soldiers to lye in the towne (not knowing what the Portugalls might attempt to gett theire man) and order that out of hand he shoold be put to death. But wee woold willingly have repreivd him untill the President of Surrat had been made acquainted with it, in regaurd of [y]our servants and estate in Goa; but the importunitie of our Naique and our people here woold not suffer us longer to deferre it.'

as aforesaid, wee shott him to death before our corps du guard. Since when wee have byn wonderfull at ease in respect of the Portugalls,[1] for till then wee were dayly troubled with one or other. And now in this place it will not be impertinent, before wee conclude, to say somewhat of St. Thoma; where from the time the armado arrived, which was in May last, to the time they parted, which was the 28th of August, it is not to be spoken what a many murthers and other crimes, which in any part of Christendome deserved death, were committed by the soldiers; yet no one man suffered for it among them. This homicide Myrando about the prime of August kild a man in St. Thoma and rann hither for sanctuary; and being wee woold not protect him, he not having made his peace, he vou'd in some of our hearing to be the death of some English man ere he left the Coast. The said Myrando further confessed, ere he suffered, that this was the seventh murther he had committed. But now, say the Portugalls of St. Thoma, or rather the Capt. More [*Capitão Mór*, or Captain-Major] (for all the citizens rejoice at what wee did), the peace is broke and they expect order from the Viceroy to fall on us; which were it so (or wee faile much in our judgements) St. Thoma woold not continue a month more in the hands of the Portugalls. The Naique of Armagon is absolutely beaten out of all his country, it being possest part by the King of Golquondah[s] people and the major part by Raylawar. The Moores have encamped themselves, or rather seated themselves for the warr, at a place called Cowle Geldancke, the cheifest place in all that country; and Raylawar hath a strong garison in Vinquatagery and Armagon.[2]

[1] 'For and now none of our people doe so much as desire to goe to St. Thoma; nor come any, or very few, Portugalls hither' (*O.C.* 1792).
[2] The following is the version given in *O.C.* 1792: 'The Naique of Armagon is absolutely drove out of his country by the Kinge of Golquondah and his neig[h]bour Naique Raglawarr [*sic*]. The Moores have seated themselv[e]s for the warre in a stronge place and the best part of his country, by name Cowle Geldanke, and Raylawarr is with his strength at Vinquatagery and Armagon.' *O.C.* 1799 has the same wording, but in that 'Raylawarr' becomes 'Rayla Warra'.
'Cowle' indicates that there was a temple (*koil*) at the place; and 'Geldanke' may be Gadanki, a village in the taluk of Chandragiri (North Arcot). 'Vinquatagery' is obviously Venkatagiri, about 80 miles north-west of Madras. The progress of the invasion may be traced in the *Dagh-Register*, 1641–42, pp. 272, 274, 288, 295. Mention will there be found (p. 274) of the attack made upon the Nāyak of Armagon (whose name is given as 'Willegotij') by 'a certain Rauweleware, who was lord of Caleteura' [i.e. Calitore, now Kistnapatam, in Nellore District]. This in all probability was Śrī Ranga Rāyalu, who in

Indeed, wee are of opinion that the Moores will have all this country ere many years; for what with the Kinge of Vizapore [Bījāpur] on one side and the Kinge of Golquondah on the other, the Gentues themselves being divided among themselves, it is even impossible their country cann continue.' (*Copy*. 2¼ *pp.*)

ANDREW COGAN, HENRY GREENHILL, AND JOHN BROWN AT FORT ST. GEORGE TO THE COMPANY, SEPTEMBER 20, 1642 (*O.C.* 1792).[1]

Wrote last by the *Reformation*, which sailed August 31, 1641. Have since received from Surat on November 18 a transcript of the Company's letter of March 12, 1641, the original of which came to hand from Bantam on May 19[2] last; and to this they now reply. Declare that 'there neyther hath byn hitherto in our time, or shall be, conveyed away any originall letters or elce out of your principall factory.' Acknowledge the receipt of the cargoes of the *Hopewell* and *Reformation*, amounting together to 19,559*l*. [0*s*.] 3*d*. 'Wee read your pleasure concerning our reaccompting with Bantam. To us it is all one. Wee for our parts promise conformitie, and shall subscribe to whatever the President of Bantam shall command and not in the least neglect the President &c. of Surrat.' As regards the charge of 'ryotous living', they refer to the accounts, which will show their monthly expenditure. 'For private trading, if any, it is very private, for the Agent can know of little or none.' Cogan denounces as 'most abominable false' the statement that he invested 20,000 rials with Ivy in private trade [*see* p. 11]. If any one can prove that he had any more adventure with Ivy than was shown in the invoice, Cogan 'will be liable to loose his whole estate'. These accusations, he declares, are made in revenge for his exposure of the misdeeds of his predecessors. Note that the Company wish care to be taken that they 'have not the refuse of the Dutch or Danes cloath. As for the Danes, they are nothing; but, untill you have means to be doeing all the yeare, wee must have the refuse

the autumn of 1642 became 'King of Carnatica' in succession to Venkatapati. Apparently the word is really the Telugu *Rāyalavāru*, meaning 'the Rāyalu's people', but it is an easy transition from this to the Rāyalu himself.

[1] There is a duplicate under *O.C.* 1799. From this a few corrections have been made (in brackets).

[2] 9th (*O.C.* 1799).

of the Dutch and it is not to be holpe, or your shipps must away as they came; for a cargazoon of cloath, espetially paintings, are not procurable under 9 or 10 months time. Wee know to our harts greife how you have suffered by trusting pore painters and weavours. But experience tells us it cannot altogether be avoyded, unless [we] had on pr[ime] merchant (as have the Dutch), who secures all. Such a one wee had some time with us, with his wife and familie; but when he sawe wee had more occasion to borrow of him to feede ourselves then any way to drive a trade, other then some few months after the arrival of our shipps, he left us, not to be found againe unless [we] had means to continue a trade.' Golconda factory is dissolved, though the debts owing there have not yet been recovered. As Elchi Beg, the chief debtor, denied liability, Rogers was sent thither; but after remaining there many months longer than he was authorized to do, he died, and thereupon Elchi Beg swore that the English owed him 500 pagodas. However, Collet, who had been sent to fetch away Rogers, petitioned the King on the subject. The latter ordered certain 'Brammoneys' [i.e. Brahmans] to go through Elchi Beg's papers, and they reported that the English claim was correct. 'Thereupon order was made that within certeine dayes he shoold make payment; and now he hath no plea left but povertie.' A letter recently received gave hopes that 'all will be paid presently', and stated that Collet was preparing to return to 'Bandar' [Masulipatam]. 'As for our priviledges, there is no feare but they will continew. But to what purpose are those privilidges, if wee make no use of them? The Kinge and nobles they conceive you are as much obliged to them, doeing nothing, as if you delt for as much as doth the Dutch. Your Worshipps are forced to pay what is oweing in the King of Goldcandahs country, but nothing can be recovered of what is owing you, being many thousands of pagodas; nor indeed ever will they pay unless forced unto it.' Have written to Surat and Bantam for advice on the latter point. The presents sent out in the *William* for the King of Golconda are expected shortly from Bantam. 'When wee doe (as that wee doe often) fall into consideration how much Your Worshipps are displeased with us for proceeding on this worke [i.e. the building of the Fort], it even breaks some of our hearts. Tis now too late to wish it undone;

and yet wee may not but tell you that, if so be Your Worshipps will follow this Coast trade (or rather the Karnatt [1]), this place may prove as good as the best; but all things must have its growth and time. But on the contrary, if Your Worshipps will not continue it, you may doe it away to profit, and not hazard the losse of a man.[2] It may with ease be effected, unlesse the Moores conquer the country before. Our vicinitie with St. Thoma is no impediment, at least to us; for only the towne of St. Thoma belongs to the Naique of Tanjour, and round about, even to their very dores, is our Naiques, who keeps them in such awe that they must eat and drinke uppon the matter when he please. What time may worke our Naique to, wee cannot devine; but hitherto wee have found him still as good as his word, onely [i.e. except] in the Forts erection (the mayne thing of all); but in that thing he excuseth himself, and did excuse himself ere Mr. Day left this place, for he professed never to promise Mr. Day any such thing; which caused Mr. Day to profer freely to pay the interest of all the monies that shoold be expended till the Forte was finished; and so much was written to Surrat before Mr. Day went thither and when he went. But Your Worshipps will not allow of any charge of [at] all, neyther in biulding or payeing of garrison, but will that all the charge be bourne by the Naique that invited us hither; for to answere which clause, if wee doe appeare too prolix, doe hope Your Worshipps will excuse us. In the first place it is our opinion, in regaurd the Moores and Gentues are false and not to be trusted, and that at all times you may command your owne uppon all this coast, 'tis very necessarie you have a place to retire to under your owne command. 'Tis not only our opinions, but the opinions of your Presidents of Bantam and Surrat; for from the first it hath byn written hither "Tis not good to leave on place till possest of another"; then from Surrat twas said "Biuld (when you biuld) no such mocke forts as was Armagon." The Dutch saw the necessitie of it thirty years since; which made them proceed uppon Pullicatt, to theire unreasonable expence in moneys, besides losse of men,

[1] Sanskrit *Karnāta*, which forms the basis of the later term 'Carnatic'. It is here equivalent to the Hindu kingdom of Vijayanagar.
[2] *O.C.* 1799 interpolates here: 'If you resolve upon the latter, after advice given once within a 12 mo[nth].'

ere brought to perfection. The Moores in Messilupatam have began to practize a most unconscionable way; nay, they have declar'd themselves to perseviere in it; which is that, whatever Christian shall molest the juncks belonging to Messilupatam, the other Christians resident shall make it good.' Instance the embargo placed upon the lading of the *Diamond* because the Danes had seized the Sar-i-Khail's junk. 'The Dutch, to prevent the like, and that theire shipps may not be stopped (or rather that their goods may be readie at all times when they please), they imploy small shipping continually to fetch there goods into theire owne command; and so must Your Worshipps if you meane to continu a trade. But, wee beseech you, if these people biuld us a forte and pay the garrison, in what securitie is your estate and our lives? Suerly, in none at all; for it is farr more freedome to live without a forte then within, unless the forte be at its owne devotion. But this forte of yours, if Your Worshipps did butt followe this trade as it might be followed, or that you had but two or three small vessells to voyage it too and againe to draw trade hither, all your charges woold bee bourne with advantage. But if Your Worshipps are resolved absolutely to leave this trade of Karnatt, advise us and you shall not be a pice looser for what worke is done and monies disbursed; which being so, and that Your Worshipps conclude of one of the two wayes, wee hope to heare of noe more of the forte. Wee see kingdomes have their risings and fallings, as appeares by Portugall in Europia and Karnatt in thes parts. So the nature and condition of people doe better or worse it. Formerly it was very secure and necessary to have your cheife residence at Messulapatam; but now not, for the reasons aforesaid; for farther and now wee are informed (and wee beleive its truth) that shall your Agent but sett his foot ashore in Messilupatam, he must perforce goe for Golquondah, and there continue untill another supply his place. The like they intend with the Dutch, if the Governour of Pullicat come there; for by that means they conceive they dare doe anything to us, and wee dare doe nothing to them. When wee said Armagon was not a fitt place for the cheife residency, it was in respect of the seat ['site' *in O.C.* 1799] of the forte and the small defence it coold eyther make by sea or land; if which be not motive sufficient (or however) wee referre our selves to your better judgement. Wee now are and have byn a 12 mo[nth] constant resident at Maddaras[patam], and have made that the cheife place for your other factories to acco[unt] to. What condition hath byn made with the Naique long since hath byn sent you by severall conveyances; and therefore forbeare them at present. Wee have in a foregoeing clause shewed you that St. Thoma belongs to the Naique of Tanjour; who putts in almost monthly (to him that will give most) a new governour, unto whom even the Portugalls themselves pay custome. How then shoold wee expect to live there free? Noe; thes Naiques, although they abound in wealth, yet will they not part with a cash but uppon a certeinty, or mighty great hopes, to have ten for it. Again, had it byn otherwise, and that wee had imbraced theire proffer to reside in that cittie, you must have sought out for such servants to doe your busines as were both stick free and shot fre, and such as coold disgest poizon; for this is their dayly practice in St. Thoma, and no justice.' Have paid all their debts at Armagon; 'but to our greifs wee must say wee shall never gett what is due to you there.' Note that the Company express doubts whether all the debts on the Coast were real. Explain that these were recognized by Ivy before Cogan arrived, and that in each instance the former inquired of Clark and Hudson 'whether they were reall debts or no, because no mencion of them in Clarks books'; and, on getting answers in the affirmative, Ivy promised payment. The bills were again presented to Cogan on his arrival, and he also, learning that the money was really due, promised that it should be paid as soon as possible. Answer in detail Pinson's charges that some of the bills had been paid. As for house-rent [at Masulipatam], since no agreements could be found, 'wee concluded with all our landlords and had new writings drawne on boath sides to content.' The *Reformation* spared them ten sailors, and so they have since made little use of 'thes country mariners'. Grimstone and Greenhill were duly called to account for wasting powder in a salute at Gombroon [*see the previous volume*, p. 176]. The quick passage of the *Caesar*[1] was due to favourable winds. As for her stowage, it is reported that the

---

[1] A vessel which the Company had freighted and dispatched to Bantam in the spring of 1640. She was back early in the following February—a quicker return than had ever been made by the Company's own ships.

captain filled even his gunroom and great cabin with bags of pepper; and that he left Bantam ' with so little water and so logg laden that, had he mett with any blustering weather within or without the Streights, it would have indangered all'. Much regret the wreck of the pinnace *Eagle* [*see the preceding volume*, p. 266]. ' Shee was the most basest lost as ever was vessell; and all by the means of a druncken master. Wee have recovered little or nothing of what was in her when she was wrackt; for whilest they deferr us from weeke to weeke, in hopes to get a large some of moneys (more then the goods were worth), the sea hath so worked her into the sand as all the best ordnance that were on boord her are with the hull vanished. So basely haveing [i.e. greedy] are al thes people; but, being so, it happens with them often as with those who, whilest they think to have all, loose all. Your Worshipps, wee perceive, have never beene truly informed with the goverment of Karnatt; for our Naique hath no more to doe, or is more cared for, where the *Eagle* was wrackt, then is the Pope of Roome, or is that Nauge respected here. For Your Worshipps may please to understand that every Naique is a king in his owne country, and will attend the Greate Kinge at theire pleasure (which will be the losse of this country); and according to the custome of Karnatt, whatever vessell doe but touch the shoare (er a coule being granted) is absolutely lost.' Wish the *Eagle* had stranded ' within our Naigs command, for then wee shoold at most [have lost] the hull; for it is one article in our cowle that if any our shipping (as God forbidd) shoold be cast ashoare in his country, all that cann be saved is to be restored. The like is to be done with those who shall come to trade with us. Well might Mollay [1], the merchant that deals for the Dutch (for so wee have beene told), invite the Naique underhand to doe as he did. But for the Portugalls, they never stired in it, they having not wherewithall; for without a present there is no speech with thes great villians; no, although it concerns their owne profitt '. The Company need not fear that they will brawl with the Portuguese, as until the recent trouble ' wee lived as freindly as brothers, for wee have still binn helpfull unto them on all occassions '. ' Wee (as said formerly) have hitherto found our Naique and his people

---

[1] Chinnana Chetti, also known as Malaya, for whom see the 1624–29 volume (pp. 358, 359).

very faire conditioned and indifferent honest. As for your Forte, which is better then half finished, tis of such force, with the few wee have, that wee feare not what any can doe against us, espetially so long as wee have our Naique to our freind, or the sea open to furnish us with food.' More ordnance promised from Bantam. Cogan denies the charge of private trade. As for his taxing his predecessors with this offence, he did so because he conceived it to be his duty to inform the Company of what he had learned from the other factors here. It would have been more to his own interest to be silent on the matter, for then he could not have aroused the enmity of those concerned, and he 'might have private traded for 40,000 pagodas and Your Worshipps never have knowne it'. Again, it is unfair to blame Cogan solely for the building of Fort St. George. He did not act alone, 'for all matters of consequence and novell hath byn first maturely considered of in consultation and then put in practize.' Authority for the dismantling of Armagon was given from Surat, 'for they writt us in this manner concerning Armagon. "The forte in respect of its quallitie, for ought wee have yet heard, can as little resist any ordinarie force as secure goods or any thing else subsistant therein or [our] shipps without in the roade, in regard they are forced thorough the shooldnes of the water to ride at such distance. Wee have beene onely informed that excellent kind of paintings are there onely procurable for Macasser, &c. What other conveniencies redound unto the Company for so vast an expence requisite to its maineteynance wee are wholey ignorant of. If, therefore, acquirie of some sorts of goods there, not else where atteyneable, be the most important benifitt accrewing, you may doubtless as well there, and with as much safetie as in other factories, procure them. And then, though your factory continu to inhabitt the house, yet may the amunition and those called soldiers (of all which pray send us the perticulars) be disposed of into the Companies shipps," &c. Dated 1 October, 1639.[1] Wee in answere to which said that Armagon was better lost then found, " of which place you are not misinformed", &c.; and say farther that "the house and forte is so decayed that to continue it but on yeare longer it will cost a 1,500 or 2,000 pa[godas], which monyes woold halfe biuld a [very] defenceable place in a Naiques country adjoyning to

---

[1] The correspondence here cited is no longer extant.

St. Thoma, concerning which be pleased to peruse seriously the inclosed to that effect and, according as you finde the Company inclyned, give order for its goeing foreward; for (for the supply of the southern parts) that or such a place must be had ". Dated the 8th November, 1639. Then the 18th ditto, after the receipt of severalls from Mr. Day which importunes us to goe for Maddaraspatan, wee say: " Wee know obedience exceeds sacrifice. To our power wee have and shall practize it; but in a busines of such consequence, wherein celerrity is required or hazard to lose all, it even staggers us. For willingly wee woold proceed uppon it, as Mr. Day desires; but wee are very sencible how dangerous 'tis to breake a commission, and (prove how it will) must be subject to sensure." Then the 14th of December wee writt againe and intimated to Surrat that the Naique of Armagon takes notice of our intent to leave that place, &c., and that, he being now imployd in the warrs, is a good time to get away our people and elce with little prejudice; and, but in expectation of an answer to ours of the 9th [*sic*] of November, the Agent woold have gone away on the *Eagle*, to lessen our charge and to avoid the clamour of our creditours. Then, by conveyance of a Dutch pattamar the prime February, wee writ againe to Surrat in thes words: " Wee have been long in expectation for order to remove our people from Armagon; where, unless it be done very suddainely, wee must be forced to expend a good some of monyes in repairations; but being almost confident that that place is doomd for desolution, especially the forte, wee have yesterday enordered Mr. Day to put on boord the shippe *Eagle* some of the ordnance, &c." By which Your Worshipps may perceive that still wee expected order from the President, &c., unto whom wee were subordinate; for without order from them wee might not, nor did, stirr. Then about the 6th February came a letter to hand from the President and Councell aforesaid, which said letter hath thes words in one clause: " Touching the dismantling of Armagon, you received the Companies positive order, when they knew not that it was so decayed and woold require so great a some of monies as 2,000 pa[godas] to make it habitable onely, not defencible. With those our masters directions, our duties prompt[ed] us to inviate our opinions, which then assented to what they had byn pleased to determine, provided you discover no maine inconveniencie, hinderance, or dammadge to their affairs in its execution. Such nor your advises nor Mr. Dayes relation intimates, but on the contrary present unto us faire hopes of fortifying at Madraspatan; which wee conceive, according to the import of your letters" (which are no other then those before inserted) "will be so farr advanced that our directions will come to late to improve the action. If you have gone thorough with it, wee doubt not but all fitting and cautionall conditions were seasonably thought on; provition made as well for recovery of debts at Armagon as exporting thence whatever belongs to the Company; which neyther shoold not be compleated untill you are well assured of the other Naiques resolution to receive you and assist in the fortification. That some such place is very necessarie unto you for provision of paintings for the South factories, wee are by your information induced to credit. That the Naique of Armagon hath abus'd you and rob'd those that trade with you, your confession publisheth. That notice of your intended desertion of his precincts will exasperate him against you and incite him to impediate the gunns exportation, is most probable. How you can prevent his designes and force them from thence will be a matter (wee beleive) of some difficultie. Then doth the whole action require no lesse then a most serious deliberation and propention for its contrivall and performance; therefore wee coold wish the Agent had byn present to assist and further with his ableler advice the progression and perfection of the whole machin. If you goe foreward with it, doe what you resolve on to purpose, and biuld no such mock forts as that of Armagon, &c. And so wee wish you good sucess to your undertakings." Upon receipt of which lines abovesaid, Andrew Cogan imbarqu'd himself and went uppon the worke, taking that letter for his warrant; for being subordinat he dirst not stir (as beforesaid) till order; if which be (or bee not) warrant sufficient, Andrew Cogan referrs himself to Your Worshipps.' He defers further explanation until he comes to give an account of his actions at Bantam and afterwards at home. Now answer the letter of November 30, 1641, brought by the *Hopewell.* Here again Cogan is unfairly singled out for censure. He reiterates his denial of 'vast private trade' and prodigality of expense. 'At present here wee have two horses, boath not worth their meat; and at Messilupatam they have only one and a coach with two old oxen past labour, insomuch as about à month since wee enordered them to give them their libertie to graze and fatt themselves against some shippe came, or eate them in the factory. Thers all the Coast pride; for the Agent hath neither his flaggs, his rundalers [*see the preceding volume*, p. 48], his torches ['torcheirs' *in O.C.* 1795], his fencers, his drumes ['drummers'] on horseback, his fidlers, his horses, or horse of state, nor (and which is not a little admired at) his pallenkeine; nor are your servants in Messilupatam allowed any for their owne occasions. As for our expence of diett, it cannot possible be brought lower then tis; for at Massilupatam they spend about 20 pa[godas] old per month (all things accompted) for matter of dyett; and wee (being here at table constantly nine, oftentimes twelve, besides strangers, commers and goers) expend about 30 pa[godas] new a month; with which some wee cannot often feast it.' As for servants, they cannot have less 'and doe your busines'. Particulars will be found in their accounts. Are still of opinion that money would have been saved formerly, had these factories been under Surat; because then their cash accounts would have been transmitted monthly, and the President and Council could have checked any extravagance. The King of Golconda can, of course, withdraw their privileges; 'but in respect of ourselves wee shall give him no just occasion'. Explain an obscure reference in their former letter. Reasons for sending the *Expedition* to Surat. The factors were as much offended that her cargo was no larger as the Company are that it was so large. 'Surely Your Worshipps cannot but know that ever since August in 39 to this time, which is now compleate three years, wee have payd for interest upwards of 10,000 pa[godas]: for shipps expence no small some: besides expence of housekeeping, &c. Acco[unts] of biulding will appeare at large, for you had not a house on all this Coast for your servants to shelter dry under. Also acco[unts] of sallerie helpe to fill upp; for, whither Your Worshipps have imployment or no, men cannot goe naked, as the Gentews [Hindūs] doe. But seing Andrew Cogan is so unhappy and unfortunate, his humble desire is to leave this imployment, for he professeth it twere a thousand times better for him to live at home in a prison then as he doth.' He has therefore asked the President and Council at Bantam to appoint a successor. He will then remain a year at Bantam to answer any charges that may be made against him, though he fears none; 'and so much by way of digression to ease his overburthned heart.' Note the termination of the Third Joint Stock and the inception of the General Voyage; also that Day is ' factor for the Voyage and must be made acquainted with all buyings and sellings'. Explain why, contrary to instructions, part of the money has been used to pay their debts at Masulipatam. The goods ordered for Bantam will be provided and sent thither in the *Advice*, as soon as she returns from the Bay. Will find it difficult to dispose of the cargo of the *Hopewell* here, ' chiefly by reason of the warrs'; so will send the lead and most of the broadcloth to the Bay. Advices from Masulipatam say that scarcely any freight will be procurable for Persia, because ' the Serkaile sends this yeare his great jouncke thither'; they have accordingly sent word of this to the Bay, 'that if so be Mr. Day coold procure a fraight, not to refuse it'. It is untrue that goods from Masulipatam to Persia pay freight according to fineness. All cloth is weighed at the ' Bancksall ' [custom-house], and ' according to its weight payes both freight and custome '. The following is the scale for freight: cloth, 1½ pagodas per maund; Bengal sugar, 8 pagodas the candy of 500 lb.; coarser sugar, 4 pagodas the candy; gum-lac, 7 pagodas the candy; benzoin, 12 or 15 pagodas the candy, according to quality; cloves, 16 pagodas the candy; tin or 'tottanaga' [see p. 36], 8 pagodas, and steel 6 pagodas, per candy; sugar candy, 10 pagodas per candy. Passengers pay 10 pagodas; but if a man lades goods paying 100 pagodas, he gets his passage free; 'if 1000, then himself and another'. A bale of goods found missing in the *Expedition*. Explain their action in asking that certain goods from Masulipatam should be excused the payment of customs at Gombroon. By so doing they ' gayned the love of the King and Serkayle; and, whether our letter or no, they had not pay'd a pice custom; for there is small hopes to gett your customs from the Moors and Persians that trades in juncks, when you cannot get the custome of goods that comes uppon your owne shipping'. However, they long since promised Surat 'that neyther Kinge nor Serkayle shall ever prevaile againe with us for any such letter'. Note the caution about keeping the *Hopewell* prepared to fight the Malabars on her way to and from Persia. 'Let the maister goe which way he please, tis very necessary the shippe be cleare of all lumber betweene decks; but if hee'l voyage it the way[1] that Dowle, the master of the *Advice*, did by our order (for the other way wee durst not hazard him), ther's no feare of a safe and quick passadge. 'Tis the way that all jounks that goe from this coast take; and seldome any of them miscarry, and never by the Mallavars.' Note that Courteen has sent out three ships; also their cargoes, 'as you finde them in the Custome House. If any of them come wher wee have to doe, they shall finde colde interteinment.' The Company's letters for Surat were dispatched from Masulipatam on July 20. 'So that wee make acco[unt] by the 20th of August they were with the President; for all the ways from Massilupatam to Surrat are free from all troubles, unlesse some rains at that times of the yeare peradventure may hinder them 4 or 5 dayes; but from hence to Messilupatam is very difficult, by reason of the warrs, for many times our servants are stopped 10 and 20 dayes in the armies ere suffered to proceed on their journey; and therefore wee sent your letter to Messilupatam on the *Advice*, who was 5 dayes in her way thither from hence.' Neither Hudson nor Clark left any books balanced, and what books there were abounded in errors. Send accounts of the estates of all who have died on the Coast, and a list of the Company's servants here and at Masulipatam [*missing*]. Express their thanks for the pipe of wine sent them in the *Hopewell*. 'It came in good time to comfort us; for a long time before our best drinke was bade water.' It is desirable that Day should continue on the Coast 'to see the investment made for England', and so Cogan has decided 'to leave this imployment to Mr. Day, who of all men in the world deserves it, and with the first shippe (which will bee in December next) to goe for Bantam.' This will lessen the charges here, 'for two 200*l*. men is to great a burthen, as the times are'. Narrate the events that have occurred here since the dispatch of the *Reformation* in September, 1641.[2] A letter from St. Thomé, received yesterday, announced the arrival of one English ship at Tuticorin and of two others at Cochin. These are probably Courteen's ships, 'for they say they came immediately from

---

[1] Apparently this was the route past Minicoy, between the Laccadives and Maldives (cf. pp. 71 and 73).

[2] This section is practically identical with *O.C.* 1791 A. Any differences of importance have been noted on that document (see p. 42).

England, and most parte of the way in company of six Portugale shipps, which they left at Mosambique; in one of which shipps is a new Vice Roy[1].' (*Copy*. 16½ *pp*.)

EDWARD KNIPE, ABOARD THE *CRISPIANA* [AT SWALLY], TO 'BENIDAS' [BENI DĀS] [AT SURAT], SEPTEMBER 25, 1642 (*Factory Records, Miscellaneous*, vol. xii.[2] p. 17).

Thanks him for the provisions he has sent, and promises him employment. Begs that he will supply him at once with some cotton goods to make into clothes; also 'a taylor that knowes to worke after our English manner'. Would be glad to see him, if he can come down. (*Copy*. ¾ *p*.)

WILLIAM THURSTON, EDWARD PEARCE, AND MAXIMILIAN BOWMAN AT BASRĀ TO THE COMPANY, SEPTEMBER 26, 1642 (*O.C.* 1793).

Answer briefly the Company's letter of February 18 last, just received by way of Aleppo. Will observe carefully the cautions given concerning 'treating with this Bashaw and people', or building a factory house. It is certainly better to hire than to build, for, should the trade be abandoned, 'the Bashaw would claime the howse as his owne.' 'Wee have in this our 15 or 16 monthes residence throughly experienced the trade of this place, and doe finde that the first markets at the begining of the monzoane is most proffit-

---

[1] An unfounded rumour.

[2] This is Edward Knipe's letter book. It opens with a note to the Company from Torbay, April 10, 1642, mentioning their departure from the Downs on the 6th idem and their being obliged to take shelter in Torbay, together with three of Courteen's ships. Then comes another short letter to the same, dated May 16, evidently sent home by the *William*, which had just been met. Next is entered Knipe's instructions from the Company, followed by a copy of the charter party of the *Aleppo Merchant*. Knipe has also copied two letters written on his arrival at Swally to two unnamed persons at Surat, one being perhaps Fremlen, the other a chaplain; these, however, contain only commendations and compliments.

Knipe was one of those former servants of the Company who were enticed into the employment of Courteen's Association. After his first voyage under his new masters, however, he quarrelled with them (see the House of Lords papers in the Fourth Report of the Historical MSS. Commission, pp. 75, 81) and again took service with the Company, who sent him out in the spring of 1642 as merchant or supercargo of the *Crispiana* and *Aleppo Merchant*. His account of the voyage will be found under date of July 18, 1643.

ablest, and so the proceed to bee sent to Suratt at the end thereof, for that afterwards here offers not fraequent transport for our monie to India but by boates to Gomroon, whereby to ease the great charge that doth accrew by its so long detention here. Besids, the country people, having then fully supplyed themselves, retorns not till the next moonzoane to replenish their wants. The chiefest buzars[1] that the winter affords is through the arrivall of the few merchants that comes then hither from Aleppo, Dealbuckeer, and Munzull[2], with a few janazaries[3] from Bagdat; and the goods that they buy are chiefly white cloath, indico Agra, some small quantitie of indico Surques [Sarkhej], Chyna ware, pepper, cowho [coffee] seed, gumlack, suger, &c. [i.e. and other] poyzed goods; and of them in these barren tymes noe great quantitie. So that in our weake judgments the first yeares pattern will suite best with your desires and profitt; although this yeare it is not dispissable.' Refer, however, to the opinions of the President and Council at Surat, who will advise the Company on these points by the next ship. Of the English broadcloth they brought with them, two bales were returned on the *Seahorse* in her last voyage, and the other two (except some pieces sold here at 4½ rials 'this covid') they will leave at Gombroon on their way to Surat. 'They are too high prissed for these griping Arabs, who are openmouthed in promising but closefisted if come to performance more then what of necessity they must. However, thus much wee can justly boast of, that there is noe nation here resident which is made capable of one halfe the respect or faire dealeing that wee have hitherto enjoyed, as well from the highest as the lowest.' All their India commodities have been disposed of, except the Dholka lungīs, which are not vendible here, though they are said to be in demand at Mokha. The proceeds of the sales amount to about 71,300 rials; for details they refer to their books, which will be sent home from Surat. 'Wee have lately received newes by the Portugall caphila that come from Syndah of the distracted estate of the Mogol, as having at present theire [three?] powerfull enemie[s] agaynst him, vizt., the Perrsian, in endevouring the recovery of Candhore [Kandahār], his strong rebellious Rajaes about Agra [see p. 18], and

---

[1] *Bāzār* is here used in a wider sense than its ordinary meaning of a market-place.
[2] Diarbekir (in Kurdistān) and Mosul.
[3] Turkish soldiers, especially those employed in escorting travellers.

his unduetifull second sonne [1] in Bengala; so that, whilst hee goes to repulse the Persian, hee is affraid his sonne will seiz on Agra, the chiefe place of his unspeakable treasure, or elce that the Rajaes will doe as much for him before hee retornes; therefore is forct to keep his lascar [i.e. army] about Agra.' They intend to repair at once on board the *Seahorse*, which will then sail (accompanied by the *Prosperous*) for Gombroon, where the *Francis*, laden with coffee from Mohka, is awaiting them. Would have ordered her to come hither, but this would have detained them a month longer. All three vessels are then to proceed to India together, 'to prevent the least of dainger, either by the French or Malavars, with whom the India coasts are very much infested.' *PS.*—Trust the Company will satisfy the Consul at Aleppo for the charges incurred in the correspondence. Have agreed to pay the messenger 420 lārīs for his journey thither. (*Copy, received via Surat.* 2¾ *pp.*)

THE PRESIDENT AND COUNCIL AT SURAT TO JOHN MILLET, MASTER OF THE *ALEPPO MERCHANT*, OCTOBER 10, 1642 (*Factory Records, Miscellaneous*, vol. xii. p. 37).

The management of the intended voyage has been entrusted to Knipe, whose instructions he is to obey accordingly. (*Copy.* 1 *p.*)

COMMISSION AND INSTRUCTIONS FROM THE PRESIDENT AND COUNCIL OF SURAT TO EDWARD KNIPE, OCTOBER 12, 1642 (*O.C.* 1794).[2]

He is to proceed to Goa, and thence to Cochin, on the *Aleppo Merchant*, the master of which has been directed to follow his instructions. On arriving at Goa he should send on shore for Pitt or Thomas Hill and inquire from them of the state of affairs, particularly as to the Viceroy's intentions regarding 'that unseasonable execution of Ant[onio] Pereira de Miranda' [*see* p. 43]. If the Portuguese are likely to 'raise a generall quarrell' with the English about this, it may be necessary to 'withdraw our people and our masters goods out of their reach.' Otherwise he may land and proceed about his

[1] Sultān Shujā, who was in charge of Bengal. The rumour of his revolt seems to have been unfounded.
[2] This is the original document, signed by Fremlen, Breton, and Merry, and bearing an excellent impression of a seal with the Company's arms. For a copy of the commission see p. 27 of Knipe's letter book (*Factory Records, Miscellaneous*, vol. xii).

business. Should a new Viceroy have arrived, Knipe is to seek an interview, present him with the pair of carpets sent for that purpose, and beg the delivery of the cinnamon due from the state. If, however, he finds the old Viceroy still in possession, he is to present him with those carpets and with the accompanying letter, in which the Viceroy is requested to permit the English to purchase a quantity of cinnamon in addition to that due to them. He is also to deliver to him a bale of carpets, ' being his propper goods, provided for him in Lahoar or Agra by the Jesuits there resident.' Should anything be said about the execution of Miranda, Knipe may pretend not to have heard anything of it until his arrival at Goa; or, if this attitude cannot be maintained, he should labour with his ' best rhetorick ' to excuse the Coast factors herein. Coral, cloth, and lead to be sold if possible; prices of these at Surat. Letters to be delivered to the Jesuits and others. His main purpose is to take in at Cochin a quantity of cinnamon, which Francisco de Brito da Almeida, a gentleman residing there, has covenanted to deliver. As this is a prohibited commodity, the utmost secrecy must be observed; and they should clear up all accounts at Goa and take Pitt and Hill on board, in order that there may be no need to call there in returning from Cochin. If, however, they are obliged to go back to Goa, precautions must be taken against discovery of their cargo. Including 4,000 xerafins repaid for a similar sum advanced by Cogan at the Viceroy's request 'to the Capt. Mor [*see* p. 44] of the armado sent to St. Tomees succour', and another sum due from ' Padre Gonsalvo Martyns, Procurador of the Jesuits Colledge, for so many rupees we have made good unto his fellow padrees in Agra', Pitt ought to have more than enough (with the money now sent) to pay for the cinnamon at Cochin; so with the surplus cardamoms, cinnamon or pepper may be bought. From Goa the ship is to go to Calicut, and land two of Vīrjī Vōra's servants; next to proceed to Ponnāni and land the other two; and then to go on to Cochin. After taking in the cinnamon there, they are to return, calling at Ponnāni and Calicut for the pepper which Vīrjī Vōra has promised to have in readiness for them. Pitt is to be lodged with Knipe in the great cabin, and both he and Hill are to be consulted on all matters affecting the Company's business. But there is some fear of 'Mr. Pitts miscarryage, since the V[ice] Roy himself hath spoken him dangerously wounded, though as yet the cause and actor of such mischief are not known unto us.' The Bantam factors have promised to send to Surat a ship laden with pepper, &c., and she is expected to call at Goa on her way to land some 'damar' for which the Viceroy has undertaken to give cinnamon, &c. Arrangements to be made should this ship be found at Goa or met at sea. The master of the *Aleppo Merchant* must be reminded to keep his vessel prepared in case of an attack by the Malabars; also to be careful lest his men desert at Goa or Cochin. Arrack to be purchased at the former place. Inquiry to be made concerning a parcel of opium left at Ponnāni by the *London*. 'Our sheraff, Tapidas Parrack,' has been allowed to send two casks of 'roxamalla' [*rasa-mālā*, i.e. storax] to Goa. Some 'taffataes' to be delivered to the Vedor da Fazenda, Andre Seleina. Should Knipe find it advisable to call at other ports on the coast to sell his goods, he may do so, provided it does not delay his return by December 20 at latest. (6¾ *pp.*)

PRESIDENT FREMLEN AND COUNCIL AT SWALLY MARINE TO WILLIAM PITT AND THOMAS HILL [AT GOA], OCTOBER 12, 1642 (*Factory Records, Miscellaneous*, vol. xii. p. 38).

Announcing the dispatch of Knipe, under whose orders Pitt and Hill are placed. They are required to give him full information and to assist him to the best of their ability. (*Copy.* 1 *p.*)

PRESIDENT FREMLEN AND COUNCIL AT SURAT TO THE FACTORS AT FORT ST. GEORGE, OCTOBER 17, 1642 (*O.C.* 1795).

Arrival of the *Crispiana* and *Aleppo Merchant.* Account of their voyage. News brought by them concerning Courteen's shipping. Edward Knipe is in charge of the cargo, consisting of 200,000 rials of eight, 92 chests of coral, 600 pigs of lead, 33 bales of broadcloth, four bales of 'bayes', and one bale of 'perpetuanaes': total value, 58,947*l.* 7*s.* 4*d.* Have decided to send back both vessels by the middle of January with the full value of the cargo received. Meanwhile the *Aleppo Merchant* sailed on the 13th current for Goa and Cochin to fetch some cinnamon; while the *Crispiana* is to proceed to 'Sinde' about the end of this month for indigo and piece-goods. The *Discovery* has not yet returned from Mokha, though a Dutch vessel which left there eighteen hours after her has arrived, and so have all the country ships. 'Besides the men and shippe, wee computate the Old Joint Stocke hath on boord her in indico, rialls, and other goods nere 20,000*l.* sterling ; and the merchants of this toune more then ten times as much. Soe that with us this whole towne is much grieved and frighted with this her unwonted retardance, consideringe the shortenes and few hazards in this soe easie and well knowne passage.' (*Copy.* 2 *pp.*)

EDWARD KNIPE, SIX LEAGUES NORTH OF GOA, TO [THE PRESIDENT AND COUNCIL AT SURAT], OCTOBER 22, 1642 (*Factory Records, Miscellaneous*, vol. xii. p. 18).

Has just met the *Swan*, but has little to report. ' The 19th present betwixt Chaul and Dabull wee mett, plying to the northward, Mr. Durson in the *Loyallty*, belonging to Mr. Courten, bound to Rajapore, not beeing above 30 leagues shott beyond his port; from whome wee understood thus much : that the 14th present [he] departed Carwarr [and the] 16th mett of Goa, in company of the Dutch shipps, Mr. Hogg in the *Hester*, bound to Carwarr from Rajapore, where shee left their small shipp, the *Unity*, Mr. Farren, who came this yeare from England. The Squires Agent [*see* p. 8] was then att Carwarr, expecting the *Hesters* arivall, intending to proceed on her for Cochine in quest of such synamon as may bee there procureable.' Thinking, however, that there is no fear of his getting hold of the cinnamon contracted for on the Company's behalf, Knipe has decided not to alter his plans but to put into Goa as arranged, though it appears from Pitt's letters that the quantity of cinnamon there is scarcely worth the trouble. Will use all possible diligence to get away from Goa and continue his voyage. (*Copy.* 1 *p.*)

DECLARATION BY JAN DIRKSZ. GALEN, CORNELIS VAN SANEN, AND JACOB JACOBSZ., ABOARD THE *AMBOINA*, OCTOBER 23, 1642 (*O.C.* 1796).[1]

Having been sent to blockade Goa and expressly charged to prevent the entrance of supplies and merchandise, and having found

[1] Endorsed: 'Hollanders writeing given us before Goa.' It is dated November 2 (N. S.). For the circumstances in which this document was given to Knipe, see his letter of July 18, 1643. There is a copy among the *Hague Transcripts* (series i. vol. xiii. no. 418).

that the English ship *Hester* (which got into the port without their being able to prevent her) supplied the Viceroy with brimstone in exchange for cinnamon, and that the *Swan,* which was permitted to enter for the purpose of obtaining water, &c., under promise not to trade, nevertheless took in 300 quintals of cinnamon, they have now acquainted the commander of the *Aleppo Merchant* with their instructions and have forbidden him to take his ship into the port. They have, however, willingly consented to his sending his goods on shore by boat and bringing off his people and merchandise (except cinnamon, which is the King's commodity), the ship meanwhile remaining in the Road. This is permitted because the said English have declared that there is but little cinnamon now there, and that they have only come to remove their factory and stock; and in token thereof the undersigned have delivered to the commander this document. (*Dutch.* 1 *p.*)

EDWARD KNIPE IN GOA ROAD TO [THE PRESIDENT AND COUNCIL AT SURAT], OCTOBER 30, 1642 (*Factory Records, Miscellaneous,* vol. xii. p. 19).

Anchored here on the morning of the 23rd among the Dutch ships. The admiral of the latter, 'John Dirkgalen', declared that he had orders from Batavia to prevent English vessels either entering the port of Goa or carrying any cinnamon from thence; but, after a great deal of debate, permission was given to bring off their cinnamon, which has only now been accomplished. 'The carpetts sent by you from the Padries in Agra gave to our seeming gratefull acceptance from the V[ice] Roy, allthough wee found not any such reciprocacion as to connive at any mans particular synamon as might have byn so advantagious as expected. Mr. Cogans buisness, wee heare, caused a great deale a muttering amoung them, allthough by the descretion of the V[ice] Rey much appised; but although he seemes silently to passe it over, yet he hath secreet[l]y voued, if not satisfaction here made him, to appeale to His Majestie of England for justice; afferming that by severall good testimonies the English man that was slaine was by reason of his willfull entring, not to part the fray betwixt the Portingalls and Daines but to side against the partie shott to death. Nevertheless, the V[ice] Rey hath byn so modest in procecuting his revenge as [he] hath laboured with all stiffe injunctions towards the freindly entertainment of our nation to his port; by which means have wee not received the least affront, till last night one of our men, beeing in our long boate, laden with water, staing (as now the costom is) for a chitte [i. e. a *chit* or permit] from the V[ice] Rey to depart, was by some deboyst souldiers daingeriously and couerdly wounded in the head, but by relacion of our chirurgion [there?] is hopes of recovery.' Some inquiry has been made by Banyans for their coral, but there is now no time to come to terms. Pitt's books will show the reason why he had not the expected money in hand. Since coming on board, they have sold to Lewis Ribeiro [*see* p. 26] five chests of coral at a gain of ninety per cent. on the cost in England, reckoning the 'tango' at sixpence. Pitt and Hill have 'cleared themselves from Goa' and are now on board; they have got in all the money owing, except about 100 xerafins. (*Copy.* 3 *pp.*)

EDWARD KNIPE IN GOA ROAD TO [PRESIDENT FREMLEN AT SURAT], OCTOBER 30, 1642[1] (*Factory Records, Miscellaneous,* vol. xii. p. 23).

Has done his best to carry out all his instructions. Could not find a customer for the two remnants of cloth. Has delivered his correspondent's 2,000 Venetians to Pitt, but no opening has been found for the investment of the money, as Pitt will no doubt advise. Neither Francisco de Souza de Castro nor Manoel Morais appears to have money to lend at interest, 'allthough the latter was motioned by Mr. Pitt; whose chubbed[2] answer was he had too much their [at Cochin?] allready. It is thought that his churlishness proceeds from a deniall of his sending must[3] for England on our shipps.' The letters &c. from Padre Leno at Surat to the Padre Procurador of Madre de Deos have been duly delivered; also all the presents sent by Fremlen to various persons. To the Vedor da Fazenda, however, they gave the smallest instead of the largest of the carpets, chiefly because he had treated Pitt so shabbily. All the goods intended for Gonsalvo Martins de Castello Branco were handed over to him, except the case of bottles, which he failed to

---

[1] A separate letter to Fremlen, dealing mostly with matters of private trade.
[2] Blunt or rude. 'A churle, a foole, a chub' (Cockeram, *Gnoffe*, 1623).
[3] Probably 'musk' is intended. 'Must' is an old form of that word. '

send for; this they hope to leave at Chaul on their return. Money received from Francisco de Souza de Castro on behalf of Tapī Dās. (*Copy.* 3½ *pp.*)

FRANCIS DAY AT 'BALLASARA' [BALASORE] TO THE COMPANY, NOVEMBER 3, 1642 (*O.C.* 1797).

The *Hopewell* reached 'Madrasapatam' safely on July 5. There, contrary to the Company's orders and in spite of Day's opposition, it was decided by consultation to use part of the money she brought to pay off the old debts. The ship sailed on July 19 and proceeded to Masulipatam, where she landed some broadcloth and eleven chests of silver. 'The latter was wellcome; but, for the cloth, it found noe such acceptance as in former yeares, by the occation of the great warrs in those parts.' Finding that the indigo of Masulipatam is far better than that of 'Madrasapatam', he has asked Peniston to send a sample to Surat; if approved there, no doubt a good quantity will be provided against the return of the *Hopewell* from Persia. On the other hand, the 'murrees of Madrasapatam' are far better and cheaper than those of Masulipatam, and so the former should be 'the place of provition'. Sailed from Masulipatam on August 7, and reached Balasore six days later. Here they have sold or bartered their glasses, knives, lead, broadcloth, &c., for sugar, 'gurras', 'sannoes', 'cassaes', iron, and ginghams, all but the last being intended for Persia. Some 'sannoes' and 'cassaes' are being provided at 'Harapore' [Hariharpur] for Europe; but 'many you may not expect, the raines havinge bin soe late and soe violent.' Yard and Travell both intend to proceed in the *Hopewell* or *Advice* to 'Madrasapatam' and so to Europe. 'Mr. Hatch only remaines, and very much discontented, in regard his contracted time is expired and the small imployment that hee is like to have. Accordinge to that small time of my being heer and that little observation that I have taken, I thinke Ballasara (with the adjacent places) is not to bee totally left; for it is noe such dispisable place as is voted, it beinge an opulent kingdome, and you haveinge bin already at great charges in gaininge the free custome of all sorts of goods. Beleive it, if you had but an active man, two or three, in these parts, you would finde it very proffitable; provided you double stocke the Coast, without which tis impossible to comply to your desires. Since I have knowen these parts, for the most parte you have had servants and little or noe meanes to imploy them. If you should inlarge your trade, you may happely have meanes and noe servants, especially such that should know how to imploy it to best advantage. Mr. Winter this yeare goes for Bantam, and soe intends for Europe.' They are promised by the natives sufficient freight to fill both the *Hopewell* and the *Endeavour* for Persia; but he doubts this, at least as regards the latter vessel. Any money received on that account will be invested in goods suitable for Persia, 'for to carry rupees to Mesulapatam there would bee too great loss.' (2 *pp. Received July* 20 [1643].)

THE CONDE DE AVEIRAS, VICEROY AT GOA, TO [THE PRESIDENT AT SURAT], NOVEMBER $\frac{4}{14}$, 1642 (*O.C.* 1798).

Thanks the President for his two letters and for the present which accompanied them. As regards the 'chandaros[1]' which is to be sent from Surat and the cinnamon which the English desire to have in exchange, the Vedor will write. A special effort shall be made to supply the cinnamon, in spite of the difficulties mentioned in the Viceroy's former letters. Up to the present no vessel has arrived from Portugal. Is much obliged to the President for transmitting to him the letters from the Portuguese ambassadors now in London, which contained much pleasing intelligence. Has delivered to Captain 'Knarp' [i.e. Knipe] a packet of letters for the said ambassadors, and begs the President to arrange for their safe delivery. The bundle of carpets belongs not to him (the Viceroy) but to the Jesuit Fathers; refers to the Captain of Damān, who will tell the President how they should be sent. Thanks the latter for the two carpets he has given him, which are excellent. In return he forwards a diamond ring from his own hand and two 'boyōes[2]' of Chinese porcelain, containing citron preserves made in this house. Has forgotten to mention that in their

---

[1] Dammar or resin (Hind. *chandras*). This corrects the notes on p. 296 of the 1618-21 volume and on p. 70 of the 1622-23 volume.

[2] Port. *boyão*, a jar used for preserves. The word, which is possibly derived from Malay *buyong*, has passed into Hindustānī as *boyām*, and is still in general use.

letters of March $\frac{4}{14}$ the ambassadors of King John in London announce that twenty days earlier they had concluded an arrangement with the King of Great Britain for a treaty of peace up to the Cape of Good Hope, while as to India the truce concluded in the time of the Conde de Linhares is to be maintained pending the appointment of commissioners on both sides to settle a peace in these parts also. This agreement has been sent to Portugal for approval, and the Viceroy trusts that it will be duly confirmed. (*Portuguese.* 1½ *pp.* Received December 16.)

MESSRS. COGAN, GREENHILL, AND BROWN AT FORT ST. GEORGE TO THE COMPANY, NOVEMBER 5, 1642 (*O.C.* 1799).[1]

Forward a transcript of their last, which went by a Dutch ship to Bantam. Their investment for that place is now awaiting the arrival of the ships from the Bay; but it will not be so large as was expected, for they have been unable to dispose of their coral, quicksilver, and vermilion, 'by reason of the warrs, which now upon the matter is ended among the Jentues within themselves, by the death of the old Kinge.[2] What the Moors and Jentues will doe, tyme must shew.' Have heard from the Dutch that the *Hopewell* and *Advice* have safely reached the Bay. Have written to Day to accept freight there for Persia, as he cannot expect any at Masulipatam, where 'the Serkailes great jonke' will monopolize all that is available. If no freight be procurable in the Bay, they hope that he will at all events be able to procure some sugar, &c., there for Persia, and then fill up with goods of these parts. Have arranged for the purchase of some at Masulipatam, and have also bought a quantity of cinnamon here. (¾ *p.* Received in London July 20, 1643.)

[1] This is appended to a duplicate of the previous letter, printed on p. 45.
[2] The Batavia *Dagh-Register*, 1643–44 (p. 244) records the receipt of intelligence rom Pulicat that the Carnatic King '.Weijneketapatij' [i.e. Venkatapati] was dead, after lying sick of a fever for five or six days, and that his body had been burned on October 12 [N. S.] at 'Narrewarom' [Narayanavanam, 50 miles west of Pulicat]: that he left no children except an illegitimate son, who by the law of the land could not succeed: and that after much dispute his brother's son, Sri Ranga Rāyalu, had been elevated to the throne on October 29 [N. S.], but many of the chiefs were displeased at this choice. A letter from Pulicat to the commander of the Dutch fleet off Goa (*Hague Transcripts*, series i. vol. xii. no. 402) gives the date of Venkatapati's death as October 10 [N. S.].

MESSRS. COGAN, GREENHILL, AND BROWN AT FORT ST. GEORGE TO THE PRESIDENT AND COUNCIL OF SURAT, NOVEMBER 5, 1642 (*O.C.* 1800).

Reply to theirs of August 6 and September 13, both received at the end of last month. Arrival of the *Diamond* at Bantam. Expect to be blamed for not sending the *Advice* instead. The clamours of their Masulipatam creditors have been stopped, but only 'by robinge Peter to pay Pawle'. 'Wee hope to heere noe more of the Fort in the old dialect, espetially after the arivall of these our last letters, for tis put to the Companies choice whether theyle keepe it, or leave it and bee noe loosers by it. Tis againe battred from Bantam, because they would have somewhat to say.' Disposal of the *Advice* and *Hopewell*. 'Mr. Markham[1] (good man) hath had but small comfort in his sonns that hee hath sent for India; for the elder death tooke from us the last yeare in Mesulapatam, and the younger (it seems) helped to make up the nomber with you in your last generall visitation.' A small horse has been provided for the Queen of Jambi, but perhaps a better one can be sent from Surat. Dispatch of letters and transcripts. The payment of their debts has saved the nation's reputation, but they can hardly hope that it will please the Company, since 'all our actions are displeaseinge'. What Rogers owes the Company they cannot yet say. His dispatch to Golconda was absolutely necessary to prevent the loss of the debts there. 'As for his beinge Accomptant, twas but litle before his death (by the death of Mr. Markham) conferred upon him; and that alsoe for want of another of abillity to performe it, for Mr. Winter was setled in Pettapollee, to negotiate the Companies affaires there, and could not accomplish the busines in both places. But when Mr. Peniston came, or soe soone as wee could gett the acco[un]ts from Rogers, hee had them delivered to him.' Have had no letters from the Bay, though they know the ships have arrived. Cannot sell their coral, &c. Enclose copies of their letters to the Company and to Bantam. The Dutch sent in September two large ships to Batavia laden with Coast goods. Cogan's intended departure. (2¾ *pp.*)

---

[1] Valentine Markham, the Company's Auditor at home. His son Robert went out to the Coast in the *Hopewell* (1639), and another son, Thomas, proceeded to Surat in the *London* (1641).

CONSULTATIONS HELD IN MASULIPATAM BY FRANCIS DAY, THOMAS PENISTON, AND THOMAS WINTER, DECEMBER, 1642 (*O.C.* 1801, 1802).

December 10. On the perusal of letters lately received from the Agent [Cogan], it is agreed that the reasons he gives for desiring to surrender his post to Day are insufficient: that such action on his part would prejudice the Company's affairs, and probably make it impossible for them to borrow afresh: and that in any case he 'ought not to leave his imployment without order from England or Bantam, or at least advizeing thither.' Moreover, Day, by the Company's order, is not to remain on the Coast beyond the time of the ship's departure for Bantam or England; and it is necessary that he should proceed to Persia on her, as the returns from thence are their chief reliance for making up the investment for Europe. As regards borrowing, no money is to be had here, but they learn from Golconda that the Sar-i-Khail is willing to lend four or five thousand pagodas at $1\frac{1}{2}$ per cent. for four or five months. This will be sent after the *Hopewell* to Madraspatam, either by the *Advice* or the *Prosperous*. (*Copy.* $\frac{3}{4}$ *p.*)

December 11. Although the Agent has refused to allow a pilot to be lent to take the Sar-i-Khail's junk to Mokha, it is decided, in view of the proposed loan from him, to spare Roger Adams for that purpose. (*Copy.* $\frac{1}{4}$ *p.*)

December 19. It is resolved to send 5,000 pagodas (when procured) to Madraspatam for investment in piece-goods for England. Then, if more money can be obtained at reasonable rates, to make an investment here in certain specified goods of the same kind. (*Copy.* $\frac{3}{4}$ *p.*)

CONSULTATION HELD IN SURAT BY PRESIDENT FREMLEN AND MESSRS. BRETON, MERRY, BORNFORD, AND KNIPE, DECEMBER 26, 1642 (*O.C.* 1803).

In the recent voyage of the *Aleppo Merchant* down the Malabar Coast, Knipe succeeded in selling a considerable quantity of coral at better prices than have of late been obtained here, 'wheare wee finde the comon buyers so confederate with the Kings ministers that they will have it at theire owne price or lett it lye on our hands.' It is therefore decided to put aboard the *Swan* all or most of the remaining coral, to be by her landed at Cochin in her voyage to Bantam next month; and to send in charge of it, as also for the purchase of cinnamon and pepper, William Thurston and Luke Pynn. It is further determined that the *Discovery*, on her return from Mokha, shall call at Cochin to fetch away them and their goods; and orders are accordingly to be given to John Wylde to dispatch her from Mokha in good time. As regards Persia, since Messrs. Adler, Hall, and Wheeler are expected to return next year, it is agreed to send William Pitt thither to succeed Adler as chief; also Philip Wylde as assistant. Thomas Codrington is to be made Third in Council there, with an increased salary. Finding themselves unable to sell their broadcloth, &c., at Surat, Agra, Lahore, Cochin, or any other place in India, they decide to send it to Gombroon. (2¼ *pp.*)

CONSULTATION HELD IN FORT ST. GEORGE BY MESSRS. COGAN, DAY, AND GREENHILL, DECEMBER 29, 1642 (*O.C.* 1804).

The present Agent [Cogan] has signified his wish to resign his post to Day; but the rest of the Council are opposed to this, on the ground that without him they would be unable to raise the necessary loan, 'because of the Agents respect with those people.' It is further decided to send the *Hopewell* to Persia instead of to Bantam, under the charge of Day; also to ask for pepper from Bantam, in order that the ship may upon her return be sent to England direct from this Coast. The *Hopewell* is to spare a master's mate to the *Advice*. 'The warrs and broyls increasing in this countrey, and now (by reason of our Great Naiques imprisonment[1]) drawing nere to us, wee latelie raised a third bulwarke of turfe; and wanting gunns to mount thereon, have resolved that the *Advice* shall spare us foure minion for that purpose, because there is noe danger of enemie in her way to Bantam, and when shee comes there shee may be againe supplied.' Yard having arrived with the *Endeavour*, her disposal is taken into consideration. She has been surveyed by the carpenters of all the vessels here and pronounced unfit for a voyage

[1] Damarla Venkatappa had been detected in intrigues with Golconda and had thereupon been imprisoned by the new King and deprived of all his territory, with the exception of Punamallee and the surrounding district (see p. 80; also the *Dagh-Register*, 1643-44, p. 244).

to Persia. As Yard bought her without authority, and after so much has been laid out on her she is found useless for the Company's purposes, it is resolved to make an inventory of his estate and to refer to Surat and Bantam the question of confiscating it towards the damages and losses suffered in consequence of his action. *Annexed*: Certificates of the masters and carpenters, dated September [December?] 28, 1642, that the *Endeavour* is unfit for a Persia voyage. (*Copies.* 3 *pp.*)

THOMAS DOWLE, MASTER OF THE *ADVICE*, AT FORT ST. GEORGE TO THE AGENT THERE, DECEMBER 31, 1642 (*O.C.* 1804).

Requests a supply of ropes and blocks for his ship. (*Copy.* ½ *p.*)

THE VOYAGE OF THE *HOPEWELL* FROM THE COAST TO PERSIA AND BACK (*Marine Records*, vol. lxv. p. 26).[1]

1642, *December* 21. Sailed from Masulipatam. *December* 23. Passed Pulicat.[2] *December* 30. Left Madras. 1643, *January* 9. Passed Colombo. *January* 28. Saw 'Cubella[3]'. *March* 6. Were in latitude 26° 33'.[4] *April* 13. Sailed from Gombroon. *April* 28. Anchored off Dābhol. *May* 1. Departed. *May* 18. Were in latitude 11° 41'.[5] *August* 28. Sailed for Masulipatam. *September* 1. Anchored at Petapoli. *September* 2. Sailed. *September* 3. Reached Masulipatam. *September* 22. Departed, and went to 'Emeldee' [*see* p. 75]. *October* 1. Sailed for Bantam.[6] (15½ *pp.*)

ANDREW TRUMBALL'S 'DECLARATION OF SOME PASSAGES AND OBSERVATIONS' MADE BY HIM IN THE VOYAGE OF THE *HOPEWELL* (*O.C.* 1784).[7]

Sailing from the Downs on the last day of 1641, they reached 'Madraspatan' on July 4, 1642, and during a stay of fifteen days

[1] Continued from p. 32.
[2] They got to Madras next day, but the writer omits this.
[3] Apparently Minicoy: see the 1634–36 volume, p. 69.
[4] Their arrival at Gombroon (the next day) is not recorded.
[5] They reached Madras next day, but there is no entry to that effect.
[6] They arrived there at the end of November.
[7] Dated September 18, 1644. This is the date at which the charges were submitted to the Company at home: see the Court Minutes for September 13 and October 4. Here, however, they have been placed with the papers of 1643, as they relate mostly to that and the preceding year.

unladed part of their cargo. On the 24th they anchored at Masulipatam, where they remained twelve days, landed more of the cargo, and Day embarked some cloves, 'but none of them belonging to the Company.' Balasore was reached on August 14 and there they landed the rest of their English goods and the cloves. They stayed three months and sixteen days, at a cost of 180*l.* per month. Day made an agreement to carry freight goods and passengers to Masulipatam and Persia, though Trumball pointed out to him that the voyage would occupy fifteen months and the receipts would not cover the charges, whereas if they started at once for Bantam they might hope to be in England within the same period. Day, however, insisted; and so they took in sixteen passengers for Masulipatam at 15 rupees per head; thirty-five for Persia at 40 rupees per head; 76 bales of cloth at a freight of 15 rupees per maund of 64 lb.; and 355 bales of sugar at 7 rupees per maund of 128 lb. Further, they embarked 118 bales of calicoes (at a freight of 15 rupees per maund) on joint account of Messrs. Day, Peniston, Winter, and Greenhill, ' as is supposed'; and only 700 bales of sugar and 34 of calicoes for the Company. Moreover, Day 'caused to bee putt aboard such quantities of provisions (as hee termed them) for the Persians in hampers, bales, chests and fardells (for the which, though noe freight was paid to the Company, yett hee in liew thereof received divers guifts from them)' that sixty bales of the Company's cinnamon had to be left behind. Though the freight money amounted to 17,854 rupees, Day only brought to the Company's account 6,345 [*cf.* p. 77]; and during the ship's stay at Balasore he charged 1,400 rupees for her provisions, whereas ' by the estimation of all men that knowes the place hee could not expend above 60 rupees per moneth ... a beefe being constantly bought there for one rupee or one rupee and a half at the most, and all other provisions accordingly as cheape.' At Masulipatam they arrived on December 8 and remained thirteen days, though they only took in 22 bales of cloth and 100 of sugar for the Company, besides 76 bales of cloth for Day (part of the 118 already mentioned). 'Madraspatan' was reached on December 24 and six days were spent in embarking 11 bales of cloth and 39 of cinnamon for the Company, to make room for which they were forced to land the 100 bales of sugar. Departing so late, they were obliged to 'looke for a new passage [*see* p. 56], partly in respect of the winds and principally to avoyd the theevish Mallabars', as owing to the amount of passengers' lumber on board they could only use four pieces of ordnance. On their arrival at Gombroon (March 7, 1643) the Company's goods were made over to the Agent, and Day's calicoes were also landed. 'For the sale whereof hee tooke (at his first goeing ashore) a house next doore but one to yours, and there hee carryed them, and enterteyned the most part of the broakers there to goe abroad to sell those goods and to bring merchants unto him; by which meanes his house was soe filled (though large of itselfe) with buyers that, if I had any thing to doe with him about the dispatch of our shippe or about the shipps provisions, I was forced to have two men to make way, as in a great croud or fayre, before I could come to him; hee sitting in the midest with his bales open, receiving money and delivering cloth. Besides, for his assistance in the sale of his callicoes, hee tooke Thomas Clarke, one of my mates, and the purser, with two more of our shipps company, ashoare with him, and kept the said Clarke untill all his goods were sold; soe that I could not have his helpe in tryming the shippe at Ormous.' Though Day disposed of all his calicoes, the Company's small quantity was returned unsold to Madras. 'And in regard I tooke the weight of the Persians goods as they went out of the shippe, because hee should not wrong the Company in the freight of them, Mr. Day having heard thereof, as I was walking to a small fort out of towne, hee followed mee with his weapon, assaulted mee and wounded mee, I having nothing then in my hand but a rattan.' Day accepted a freight for Dābhol, but he waited so long to get in the money for his calicoes that it became doubtful whether they could without danger touch there. However, Trumball undertook to make the voyage, provided the ambassador[1] would agree that the *Hopewell* should not stay at Dābhol more than two days. This having been arranged, they sailed on April 13, with 95 passengers, a quantity of goods for the Company,[2] and the return investment of Day and his partners (in rūnās and rosewater). They got to

---

[1] From a later document it appears that this individual had been sent to Persia by the King of Golconda, probably to solicit assistance against the Mogul Emperor.

[2] Viz., rūnās [madder], rosewater, pistachios, almonds, āchār [pickles], leather, 'simoranees' [possibly materials for rosaries (*smaranī*)], 'soerts', and carpets.

Dābhol on May 1, 1643, landed the ambassador and the passengers, and then sailed the following night, to the annoyance of Day, who had counted on selling his private goods there. The freight between Persia and Dābhol came to 21,738 lārīs, but Day only brought 9,385 to account. The *Hopewell* reached Madras on May 19. There Greenhill told Day that great benefit might be made by bringing betel-nuts from 'Trickumbar' [Tranquebar]. Knowing that Trumball was determined to prevent private trade, Day now endeavoured to remove him from the ship. To this end he incited all those with whom he had dealings to refuse to embark on any voyage with Trumball, and he himself took an oath to the same effect. Moreover, on the voyage from Persia he plotted with the ship's officers 'to draw a head against mee, intymating unto them that it was impossible for them to make a voyage or gett money as long as I was in the shippe; for indeed those that they make masters there they place or displace as they respect or disrespect their private bussinesse, for they must bee their carriers or els leave their charge.' The pretext was Trumball's harshness to his crew, though he never 'whipped or ducked [a] man in all the voyage or ever did exceed eight blowes with an inch rope for any fault by them committed.' His removal having been ordered by the Agent and Council at Madras, he submitted quietly and remained on shore till the vessel returned from Tranquebar, a period of two months and seventeen days. To secure Cogan's consent to that voyage Day declared that 'payntings' could be bought there far cheaper than at Madras; and he was accordingly dispatched thither, in command of the *Hopewell*, on May 31, 1643. After nearly capsizing the ship on the way, he reached his destination about June 16. There Day gave a great feast aboard the ship, when 110 guns were fired in salutes. The same night a gale arose and, 'in regard all the ports were open belowe and themselves drunke', the ship was in great danger. For this William Hills, the chief mate, was kept in irons for six weeks. Day spent in a short time two butts of Canary wine and two of arrack, besides giving away to the Danes a quantity of butter and sugar from the Company's stores. Cogan had ordered him not to remain more than thirty days at Tranquebar, but he stayed forty days longer. On July 10 a small vessel arrived at Madras from Tranquebar, laden with betel-nuts on Day's own account. The *Hopewell* returned on August 13, bringing 30 bales of calicoes for the Company and 400 of betel-nuts belonging to Day; in addition to which the latter had engaged another small vessel to follow him laden with the same commodity, under the charge of Edward Hemingway. The day after the ship arrived Trumball was reinstated as master. Cogan can tell the Company that Day left a thousand rials of eight of theirs in the hand of the Danish President, 'who is never like to pay the same againe'; while the calicoes he bought at Tranquebar would not yield at Bantam the money they cost. Had almost forgotten to mention 'another kinde of private trade' Day had in the second small vessel, of whose arrival they heard at Masulipatam. 'There is one Captaine Sampson[1] belonging to the Danes, who was gone for them upon some employment to Maccassar; but his wife and two wayting gentlewomen were brought upon that vessell from Trinckumbar to Madraspatan for the perticuler account of Mr. Day; for whose residence there I beleive Mr. Day must build a house equall to that shee lived in at Trinckumbar. Neverthelesse, I am of opinion the Company must pay for it, for his condition is to make what benefitt hee can of others and keepe that hee calls his owne fast. The aforesaid Sampson is the cheifest and richest seaman the Danes have in all India; whose wife and servants and jewells, and what els portable, Mr. Day hath now at Madraspatan; whereby it is thought, if there bee not a gennerall quarrell betweene the Danes and English, yett a private betweene Captaine Sampson and Mr. Day will hardly bee avoided.' Trumball left Madras in the *Hopewell* on August 28, carrying for the Company's account a quantity of 'Madraspatan payntings', and the 30 bales bought at Tranquebar; also 109 bales of calicoes belonging to individuals. At Masulipatam they took in more private trade, besides some calico and cinnamon for the Company; and at 'Ameldee[2]' they embarked 44 bales of calico on the account of the latter. All these goods were delivered at Bantam on November 30. Besides the 4,000 rials of eight Day laid out in betel-nuts as aforesaid, he had an equal sum in private trade at 'Gingerlee[3]'; 2,000 rials 'upon Mr. Greene-

[1] See the previous volume, p. 259. His name also occurs in the *Dagh-Register*, 1643-44 (p. 255).
[2] A roadstead near Masulipatam: see the preceding volume, p. 314.
[3] The Gingeli coast extended from the Godāvari Delta to Jagannāth. Where the term

hills shippe which is gone for Pegu'; and a horse at Goa which had cost in Persia 1,000 abbāsīs. This was apart from the cash he had by him; and it was all made in eleven months, though he carried out not more than the value of 100*l.* in money. 'Sometymes I have familiarly asked him whether hee thought, if our masters should heare of his actions, they would not keepe his wages and adventure. His answeare was hee would at all tymes give 100*li.* for 150*li.* And moreover hee said to mee at one tyme hee would private trade soe deepe that hee would neither value his wages nor his stocke that hee putt in with the Company; and at another tyme hee said that hee came from England purposely to make a voyage for his wife and children. Mr. Thomas Penniston, another of your factors on the Coast, is by estimacion worth 80,000 ryalls. Hee hath marryed two gentlewomen to two souldiers and a third is resident with him, who when wee were there was with childe. Mr. Thomas Winter, another of your factors on the Coast, is by estimation worth 20,000 r[yall]s, besides in adventure upon the *Hopewell* in goods sent to Persia, 10,000. Hee hath marryed his gentlewoman to a souldier; by whome hee had two children, one of which came into England in the *Mary.* And Mr. Day and hee are very well versed in game-ing, and noe day comes amisse to them for that exercise. Mr. Henry Greenehill, another of your factors on the Coast, is by estimacion worth 12,000 r[yall]s. Hee keepeth a gentlewoman, by whome hee hath had two children and shee was at our being there with childe of her third by him. At the christening of his second childe there was shott off 300 brasse bases, with three vollyes of small shott of all the souldiers in the castle and 13 gunns from the fort; but the powder was paid for by him. Hee hath built for this gentlewoman (who was formerly belonging to Mr. Day) a very faire house with orchard and garden; in which house hee himselfe lodgeth every night. These foure gentlemen are all sworne brothers; and when they perceive they may benefitt themselves in any project, they passe an oath one to another to prosecute their intend-ments and not dissent one from another untill their ends bee obteyned. And one principall cause of raysing these men to that heigth of pride and riches which they now possesse is the keeping

is intended for a definite place, it probably means Vizagapatam (see Bowrey's *Account,* p. 123).

of such mighty stockes of money, which they call their owne, and with which they buy upp all cloth and paintings that are vendible either in the South Seas or in England at certaine tymes and seasons; and when your shipps come to the Coast in June or July, they must have 50 per cent. proffitt; nay, if your shipps arrive upon the Coast in May, there is order given by them to all the broakers and weavers dwelling about 14 or 16 miles compasse not to sell under the price that is sett by these men. And if any weaver bee soe needy that hee doth undersell their price, if they heare of it, hee is presently rebuked and money lent him for his present necessity. And this is done that the price of cloth and their pollicy shall not bee found out by those they thinke will give you notice.' (11½ *pp.*)

MESSRS. COGAN, GREENHILL, AND BROWN AT FORT ST. GEORGE TO THE PRESIDENT AND COUNCIL AT BANTAM, JANUARY 4, 1643 (*O.C.* 1805).

Enclose a transcript of their last, dated September 20. The pinnace *Advice* left Balasore on November 7 and reached Masulipatam ten days later with a cargo for the Joint Stock amounting to 5,333 rupees, 12 annas, and freight goods paying 486 rupees. Having landed her goods and taken in others for Bantam, she was sent to fetch a further supply from Narsapur; then she was dispatched on December 22 for this place, where she arrived on the 25th. The *Hopewell* quitted Balasore on December 1 with goods for the General Voyage invoiced at 15,879 rupees 12 annas, together with passengers and freight goods paying 6,345 rupees. She got to Masulipatam on the 9th, left on the 19th, and anchored here on the 24th. At Masulipatam she took in freight for Persia producing 374 pagodas. The *Endeavour* sailed from Balasore on November 25, and, after calling at 'Harrapore', reached Masulipatam on December 18 and Fort St. George on the 27th. Her cargo included 4,857 rupees 3 annas for the General Voyage, 209 rupees 12 annas for the Joint Stock, and freight goods 745 rupees. Yard came in her as far as Masulipatam and thence in the *Advice* to this place. There being more goods for Persia than the *Hopewell* could hold, he was questioned about the *Endeavour*, and declared that she was now fit for a voyage either to Persia or to Bantam. Thereupon they resolved 'to put a mulct of 1,000 pieces of eight on him for not following comission, and imploy the shippe for the Companies use.' However, on the arrival of the *Endeavour* her master gave so bad an account of her that a survey was ordered, with the result that she was declared 'not fitt to navigate the seas'. The President and Council of Surat had written on August 18, 1641, directing that Yard should be told to sell her 'as for himselfe', and that all the money spent on her, with suitable interest, should be charged to Yard's account, with due deductions for any freight earned by her for the Company. This course has been followed, but confirmation is requested. Finding that the *Endeavour* was not available, the *Hopewell* was dispeeded alone to Persia on December 30. Fear that after her return the time may be so short that she will have to go home direct from the Coast; and therefore they request a supply of pepper 'to fill upp betweene the bales'. If not required for that purpose, it can be sent to the Bay for sale. Day has gone in charge of the *Hopewell's* cargo; it is hoped that the goods will sell to good profit, but at all events they were taken in barter for English commodities at rates yielding 100 per cent. advance. ' Here with us the times are soe badd, in regaurd of the warrs, that nothinge will sell at any rate ; that makes us wish now (too late) that wee had sent all the corrall, quicksilver, and vermillion which wee tooke ashore here into the Bay. Indeed, if the state of this countrie doe not better itselfe ere the monsoone serves, wee must send it thither unto Mr. Hatch, whoe is left in Bengalla to looke unto the Companies houses, &c., or rather to continue our priviledges untill further order from you for our absolute abandoninge those parts or furnish it as it ought to bee. For ought wee can perceive by the relation of Mr. Day, &c., Mr. John Yard hath but said the truth in all his letters concerning the fruitfulnes of Bengalla and the profitt that may be made to and from that place, if 'twere stocked as it ought.' Now send to Bantam the *Advice*, with a cargo for the General Voyage amounting to 16,400 pagodas 15 fanams. A larger quantity of gunpowder might have been forwarded, had they had casks to put it in. As it is, they have been forced to use iron-bound casks, which is a dangerous practice; but they have covered each one with mats and gunny. Intended also to send the horse they had promised; but the master represented that there was no other place to stand him in than upon the upper deck and that he would not be likely to survive the voyage, whereupon they abandoned the idea. They hope, however, that the President at Surat will supply the want, as promised. Messrs. Collet and Winter, their covenanted period of service being expired, proceed to Bantam on this ship. The latter could hardly be spared, but his health is bad, as he 'of a long time hath byn troubled with a kinde of convultion fitts, insoemuch as wee have often feared his safetie.' Cogan himself had intended to embark in the *Advice*, ' but findeing a general opposition . . . hee is content to continue till the Company or you shall enorder his removeall, which he hopes, nay, he desires, may bee by the next.' The reason why no merchandise is sent on account of the Third Joint Stock is that all the funds available are needed for ordinary expenses, 'for beinge borne wee must bee kept '. Are now endeavouring to borrow money at Masulipatam to begin an investment for England; but find it difficult to do so, 'in regaurd the monyed men have for the most part left that place, and the reason of it is the Serkails hard usage, for to his power he'le suffer noe merchant to buy or sell there, but such as deale for him '. He lately promised to lend them 10,000 pagodas, and if he keeps his word they doubt not to lay out the money to advantage, for goods were never cheaper, as will be seen from the present consignment. 'Onely three small bales of fine tappies will appeare deare, because spoyl'd in the chay [1]; for you may please to know the cloath was bought in Messilupatam and here delliverd out by us on cooley [2], wee allowing them chay, &c.; which was all done in the Fort. At first it appeared excellent good; but after, what with boyling out the waxe and often challowing [3], the chay is decayed and not now to be remedied by us.' This was due to the unskilfulness of the 'paynters'. Their books will show how heavily they are indebted in these parts. Unless money soon arrives from England or Bantam, the liability will be a huge one, for interest will 'eate deepe, espetially now that the usurers must bee paid theire interest everie sixe months, being a custome brought upp by the Dutch, now not to be broken.'

---

[1] Dyeing (see the 1630-33 volume, p. 55).

[2] Tam. *kūli*, 'daily wages'.

[3] Mr. C. Hayavadana Rao derives this term from the Telugu *chaluva*, meaning the bleaching or washing of cotton cloth. He also states that *tappi* is a Telugu word, meaning a bleached or washed cloth.

The Company only ordered an investment here of 5,000*l.* for Bantam; but more than this has now been sent, to provide for the pepper required. If this cannot be supplied, the surplus should be returned in gold; 'for as for other comodities, they will not of [f] of our handes, this countrie being all in broiles, the old Kinge of Karnatt being dead. Soe is the Naique of Armagon, whose countrie is all in the handes of the Moores, and [*sic*] whoe will ere long by all likelyhood bee maisters of all this countrie; for our Naique, not findeing the respect from the new Kinge as he expected, did make profer to assist the Moores; but ere he could bringe his treason about, 'twas discovered [and] he apprehended by the Kinge, who hath seaz'd a greate parte of his countrie. But wee beleve hee will be forc'd suddainely to restore it againe and release him, for our Naiques brother and kindsmen ar levying an armie for his rescue; whoe, with the helpe of the Moores on the other side (whoe are within halfe a dayes journey of each other [1]), will force his libertie or ruine the whole kingdome.' Letters from Goa announce that the *Swan* has arrived there, has discharged her 'dammer', and has taken in the cinnamon, &c., provided by Pitt. 'Our masters busines goes on with the Portugals in Goa verie faire, and here farr better then formerlie, for they neyther come to us nor wee goe to them, which is noe small ease.' At the request of some great personages in Goa, a Capuchin father has been permitted to embark in this ship for Bantam; likewise two Dutchmen, who are bound for Batavia. The wars have obliged them to take four small pieces of ordnance out of the *Advice*; these will be utilized for the small vessels when bigger guns arrive to replace them. A bale of cloth belonging to a debtor sent for sale. Transcripts forwarded of letters from Surat. 'The Dutch on this coast, for ought wee can perceive, hath some greate matters to act; for, notwithstanding the Serkaile did last yeare seale upp theyr warehouses, not suffering them to sell their spices &c., with many other affronts to their unspeakeable prejudice, yett now have they lent the Serkaile, to saile his jounke for Persia, nine men and two pieces of ordnance [2], [and] prepared a pishcash for Gol-

---

[1] Some particulars of the advance of the Golconda invaders will be found at p. 244 of the *Dagh-Register* for 1643-44. They had just occupied Venkatagiri. The release and reinstatement of Damarla are mentioned on p. 259 of the same volume.

[2] *Dagh-Register*, 1641-42, p. 306.

quondah worth 10,000 pieces of eight. The piscash consists of two faire eliphants, two Persian horses, a large branch of candles (poiz about a candie) of copper, with sandall and spices in aboundance; all which (by estimate of our people in Messilupatam) may amount unto the some abovesaid. And from Pullicat about a moneth since a piscash was sent by the hand of their merchant Molleya (alies Chinana Chitty) unto the present King of Karnatt, estimated to be worth 4,000 pa[godas].[1] The Portugauls from St. Thoma have likewise been with theire piscash with the Kinge; but it comes far shorte of the former, for all that they carried coold not amount to full 200 pa[godas]. Somewhat is expected from us; but untill our Naique and the Kinge bee eyther reconcyled or absolutely outed, wee intend to stand uppon our gaurd and keepe what wee have. The Serkailes importunitie hath prevayled with us for a pylott and one other English to sayle on his jounke for Mocha [see p. 69]. The pylott is the same Adams that was bound for Chyna uppon the Portugall shippe the last yeare; which said shippe, goeing from hence for Goa, was cast away nere Nagapatam; where the Portugalls are and have byn put to a greate strait, for the Naique of Tanjore hath beseiged them now upwards of seven monehts.'[2] *PS.*—A small bale of silk returned as unvendible. Send also two slaves; 'the man, being a lustie slave coffer[3], was sometime a slave to the Portugauls of St. Thoma, but running from them to us wee bought him, and for him the woeman; and both whome indeavouring to give us the slippe are sent for prevention as aforesaid.' Have likewise permitted an 'antient sarango[4]' to return to Bantam with his wife, child, and goods. 'Our merchant Sesadry Chittie' [*see the previous volume*, p. 316] has been allowed to send a bale of 'skate skinns' in the ship for sale on his own account. (*Copy. 6 pp.*)

[1] The Dutch merchants at Pulicat wrote, in January, 1643, that Malaya [see p. 50], having been summoned to Tirupati by Srī Ranga Rāyalu, had been graciously received and given the charge of certain districts; and that Gardenijs, the Governor of Pulicat, had taken the opportunity to send a complimentary letter by him to the new King, accompanied by the gift of a fine telescope (*Dagh-Register*, 1643-44, p. 244).

[2] *Dagh-Register*, 1641-42, p. 302, and 1642-43, p. 248; *Hague Transcripts*, series i. vol. xii. no. 394.

[3] Arabic *kāfir*, 'an unbeliever'. The Portuguese, following the Arabs, applied the term especially to pagan negroes, and this is probably the meaning here.

[4] A *serang*, or chief of a lascar crew.

President Cartwright and Council at Bantam to the Company, January 13, 1643 (*O.C.* 1807).

... Intend to dispatch a ship in May or June next to Surat with pepper, &c., to return with suitable Indian commodities. ... The papers now forwarded will show the 'strange and unwarrantable proceedings' of the Coast factors. 'Noe sooner had they notice of Your Worshipps injunctions for their resubordinacy and accompting to Bantam (as in former times that place was accustomed) but a new found way of accompts was contrived (by whose order we know not) and all the charges they had byn at in three yeares time with their buylding their Madrasapatam Castle, and accompt of interest, &c., they would writh and twist in our generall accompts, thereby to avouch and make good, or at least to cover and hide their own (as said) unwarrantable actions.' Do not intend, however, to admit any such charges, unless the Company expressly orders them to do so. The accounts will show 'what a chargeable place that Madraspatam hath byn to Your Worshipps.' ... Aaron Baker has resigned the Presidency to Ralph Cartwright and now takes passage in this ship, the *Ulysses*, for England. ... (*Copy.* 1 *p.*)

President Fremlen and Messrs. Breton, Merry, Bornford, and Knipe at Swally Marine to the Company, January 17, 1643 (*O.C.* 1808).

In their letters (sent via Basrā) of February 8 and March 2, 1642 [*not extant*], they related their difficulties for want of money; 'which, growing upon us, rendered us miserable in ourselves, despicable to others, uselesse to you, otherwise then in our sufferings; for, enjoying nothing but disgraces and revilings, we were driven to such extremities that not without infinite difficulties such monies as are absolutely wanting to defray your factories expences became acquirable. So that from the time of your ship *Londons* departure your cloth investment ceased in the severall residences' until the arrival, on August 28, of the letters [*see the preceding volume*, p. 310] brought to the Coast by the *Hopewell* in the previous month. Then, finding that the Company were sending them

THE ENGLISH FACTORIES

'a fuller carga[zoon] then of late years you have been accustomed to destine to these parts', they at once ordered the various factorise to set about the provision of the goods required. The *Aleppo Merchant* and *Crispiana* duly arrived at Swally on September 21. Now answer the letters brought by them. Are doing their best to close the accounts of the Third Joint Stock, but they must await further particulars from Persia and Mokha before they can complete them. Rejoice that the silk sent home in the *Crispiana* was found to be so good; regret, however, to learn the 'continued disesteem' of that commodity in England. The price is still high in Persia; yet 'the Dutch continue to convert the provenue of those vast quantities of merchandizes yearly landed by them in Gomroon into that specie.' In October last the *Seahorse* and *Francis* brought hither four bales, purchased in Ispahān for ready money, which cost in all 5s. 6d. the small pound; and at this rate, if they had funds to send Indian commodities to Persia (English goods being in no demand), they think the trade might be continued 'with a competent gain', even if the price in England remains at its present level. A quantity of silk is still due from the Persian King, but his officials deny this and there is little likelihood of its recovery. 'In the meane time we are from Mr. Adler advized that Shaw Suffe, late King of Persia, being in May last advanced as far as Cashone [Kashān] in prosecution of his intendments for reducing Candahar to his obedience, dyed there unworthily, whilest overmuch drinking and other ryots hastned his end, and consequently gave beginning to his sonnes enthronization, who by the name of Sultan Abass was saluted and proclaimed King of Persia, and is reported to be a prince of very great hopes;[1] towards whom the Dutch Comandore was in August last journying to visit him, and with him to stipulate a new contract for silk. To him also (and that we conceive not unnecessarily) Thomas Adler was . . . intended to travail, not only to congratulate his happy inauguration but also to procure the confirmation of those imunities you enjoy in his

[1] Shāh Abbās II was only ten years of age when he succeeded his father, Shāh Safī. The Dutch President, Wollebrant Geleijnszoon (de Jonge), started to visit him, but found, on arriving at Ispahān, that the new monarch had departed some time before. The present was therefore sent after him under the charge of Hendrik van Thuijnen, who succeeded in obtaining from the Shāh the renewal of the Dutch privileges (*Dagh-Register*, 1643-44, p. 174; Heeres' *Corpus Diplomaticum*, p. 370).

country;[1] which cannot otherwise be done then by acquiry of sundry firmaens under his seal, which, as they are absolutely necessary to your occasions, so they will prove somewhat costly, that court and countries customes (which may in this particular be justly declared unalterable) not affoarding, but on dear rates, the least of courtesy.' Pitt and Wylde to be sent to Persia to replace Adler, Hall, and Wheeler, who wish to return to England. Codrington's salary raised. During last year the goods sent to Persia from Surat and Masulipatam produced '85,132 m[ahmūdī]s advance, though their prime cost and charges exceeded not 392,152 m[ahmūdī]s.' This year they have no Indian goods to send, owing to their poverty having prevented the necessary provision and to there not having been time, since the ships' arrival, to procure any considerable quantity of 'Agra cloathing, the now most gainfull sortments India affoards.' Consequently little is to be expected from Gombroon, except 'the poor pittance those unjust, inhospitable Persians think fit to affoard you in lieu of your moiety of customes.'[2] No satisfaction has been given for the wrongs sustained there; 'so that we hope, and earnestly desire, to receive your resolutions and directions to right yourselves on this ingrate and unjust people. And untill you are pleased to pitch upon this course, it is as hazardous as dishonourable to continue a residence among them, unlesse you can resolve to expose the nations honour, your own estates, and your servants lives to certain disgrace, damage, and ruine.' As regards the Indian commodities required for England, they regret to learn that the price of Biāna indigo had fallen so much in England; and it is to be feared that the quantity sent home in the *London*, together with the vast amount (over 2,000 bales) exported last year by the Dutch, will debase it still lower. Have now sent 439 bales of it, and would have provided a further quantity, but could not get any more of the requisite quality. Have bespoken 500 bales, 'or 2000 Eckbar maunds', for the ensuing year at very cheap prices, viz. about 35 rupees per maund. Have not heard for a long time from John Turner, who succeeded Bornford

---

[1] According to the *Dagh-Register*, 1643-44 (p. 176), the English presented the Shāh with 700 gold ducats.

[2] Cf. p. 185 of the *Dagh-Register*, 1643-44, from which it appears that the English in 1642 got not much more than a fourth of the total receipts.

[at Agra], but they do not doubt that he will make good their expectations. Much of the Sarkhej indigo now sent is but little inferior to the Biāna. 'This year the indico makers about Ahma[dābād] begin to frame indico of the green leaf, as in Agra, and so it becomes very pure and good; yet the price thereof is pitcht so high that we are resolved not yet to buy more then 100 f[ardle]s of that making.' Have, however, instructed George Tash (who has been chief there ever since Robinson's departure) to buy up to 500 bales of 'the last years round indico', which is much cheaper and yet very little inferior to that made from the green leaf. This they have done now, not only because Dutch competition will raise the price later on, but also because they anticipate some scarcity, 'in regard of the small quantity of seed sowed the passed year.' Rejoice that, in spite of their difficulties, they have found it possible to send back without delay both the ships, with almost all the goods requisitioned by the Company.[1] Particulars of the Agra piece-goods now sent. No investment made in Broach or Baroda baftas. Had bought some at Nosārī, but have since decided to send these to Bantam. The *Supply* was dispatched to 'Scinda' on October 29 with lead and other goods, but as yet nothing has been heard of her arrival; still, they hope soon to see her back from thence with calico. Have also remitted thither from Ahmadābād a good sum of rupees to commence an investment, and have ordered the provision of 20,000 pieces of 'Nussurpore joories', and 4,000 of 'Sehwan[2] joories'. Will do their best to remedy the defects of which complaint has been made. The Guinea stuffs sent were bought in Baroda. Could not procure in time any 'Semana cloth', 'gooldares', or 'seribafs'. No more 'tapseels' will be provided, as they are found to be dear. Quilts and 'chints' forwarded; also cotton yarn. Have embarked a quantity of gum-lac, olibanum, turmeric, and 'tincal' or borax; while, if the unexpectedly large consignment of cinnamon will leave room, they will add some dry ginger. Know not how to remedy the loss in the weight of pepper. Complain of an 'injurious' letter received from Bantam in the *Swan* about the cargo of the *Michael*. 'Since they shame, or refrain, to speak their meaning

---

[1] A summary of their lading is given at p. 171 of the *Dagh-Register* for 1643-44.
[2] Sehwān: see a note on p. 129 of the 1634-36 volume.

otherwise then what a scurvy, silent dash might intimate [see p. 34], we heartely desire you to command them to expresse in some planer character, that so we may endeavour to acquit ourselves of their malitious suggestions and vindicate our inocence and reputation against such treacherous, injurious detractations.' At all events they hope that the Company will suspend judgement until Fremlen's return. The pepper brought by the *Swan* has been transferred to these two ships and invoiced at the price offered for it here, viz. 22½ mahmūdīs per maund of 36⅔ lb. Point out that on balance the Bantam factory owes Surat 133,986 mahmūdīs 29¼ pice, and yet the *Swan* is to be sent back to the former place shortly with as large a cargo as last year. 'These are no fictions, but such truthes as your acco[mp]ts speak and themselves should acknowledge; and therefore, if they have prepossessed Your Worships with any other stories, we must declare them falce, and presume you wilbe pleased to credit us, who have beggered ourselves to fatten them, and yet are recompensed with these unkind and unjust offices; which yet we should not vallue nor resent, if we perceived not in your letters some appearance of discontent in you raised against us by their calumnies.' Now daily expect from Bantam the *Diamond*, with cloves, tortoise-shells, and dammar. Cinnamon obtained from the Viceroy at Goa in exchange for dammar, anchors, &c. The *Aleppo Merchant* sent to Goa and Cochin under Knipe. At the latter place he sold most of his coral and procured a good quantity of cinnamon; while at Calicut he received 550 bags of good pepper from Vīrjī Vōra's factor. These results were so satisfactory that they have determined to dispatch a fresh stock of goods to that coast by the *Swan*, the proceeds of which will be fetched by the *Discovery* on her way back from Mokha. Suggest that in future one of the ships from home should go direct from the Comoros to Cape Comorin and 'range all that coast along, even as high as Goa', to sell coral, &c., and procure pepper, cinnamon, &c., and then to proceed to Surat. Among the goods now sent are cardamoms, 'motoota[1]', and Bantam sugar. As regards other points in the Company's letters, they grieve to learn that the *Jonas* is still missing. Care will be taken to prevent the decks of vessels being pestered with goods, though there will be some loss of freight in

---

[1] Copper sulphate: see the previous volume, p. 87.

consequence. Note the directions given concerning the accounts of the Third Joint Stock and of the General Voyage. Methwold's proposal to Fremlen to borrow 200,000 rupees at interest was fruitless; but the provision of return cargoes was effected in spite of all difficulties. Have only heard once from the Coast since the arrival there of the *Hopewell.* Excuse the factors there for sending the *Advice* to Persia and dispatching the *Diamond* to Bantam in her place. The present ships carry nothing on account of the Third Joint Stock. Understand that the *Blessing* did not reach Bantam until September 14. 'The Coast Agents advices that the months of July, August, September, and so forth untill the fine [i.e. end of] November are most dear and incomodious seasons for buying and curing Coast goods are well grounded. For the Persians and Indians, traders to Gomroon, coming thence in April and arriving on the Coast in May and June, presently disperse themselves into the country and then begin and continue to provide merchandizes for their return to Gomroon; which happening usually about the fine December, they then embarque themselves and goods. Now whilest their affaires are thus agitating in all the places of trade in that country, clothing continues dear; and though it may (and that justly) be alleadged that they buy and carry little whited cloth to Persia, yet the weavers fit their loomes and labours to the seasons and markets, and so make not much cloth for whiting, but divers sorts of alejaes, shashes, and other kind[s] of stuffes most vendible in Persia. Besides, the time of raines (at least we find it so here), we mean the most violent part of them, falling from the fine June to the 20th August, is not seasonable for whiting of cloth; for, besides the want of the sunns heat through the couldes interposition, the rivers, overswelling their bankes, become in their courses more impetuous, their waters muddy and unfit for washing; so that the Agents intimation, touching buying and curing cloth in January and so forwards till June be expired, is very reasonable, for then there are few other buyers then ourselves and the Dutch; for the vessels being once gon to Persia, few or no investments are made untill their return, because till then, wanting notice how each sortment is esteemed in Persia, the buyers sit still.' This was why Surat previously furnished the Coast with 14,000 pagodas for the timely purchase of goods; and similar assistance would have been afforded this year had it been possible; 'for indeed the Coast goods in Persia produce so competent profit to you, and consequently such encrease to our stock, that we would not willingly want them, if your mean carg[azoon]s from England had not rendered you wanting to yourselves. And this maxime, that your trade cannot be made gainfull to you in any competency untill you can resolve to continue an ample stock in India, is infallible, undenyable.' Approve the dispatch of the *Hopewell* to Persia. She is not likely to lack freight either way, 'though the alruling Sarkail or Vizier in the King of Goolcondaes court hath built and yearly sends one or more vast jounckes to Persia, and that other vessels may not lade there untill his be impleat.' Note the allowance to be made by the General Voyage to the Third Joint Stock for the use of the latter's factors, warehouses, &c. Fremlen thanks the Company for permitting him to adventure in the General Voyage, and has paid the amount into the Company's cash here on September 1, 1642. He intends to return in the *Discovery* next year, leaving Breton as President and Merry as Second. The latter left Persia in the *Supply* on April 22, 1642, and reached Surat on May 6. 'We find our disposure and employment of your small shipping is gratefull to you. They are indeed very usefull and serveceable vessels, with which a great deal of mony may be pickt up, if you could (as foreadvized) resolve amply to stock India, and furnish one or two such small vessells as the *Eagle* was; rather indeed 50 tonns bigger, yet contrived so as not to draw above 10, or at most 11, foot water. These, being built very strong, that so they may endure grounding and trymming on Swally Marine or in this river, would for many years do Your Worships a great deal of good service.' Thomas Steevens will be able to advise the Company how best to suit local conditions. As yet, nothing has been recovered from the Malabars. 'However, as you have not gained, so neither, since the *Hopes* surprizall, you have not lost anything. Nor indeed have they of late dared to assault your vessels, notwithstanding that the *Francis* was met with 11 sale of their frigatts; who [i.e. the *Francis*] being as well manned and munited as indeed your *Supply* and *Seahorse* now are, chased them as long as daylight directed her; and by accident, standing in the night into the shoar to gain the benefit of the mornings land breez, happened among them, and so distracted them that, cutting their cables, they rowed away to windward and so left her.'[1] The *Seahorse* was sent last February to Gombroon and thence to Basrā, where the goods she carried, and those the factors had already there, were sold at about forty per cent. profit. For particulars they refer to the factors' accounts and letters. It is intended to dispatch the *Seahorse* again to that port this year, with a small stock on the Company's account and a cargo of freight goods. Merry's departure from Ispahān does not seem to have been actively resented by the Persians, but this may be partly due to the King's death. Knipe commended for his services on the Malabar Coast. Bornford, who now returns on the *Crispiana*, has for eight years honestly and ably served the Company 'in very eminent employments'. Have little to say of Mr. Panton[2], save that they find 'his conversation agreable to his profession'. 'Of Esquire Courtins three first ships we have no more notice then what Your Worships letters specify. His three latter ships are (for ought we hear to the contrary) arrived upon the coast of Decan and Mallavar, where they were met by Mr. Knipe, busied in gathering up their lading. The *Hester* had been at Goa and put off to the V[ice] Roy, in barter of cinamon at 50 xera[fins] the quent[al], brimstone at 20 xera[fins] the quent[al]; where whilest her master, Hogg, was busied in agitating these affaires, the *Loyalty* comming thither, they disagreed about the wearing of their flags; and so, having interchainged some shot each at others flag-staff, they were in fine, after they had rendred themselves rediculous to the Portugals and Dutch, (upon what tearmes we know not) reconciled.' Enclose a note of what they can discover regarding the 'warranted private trade outward' of the owners of the *Aleppo Merchant*. Praise her master [John Millet]; but the ship herself is said to be 'a very laboursome vessell in grown seas'. The *Crispiana* has been much improved by her recent repairs at home. Advise the Company not to persist in employing freighted ships, 'unto this people raising suspicions and jealousies [which?] are not (in these declining times of your trade) easily removed. Nor indeed can fraughted ships be so convenient nor apt for your occasions in

[1] See the *Dagh-Register*, 1641-42, p. 198.
[2] Anthony Panton went out and returned as chaplain in the *Crispiana* (see p. 28, and *Court Minutes*, 1640-43, pp. 236, 336). 'Conversation' is of course used in its old sense of 'behaviour'.

these parts, when, if we want men either to convoy your treasure unto, [or?] your caphilaes from, Ahmuda[bād], we cannot expect them from fraughted ships; nor, when we are upon sundry occasions enforced in a manner to convoy the Kings and other eminent merchants shipping free of the Mallavars danger, can we command them thereto, who pretend not to be obliged beyond their charter-parties extent to the least of service. Many other inconveniencies depend thereon then we intend here to muster. In a word, we find fraughting of ships a dishonourable, and we believe Your Worships will not find it a profitable way. ... . We heartely wish and nevermore hope to see a fraughted ship of the Honourable East India Companies employing.'[1] Express their gratitude for the chests of 'chyrurgery' and drugs, and beg for an annual supply of these 'comforts'. Some of the contents found to be missing. Regret that the Company has reduced the supply of Canary wine for their use 'to one only butt'; they beg that in future more may be sent, and meanwhile they have helped themselves from the *Crispiana*'s stores. Robert Tindall cannot be spared at present; but he has written to his wife and sent her somewhat towards her maintenance, in order that her clamours may be stopped. 'We have many monthes (rather some years) since, upon the first notice that they were not extant in Persia, made diligent inquisition for the artickles of agreement stipulated twixt the English and Persians at taking Ormooz; but we find our endeavours fruitlesse, and so much we did then advize our Persian friends. More we cannot say to you. In our times (we are sure) none such came hither; and so much the Persian factors do now in their late letters witnes for us.' The Company's business in these parts 'is indeed very much declined'; yet the number of factors cannot well be reduced, so long as the demands from home include goods (though in small quantities) from many different parts. However, Bornford returns this year; and by the next ships Fremlen, John Wylde, Adler, Thurston, Hall, and Wheeler intend to go home. It will be necessary, therefore, for others to be sent out to take their places. Their consultation of October 1 will show what they have determined in pursuance of the instructions to borrow 20,000*l.*, in order to provide cargoes for

---

[1] Yet eight years earlier the President and Council were urging the Company 'to make triall of the freighting of shipping' (see the 1634–36 volume, p. 95).

the *Discovery* and the ship intended to be sent out this year. The letters for the Viceroy were duly forwarded to Goa. Letters from him, and from others there, are sent home, as showing his determination to continue the truce. The diamond ring mentioned in his letters [*see* p. 66], as also some cinnamon presented by the Vedor da Fazenda to the President, are forwarded to the Company. The Viceroy's letters to the Portuguese ambassador in London are in the custody of Knipe. The rials brought by the ships were eight short in number and lost in weight 25 per cent. more than any received before; moreover, the silver was so much 'courser' than usual that the shroffs pretended that they lost one per cent. by the bargain. Disposal of the rupees into which the rials were converted. Most of the broadcloth must be sent to Persia. There were too many reds and too few greens. In future, six or eight pieces each of grass greens, 'popenjaes[1]', and very fine scarlets should be sent; but no coarse cloth. Disposal of the coral, and the prices obtained. Part of the lead was sold here, and part they will forward to Mokha. The 'perpetuanaes' received are good, but a finer quality would sell better. The 'baies' are extremely coarse, and must be sent to Persia, for they are unvendible here. They could, however, dispose of some 'of the suprafine sort, dyed into very good scarlets'. The knives will be given away, as occasion requires. It has also been necessary to buy here some fine broadcloth for presents, since the Company refuse to send any for that purpose, though it would surely be cheaper to do so. Forward a list of the present prices of European goods in India. Their letters via Basrā intimated the dispatch of vessels to Bantam, Mokha, and Basrā; also the return of the *Supply* from Persia. The next to arrive here was the *Discovery* from Gombroon, whence she sailed on February 2, 1642, and reached Swally a fortnight later. Goods to the value of 385,000 mahmūdīs were then put on board, and by March 5 she was ready to sail for Mokha. Very little freight could be obtained, as the Governor had prohibited merchants, under great penalties, from lading goods on any vessel 'untill the Kings great jounck was full'. Further, as there was no other Christian vessel left 'to convoy her free of the Mallavars danger', the Governor and other officials prevailed upon the President to order the *Discovery* to attend on the junk. Accordingly

[1] Parrot-green cloth.

they departed together on March 12, and kept company until they were out of sight of land. The *Discovery* anchored at Mokha on April 13 and landed the greater part of her cargo; 'though, in respect of those markets dulnes and badnes, so little thereof was sold that Mr. Wylde, the better at more leysure to dispose thereof, resolved (since William Fursmans untimely end and the other factors mean experience thereunto enforced it) to dismisse the *Discovery* (the season so inviting) and remain himself at Mocha to vend your goods after ships departure.' She sailed accordingly on August 22, but met with such adverse winds that she was much delayed. In consequence her safety was generally doubted at Surat and the rate of insurance rose from 3 to 30 per cent. Moreover, suspicions were roused that she had gone to England 'with all that mass of treasure these merchants pretended to be embarqued on her, amounting unto (as they shamed not to advize the Governor) ten lack or 1,000,000 r[ial]s.' However, she arrived here in safety on October 31, though with her crew 'very weak and crazed' owing to their food supplies having run short. This was partly due to carelessness or dishonesty, for at her departure, according to her list of stores, she should have had 110 cwt. of bread on board, whereas only 44 cwt. could be found. Had it not been for some 'cuskus[1]' obtained from the passengers, the ship would have been forced either to return to Mokha or to put into one of the Arabian ports, in which case she could not have arrived here until February or March. She is now awaiting a lading of freight goods for Gombroon, whence she will proceed again to Mokha to fetch away the factors and their goods. In returning she will call at Cochin to embark such goods as Thurston has ready. The *Supply* was dispatched to Gombroon on February 25, 1642; arrived there March 19; sailed again April 22; and on May 6 'moored at Umraw [Umra], a town three miles short of Suratt'. There she was docked and repaired; after which, on October 29, she departed for 'Scinda' with lead, broadcloth, tobacco, &c. She returned on December 31, bringing back her English goods unsold, together with 71 bales of piece-goods now sent home. She will probably make another voyage to Persia, and will then be freighted to Achin by certain merchants of this town, returning in November

---

[1] The grain of the African millet (*Holcus spicatus*). This corrects a note at p. 198 of the 1630-33 volume.

next. The *Francis* was dispatched to Mokha on February 5, 1642; reached that port March 3; 'was again fruitlessely sent forth in search of Mallavars'; and left Mokha on July 12 with a freight of coffee for Gombroon. She anchored there on July 30, and was joined by the *Seahorse* and *Prosperous* from Basrā on October 3. They left Gombroon in company on the 7th, and reached Swally on the 29th of that month. The *Francis* is now to be sent either to Gombroon or to Basrā. The *Seahorse* and *Prosperous* sailed hence on February 16, 1642, and arrived at Gombroon on March 14. Three days later the *Prosperous* proceeded to Basrā. The *Seahorse* followed her on April 22 and reached the same port on June 13. They remained until September 26, and then returned via Gombroon to India. On November 14 the *Seahorse* was sent to Diu, 'and ordered to coast alongest that shoar untill Salbet Iland [1] should be discovered; ... but the iland no way answering our expectations, nor agreeing with the report famed of it, so much time and labour was fruitlessely expended.' On her return she was beached in Surat River for examination; and, being found to be much worm-eaten, was 'doubled' with $2\frac{1}{2}$ inch plank. It is hoped that she will be ready by the end of February for a voyage to Mokha, Basrā, or elsewhere. The *Prosperous* is also under repair at the same place. The *Swan*, under Michael Yates, left Bantam for Surat on July 25 with a cargo amounting to 16,123 rials 16d. She 'anchored before Goa (under the Dutch admirals stern, forced thereunto by her commandores insolence) the 19th September; who having searched her and threatned to take her dammar from her, kept her there four daies and then, having (it seemes) better considered with himself, licensed her nearer approach to Goa; where, after landing her dammar, it became the 20th October before the 227 bales cinamon were embarqued; with which then hastning towards us, the busy Dutch again invested, searched, and suffered her not to depart untill the 21th following at midnight,[2] when, being freed of their disturb-

---

[1] Salbet or Shiāl Bet, a small rocky island seven miles east of Jāfarābād. It was at this time in the occupation of the Portuguese.
[2] Among the *Hague Transcripts* (series i. vol. xiii. no. 418) will be found a note of a debate among the Dutch commanders on this subject. It appears that the Dutch objected strongly to the exportation of the cinnamon, and even offered to buy it at cost price; but the English refused to agree to this and insisted on their right to carry it to Surat, pointing out that it had not been bought at Goa but merely taken in settlement of debts.

ances, she prosecuted her voyage and the 9th November anchored in this port of Swally.' Hope to dispatch her to Bantam again by the 20th current. For the proceedings of the Portuguese and Dutch they refer to the President's journal [*not extant*]. Advices from Ahmadābād, Agra, and Tatta show that the investments are well forward and they 'make no question to have in readines for embarquing, before November ensuing be expired, (if at least you please by the way of Messlipatam to preadvize us of your resolutions to send forth a full carga[zoon] to disengage us) a good ships lading of such merchandizes as have been this year inlisted to our provision; unto which (though you have not been pleased to name or desire it) we intend, seing saltpeter is become very cheap and that the Court of Parliament have enfranchized divers comodities which were formerly restreined within the bounders of monopolies, to order the buying of three or four hundred f[ardle]s thereof; for your sea commanders are not only infinitly desirous of such kintelage but the fraught thereof is as good as gained unto you whilest in place thereof, and for want of such ponderous goods for stifning, they are necessarily enforced to lay [in?] and carry hence so much ballast. We know it is an evill neighbour to other goods; yet we will hope so to prevent its maligne condition that no damage shall therefrom redound unto Your Worships, especially whilest we confide to have 200 tonns [of] pepper to shoot amongest it and your other goods.' Details of the pepper now sent home. The Malabar pepper is here worth 1*d*. or 1½*d*. per lb. more than that from Bantam. Stores supplied to the homeward-bound ships. 'This passed year we have at Mocha and in Suratt buried William Fursman, Thomas Markham, Thomas Timberlake, and Thomas Veal'; in their places Luke Pynn (purser's mate), John Mantel, and Thomas Clark have been taken on shore from the *Crispiana*. The wages of 'divers young men' who have been employed for some years have been augmented. At the pressing request of the Viceroy and his Council, passages in the *Aleppo Merchant* have been granted to two 'Dominican padrees', who are 'sent to negotiate some important affaires of their state'. There being still some room in the ships, they resolved to negotiate with the Governor of Surat 'about a parcell of Agra indico

In the end the Dutch deemed it wise not to use force over such a small matter, and so the *Swan* was released.

which being sometime Asaph Cauns and since his death, togither with his other goods, ceized on to the Kings use and sent for his acc[omp]t to Suratt the passed year, in search of a chapman.' They bought 301 bales at 32 rupees per Surat maund[1] and put them on board, taking out some of the cotton yarn and cinnamon to make room for the full quantity. The indigo 'hath been bought and fardled upwards of 8 or 10 yeares', and, being consequently very dry, is not likely to lose in weight. Since they are allowed six months' time for payment of the money, it will probably be in the Company's hands 'ere its proceed be due unto the King'. John Stallon, who came out in the *London* and was then made master of the *Supply*, returns in the *Aleppo Merchant*. He is commended for past services. 'Although our generall welwishes to our Sion induce us to hope that the troubles and distractions under which she laboured, when these ships left her, are fully quieted and removed, yet dare we not so certainly depend thereon as not to endeavour with utmost caution to provide for your indempnity against such mischances as may through those troubles befall you in your ships approach to and falling with our coast.' The *Crispiana* has therefore been detained until the *Aleppo Merchant* was ready, and the two masters have been required to give bonds to each other to keep company in the homeward voyage. To avoid all question, they 'could wish that Your Worships would be pleased hereafter to continuate your necessary submission of whatever vessels or men employed in your service to your President and Councels absolute direction; for so will such your occasions as depend on your ships and seamens performances be best agitated and accomodated.' *PS.*—The purser of the *Aleppo Merchant* professes a doubt as to the number of bales of Sarkhej indigo taken on board; but they have inquired into the matter and find that the invoice is correct.[2] (29½ *pp. Received July* 20, 1643.)

---

[1] 'Which is 26¾*d.* the pound' (*marginal note*). The rupee seems to be taken at 2*s.* 3*d.*, and the maund as about 33 lb.

[2] An attestation to this effect, signed by Richard Fitch, Maximilian Bowman, and William Bindlos, forms *O.C.* 1816.

THOMAS MERRY AT SWALLY MARINE TO THE COMPANY, JANUARY 17, 1643 (*O.C.* 1809).

Thanks them for their favours, expressed in their last letters. Here he has found more content and quiet than ever in Persia, and he 'cannot doubt of other in soe orderly a famylie, governed by soe worthy and able a President'. For the state of affairs in Persia when he left, he refers to earlier letters. Explains the circumstances in which he became indebted to the Company and trusts that this will not lessen their good opinion of him. Disposal of a chest of rhubarb sent home by the *London*. Requests that no further payments on account of his salary may be made to Mr. Skinner. (1¾ *pp.* Received *July* 20, 1643.)

FRANCIS BRETON AT SWALLY MARINE TO THE COMPANY, JANUARY 18, 1643 (*O.C.* 1813).

Thanks them for nominating him to succeed Fremlen on his departure, but begs that his salary in the meantime may be reconsidered. Refers to the general letter and the accounts for the state of the Company's business here. Regrets that the Third Joint Stock is still indebted upwards of 20,000*l.* more than its estate will satisfy, and that this must necessarily be increased by the 'excessive corrodeing interest'; but he trusts that the Company will send out means to extinguish the debt and stock the various factories, 'untill when it is not to bee expected your biussines should be negociated either to your proffitt or reputacion.' Excuses the use of part of the money sent out in paying former debts. In the invoices of goods the rupee has been reckoned at 2½ mahmūdīs, though it is really worth only 2¼; but this was done 'for the better clearing of those which remained upon the Stocks ballance'. (2½ *pp.* Received *July* 20, 1643.)

LISTS OF PACKET BY THE *ALEPPO MERCHANT* AND *CRISPIANA* (*O.C.* 1810, 1811, 1812).[1]

Surat letter and enclosures; invoices and bills of lading; copies of letters from other factories; journals, ledgers, &c., of various fac-

---

[1] Duplicates of the first two will be found under *O.C.* 1814, 1815.

tories (including Vīravāsaram, Hariharpur, Agra, Lucknow, and Tatta); inventories and accounts of deceased factors; will of Marles Twine; Portuguese letters; the President's journal, 1641 and 1642; arraignment of John Layton; process against John Stallon; appraisements of the *Supply* and other vessels; &c. (*In all 3 pp.*)

RALPH CARTWRIGHT, JOHN JEFFRIES, AND THOMAS WINTER, ABOARD THE *BLESSING* IN BANTAM ROAD, TO THE COMPANY, MARCH 13, 1643 (*O.C.* 1819).

... On February 5 the long-expected pinnace *Advice* arrived from the Coromandel Coast with a cargo of 24,600¼ rials of eight for the First General Voyage and 427⅕ rials of eight for the Third Joint Stock. This leaves the Coast still much indebted to Bantam, and apparently there is little more to be expected from thence. The Coast factors complain much of the burden of interest on the money they owe, but no help can be afforded them from this place, for want both of means and of shipping. The *Swan* is at Surat and the *Hopewell* on the Coast; while the *Expedition* (and probably the *Michael*) have gone to Macassar. The *Advice* is to start at once 'in her discoverie of Keeleings Islands[1], and thence for Diego Ries [Rodriguez], Englands Forrest [Réunion], Mauritius, and the back side of St. Laurence, in quest of the *Jewell* and *Jonas* and to procure slaves and some salt flesh.' ... If the *Swan* returns from Surat in good time, they hope to dispatch two ships to England in December next. They also propose to send the *Expedition* to Surat about July next with pepper, &c. ... Estate of the late Gerald Pinson and of 'Padre' Hall, who died at Masulipatam. ... Thomas Winter and Edward Collet came from the Coast in the *Advice*, intending to return to England by the first ship thither bound; but Winter has been persuaded to remain here until the next season, and Collet has referred himself 'to the President and Councell for his further disposure'. ... Understand that two of Courteen's ships are trading for pepper on the West Coast of Sumatra. ... (½ *p.*)

[1] The Cocos-Keeling Islands (supposed to have been discovered by Captain Keeling in 1609) lie about 600 miles SW. of Java Head. In January, 1642, the Company had ordered that a pinnace should be sent to visit them (*Court Minutes*, 1640-43, p. 221).

PRESIDENT FREMLEN, FRANCIS BRETON, AND THOMAS MERRY AT SWALLY MARINE TO THE COMPANY, MARCH 20, 1643 (*O.C.* 1821).

The *Crispiana* and *Aleppo Merchant* sailed on January 19. Now write by the *Seahorse*, which is bound for Basrā, whence this letter will be sent overland to Aleppo. On January 30 the *Discovery* and *Supply* were dispatched to Gombroon with cargoes invoiced at 53,810 mahmūdīs, besides freight goods and passengers paying 51,091 mahmūdīs. The former is to go on from Gombroon to Mokha, and the latter to return to Surat. Pitt and Philip Wylde sent to Persia in the *Supply*. On February 9 Thomas Hill was dispatched to Ahmadābād in company of a Dutch caravan, with a quantity of rūnās for sale there, besides five horses ('refused by this Governor') and a coach and camel brought by Bornford from Agra. Have since heard that Hill arrived in safety and, leaving the rūnās at Ahmadābād, proceeded with the horses &c. to Agra, accompanied by some Dutchmen. On February 16 two Dutch ships arrived from Persia. Letters from the English factors there announced that Adler and Codrington had been to the court of the new King at Kasbin and had been well received. Most of the Company's privileges were renewed; but the farmān authorizing the English to maintain a watch at the custom-house, and another ordering their share of the customs to be demanded from all men not expressly exempted by the King's warrant, were withdrawn, and no satisfaction could be obtained for the killing of their men by the Sultān of Gombroon. There is now no remedy but force, and they trust to receive from the Company authority to adopt strong measures. The reasons given by the Persians for 'this dishonourable and injurious abearance towards you' were 'that you were grown poor, bought no more dear silk of the King, and were not able to defend his port; but we think rather they grutch you not only the priviledg of sitting in but the poor profit which redounds to you from the custom-house and exemption of your own goods from paying customes.' Send the factors' letter on this subject, and have instructed those at Gombroon to advise the Company 'what your share of customes, rather what in liew thereof the Persians allowance or pension (for so they now tearm it) will amount to.' It will be seen that broadcloth is in no demand in Persia ; and, as there is no improvement in its sale here, the Company will do well not to exceed the quantity asked for in the last letter. On February 25 the *Swan*, commanded by Michael Yates, with a cargo amounting to 212,438 mahmūdīs, sailed for Cochin, where she was to land Thurston with part of her goods and then proceed to Bantam. They had intended to send all their coral to the former place ; but Vīrjī Vōra at the last moment bought all the 'gretzo' and 'teraglia', and made an offer for the 'recaduti'. This they consider insufficient, and so, ' finding that sort very much requested on the Mallabar Coast, we sent it thither, and ordered the bringing up of the remainder to Suratt, after we had first taken a wryting from this Governor &c. Kings ministers, not only not to demand the novel imposition of one per cent. to the Kings broker but also not to rate the coral in custom-house beyond its true vallue. And thus by discovery of this new vent for coral on the Mallabar Coast we have not only advanced its vallue here but also enforced this Governor &c. to deal more justly and respectively with us in the matter of customes, which formerly they usually overrated 40, if not 50, per cent. more then we could here advance it to.' From the proceeds of the goods consigned to Cochin, to which they propose to add a further consignment by the *Supply* on her way to Achin, Thurston is to provide cinnamon, pepper, and cardamoms, to be ready upon the arrival of the *Discovery* about the end of September. It is hoped that she will thus obtain a good part of her cargo for England, should the Company by that time have sent sufficient funds. Her master has orders to repair her at Assab, and she should then be quite fit for the homeward voyage. Have sent a large stock of goods to Bantam in the *Swan*, and trust that the factors there will return the like value and also the amount of their former debt. ' The 3d March two Dutch vessels, vizt. the *Pao* from Japon and China and the *Lewert*,[1] from Battavia, anchored in Swally Hole; the former of which, setting sail from Teiwan or Ilha Formosa, near the coast of China, about the middle of November encountred the latter at Mallacca ; who bringing that (by the Portugals) long desired and expected confirmation of peace twixt both nations, came

---

[1] The *Pauw* (*Peacock*) and *Leeuwerik* (*Skylark*). Their arrival at Swally is recorded in the *Dagh-Register*, 1643-44, p. 178.

in joint company to Punto de Gallo in Seiloan, left there a commissary, Peter Burrel [Pieter Boreel], to follow them to Goa, there by the Generals order to publish their willing assent to and observation of such artickles of truce as were from the States and their employers received. At Vingurla the vessels stayed some daies; but loosing thence hasted for this place, where the 6th current they landed 103 boxes Japon silver, with a very great quantity of tutinagle. From Japon they pretend to bring good tydings (though we are somewhat incredulous thereof, considering the small quantity of silver landed) that the Emperor is become very gratious to their nation, which, being now freed from all former dishonour and disturbances, enjoy a most gainfull trade, such as produced this year 80 per cent. advance. On the Ila Formosa they boast also to have taken from the Spaniard a small fort[1] without any great resistance; which is probable enough, for the Spaniard, determining long since to have abandoned it, left only 35 men to defend it.' By the *Leeuwerik* came a letter from the Bantam factory, intimating that neither the *Blessing* nor the *Diamond* could be spared for a voyage to Surat, but promising to send such goods as they had in July next. 'Thus they take pleasure to sport themselves with us, whilest we (awed by your mandats) send them yearly even as much as they inlist unto us; which it seems must rather help to fill the *Reformation* for England for the Third Joint Stocks accompt then extinguish its engagements here, where the said Stock paies costly and constant interest.' The *Francis* was dispatched on March 13 to Mokha with a few freight goods and with provisions, stores, &c., for the *Discovery*. Would have sent some pepper, had not the Dutch dispeeded a very great quantity thither shortly before. Wylde has been directed to take with him in the *Discovery* to Cochin 'as much of your estate in Mocha as exceeds 3,000*l*. sterling.' The *Seahorse*, after being substantially repaired, was brought into Swally Hole on March 12, and is now being laden for Gombroon, 'Cattife[2]', and Basrā. Edward Pearce goes in charge of the cargo. Investments have been made at Agra, Ahmadābād, and 'Scinda' in piece-goods and indigo;

---

[1] The fortress of San Salvador at Ki-lung, on the northern coast of Formosa, was captured by the Dutch in August, 1642: see *Hague Transcripts*, series i. vol. xii. no. 388, vol. xiii. no. 407; also Heeres' *Corpus Diplomaticum*, p. 368.

[2] Al-Katif, near Bahrain.

and they trust by the middle of next December to have enough to fill the *Discovery* and dispatch her to England. The *Advice* left 'Madrazpatam' for Bantam on January 4. The *Hopewell* quitted Balasore on December 1, anchored at Masulipatam on the 9th, and at Fort St. George on the 24th. She sailed thence for Persia on December 30, with orders to return as speedily as possible, that with the proceeds of her cargo the factors 'may perfect their Europe investment', as they find it difficult to borrow the money they need; they have also applied to Bantam for a consignment of pepper, with the idea of lading the *Hopewell* for England direct from the Coast. Omitted to advise in their last letter that Merry is charged in the Persia accounts with a debt of 150 tūmāns, but, as he queries the correctness of the amount, particulars have been sent for; he avers his readiness to pay whatever is found to be owing. *PS.*—Cannot give the total received for freight on board the *Seahorse*, as this includes '36 bales of cloath belonging to this King'; the payment for which cannot be settled until they return to Surat. (7 *pp.*)

DECLARATION BY HENRY BASSANO, STEWARD OF THE *HOPEWELL*, AT FORT ST. GEORGE, MAY 30, 1643 (*O.C.* 1823).

Charges Trumball with excessive use of the wine on board, 'haveing sometymes a gallon, but never less then a pottle a day for his owne perticuler', besides an extra quantity 'when hee hath byn disposed to bee merry'. All of this, or the greater part, Trumball directed Bassano to charge to the ship or as sent on shore to factories; and he was forced to comply, having 'severall times byn strocke and beate by him and threatened divers tymes to bee displaced.' Alleges also that two of the Company's butts of strong beer were used to fill up the seven butts brought out by Trumball and sold by him on his own account. (*Copy.* 1 *p.* Received in Surat October 13.)

COMPLAINT BY THOMAS CLARK AGAINST ANDREW TRUMBALL [MAY, 1643?] (*O.C.* 1825).

Recounts seven instances of Trumball's striking and abusing him, the last being when Leigh, master's mate of the *Advice*, desired to carry on shore certain cases belonging to Clark. (*Copy.* 1½ *pp.*)

ATTESTATION BY SEVEN SAILORS AGAINST TRUMBALL, ABOARD THE *HOPEWELL*, JUNE 14, 1643 (*O.C.* 1824).[1]

Declare that, when ashore at Madraspatam they heard Trumball command them to go aboard, they instantly prepared to do so; but 'presently hee gave us a counter checke, that, notwithstandinge hee bid us goe, yett wisht us not soe to doe, but for to sticke close to him, and that wee should not want for any thinge, if it were a thousand pagothas; and bid us goe and call for a case of wine, or what else wee would, and hee would pay for the same.' (*Copy.* ½ *p.*)

ANDREW TRUMBALL'S ANSWER TO THE CHARGES MADE AGAINST HIM BY FRANCIS DAY, JUNE, 1643[2] (*O.C.* 1824).

Denies that he used the chirurgeon[3] 'in a cruell horrid manner'. The latter charged Trumball's servant eight pounds for treating him and, on Trumball remonstrating, told him 'hee would make what rates hee thought fitt.' Being further asked why he carried medicines ashore when there were no sailors sick there, 'hee replyed I should never know; which mooved mee, seeinge his infinite pride, to stricke him three or four blowes with an inch rope.' As for the purser, so far from being unkind to him, Trumball gave up his own cabin to him when he was sick. The boatswain was not ill an hour, and has never once been beaten by Trumball, though at times the latter has 'reprooved him for his slow proceedings with such termes as best befitted him.' The said party is so far from being 'charritable' that he refused to be reconciled to one of the gunner's mates, who had begged this on his death-bed; while as for his sobriety, he was 'a meere sott' at the time of sailing. The quarrel

---

[1] There is another copy among the *O.C. Duplicates*.

[2] Undated, but noted as received in Fort St. George on June 20. There is another copy in the *O.C. Duplicates*.

[3] In an article contributed to the *Indian Antiquary* for Sept. 1911, I suggested that this unnamed surgeon might possibly have been Gabriel Boughton, who certainly held the post a few months later; but I am now inclined to identify him with the John Reynolds mentioned on p. 111, who is described in the Court Minutes of Nov. 19, 1645, as a surgeon. He had at that date been dead for some time, and an acconnt of his estate had been sent home from Bantam; so the probability is that he died before the *Hopewell* quitted Madras.

between Trumball and Beck was settled by the latter apologizing; 'but, indeed, to say truth, Mr. Day could never indure there should bee any unity betweene mee and my mates all this voyage, hee haveing an old grudge at mee and would have undone mee before I came home the last voyage, if possible hee could.' Had Day been entertained by the Company before Trumball, the latter would have declined to go to sea in the same ship for this reason. As regards John Leigh, he came aboard in Balasore Road to fetch the Company's goods and money ashore, and wanted also to take some cases of strong waters which he alleged he had bought on board, though they were really still the property of Thomas Clark. Trumball prevented him from so doing, as the boat was already full, and Leigh thereupon 'went forward and aft upon the decke, abuseinge mee with what words hee pleased.' He refused to go into his boat when ordered, until Trumball called for his 'rattan'; but it is untrue that Trumball either abused him as alleged or struck him. The accusation that Trumball 'went about to displace Mr. Hill' is entirely false. It is true that he was warned by Cogan and Beck that Hill 'did in his ordinary talke call mee nothinge but Scottish dogg, and why should they bee comanded by a Scott', and he then drew up something 'to have bridled his tounge'; but Cogan and Beck refused to sign this. When the sick men went on land at Balasore, Trumball took precautions to keep them dry, but left their diet to the chirurgeon who accompanied them. If anything was wanting in this respect, it was the fault of the latter. 'There is not a day past since wee came out of England but our men had either beere, wine, or aracke; unless it were in our passage to Persia, [when] they kept their drinke tell they had a quantitie together and made themselves drunke with it and quarrell'd and fell out one with another; then I gave order they should have it but foure tymes a week for the space of about 10 or 12 dayes. But had I knowne that a cupp of sacke had bin such a prevalent medisine to have made men well assoone as they came ashore, they should not have wanted; but I beeleeve (nay, I dare say) that Mr. Day was the sicke man that wanted sacke.' Day's fifth charge is a repetition and needs no further answer; but it is to be noted that he thus shows his desire 'to make a great harvest of a litle corne'. The sixth charge concerns Hill. He was so addicted to drink on the voyage out that Trumball was weary of reproving him. At Masulipatam he stayed on shore six days and contracted a disease, for the cure of which he asked leave to go on land at Balasore, 'tellinge mee the chirurgion was to deare.' 'There hee stayed 10 dayes, and abus'd all the merchants; and the Cheife fetch'd him out of the whorehouse at 12 a clocke at night all bambord[1].' On the voyage from Balasore to Masulipatam his behaviour to one of the women passengers led to the Persians threatening to leave the ship. Trumball reproved Hill for this in their presence and in reply the latter 'abused mee with very ill words'. A consultation was called; but Day took Hill's part and 'through his example the rest would not speake'. Notwithstanding, Trumball thought it necessary to punish the offender, in order to avoid scandal and complaints at Masulipatam; so Hill was set in the bilboes for eight hours. 'Seventhly, in our passage to Persia the Moores invited Mr. Day, myselfe, and the purser to a feast with them, which wee excepted of. And when they had eate, they fell to drinkeinge, tell Mr. Day had soe much hee could take noe more, for in my contience hee had betweene 20 and 44 [24 *in the other copy*] cups of strong waters in him. After hee was gone wee tooke our leaves of the Persians; and about five howers at night wee went to supper, where the purser fell out with mee and strucke at mee, as I have wittnessed under my mates hands. Mr. Day, beinge in the round howse, came out betweene drunke and sober and called the purser, sayinge: "Ned, come hether; the master shall have nothinge to doe with thee." What remidy could I use in this case, onely patience? Nevertheless, I comanded the purser to leave his raileinge att mee and goe to his cabbin; neither of which hee would doe. Then I tould Mr. Day hee did ill to countenance any man thus against mee; neither use[d] I any other words to him then these, for I know well what manner of man Mr. Day is.' Confesses that, on Thomas Clark absenting himself from the ship at Gombroon for '26 dayes upon a bord [2]', he 'gave him a cuff on the eare'; but cites instances of Clark's carelessness and inefficiency. As for Barker and Richards, 'their perimtory carriage and unbe-

---

[1] Drunk. The word seems to be 'bombard', which meant first a small cannon, then (from its shape) a black-jack for holding a large quantity of liquor, and then a toper. Instances also occur of its use (as here) adjectivally.

[2] This seems to be equivalent to 'at a stretch'—a metaphor derived from a vessel sailing for some time on one 'board' or tack.

seeminge behaviour is very well knowne to all, both this voyage and the last.' Roger Barker stayed on shore against orders for twenty days in one place and sixteen in another, giving as a reason that Day's business was not finished. Those who have joined in the complaint against Trumball are themselves under accusation; and their testimony is 'most faulce', especially the allegation that they were forced to sign consultations against their wills. Day himself is often drunk, both at sea and on shore. 'Drinkeinge with the Moores and Persians att Ballisara, hee soe disguis'd himselfe in theire presence that they sent him away in a pallankeene, out of which hee fell by the way. Att Persia hee fell out with the Dutch and abused them soe, when hee was drunke, that hee had like to sett the English and Dutch by the yeares, as wee terme it. I am sure they came not to one another in five dayes after. And another tyme hee made himselfe soe drunke at Persia [that] hee rann into the sea and [was] like to have drowned himselfe.' (*Copy.* 7 *pp.*)

EDWARD KNIPE, ABOARD THE *CRISPIANA*[1], TO THE COMPANY, JULY 18, 1643 (*Factory Records, Miscellaneous*, vol. xii. p. 77).

Being unable in person to bring them 'the first tydings of our arrivall', he sends the following diary of the voyage. 1642, *April* 6. They sailed from the Downs, with two of Courteen's ships. *April* 10. Contrary winds forced them to put into Torbay. *April* 12. Sailed again, 'in the said company'. *May* 3. Saw the Peak of Teneriffe. *May* 4. Passed between Teneriffe and Grand Canary, three of Courteen's ships being still in their company. *May* 15. Met the *William*, from Bantam, and spared her some provisions. *June* 3. Crossed the Equator. *July* 12. 'By judgment passed by Cape Bona Spei, but no land seene.' *August* 2. Anchored in St. Augustine's Bay. Learned that the *Hester* had departed the previous day, having stayed 24 hours. *August* 6. Sailed. *August* 16. Reached Johanna and found there the *Hester*. She had been at Mozambique and had there sold lead and broadcloth for gold. *August* 17. The *Unity* and *Loyalty* arrived. *August* 23. Departed, in company with the *Unity* and *Hester*. The

---

[1] 'In sight of Fair Lee', i.e. Fairlight, near Hastings. An alternative name of this place was 'Fairleigh' (Carlisle's *Topographical Dictionary*).

Loyalty remained to mend a topmast. *August* 24. Lost company of 'the Squires shipps'. *September* 19. Landed the purser at the mouth of the Tāptī, with letters for Surat. *September* 21. Anchored in Swally Hole. *September* 22. The President and Council came down, and two days later a voyage to the Malabar Coast was decided upon. *October* 13. The *Aleppo Merchant* sailed accordingly. *October* 22. About ten leagues from Goa met the *Swan*, which had that morning left Goa with a quantity of cinnamon. Her master, Mr. Yates, reported that there were seven Dutch ships in that road, 'who, notwithstanding the peace, [were] excercizeing as much violent hostillity against the Portugall as ever; and how that the *Swann* with much difficullty gott cleare of them, they alleadging that no English shipp ought to trade there while their shipps were in the roade; and that they vowed to hinder and putt by the next English shipp that came thither uppon any affair whatsoever.' This made Knipe doubtful whether he ought to go into Goa, as the small quantity of cinnamon there was not a sufficient inducement to lose time in contention with the Dutch. Before starting from Surat, he had urged the President and Council to allow him to go straight to Cochin, calling at Goa on his return; but their answer was that, owing to the recent execution of a Portuguese by the English on the Coromandel Coast, 'they knew not what extremity of revenge they might seeke against our people in Goa', and accordingly he was enjoined to go thither first of all. This order he felt bound to obey. *October* 23. 'About five in the morning wee came to an anchor in Goa Road, near the Dutch shipps; where suddainely wee were enterteined with a mallapert message from their Generall, John Dirrick Galen; where beeing come, fownd them monstrous peremptory in their speech, farr exceeding the relacion of Mr. Yates; demanding what wee meant to come thither, flattly telling us [there was] no synamon uppon any tearmes for us to bee had from the Portugall, and that their Generall of Battavia had so enordered them; proferring mee to veiw their commission. I tould them I never yett knew the States of Holland have the bouldnes to order deniall of any the King of Spaines ports to any the King of Englands subjects (allthough Goa was not the Spaniards port) so long as wee brought not either municion or provicion; which if they doubted by us, [they] might freely satisfie themselves by sending whome they pleased aboard our shipp to search. They begann to bee somewhat rigorous in their common insolent language; but I after very much debate tould them that, if they would faithfully promise us that wee might doe our bussiness where the shipp roade, without any molestacion att all by them, and give under their commanders hand that the Generall of Battavia had given such order as not to suffer us to bring off synamon, then should our shipp continew where shee then roade; if not, wee should bee forc't to hazzard what they threatned. After consulting with themselves, [they] were more moderate in their speech towards us, giveing us licence (while our shipp roade amoung theirs) either to carry on shoare or bring aboard our goods as wee pleased; likewise gave under their hands the authority they had from the Generall of Battavia.' Thereupon Knipe went himself to Goa to hasten matters; but it was not until the 30th that he got the cinnamon aboard, together with Pitt and Hill. The cinnamon was old and very dear. Pitt had contracted with a Portuguese for a further quantity to be received at Cochin. Knipe did his best to make void this contract, believing, from his previous experience, that he could buy the cinnamon there at a cheaper rate; but this was impossible, as Pitt had paid a deposit. Knipe succeeded, however, in selling a quantity of coral to the said Portuguese. Rials of eight were worth at Goa eleven 'tangoes' and 'chickeens' nineteen; so there was a loss of at least 14 per cent. on the latter at the price they cost in rials at Surat. 'Att my returne from Goa the Dutch commanders were earnest with mee to redeliver their writing given concerning their commission by the Generall of Batavia; which I would not doe, because it should somewhat confirme the insolencies which dayly they practise against us in those parts.' *October* 31. Sailed. *November* 6. Anchored before Calicut, and landed Vīrjī Vōra's servants. *November* 7. They returned with news that most of the pepper was at 'Punneanna' [Ponnāni], whence Knipe agreed to fetch it. *November* 8. Anchored in Cochin Road, and found there the *Hester*, which had arrived three days before. Her master had contracted for a quantity of cinnamon at 40 xerafins a quintal, a third of the amount to be paid in red cloth at 5 xerafins a yard. *November* 9 *and* 10. Received the cinnamon contracted for at Goa. During his stay Knipe also bought a quantity from other merchants, which was of excellent quality and nearly fifty per cent. cheaper than that purchased at Goa. He sold most of his coral and bartered part of his cloth; the net gain was 1,547*l*. 8*s*. 3*d*. Had he had more goods and longer time, he could have sold large quantities at a good profit. The 'recaduta' coral proved reasonably good, but the 'teraglia' was 'extraordinary bad'. *November* 24. They set sail. *November* 29. Cast anchor at Calicut. *November* 30. By night they had received 550 bags of pepper. Knipe was 'sent for to the King; where I found very courteous enterteynment, with many proffers concerning trade.' 'I understood that Virge Vora yearly sends downe his people hither to Callicutt with cotten and opium, by which hee doth not [gain?] less then double his mony to those people hee buyeth his pepper off, [and] afterwards disposeth of his pepper to us for double what it cost him; for I finde pepper to bee worth here but 15½ and 16 fannams the maund, which is not halfe the rate hee usually valleweth it to our people in Suratt.' It would obviously be cheaper to deal direct; 'but indeed Virge Vora, by reason of our continuall mighty ingagements, must not bee displeased in any case. I confess him to bee a man that hath often supplyed our wants in Suratt with moneys, for his owne ends. Notwithstanding, I hould him to have bynn the most injurious man to your trade in all the Mogulls dominions; for what ordinary Banian merchant dare come to the English howse to look uppon corrall or any other comodity, hee by his potencye and intimacy with the Governour forgeth somewhat or other against the poor man, utterly to ruine him; so that no merchant in the towne dare displease him by comeing to our howse to look uppon any comodity, except some or other sometymes whome hee sends purposely to bid for a comodity (that hee is about) little or nothing, onely to make us weary of our comodities. Hee knoweth that wee (in regard of our extreame ingagement) must sell, and so beats us downe till wee come to his owne rates; and thus hath bynn his proceedings this many yeares. And I conclude that, so long as Virge Vora is so much our creditor, little or no proffitt [is] to bee made uppon any goods wee can bring to Surratt.' Knipe bought also at Calicut a quantity of cardamoms. *December* 1. Sailed. *December* 2. Passed by Cannanore, the wind not suffering them to put in; otherwise Knipe had hoped to sell coral and buy cardamoms there.

December 5. Anchored in 'Bassalour[1] Road', where they sold two chests of coral. *December* 7. The buyers fetched away the chests. 'Wee were now the first English that ever came to this port. I have formerly endeavoured it in the Squires [i.e. Courteen's] ymployment (but our seamen could not finde the place), because I heard often (as I beleive) it is the best place for sale of corrall on all the coast of India. Had you bynn pleased to grant (uppon a motion I made per Mr. William Methwold at our comeing out) one shipp to come first for Cocheine, then might wee very easily [have] made sale of all your corrall (att better rates then now I did), fully laden the shipp with synamon and pepper, and (with Gods blessing) bynn att Suratt by the middle of November att farthest. The Squires people are againe settled at Battaccalla[2], where they part with their cloth and lead for neare about as much as the cost, and buy pepper very deare, giveing 33 dury[3] pagothaes per candee. One pago[tha] is 16½ fannams. Battacalla is not above 10 or 11 leagues to the northward of this place, under the same Naiques government; from whome came a messenger, tendring us the place to settle in, and many other courtesies concerning trade.' *December* 8. Set sail. *December* 22. Anchored in Swally Hole. Regrets that the President and Council would not agree to buy the whole of the 900 bales of indigo formerly belonging to Āsaf Khān; there are 'some other passages I conceived injurious to the wellfare of this Voyage', of which he will inform the Company, if desired. [1643, *January*] 19. The *Crispiana* and *Aleppo Merchant* sailed from Swally. *February* 17. Nearly ran on to a shoal called 'Mallha' or 'Mallhu'.[4] *March* 31. Anchored in 'Souldania' [Table] Bay, meeting the *Hester* standing out. *April* 6. Departed. *April* 26. Reached St. Helena, and found there the *Reformation*, which had been ordered by the President and Council of Bantam to wait for the *Ulysses* until May 10; but it was decided by consultation that she had better sail with them. *May* 1. All three set sail. *May* 19. Crossed the Line. *June* 31 [*sic*]. Passed the Azores. *July* 17. Sighted the South Devon Coast. Knipe gives an account of

---

[1] Basrūr, in lat. 13° 38′ N., and four miles east of Coondapoor.
[2] Bhatkal: see the 1637-41 volume, pp. 4, 206.
[3] Perhaps Dhārwārī pagodas. Lockyer notes that 'all considerable bargains with the country merchants [at Kārwār] are made for pagodas Darwar.'
[4] Now termed the Saya de Malha Bank. It lies to the SE. of the Seychelles.

private trade brought home in the *Crispiana*, including his own. (*Copy.* 8¼ *pp.*)

CONSULTATION HELD AT FORT ST. GEORGE BY [THE AGENT AND COUNCIL], AUGUST 13, 1643 (*O.C.* 1829).

In a former consultation, held May 29, they suspended Andrew Trumball from the command of the *Hopewell* while the ship was on this coast. Now, as no advice has arrived from Surat, and fearing lest they should be blamed at home or at Bantam should any mischance happen to the vessel, they decide to reinstate him until his arrival at Bantam, though they consider him unworthy of this trust. His actions are referred to the censure of the President and Council at Bantam. (*Copy.* ½ *p.*)

FRANCIS DAY'S ANSWER TO TRUMBALL'S CHARGES, FORT ST. GEORGE, AUGUST 13, 1643 (*O.C.* 1828[1]).

Has received, on his arrival from Tranquebar, Trumball's reply to the articles presented against him in May last. The latter, he conceives, are all sufficiently attested; and when Greenhill was sent on board for the purpose, the subscribers all acknowledged that they had signed them. Will neither admit nor deny the charges Trumball has now made; but desires that they be read on board the ship and that any one who will support them should be invited to sign accordingly. 'Such slaunders is familliar with him', and that he will not hesitate to back a lie with an oath is known to the Agent and Council from four instances cited. His accusations against Day of drunkenness are false, but Trumball himself is guilty in that respect, and several times the ship has been exposed to imminent danger owing to his being intoxicated. Could further enlarge on his offences, 'but charitie and Christiainitie binds mee to requite evill with good'; and therefore will only mention Trumball's presumption in breaking open the purser's cabin and ordering his servant to 'make entry of parcells in his booke'. (*Copy.* 1¾ *pp.*)

[1] For another copy see *O.C.* 1824.

PETITION FROM FRANCIS DAY TO AGENT COGAN AND HIS COUNCIL [AT FORT ST. GEORGE, AUGUST 14 (?) 1643] (*O.C.* 1824).

Desires leave to proceed to Europe by way of Surat, if Trumball is to be restored to his place in the *Hopewell*, as he cannot go with him to Bantam or any other port 'without perrill of my life'. Trusts that Trumball will not even be admitted to the ship as a passenger, for he no doubt intends to take revenge upon Day; and his 'inhumanitie and tyrany' are evidenced by his cruel treatment of John Reynolds. (*Copy.* 1 *p.*)

A SIMILAR PETITION FROM CERTAIN OFFICERS[1] OF THE *HOPEWELL* (*O.C.* 1824).

Have already represented Trumball's tyranny, and now implore that he be not permitted to resume his former authority, or that in such event they may be allowed to repair on shore, even if this entails the loss of their wages. (*Copy.* 1 *p.*)

ATTESTATION BY ROBERT WYCHERLEY[2], ABOARD THE *HOPEWELL*, AUGUST 14, 1643 (*O.C.* 1830).

That at Trumball's command he brought him 'the Kings comission to him', which was then whole; but on Trumball's going over the ship's side, 'I, seeinge in what case hee was, tooke the comission out of his hand, and carried into my cabyn, where the ratts eate it'. 'Likewise the said Mr. Trumball wished mee that, if any bodie asked mee how the comission came torne, that I should tell them it was torne in the combustion.' (*Copy.* ½ *p.*)

PETITION FROM EDWARD HEMINGWAY, PURSER OF THE *HOPEWELL*, TO AGENT COGAN AND HIS COUNCIL, AUGUST 16, 1643 (*O.C.* 1824).

Expresses his fear that Trumball, having been restored to his place, will find means to revenge himself on those who have

---

[1] Thomas Clark (master's mate), Alexander Reynolds, Richard Harsfield (boatswain), Roger Barker (carpenter), Henry Bassano (steward), and John Richards (midshipman).
[2] Trumball's servant. There is another copy of this document in *O.C.* 1824.

opposed him. Begs therefore to be released from proceeding to Bantam in the ship; 'if not, I feare twilbee the loss of my life.' (*Copy.* ½ *p.*)

CONSULTATION HELD IN FORT ST. GEORGE BY [THE AGENT AND COUNCIL], AUGUST 20, 1643 (*O.C.* 1831).[1]

It is debated how best to satisfy their creditors, who are very clamorous for payment, because of the Agent's approaching departure. No funds are likely to be available until next year; and they therefore decide to borrow, if possible, enough money for this purpose from Portuguese or others at San Thomé, to be paid in England, at about 10*s.* or 11*s.* the pagoda. This rate will not be excessive, for the interest of the debt, 'added to the principall, at each yeares end rayses every pag[oda] to very neare ten shillinges.' A similar attempt will be made at Masulipatam, 'that this devouringe interest may bee extinguished and the trade of this coast once more staund upon itts owne bottome.' (*Copy.* ½ *p.*)

CONSULTATION HELD AT FORT ST. GEORGE BY THE AGENT AND COUNCIL[2], AUGUST 23, 1643 (*O.C.* 1832).

The recent decision to reinstate Trumball has produced a series of protests from Day and the officers of the ship, and it is now debated what course to pursue. To a suggestion that Day should be placed in charge of the *Hopewell*, and Trumball proceed in her, either as master or as a passenger, it is answered that the latter would probably endeavour to regain his former place with the aid of the crew as soon as the vessel got away to sea. It is then proposed to replace all the protesting officers by others, and leave Day to carry out his threat of proceeding overland to Surat. Hereupon the Agent declares that, if Day will take his place on shore, he himself will proceed to Bantam in the ship as commander. It is further considered that (1) a new Agent is likely to arrive by July or August, as Cogan last year intimated to the Company his intention of repairing to Bantam : (2) there will be no business of

[1] For a second copy see the *O.C. Duplicates.*
[2] Cogan, Day, Yard, and Greenhill sign. There is a second copy among the *O.C. Duplicates.*

importance to transact here, owing to lack of funds, and Cogan will be better able to inform the President and Council at Bantam and the Company 'of the Coast affayres' personally than 'by penn': (3) such representations of their situation are urgently needed to save the trade here from ruin: (4) Cogan will be able to clear himself and the agency 'of those aspertions and imputations laid thereon, and touchinge the Forts erection and transferringe our masters estates thereon, contrary (as is said) to order.' For these reasons Cogan's proposal is approved. (*Copy.* 1¾ *pp.*)

ANDREW COGAN, FRANCIS DAY, HENRY GREENHILL, AND GEORGE TRAVELL AT FORT ST. GEORGE TO THE PRESIDENT AND COUNCIL AT BANTAM, AUGUST 25, 1643 (*O.C.* 1833).[1]

Received their letters of March 24 and May 31 by a Dutch ship on July 21. To the charge that they have, contrary to order, used the money of the First General Voyage, sent in the *Hopewell*, to pay off the old debts, they answer that, if this had not been done, 'our case had byn no better, but rather worse, then the Danes; for our people must eyther have fledd or submitted themselves to prison. If eyther, then had we suffered not onely in our reputation (which yet is sound) but in estate; for of necessitie the stocke that came on the *Hopewell* must (or the most part) have layen uninvested.' It is all one to them whether their accounts are cleared 'on Bantam, on Surratt, or England'; while, as for referring their proceedings to the Company, this 'doth not in the least displease us', for they hope to make their actions appear fair and just. Deny that they have made use of the Company's servants or means for their own purposes; and as for sending the Company's shipping to Persia, they had orders so to do. 'We have not in any kinde gonn about to adultriate your actions, nor in the least writt a misbeseemeing word of you or your actions to Surratt, much less to England; sure we are we have writt no untruth.' Reiterate their former account [*see* p. 77] of their dealings with Yard and his ship *Endeavour*, and deny absolutely that they ever gave him authority to build any such vessel. As desired, he shall be sent to Bantam at the first opportunity. On Yard offering to give a fair price for the

---

[1] For another copy see the *O.C. Duplicates*.

Endeavour for breaking up, she was hauled ashore and the upper works dismantled under his direction. The hull now lies 'in the wash of the shore, ready to be broke all to pieces with the first fowle weather', and is worth no more than so much firewood. Day's employment to Persia in the *Hopewell* was quite in accordance with the Company's instructions. The dispatch of that vessel straight to England was only contemplated in the event of her returning to the Coast too late to be sent to Bantam; and as she has now got back in good time, she will be duly dispatched to the latter place instead. The 'red earth' might well have been written off at Bantam, but, as it has been re-charged to the Coast, 'wee'l cleere it on our bookes, where no proffitt appeares in any accompt.' The horse will be sent in the *Hopewell*; also the butter, coffee, goats, and buckets desired. Rejoice that Winter and Collet arrived at Bantam in good health. Note that they have been detained there, 'for want of able men', until next shipping, when the former is to be allowed to proceed to England, while the latter, 'haveing incouragement, is content to stay.' 'It seems Bantam ayre hath purg'd them that now they can see wherein they have abused the Company. We hope the English ayre, or the ayre between England and Bantam, being more sereene, will soe purge their consciences that theile bee able to speake all the truth when they come home, for (or we miss our marke) they will be called to accompt and be forced eyther to deny or justyfie what they have, like course friends, put theire hands unto.' The letter of May 31 requires no lengthy answer; but they deny emphatically the charge of insubordination. 'One of the two books touching the peace and articles of agreement 'twixt the English and the Portugalls we have according to your order dispeeded to Surratt. But forasmuch as concernes the Dutch and the Portugalls, 'tis here in these partes warrs as formerly. For in Caelon the Dutch and Portugalls have fought and (as reporte goes) the Dutch lost in that land fight 400 men, besides many taken prisoners.[1] At Goa the Portugalls tooke lately a greate shipp belonging to the Dutch, ritchly laden from Pertia, wherein was Comandore Willbram [2].

---

[1] This refers to the defeat of the Dutch near Galle in May, 1643; but their loss is exaggerated (*Hague Transcripts*, series i. vol. xiii. no. 410; *Dagh-Register*, 1643-44, p. 221).

[2] Wollebrant Geleijnszoon: see above, p. 83, and a note on p. 240 of the previous volume. The capture of his ship is related in detail later (p. 150).

And here in sight of us last moneth the Portugalls tooke a small vessell, belonging to the Dommini[1] of Pullecatt, that came from Caeloan; but being he is mutch in favour with the Jesuitts, after a 10 or 15 dayes she was retourned him againe. Since when the road of St. Thomay hath seldome been free of a Dutch shipp, to keep iñ those that would to sea or to surprize such as are bound in thither. ... Speakeing of our priviledges in this place, you say you doubt they will not be many or greate. To free that doubt, we say they are many and greate; for did the Company but drive any indifferent trade, the customes onely would more then defray all the charges of the garrison; and this we shall be able to make appeare in convenient time. But it seems the particulers of the piscash sente our Naigue, or rather the King, thereby to have our priviledges confirmd, was not incerted; which we wonder at, for the transcript of ours to you tells us it was 7 yards scarlett, 16 yards greene, 16 yards redd cloth; 10 maund sandall; 3 lookeing glasses; and one chest rosewater. Tis a miserie unsufferable to be deplored by those that can, ought, and will not helpe. You have of a long time knowne how 'tis with us. 'Tis like to be rather worse then better, unless you or our masters helpe us; for we doe dayly increase our ingagements.' Should sufficient means arrive to pay their debts and make an investment, the resulting goods shall be sent to Bantam without delay; 'but our debts in the first place must be payd, and with the first meanes that comes on this coast: elce our masters or you were better to withdrawe us all from hence.' The master of the *Advice* shall be told of the damage done to certain bales, and warned to be more careful in future. Note what is said concerning the Macassar trade. Finally, 'Andrew Cogan saith that, with as mutch patience as a dejected man may, he awayts the Companies pleasure for his removeall from this uncomfortable imployment, being you say you cannot condiscend unto it.'[2] Now relate what has happened since the departure of the *Advice*. 'This countrey hath byn, and still is at present, all in broyles, one Nague against another, and most against the King; which makes all trade at a stand. But the King, by meanes of the King of Vizapore, whoe for 15 lacke of

---

[1] *Domine* or *Dominus*, a chaplain or preacher. His name appears to have been Carolus de Ladossa (*Dagh-Register*, 1643-44, pp. 251, 260, &c.).
[2] Evidently this was written before Cogan decided to proceed to Bantam in the *Hopewell*.

pagothaes and 24 eliphants hath sente some thousands of horse for his assistance, is like to have the better.' On May 6 Jacob Fuddle arrived; 'by whome we understood of your healths, &c.' On the 20th came in the *Hopewell* from Persia. She had there procured 'a fraight for Dabull, the King of Gulquondahs ambassador, which paid fraight 31,557 sha[hees]: all which, with the proceed of such goods as were sold in Gombroone, Mr. Day brought with him, all amo[unting] to 9,398 pago[das], 5 fa[nams]'. Certain goods were returned as unvendible; others were left at Gombroon for sale, and the proceeds were subsequently sent in the Dutch ship which (as already related) was captured at Goa. The *Hopewell* was then dispatched on June 1 to Tranquebar and other places in quest of longcloth, Trumball having been first removed from her owing to the refusal of his crew to sail with him. Day was put in charge, with orders to start back not later than July 25; 'but the President of the Danes abusing his trust, caused him to stay till the 9th current, when then he was forced to bring away all such goods as he had bought unsorted and unimballd.' She anchored in this road on the 11th at night; and the packing of her cargo has taken until the 24th. Trumball was restored to his post; but this 'caus'd all or the most parte of the shipps company to leave the shipp, vowing rather to leape into the sea'. Cogan therefore offered to proceed in the ship to Bantam, leaving Day in his place, and this was approved in consultation. No other solution was possible, for they could not obtain sufficient men from the shore to replace the mutineers, and no help was to be expected from the master of the *Advice* (which arrived on the 15th current), 'because not consign'd to us.' Refer to Cogan for further details. (*Copy.* 6½ *pp.*)

FRANCIS DAY AT FORT ST. GEORGE TO THE COMPANY, AUGUST 30, 1643 (*O.C.* 1834).

Wrote last from 'Ballisarra' (by way of Surat), advising that most of their cash had been perforce employed in clearing off old debts. It was then expected that fresh loans would in consequence be forthcoming when money was needed; but time 'hath discovered the contrary.' This will probably cause 'an unmerritted censure of the Coast'—an outcome which he feared at the time of his engagement, and he now regrets that he did not make matters clear before he accepted the employment. Trusts that the little now sent will give sufficient profit to encourage the Company to prosecute the trade and send funds to clear their debts and save them from 'that devouringe canker of intrest which hath impoysoned all the best indeavours of those that have had the manninge of your estates. Untill such time, I say, and your resolution for duble stockinge the Coast, tis impossible to comply with your desires or give content to your Presidents.' Cannot tell why the trade on the Coast has been so unsuccessful; 'but sure, yf you please but to cause an exact calculation of Dutch affaires, you will then finde that this Coast is the nerves and life of all their great undertakings, and yf they lade a shipp, two, three, or more, at Surratt annually, they doe more then trible it on this Coast.' Feels it his duty as a loyal servant to offer advice as to the measures necessary to be taken to improve matters. First, the Coast must be double stocked, as already recommended. Secondly, two or three ketches of from 30 to 50 tons should be sent for use here. These would assist in 'the congregatinge of all goods to this port, wheare they may be in securitie till shipps arrivall', thus facilitating the dispatch of the latter to Bantam. They might also be employed in carrying goods to other ports for sale; and their charge would be very little, 'beinge manned out of your foart'. Thirdly, more should be left to the Agent's discretion, and the Company should not 'looke more on the success then on the intent'. These measures, if adopted, would produce results which would 'vindicate the lost repute of this Coast'. Refers for further details to Cogan, 'whose abbillities and knowledge of this Coast may not be questioned'. The accompanying accounts will show what Day has done at Balasore and at Gombroon. Cannot now say how far the Third Joint Stock will be indebted to the First General Voyage, but fears that the remains will be too large 'for your proffitt'. Will write on this subject to the President at Bantam. Owing to his recent voyages and the short notice at which he has accepted 'this unthankfull imployment', he cannot give a full account of the present state of affairs here; but he hopes to do so shortly, by way of Surat. The company has repeatedly censured this Agency for building the Fort, at great charge and without authority. On the latter point he will say nothing; but, as regards the former, he is prepared not only to excuse but to commend the action. 'For, compareinge the price of Armagon and this place, there is such an unequallitie, which, yf you please throughly and truly to have calculated, you will then finde that what hath been done was noe more then necessary, and very proffittable for you. For such goods that is now heare bought for 8½ and 9 pag[odas] I have paid there 11½ and 12; besides hazard [to?] your estates in intrustinge it to uncertayne merchants, six, seven, eight, and sumtymes more monthes.' Refers to the enclosed papers for an account of Trumball's abuses and threats, which forced Day to decide to proceed overland to Surat rather than run the hazard of a further voyage with him. Had Day considered merely his own interests, he would have persisted in this intention instead of accepting his present post. As it is, he hopes the Company will relieve him of his charge at the earliest opportunity. In the meantime, he assures them of his best endeavours in their service. (3¼ *pp*. *Received by the* Mary, *June* 15, 1644.)

FRANCIS DAY AT FORT ST. GEORGE TO THE PRESIDENT AND COUNCIL AT BANTAM, AUGUST 30, 1643 (*O.C.* 1835).[1]

For an account of matters here, he refers to the general letter and his own letter to the Company. Desires them to consider what is to be done about the indebtedness of the Joint Stock to the Voyage. Suggests that the officers and crew of the *Hopewell* should be interrogated as to the truth of the charges made against Trumball. Begs that they will speedily relieve him of this 'inforced imployment' by appointing a successor. (*Copy*. ¾ *p*.)

THOMAS DOWLE, MASTER OF THE *ADVICE*, AT MASULIPATAM TO [THE PRESIDENT AT BANTAM], SEPTEMBER 19, 1643 (*O.C.* 1837).

Narrates the events of their voyage since their departure from Bantam. On April 7 they reached the supposed latitude of Keeling's Islands [*see* p. 97] and then ran west along that parallel until there was no longer any hope of seeing them. Proceeded therefore to Rodriguez, which was reached on April 23. Sent a boat on shore 'to discover any signe of our shipps being there;

[1] There is another copy among the *O.C. Duplicates*.

THE ENGLISH FACTORIES 119

but could find none but a crose and a plase where fier hadd binn made by a French and Dutch shipp that hadd binn there four monthes before us', as they afterwards learnt at Mauritius. Departed next day, and went in search of the island called 'the English Forest' [Réunion], but without result. On April 28 they anchored at Mauritius, where the Dutch came on board, and also three men that had been in one of Courteen's ships, called the *Harry Bonaventure*, which was cast away in a hurricane while homewards bound with a cargo of pepper. Could hear nothing of 'our lost shipps' [i.e. the *Jewel* and the *Jonas*]. Having obtained wood and water, they sailed on May 7 and next day reached the island of [ ][1]. Went ashore there on the 9th and found many turtles and hogs[2]. On May 17 they sighted Madagascar; but, owing to contrary winds and currents, they did not attain St. Augustine's Bay until the 23rd. Could only get a small quantity of beef to salt; and then the attitude of the natives became so hostile that they were obliged to embark their goods and men, all further trade being conducted on board. Sailed on June 10 and, after attempting in vain to make the NW. coast of Madagascar, anchored at Mayotta [in the Comoros] on the 24th. Had hoped 'to have gotten lustie blacks there; but they had kild theire king 22 dayes before that we came there and they hadd made another king, but he could not come to the crowne before the next moone; soe that we could gett but three blacks there.' On July 3 they departed for Johanna and reached it two days later. Found that they could not get there any 'blacks' (except one woman) under 20 rials of eight apiece; this would soon have exhausted their scanty stock of money, and they had nothing else available, 'for all our barambaram[3] we have left behind us.' Sailed on the 7th. Reached Tranquebar on August 12, and the next day John Jeffries died. Arrived at Madraspatam on August 15. Has now been ordered to proceed to the Bay, though the time of year is far spent. Will not fail to start on return voyage to Bantam by December 31 at the latest. The lead cannot be sold here and, if they fail to reach the Bay to dispose of it there, he cannot tell how

[1] Blank in the MS.; but it seems to have been Réunion, the very island they had been looking for in vain (see the 1624-29 volume, p. 263).
[2] Herbert, who was there in 1629, says that his ship left some goats and hogs on the island (*Travels*, 1638, p. 351; also the 1624-29 volume, p. 332).
[3] Malay *barang-barang*, 'goods'.

to get money to buy the provisions wanted for Bantam, as the factors on this Coast will not provide him with funds. Jeffries' goods and clothes have been sold, and the proceeds entered in the purser's book for payment in England. Some ambergris belonging to him is sent herewith; also his books and papers. Has forwarded by the *Hopewell* to Bantam some beef salted at Madagascar, and four 'cofries' [*see* p. 81], viz. two men (cost 10 rials each), one boy (6 rials), and one woman (9 rials). Refers to his journal (sent herewith) for particulars of his voyage. (*Copy.* 3½ *pp.*)

FRANCIS DAY, HENRY GREENHILL, AND GEORGE TRAVELL AT FORT ST. GEORGE TO THOMAS PENISTON AND OTHERS AT MASULIPATAM, SEPTEMBER 22, 1643 (*O.C.* 1838).

Enclose a letter received from Bantam on the 19th. The orders contained therein about the return of the *Advice* to that port must be carefully obeyed. (*Copy.* ¼ *p.*)

THE SAME TO THE SAME, SEPTEMBER 23, 1643 (*O.C.* 1838).

A ship [the *Hart*] arrived from England this morning. Now send transcripts of her letters and invoice, and will advise further by that vessel, which will be dispatched to them in two days. *P.S.*—Cannot get the letters transcribed in time, as the Danes, who will deliver this, refuse to wait any longer. (*Copy.* ¾ *p.*)

CONSULTATION HELD AT FORT ST. GEORGE BY THE AGENT AND COUNCIL, SEPTEMBER 24, 1643 (*O.C.* 1839).

The *Hart* having arrived yesterday with ten chests of rials[1] and six of coral (besides ships' stores), the disposal of her and her cargo is considered. It is resolved to land here only the coral and two chests of treasure, and to send her with the rest to Masulipatam, where the money is to be used in satisfying the most pressing of their creditors and in making an investment for Bantam. Whether the *Hart* should then go to Bantam or to Persia must be left to the factors at Masulipatam. (1½ *pp.*)

[1] This would mean 40,000 rials of eight (10,000*l.*).

CONSULTATION HELD AT BANTAM BY PRESIDENT CARTWRIGHT AND COUNCIL, SEPTEMBER 25, 1643 (*O.C.* 1840).

. . . The Company having ordered the return of Cogan from the Coast at or before Ivy's arrival, and Day being likewise expected to leave those parts, some able and experienced men will be needed there. Have accordingly prevailed on Thomas Winter to stay another three years from the expiration of his contract (which was about June 12, 1642), at a salary of 80*l*. per annum. He is to be employed on the Coast, and to rank next to Cogan, Day, and Peniston. . . . (*Extract.* ¼ *p.*)

THE COMPANY TO THE PRESIDENT AND COUNCIL AT SURAT [NOVEMBER 27, 1643[1]] (*Factory Records, Miscellaneous*, vol. xii. p. 89).

Wrote on March 24 last [*not extant*] by the *Dolphin* and *Hind*, which left the Downs on April 10. Had in addition prepared the *Mary* for Bantam, the *Hart* (with a cargo of 11,493*l*. 4*s*. 5*d*.) for the Coast of Coromandel, and the *Seaflower*, 'intended to touch at St. Laurence and Mozambique and to make some triall of trade on the coast of Soffola and those parts, and then to prosecute her voyadge for your port of Swalley.' Sent by the last-named letters dated February 27, 1643 [*not extant*] and laded on her moneys and goods to the value of 10,636*l*. 17*s*. 6*d*., a small part of which was intended for Mozambique and the parts adjacent. Had intended that both the *Seaflower* and the *Hart* should have been dispeeded earlier; but 'troubles att home and delayes from abroad, with opposition of contrary wind' prevented them from quitting the Downs until March 8. Trust they have duly arrived. The *Crispiana* and *Aleppo Merchant* reached the Downs on July 19, having brought with them from St. Helena the *Reformation* from Bantam, with a cargo of pepper, cloves, sugar, &c. On July 28 news was received that the *Ulysses* from Bantam had arrived at

[1] The date is supplied by the letters sent in reply (*O.C.* 1901, 1905). This letter was sent by the *Endeavour*, which left the Thames towards the end of November, 1643, bound for the Coromandel Coast, whence the present letter was to be dispatched overland to Surat. This vessel must be distinguished from the one of the same name bought by Yard in the Bay of Bengal.

Plymouth, and in August she 'came safe into the river of Thames'. Lastly, on October 30, the *Blessing* came in unexpectedly from Bantam, bringing intelligence of the arrival there from Surat of the *Advice* with a well-sorted cargo of goods. Now intend to dispatch to Bantam by the beginning of March next the *William* (a new ship of 650 tons) and the *Blessing* (260 tons). On October 3 received a packet overland via Basrā and Aleppo, containing the Surat letter of March 20, 1643, one from Basrā of June 30 [*not extant*], a number of documents from Persia, &c. As they are preparing for Surat the *Crispiana* and the *John* (a new ship of 360 tons), it is not necessary to write now at great length, and they will therefore only deal with the goods brought home by the *Crispiana* and *Aleppo Merchant*. These all came 'well-conditioned', except certain bales of piece-goods which had been cut open before being shipped, part of the contents stolen, and the resulting vacancies filled with 'a whitish clay'. The silk invoiced as 'Cannaree' turned out to be 'Legee'; however, it is 'a good, cleane, round sorte'. Desire in future only clean and well-conditioned silk, either 'Legee' or 'Ardasse', but no 'Cannaree'.[1] As regards the indigo, neither kind was up to the standard of previous consignments; while three of the bales described as Biāna indigo were found to be nothing but black earth or clay. As each bale should weigh 4 maunds or 220 lb., the loss is 660 lb. at 6s. 8d. Bornford, on being questioned, denied all knowledge of the matter, suggesting that these bales may belong to the portion bought at Surat. This practice of pleading ignorance is too common; 'but wee must have another reckning, for it must be satisfaction that will give us content.' Intend to send back these three bales next spring. The Sarkhej indigo was moderately good; but its 'new face or fabrique' is disapproved, as likely to lead dishonest persons to sell it as Biāna indigo. A thousand bales in all of the two sorts will suffice for the future. Complaints of the quality of the indigo sold by the Dutch suggest that in their case some Sarkhej indigo has been made up in Lahore fashion and sold as such. 'Wee therefore desire that old customes may be kept and the commodity appear in its wonted forme.' Complain of the

---

[1] For 'Cannaree' silk see a note on p. 195 of the previous volume. 'Legee' silk came from Lahijan; while 'Ardasse' is supposed to have taken its name from Arras or Arrash, a town in Georgia, now known as Elizabetpol or Ganja.

large quantity of sand found among the indigo. Markets, both here and on the Continent, are so bad that it has been decided to divide the indigo, cinnamon, and piece-goods among the adventurers in the General Voyage. Indigo is especially debased in price, owing partly to the large quantity brought home as private trade in the *Crispiana* and the *Aleppo Merchant*, nearly 40,000 lb. having been discovered, besides what has escaped detection. Evidently there is a large amount of private trade, both outwards and homewards, and yet the Surat factors do nothing to stop it. 'Since there is such a generall combination amongst all sorts of people in our imployment, both on shore in the Indies and on shipboard, for the prosecuting of privat trade, wee shall be constrayned to take some more severe course against that unlawfull practice then willingly wee would, since no faire meanes or admonition will take place amongst them.' The calicoes last received have 'for lacke of markett' been distributed among the adventurers, rated 'at 2½ upon their prime coast'. Cannot commend the 'Nursapoore jooris' from Sind; they are thin cloths 'onlie made fayre to the eye by overmuch starching, slicking, and beating. . . . They are neither good cloth or full size.' Much prefer the 'Dorbella' [Darbēlo] sort, which comes also from Sind; of these four or five thousand pieces would sell. 'So would some of them also made in Sevensteere [Sehwān]; and the indico of that place also would find vent here, if well bought and carefully chosen.' The broad baftas of Baroda and Broach are 'more substantiall and serviceable' (besides being cheaper) than the 'Echbarrees', which are only a longer and rather broader sort of 'Mercules'. The last-named were at first held in good reputation, 'being then full 15 yards long and yard wide and also substantiall cloth'; but those which came in the *London* in 1642 were one-eighth of a yard narrower, and are consequently almost all still on hand. If any more be sent, they must be full size, both in length and breadth, and 'well whited'. The 'Deerebauds', bought at Agra, 'give content', but more care must be taken in the bleaching. 'The narraw baftaes of Suratt and the Nunceree [Nosārī] making are the most true and substantiall cloth of all India'; 'but of these or any other sorts we would not desire above 20,000 pieces of all kinds, untill the market be quicker and the commodity more in request; for now they are almost out of request with every man, and this hath proceeded from their dearnesse and ill making, and unlesse both these can be amended callicoes will be at a stand, except they may be afforded to undersell forraigne linnens.' The same quantity as before of 'nicaneers' and other Guinea stuffs may be sent. The 'pintadoe quilts' sold for 50s. each; but 'they serve more to content and pleasure our freinds then for any proffit [that] ariseth in sales'. Not more than a hundred should be forwarded yearly; and, both as regards those and the 'chintes', more should be made 'with white grounds, and the branches and flowers to be in collors, and not to be (as these last sent) all in generall of deep redd ground and other more sadder collers.' The cotton yarn, being good, sold at 2s. 9d. per lb.; coarse yarn is almost unsaleable. The best was that bought in Surat and neighbourhood; and 70 or 80 bales of equal quality will be welcome. If saltpetre be sent, it must be 'refined up to the assay of proofe', as otherwise it is not worth carriage; besides, it is liable to damage other goods. Cannot sell the Roman vitriol or 'mottueta' [*see* p. 86]; so no more should be supplied until it is asked for. The 'tincall' [borax] fetched 15*l*. per hundredweight. 'Of this commodity we know there is good quantities, if you please but to make us the sole proprietors thereof in our returnes, be it to the quantity of 15 or 20,000 lb. weight. Wee therefore doe hereby againe require you to forbidd all marriners and others to meddle or bring home any of the said commodity, for wee will either confiscate the same or make them pay such freight as that the commodity shall yeild them little advance; and so much we require you to declare unto them all, for in this returne they have brought neer 2,000 lb. waight.' Of gum-lac the same quantity as before may be sent; also some olibanum, myrrh, aloes Socotrina, and cardamoms. No more beads for bartering required at present. Cinnamon maintains its price at 3s. per lb., and 500 skins may be supplied yearly. The dry ginger was sold at a loss, and no more is desired. The Indian sugar is likewise in no demand, and any stock on hand should therefore be disposed of at Surat. The turmeric had better have been thrown overboard than brought home, being so 'drie and old and wormeaten' that no one will buy it. The Malabar pepper will not fetch more than 15*d*. per lb.; if it can be bought at wonted prices, some may be shot loose among the bale goods, but otherwise it is not worth bringing. In making up the return cargo, preference should be given to indigo, but its quality must be good. Of calicoes, cotton yarn, and drugs they have already spoken. The *Endeavour* has been specially built for service in India; she is of nearly 200 tons burden, strong, and of small draught. She is now intended for the Coromandel Coast, carrying money and coral to the amount of 11,094*l*. 8*s*. 4*d*. On arrival there, she is to go into the Bay of Bengal for three or four months, and then, on her return to the Coast, to proceed with a cargo of suitable goods to Gombroon. The proceeds of these goods she is to bring to Surat, the President and Council having previously repaid to the Coast factors their full value. The ship is then to remain at the disposal of the President and Council of Surat, at whose request she has been built. Next spring the *Crispiana* and a new ship of 400 [*sic*] tons, called the *John*, will be dispatched to Surat, though possibly one of them may be directed to call at Cannanore and other Malabar ports on her way. 'These are our hopes and desires; and wee wish we may not come short in any of them. Yet wee are fearfull how far wee shall be able to performe in this troublesome tymes, when all trade and commerce in this kingdome is almost fallen to the ground through our owne unhappie divisions at home, unto which the Lord in mercie put a good end; and as the badnesse of trade and scarsity of monyes are here, so is all Europe in little better condition, but in a turmoyle, either forraigne or domestique warr; by which meanes monies are not procurable as formerly.' The two ships will certainly be sent; but, as it may prove impossible to furnish them with a sufficient stock to provide cargoes for both, and as moreover, if a large quantity of goods be brought home, 'wee might lacke sales', it will not be advisable to prepare in India beforehand more than enough to lade the *Crispiana*. In that case the President and Council may find some other employment for the *John*, on condition that they have her ready to be sent home in November, 1645. 'The divisions is growne so high betweene the King and Parliament in those [parts of?] Darbyshiere and Yorksheere where the lead was shipt off, that there can come none from those parts. So that, if things doe not suddenly accord, wee have noe hope to send you any this next spring. If therfore you have any on your hands, you may seeke to advance the price of what you have; for from hence wee can promise none but att excessive rate.' Will not absolutely decide at present concerning the making of Sarkhej indigo in the form of that of Lahore; by next spring they will be able to see 'what acceptance in the interim it hath found'. The Biāna indigo has suffered much in reputation from the bad quality of the last supply, and unless there is an improvement it may be necessary to 'give over the indico trade'. The 'pintadoe quilts' are reckoned very dear. The Roman vitriol was not asked for; and, if it still remains unsold, it will be made over (on their return) to the factors who bought it; and the same will be done with the turmeric. Trouble caused by piece-goods being found to be deficient in length; in future, 'let their length be certaine, that wee may know what wee sell and the buyer what he is to receave.' (*Copy.* 20½ *pp.*)

List of Writings received at Bantam from the Coast by the *Hopewell*, November 30, 1643 (*O.C.* 1836).

Journals and ledgers for Masulipatam, Fort St. George, Balasore, and 'Harrapoore';[1] various letters and consultations; invoices of the *Hopewell* and *Hart*; a list of English soldiers at Fort St. George; a petition from Geoffrey Bradford; &c., &c. (1½ *pp.*)

President Cartwright and Council at Bantam to the Company, December 9, 1643 (*O.C.* 1847).

... Note that the Company are not satisfied as to the origin of the debts on the Coast. Cannot give any explanation; but there is no doubt that such debts exist and have been a great hindrance to business, both there and here. ... Ivy, who is both able and discreet, will be dispatched to the Coast in May or June next. The factors there are at present 'in obscuritie, being destitute of a light to direct them, notwithstanding they have Day there all the day long. And heere wee supposse it's not amiss to lett Your Worships understand that Mr. Francis Day was the first projecture and contriver of that forte or castle in Madrasspatan; which another with a greite deale of discontent, laboure, and paines hath now

---

[1] The Balasore journal goes down to June 30, 1643, while the Hariharpur accounts close on August 31, 1642. Possibly this was the date on which the latter factory was withdrawn. It is true that on p. 65 reference is made to certain piece-goods which, in November, 1642, were being provided at Hariharpur; but this may have been managed through a native broker.

brought to some good pass; be[ing] a place of securitie on that coast, as the onelie place of secured saiftie with that title of honoure (castle) that ever our nation enjoyed in East India; and therefore in our opinions to bee highlie esteemed. And for it's cost, it's certaine that, if Your Worships continew the Indian trade, in few yeares it will not quitt onelie it's owne charge, but allsoe produce benefitt and put monies into your purses, by bringeing a trade thether, raiseing a custome there, paying of duties by the inhabitants neere adjoyning, and being replenisht with merchants weavers; whereby you may have all things necessarie and convenient for you under your owne command. And happy and gladd will manie bee (wherein you will find the benefitt) to come and live under our nation and bee protected by them.' . . . Cogan arrived from the Coast in the *Hopewell* on November 30, bringing goods to the value of 22,644 rials 20d. He now takes his passage in this ship (the *Mary*) for England. Note the dispatch of the *Hart* to the Coast. She has arrived there, and Day has paid some of the debts with the money she brought. . . . Do not doubt that the Coast factors will cheerfully obey the Court's orders touching their subordinacy to Bantam. . . . The *Swan* arrived from Surat on April 16; and the *Expedition* was dispatched thither on August 22. . . . Have discoursed with Cogan concerning the fort at Madraspatam; 'which certainlie was at first projected by Mr. Francis Day, and doubtless Mr. Cogan would never have erected it without greate incoureagment thereto by some that might then best doe it. And notwithstanding the cost bestowed thereon (which, considering it's building and strength, will not appeare too much), three yeares time questionless (if Your Worships continue this Indian tradd) will facylelie regaine what hath beene expended thereon, as hath beene allreadie said. And for the future greite hopes of benefitt and incoureagement, theirto is an iland scituated in the river, under the command of the castle, whereon is likelie to bee made a greate quantitie of salt yearelie; which is one of the constantest commodities in all theise easterne parts, and much monies are gotten thereby everie where.' The debts on the Coast were made before Cogan's time; and these, with the high rate of interest thereon, have necessarily ' clouded his actions and good intendments.' Their speedy liquidation is urgently required, for both the factors' business and their repute suffer much on this account. As Yard has been censured by the President at Surat and called home by the Company, nothing will be done in the matter here, but he will be sent to England in the *Hopewell*. Re-engagement of three factors, including Winter. The accounts received from the Coast will be examined, entered, and sent by the *Hopewell*. Some other books and writings go in the *Mary*. . . . Regret that the *Hart* was not at once dispatched from the Coast hither, in order that she might be sent home. Have written to Surat for a ship for that purpose, and hope to lade her with pepper for England, in addition to one of their own which will be dispeeded next July. The *Advice* has not yet returned, but they have learned some particulars of her voyage by a letter from Masulipatam [*see* p. 118]. They expect her in February, if Day does not send her to Persia. . . . 'The Dutch are at open warrs againe with the Portugalls, who (poore people) are like to goe by the walls, for the Hollander[s] have a fleete of 22 shipps (they say) goan for Zeloane, but, as 'tis thought, intended for Goa. They have taken on of Squire Curteenes shipps within the Streights of Malacca (her name is the *Boone Esperanza*)[1], detayned halfe their men at Malacca, sent the other halfe to Jaccatra (from whence thei have made meanes unto us for their passage home [*see* O.C. 1844, 1850]), and sent the shipp with the rest of theirs, eyther against Zeloan or Goea.' . . . (*Extracts only.* 3 *pp.*)

WALTER CLARK, ABOARD THE *SUPPLY* [AT SWALLY?], TO [THE PRESIDENT AND COUNCIL AT SURAT], DECEMBER 17, 1643 (*O.C.* 1852).

On May 25, eighteen days after leaving Cochin, the ship anchored in Achin Road. Visits were paid to the Queen and the principal men; and then great delays were experienced, owing to opposition of the Gujarātī merchants, who bribed the officials to hinder the passing of the English goods through the custom-house. In the end Clark was forced to pay a lump sum of 550 taels to get his cargo passed. On landing they were entertained by Arthur

---

[1] See the account in the succeeding letter; also *Hague Transcripts*, series i. vol. xiii. no. 410, and series i. vol. iii. nos. E 7, M 7.

Keniston[1], principall for the affaires of the Esquire Courteen', and at his suggestion they constructed for themselves a godown in the capacious precincts of his factory. The Dutch were living close by, in the Company's former building. Their chief was 'Petter Williamson[2]', who died about a month after Clark's arrival. No Dutch ship had been there for eleven months, and the factors had scarcely any funds left. The method of trading at Achin described. Prices of tin and pepper. Competition of the Gujarātī merchants. On July 28 the Dutch *Luipaard* anchored in the road, having come from Batavia by way of Malacca. On board of her was 'Peter Surry[3], commissire for the Dutch', who brought news of the capture of the *Bona Speranza*, 'beinge in the Esquire Courteens imployment and fraughted by the Portugalls from Goa to China.'[4] 'She anchored nere some of these ilands what time we anchored in the roade; yet had we not sight each of other in our navigateinge thither. William Gourly[5] was principall for the negotiateinge the intended designe; who by his letter intimateth that at the entry of Mallaca Streights thay encountred a Dutch yough [i. e. yacht] with 18 gunes, who would command them to goe into Mallaca roade; which thay refuseinge, she, beinge farr nimbler of saile, left them. And some few daies after, the *Bona Esperanca*, beinge nere clere of those streights, [she], acompanied with another ship, reencountred them and willed them as before to returne for Mallaca, to the intent thay might have there Generalls consent for there fre passage, which thay neede not doubt but would be granted, thay payinge custome for there goods. Gourlly, who speakes the Dutch language singular, returned them rough language, bidinge them looke up to there flagg: if thay had ought to opose against those coulours, he with his shipps company was there to defend them. After which the Dutch sent there boats abord with a protest that if thay would not returne for Mallaca or deliver up the Portugalls which thay had abord fairely, that then thay would force them soe to doe. All which he refusinge, the Dutch lett fly

---

[1] Or Kynaston. He had been purser of the *Roebuck* (see the 1634-36 volume, p. 266).
[2] Pieter Willemszoon (see *Dagh-Register*, 1641-42, p. 175).
[3] Pieter Souri (see *Dagh-Register*, 1641-42, pp. 153, 166, &c.).
[4] See the *Lisbon Transcripts: Doc. Remett.*, book 48, ff. 151, 294. She had on board Luiz de Carvalho de Souza, who was proceeding to Macao as Captain-General.
[5] Probably the 'William Gorle' of the last volume (p. 81).

(as thay say) a peece unshotted; the English affirme the contrary, sayinge the first shott thay made tooke place in her bowe and rackinge aftward killed a man. The *Bona Esperanca* in requitall fired a peece in her quarter, killed the comandour of the Dutch and two youths. Soe thay continued in fight untill the Dutch (as themselves report) loosinge out of both vessells 80 men, and (as Gourly writeth) 17 English (whereof one was the master) killed and soe much maimed that, if thay survive, any of them, it wilbe with the loss of some member; when the Portugalls, who will never relinquish there dasterly condition, sent one aloft with a white flagg, themselfe[s] beinge in hould secure from danger. The Dutch presently borded them; carried them for Mallaca; imprisoned all the Portingalls; the maimed men appointed to the hospitall; the sound saylors distributed into severall vessells; Gourly and Carter (who, beinge master, was displaced by him after there leaveinge the coast of India) only billeted one shore; particular invoices taken of all goods in hould; [those] without seased on and shared by the souldiers as pillage. All beinge refastned and she surely mored in Mallaca, a vessell [was] dispeeded to the Generall of Battavia.' Souri has obtained from the Queen of Achin the privilege of sole trade at Tiku and Priaman. Clark ' sumbaied[1], desiringe she would please to invest our nation with some favour'; whereupon she remitted the customs outward 'for this first voyage'. Narrates the further proceedings of Souri, who departed on August 20. Clark then endeavoured to obtain similar privileges to those enjoyed by the Dutch, but without result. If, however, the English can procure the release of an ' Achener ', who was captured by the Portuguese at Malacca and is believed to have been since purchased by Francisco de Souza de Castro in Goa, it is certain that the Queen will make in return whatever concessions they may desire. Most of the *Supply's* goods have been sold; but the competition of the Bengal, Masulipatam, and Pegu merchants much hindered the purchase of a return cargo. A piece of ground was obtained on the riverside, between the Dutch and the ' Courtenians ', and the erection of a factory building was commenced. No sooner had the Bengal and Masulipatam junks left the road

---

[1] An adaptation of the Malay *sambah*, a petition or representation.

than 'in creps those Keeling[1] junckes (soe comonly called by the natives here, and are not other than Mallavares)'; but unfortunately there was no opportunity of taking revenge upon them for the capture of the *Comfort*, as the English could not conclude their business on shore in time. Trade was restricted by the action of the Dutch, 'which continually lurke in Malaca Streights and permitt not any to pass, under pretence of payinge custome there, and soe enforce them for Mallaca; as this yeare thay have done two junckes from Rackane [Arakan] and as many from Macassar bound for Achene with some quantities of cloves. There thay enforce them to make saile of there goods; and sticke not themselves to report that thay doubt not but to make it the mart of all those parts and enforce all trade thither.' Proceedings of Courteen's agent, Keniston, who succeeded Glascock here in August, 1642. Tin bought from the Queen of Achin. Maximilian Bowman was left in charge of the factory, and with him Thomas Fitch, Francis Scattergood, and one of the ship's company; also William Dawes, a young man who formerly came from Bengal on a junk. He had been servant in turn to Thomas Faulkner and Thomas Clark, and (according to his own account) had been freed from the Company's employment by Cogan. The two brokers sent from Surat have both returned; but the brother of one of them has been left to assist Bowman. The *Supply* sailed from Achin on October 20. The weather proved so bad that they did not sight Ceylon until November 8, and ten days later they anchored at Cochin. There Clark received and opened a letter left by Thurston at his departure, and also one addressed to the latter from Surat. Bought a quantity of cinnamon, and sailed again on the 26th. On December 3 they passed a fleet of Malabars near Goa, and saw four Dutch ships and a yacht riding in the road. Four days later the *Supply* was off Bombay, and ever since she has been struggling against adverse winds. The ship, from the time of her leaving 'this road', has 'continued thite [tight] and proved stiffe of saile'. All her stone ballast was used at Achin in building the new factory. A small quantity of freight brought back, at a charge of 16 per cent. During their stay at Achin they buried five men, John Woodward amongst them; while

[1] In Malay countries Indian traders or immigrants are termed Klings (see *Hobson-Jobson*, *s.v.*).

almost every one on board, including Clark himself, suffered from sickness. (*Copy.* 10¾ *pp.*)

LIST OF MERCHANTS EMPLOYED AT BANTAM AND ITS SUBORDINATES [JANUARY, 1644[1]] (*O.C.* 1841).

... *At Fort St. George:* Francis Day (200*l.*), Henry Greenhill (50*l.*), John Brown (24*l.*), and William Minn (12*l.*). *At Masulipatam:* Thomas Peniston (100*l.*), Henry Olton (150*l.*), William Methwold (30*l.*), William Netlam (18*l.*), William Gurney (20*l.*), and William Isaacson (20*l.*). *In Bengal:* Robert Hatch (80*l.*) and George Travell (30*l.*). ... (2½ *pp.*)

LIST OF MERCHANTS EMPLOYED IN THE SURAT PRESIDENCY [JANUARY, 1644?[2]] (*O.C.* 1842).

At Surat: William Fremlen (500*l.*), Francis Breton (100*l.*), Thomas Merry (300*l.*), Richard Fitch (50*l.*), Andrew Baines, minister (50*l.*), William Thurston (50*l.*), Edward Pearce (60*l.*), John Stanford (35*l.*), George Oxenden (35*l.*), Thomas Hill (35*l.*), Philip Wylde (40*l.*), Maximilian Bowman (24*l.*), John Rymell (12*l.*), Nathaniel Tems (12*l.*), John Goodyear (12*l.*), William Wyche (12*l.*), Luke Pynn (18*l.*), John Mantell [ ], and Richard Clark (8*l.* 8*s.*). *At Ahmadābād:* George Tash (40*l.*), Thomas Cogan (20*l.*), Anthony Smith (20*l.*), and Robert Heynes (18*l.*). *At Agra:* John Turner (80*l.*), Francis Hammersly (50*l.*), William Jesson (40*l.*), and Matthew Downs (18*l.*). *In the Red Sea:* John Wylde (100*l.*), Robert Cranmer (30*l.*), and Peter Herbert (20*l.*). *In Sind:* John Spiller (133*l.* 6*s.* 8*d.*[3]), Daniel Elder (70*l.*), and Revett Walwyn (18*l.*). *In Persia:* William Hall (80*l.*), Thomas Wheeler (50*l.*), Thomas Adler (70*l.*), Thomas Codrington

---

[1] From the endorsement it appears that this list was presented to the Court on January 10, 1644. Being compiled at home, it is of course only relatively accurate. The list contains 45 names, and the total cost of salaries is given as 2,308*l.* per annum. Only the Coast factors are noted above. Of these, Netlam and Gurney had come out the previous year in the *Hart*; while Olton, Methwold (who seems to have been the eldest son of the late President of Surat), and Isaacson were being dispatched in the *Endeavour*, which did not arrive till July, 1644.

[2] Though endorsed ' October, 1643 ', this list has evidently been corrected to a somewhat later date. It is in the same handwriting as *O.C.* 1841.

[3] Altered from 100*l.*, in accordance with the Court's decision, on March 17, 1643, to increase his wages to that extent from March 25, 1644.

(70*l.*), and William Pitt (100*l.*). *Sent out in the ' Dolphin '*: Anthony Clitherow (20*l.*) and Thomas Reynardson (20*l.*).[1] (2½ *pp.*)

PRESIDENT CARTWRIGHT AND COUNCIL AT BANTAM TO THE COMPANY, JANUARY 10, 1644 (*O.C.* 1853).

... Regret the imperfect state of the Coromandel accounts. Ivy will, upon reaching the Coast, make inquiry into the matter. With the exception of Day, all the factors there that are capable of good service are desirous of returning to England, their covenants having expired; but this cannot be allowed for the present. ... The *Hart* arrived from the Coromandel Coast on December 13. Praise the frugality of Godfrey, her master. On the other hand the late master [Trumball] of the *Hopewell* appears to have been wasteful, for she came hither very poorly supplied. ... John Yard, formerly chief in the Bay of Bengal, returns in this ship, the *Hopewell*, having put his whole estate (sent herewith) into the hands of the Company. As regards the accusations made against him, they conceive him to be innocent, 'and that he had absolute order and authoritie to buy the *Endeavour*, as we have seene by a letter directed unto him in the Bay to procure a good vessell, three times mencioned in the sayd letter, besides the buying of a jelliah [*see the 1634–36 volume*, p. 43] or fiatt bottomd boate, which are not capable to transport to Mesulapatam from the Bay of Bengala the 20th part of what was desired to be sent thence in the sayd vessell he had order to procure.' ... Omitted to enclose in their last a letter from Day &c. on the Coast, dated October 3 last [*not extant*]. Nevertheless, they cannot consider the proposition made therein worthy of consideration or approbation. ''Twere better for them discreetly to mannage the busines they have now in hand then to trouble themselves with new projects and conceits of 12 or 16 sayle of shipps, pinnaces, and ketches, with a carga[son] of fowerscore thousand pounds and a yearely supply of 30 or 35,000*li.*, with an unlimitted power to doe what they pleased without any controlement.' They believe, however, that upon Ivy's arrival, 'these foggie mists will be gently dispersed'. 'The continuance of the Bengala factory,

---

[1] The total of the amended list is 2,420*l.* 14*s.* 8*d.*, or, adding Mantell's salary of 15*l.* (omitted in the list), 2,435*l.* 14*s.* 8*d.*, divided among forty persons.

if Your Worshipps intend the continuance of your trade, is soe necessary (and maintayned with soe little charge) that we desire you would be pleased absolutely to inorder its dissolution or subsisting. If the latter, the man appoynted thither by Mr. Day, namely William Nettlam, is very unfitt to have the direccion of your affayres there; where not any is soe well acquainted, or hath more abillities for its performance then Mr. Yard aforesaid.' . . . Will probably dispatch the *Hart* to Surat next May with pepper. . . . The *Swan*, on her return from Jambi, is to go to the Coast, carrying thither Thomas Ivy and Thomas Winter, 'for the resettlement of your affayres there'. . . . Dutch discoveries in the South Seas.[1] They have also found 'a second Mauritius, some 80 leagues to the northwards of the other, whose draught [*missing*] is likewise herewith sent you.' The Dutch, Portuguese, and others, trade annually to Macao and other parts of China. The Hollanders are also about to send a ship to 'Tartaria'. 'That island of Poolaroone[2], soe long in their possession, in which His Majestie of England hath soe just right and tytle, and under him our Honorable Company, we mervayle as yet that it is not redellivered upp into our possession. But we knowe there myndes, which is thus: that unlesse there come an absolute comaund in writing from the King of England, approved and allowed of by the Netherlanders States, with their order for its redellivery to us, they in these parts will never yeild it upp; which when done, perhapps they will require satisfaccion for the charges they have byn at in keeping it out of the enemyes hands these many yeares, purposely for the generall good.' Thomas Lamberton, one of the men captured in the *Bona Speranza*, was given a passage to England in the *Mary*; and now Thomas Hinton, the surgeon of the former ship, has been permitted to embark in the *Hopewell*. . . . *PS*.—Estate of John Jeffries, who died near Tranquebar on August 13 last. (*Extracts only.* 2½ *pp.*)

---

[1] Viz. Abel Tasman's discovery of Tasmania and New Zealand: see an article in the *Geographical Journal* for May, 1911.
[2] Pulo Run, in the Bandas. It had been agreed in 1623 that it should be restored to the English, but the Dutch had hitherto evaded its redelivery.

FRANCIS BRETON, WILLIAM FREMLEN, THOMAS MERRY, THOMAS ADLER, WILLIAM THURSTON, AND RICHARD FITCH AT SWALLY MARINE TO THE COMPANY, JANUARY 27, 1644 (*O.C.* 1858).

Wrote last on March 20, by way of Basrā· Need not recapitulate what was stated therein, save the dispatch for England on January 19, 1643, of the *Crispiana* and *Aleppo Merchant*, with cargoes that cost 1,175,353 mahmūdīs 20 pice. Arrival of the *Seaflower*, under Adam Lee. She left the Downs on March 8, 1643, in company with the *Mary* and the *Hart*, but parted from them on April 10; passed the Cape on June 22; sighted Madagascar on July 18; and reached Mozambique on July 27, with her men in a very weak state from having been at sea so long. After spending seven days there, without much result as regards sales, she embarked a few Portuguese and their goods, and departed for Johanna, which was reached on August 7. Two days later the *Dolphin*, *Hind*, and *Hart* came in. The last-named, having already refreshed her sick men at Madagascar, proceeded on her voyage to Fort St. George, arriving there on September 23. Thence she was sent to Masulipatam, reached that port on October 1, and departed for Bantam on the 21st. The *Seaflower* left Johanna a day after the *Hart*, and entered Bombay harbour on September 5. She 'might with equall safety have come to Surratt, because, in entring this river, to vessells that swim deeper then shee doth, there is neither difficulty nor danger.' The *Dolphin* and *Hind* anchored at Swally on September 18.[1] Now reply to the letters thus received from the Company, dated March 24, 1643 [*not extant*]. Can advise little that is satisfactory about Persia, where nothing can be effected without costly gifts. Adler, having been to court to congratulate the new King, managed in this way to procure the renewal of most of the Company's former privileges. On the strength of these *farmāns*, the factors got through the year 'without any publike affront done them', and even obtained from the Shāhbandar of Gombroon 300 tūmāns on account of what was due to the Company. When the heat rendered Gombroon uninhabitable, they retired to Ispahān. This course must be maintained, for, unless the English are in a position to make representations at court,

---

[1] According to the Dutch, these vessels brought to the value of about 700,000 rupees in money, coral, lead, &c. (*Dagh-Register*, 1643-44, pp. 196, 238).

the Gombroon authorities will never deal fairly with them in the matter of the customs; especially as the Company will not consent to 'our proposition for takeing your right on board' [*see the previous volume*, p. 272]. The only way of making the Persian trade more profitable is to augment the stock of money in India, wherewith to purchase goods in Agra, Ahmadābād, Sind, Masulipatam, &c. These, with a little English merchandize, would be likely to 'produce some good advance, and consequently procure you silke at or under 40 tomands per loade.' The Dutch recently offered to contract with the King for 400 loads yearly, if he would accept less than 50 tūmāns per load; but no agreement was reached. Sale of the broadcloth sent to Persia. Have provided 505 bales 'indicoe Agry' [i.e. of Agra], both good and cheap, the dearest portion costing not above 33 rupees per maund in Agra. Have given instructions to buy a thousand more, and also 200 bales of Sehwān indigo, though they fear the latter may not be procurable. 'This comodity hath these latter yeares bin much unrequested in the neighbouring countries of Persia, Mocho, yea, Bussora alsoe; and that hath soe admirably declined its vallue where it is made that the planters are almost beggered thereby, and therefore doe annually more or lesse reduce the wonted quaintities made by them. However, it little troubles us, whilst the accession of soe much advance thereby to our trade affordes us much greater cause of rejoyceing.' Of Sarkhej indigo they now send 722 chests and bundles; it is extraordinarily good, and has been carefully sifted and packed. These ships also bring 200 bales of cotton yarn. The finer sort required by the Company can be better procured at Surat than at Ahmadābād; but the latter place is more suitable for the coarser varieties. Note the dissatisfaction expressed with the calicoes formerly sent, and will do their best to remedy the defects indicated. The complaints regarding those from 'Scinda' have been forwarded to Spiller and the other factors there resident. It is hoped that the bales now sent will be better liked. Have bespoken from thence 10,000 pieces of the ordinary sorts for the next returning ships, besides 1,000 pieces of better quality; also a quantity of saltpetre, indigo, 'pintadoes', and turmeric for England, 'cossumba¹' for Achin, and some other drugs for Surat. Eight

---

¹ *Kusumbha*, i.e. safflower, which is much grown in India for the red dye produced from its flowers, as well as for its oil-yielding seeds.

bales of 'chints' forwarded; and in addition 'some of those made in Serongee[1] and Brampore [Burhānpur] of thinner cloth. In Tuttha cloth is well painted, but generally upon narrow guzzees; nor doe those weavers make broader, unlesse they are purposely bespoake; and they are such as the broad bastaes are, which have bin soe much disliked by you.' Of 'merhcools' 117 bales are sent; but these started so late from Agra that only part of them could be bleached at Broach, the rest being 'cured' at Baroda and Ahmadābād. This was inevitable, because 'beyond Brodera towards Barroach the deepenes of the waies at that time of yeare permitt not passages to coaches, much lesse laden carts, such as are usually imployed in transporting goods from place to place in these parts of India.' Have ordered 10,000 pieces of these calicoes from Agra for the next consignment; together with some 'eckbaries' and 'guzzees', 'which wee intend to transforme into cannekins, ardeas, byrams, selaes, and other speties of dyed cloathing for supply of Bantam, Mocho, Persia, and Bussora.' Have also sent home 100 bales of 'Derebads' from Agra, and have ordered 10,000 pieces for next season. No 'Kerebauds' are forwarded; and only two bales of 'eckbarees'. 'Semana cloth was bespoake, but its excessive dearnes hath almost lost both the use and makeing of them', and so they have sent only twenty pieces 'for a muster'. As regards 'callicoe lawns, distinguished into gooldars, salloes, and furradckaumes' [*sic*], they dispatched one of their brokers to the towns where these sorts are made, but he has not yet returned; they have therefore bought a small quantity of each for England, and will send the others (when received) to Basrā. 'Of other sorts of callicoe lawnes, as cossadees, gooldars, humony, beetelas, &c., the Coast of Choromondell and Bengala will best furnish them; but for sheerisadfs, they are extreordinary deare, almost out of use, and indeed not worth your owneing.' For three years past the dearness of cotton wool (owing to bad seasons) has raised the price of cotton yarn and cloth in these parts; and they have therefore only sent home this time a small quantity of Nosārī and Baroda baftas. They have bought more than 400 corge of Broach and Ankleswar cloth; but these are intended for Bantam and Basrā. Advise also the dispatch of narrow

[1] Sironj, in Tonk State. Its calicoes and muslins were long famous (see Ball's *Tavernier*, vol. i. p. 56).

blue baftas, Guinea stuffs, quilts, and cardamoms. Steps taken to procure borax and cardamoms from Rāybāg. Have made generally known the Company's prohibition of private trade to England in borax. Enclose particulars obtained from Ahmadābād concerning this commodity, its place of origin, and the method of refining it and reducing it to powder. Of the borax now sent home a small part has been treated in that fashion; and steps are being taken to provide a larger return by the next shipping. Vīrjī Vōra's troubles at court, and their own indebtedness to him, have hitherto deterred them from pressing him to fulfil his contract; and now, having plenty of pepper from Bantam and Malabar, they are not anxious to deal with him for any. Thurston was instructed to procure cardamoms, cinnamon, and pepper at Cochin and its neighbourhood, 'but the Portugalls wars with the Raja of Upper Cochyne, and there approved base and treacherous dealings with us, prevented him wholly of the two former, and noe lesse of the latter inasmuch as they could hinder the action.' However, the *Dolphin* has now fetched from Goa a quantity of cinnamon that had been bought there; and with it Fremlen forwards certain bales presented to him personally by the Viceroy and others; he leaves the Company to dispose of these as may be thought fitting. A further quantity of cinnamon was bought at Cochin by Walter Clark, master of the *Supply*, and is now put on board the *Dolphin* and *Discovery*. Measures taken to secure a supply for the next ships. Rejoice that the Company approved of their action in sending Pitt and Hill 'to reside at Goa for prevention of Esquire Curteens people'. They remained there from March to December and then, finding that the Viceroy was indifferent to both sides and that Goa yielded little of value for their purposes (cinnamon excepted), they were ordered to return on the *Aleppo Merchant*. Thurston and two other factors were left at Cochin by the *Swan*, but the wars between the Portuguese and 'the neighbour Raja' had put a stop to trade, with the result that they could sell nothing but a little alum and opium. They bought, however, a quantity of pepper from a neighbouring Rājā who is 'Lord of Purcatt[1]'; and this was brought to Swally by the *Discovery*. The *Expedition* then arrived from Bantam

[1] Porakād or Purakkātu, a town on the coast of Travancore, about ten miles south of Alleppi. It was an independent principality until the middle of the eighteenth century.

with 200 tons of pepper; while the *Supply* added a further supply from Achin. After filling the ships for England, the remainder has been reserved for Basrā. Have also embarked a quantity of saltpetre (packed in chests), olibanum, aloes, turmeric, gum-lac, myrrh, ginger, and benzoin. Note with pleasure the Company's approbation of their proceedings. Were they but supplied with more money, and thus relieved of the constant charge of interest, they could produce still better results, for at present their limited credit causes them to lose many opportunities of profit. Moreover, 'the sence of these troubleous times in England, which are too well knowne,' has made them the more cautious in their investments. Still, the results have on the whole been encouraging. The *Discovery* and *Francis* sold some of their goods at Mokha at a profit of 28 per cent., though the ginger and some of the dyed cloth were returned unsold. These have now been sent to Persia in the *Seaflower*. The *Seahorse*, returning from Basrā in November last, brought 'good encouragement to prosecute that trade, for there goods produced neerest 50 per cent. proffitt'; 'soe that, not to desert that place and trade, which hath yett approved its selfe advantageous to you', they have arranged a further investment of suitable goods for dispatch thither. The *Discovery*, after landing her freight goods at Gombroon, sailed for Mokha, as directed, but met with such adverse winds that the Malabars arrived before her and so that part of her design was frustrated. They intend, however, to dispatch thither immediately the *Supply* and the *Francis*, 'the former to proceede directly towards the Bab, the latter to anchor in Aden Roade; that soe the Mallabars, who use to touch at Aden and there enquire of your shipping before they passe towards Mocha, being frighted thence by sight of [the] *Francis*, may, wee hope, happily bee surprised by the *Supply*.' The goods intended for Mokha this year will be put upon a Dutch ship, under the care of Richard Clark. George Oxenden and Peter Herbert will be sent in the *Supply* and *Francis*, to prevent the embezzlement of any goods that may be taken from the Malabars. They are then to proceed to Mokha to sell those and the other goods consigned thither in the Dutch ship; 'which being according to our hopes successfully accomplished, they shalbee directed soe soone to leave that place as, if they cannot in Mocha accquire alloes and olibanum, they may seeke them at Shehr, and yett proceede thence soe seasonably as sometime about the fine [of] August they fall with Cape Comerin, and thenceforth range all that coast alongst untill they arrive to Swally, gleaning and gathering up such pepper, cinnamon, and cardamon as may bee procured conveniently.' Have instructed all masters of ships to attack the Malabars (outside the prescribed limits) on every possible occasion. Desire a supply of swords and muskets to arm their vessels; also cordage and sailcanvas. Had intended to send Merry to take charge at Ahmadābād, but Tash has exhibited such proofs of diligence and discretion that they have resolved not to supersede him; and therefore Merry remains at Surat as Accountant and Second in Council. Settlement of his debt to the Company. It is certain that vast quantities of broadcloth are landed from the ships as private trade; yet they can do nothing to stop this, as it is effected through native agents and the customs officials favour the practice. The markets are further cloyed by the quantities landed by Courteen's people at Rājāpur; 'for they not only furnish Decan and Brampoore but, haveing soe free and not much dearer nor longer passage to Agra then your goods have, are by the buyers transported thither, and soe alsoe renders this marchandize the more despicable.' Vīrjī Vōra has treated them well in the matter of their debt to him; though this year he has followed the example of their other creditors in demanding a higher rate of interest. As yet they have not agreed, nor will they if the money can be raised elsewhere. 'The encouragement you give us to expect ample supplies in the future hath animated us to ampliate your trade accordingly.' Know not what accusations have been made from Bantam against the Coast factors; but, so far as they can judge, Cogan has rendered good service in reducing expenses and checking disorder. Fear that the factors at Bantam have resented the subordination of the Coast to Surat and are inclined to behave harshly in consequence. For instance, Dowle, the master of the *Advice*, acting under instructions from Bantam, refused to allow the Agent on the Coast to have anything to do with his vessel or her cargo. Refer to letters now forwarded from the factors, and also to Cogan, for further information. So far as they themselves are concerned, it is a matter for rejoicing that they have been relieved ' from that burthen the superintendency of the Coast Agency and affaires bring with it'. 'Wee may with

THE ENGLISH FACTORIES

you congratulate the pleaseing tydeings of the French pyrates cessation of there unjust trade driven by there quondam great master[1] towards the Redd Sea Streights; whose successe in there latest designes cannot give them any great encouragement further to tempt the Almighty by such unlawfull and unworthy practizes.' Thank the Company for the stores sent for the use of their smaller vessels; but the water casks proved very defective. The *Hind* and *Seaflower*, though good sea ships, are altogether unsuitable for service in these parts. 'There decks are very low, and soe close that, if they should bee assaulted by Mallabarrs, they will rather stiffle then preserve your people.' They have no accommodation for passengers, and this occasions a loss of freight. 'They are in some measure a discreditt to our nation, whilst this people (who know noe better) enquire whether England doth not affoard shipping of its owne, that it is enforced to seeke and buy them among strangers.'[2] Desire to be supplied with 'handsome, well built shipps, framed to affoard accomodacion to passengers, and that made as airesome as may conveniently bee contrived; of burthen twixt 200 and 250 tuns; drawing twixt 9 and 12 foote water; and formed to bee of good force and defence. Such vessells will doe you creditt and service.' They should bring out arms and ammunition for themselves and for their consorts; for though gunpowder can be easily procured here or at Ahmadābād at five or six rupees per Surat maund, yet round and crossbar shot for guns, half pikes, swords, muskets, and carbines are not obtainable. A supply of cordage is much needed. As for the Portuguese, 'our correspondence with them is as fervent as frequent', and the new President promises to follow Fremlen's example in maintaining good relations with them. Grieve to learn that so much private trade was carried home in the *London*. Have done their best 'to prevent the like prejudice in these shipps', but have just heard that a large quantity of indigo has been smuggled aboard them; 'and though this is knowne for a certaine truth, yett there owners cannot bee discovered, notwithstanding the uttmost of our dilligence and industry.' The Company's approbation of Fremlen's services has encouraged him to

---

[1] The reference seems to be to the death of Richelieu, which occurred towards the close of 1642.
[2] Both the *Hind* and *Seaflower* were Dutch-built 'prams' (lighters).

hasten home to 'enjoy the much desired effects of such comfortable promises'. Approve the course adopted 'in the matter of your shipps goverment and command'; and praise both Proud and Bradbent, the masters of these two ships. Explain why little has been received of late for local freights. The native merchants prefer the Dutch vessels, 'findeing there much better accomodacion and noe less safety', with the result that 'the Hollanders in foure shipps have carried hence all the fraught goods that have bin brought to the Marryne'. However, the *Hind* will no doubt find employment when the Dutch depart; 'for wee know that, whatever inconveniences the passengers undergoe, yett they will choose to voyage on them rather then on the Moores shipping, which are now become soe numerous that for procury of employment they submitt to any, however contemptible, fraughtments; yea, some of them, soe to gaine merchants to them, furnish them gratis with monies to extinguish such engagements as customes, fraught, &c. charges involve them in; for which formerly they have paide 20 and (in these last daies) 15 and 16 per cent.' Estates of John Wylde, who deceased at Mokha in October, 1642, and of Walter Clark, late master of the *Supply*, who died suddenly on December 26 last, a few days after his return from Achin. Duarte Fernandez Correa, who 'hath bin very usefull to your occasions', returns to his own country this year and will take passage on the *Seahorse* to Basrā; he has been permitted to embark a small chest on the *Dolphin*, recommended to the care of Fremlen. To Bantam they have annually remitted far more than they have received in return. Would be glad to be supplied from thence with cloves, mace, or nutmegs; but this is scarcely feasible, as the factors there cannot obtain enough to satisfy the home demand. Account of goods received from that place by the *Expedition*, and of the consignment intended thither by the *Seaflower* about April next. Estates of the First General Voyage and of the Third Joint Stock. The Agra accounts were sent down, but the bearer was robbed on the way and his papers torn to pieces; transcripts have been asked for and shall be sent by the next fleet. Steps taken to turn over all remains to the account of the Fourth Joint Stock, and to recover the debts. Refer to a consultation of November 15 last for the re-engagement of certain factors whose covenants had expired. Would be glad to receive yearly 'two or three ingenuous young men, such as are ready and faire writers, for indeed such are very much wanting in your writeing office and compting house'; also one at least 'of greater experience in merchandizeing affaires'. Commend the factors who have arrived this year. To replace Luke Pynn, who returns home as purser's mate of the *Discovery*, they have taken on shore Joseph Cross. Fitch, who has been General Purser for the past two years, has been 'admitted of Counsell and rancked under William Thurston, who alsoe is lately preferred to that dignity'. Adler, who has been acting in the same capacity since his arrival from Persia, is now proceeding to England, accompanied by William Hall and Thomas Wheeler. Enclose particulars of the cargoes intended for Basrā and Mokha. A residence will be maintained at the former place, both on account of trade and for facilitating communications with Europe via Aleppo. Letters dispatched that way from London in October or November may be expected to reach Surat in May. ' For Bussora, this (as the passed) yeare Edward Pearce is in chiefe, assisted by three other factors designed; and seeing (as wee have bin lately informed) the differences twixt the Portugalls and that Bashaw are rather fomented then extenuated, wee doubt not the sorts of goods now in provision for your accompt for that place will vend to competent gaine, and consequently exhibitt new encouragement, not only to continuate but importantly alsoe to ampliate your trade in those parts of Arabia. Since Mocha is reduced under the Arabs goverment, the Turke[s] have bin generally expulsed from those parts and esteemed the most dangerous enemyes those petty Arabian kings have; and though such complaint of Surratt merchants to the Governor of Mocha[1], whilst that place was subjected to the Grand Segnior, bee in such cases of some use, yett now, by alteracion of goverment, they are become wholly improper and unproffitable. However these people are fully acquainted with your resolucions, yett, they being now three yeares successively frighted only, they imagine it is by us purposely contrived to advance our fraughtments in your vessels returne thence, by induceing (for more securityes sake) these merchants to put rather

---

[1] Apparently the Company had suggested that the Surat merchants should be induced to complain to Constantinople (through Mokha) of the reported depredations of French pirates in the Red Sea.

there monies on board your shipping then the Moores junks. And this, for thus much care of them, is the recompense wee received or may expect from them ; as was the passed yeare experimented, for, the *Discovery* staying from this port longer then ordinary, our old false freinde, Mirza Mahmud, would, togeather with a company of credulous Moores and Banian merchants, have perswaded (though hee lost his labor) Mierza Jam Collibeage, our then Governor, that the English haveing, by venting such reports of the Frenchmens feared comeing into the Redd Seas Streights, induced the marchants in generall to embarque theire monies on board the *Discovery*, they had thence sent her for England directly.' John Spiller and Anthony Smith thank the Company for its bounty.[1] Wish that Thomas Markham had lived to enjoy the same favour;[2] but the Almighty, 'knowing him fitter for His then your service, tooke him from you.' On the arrival of the *Seaflower*, Richard Fisher was at once made prisoner and his papers examined; yet nothing was found to inculpate him in any way, and so he was restored to his place.[3] Thomas Whatmore, some time master of the *Diamond*, reports that John Derham died in 'the river of Scinda anno 1639, when the vessell there wintered'. As regards Thomas Derham, they are making inquiry at the Coast. 'Wee are nothing sorry that Captain Bonds plantacion at St. Lawrence proceeded noe further; but wee more wonder that Mr. Corteene intermeddleth with these matters, since it might bee generally thought his trade to India might afford him worke enough to prosecute it.' Of the rials received this time the shroffs objected to 13,300, and 'would not (after exact tryall made of there alloy in the Kings mint, your owne and the Customers houses) bee induced to buy them, unless wee would submitt to part with them at 205 rupees per 100 rials.' They therefore sent part of them to Goa (where no difficulty was made) and part to Ahmadābād. 'Though the King of Spaines necessities enforce him to sett a higher price on his rials then formerly, yett this people being not soe urged, nor esteeming more of his rials this then the former yeare, seeing they serve cheifely to bee refined and

---

[1] Both had been granted an increase in salary: see *Court Minutes of the East India Company*, 1640-43, pp. 299, 313.
[2] *Ibid.*, p. 313.
[3] He was charged with taking out private trade (*ibid.*, p. 313).

there alloy made answerable to that of the Surratt rupee, wee could not advance them beyond the usuall prizes of 212¼ rupees the new, the old 215¼, and 216 rupees ½ m[ahmūdī] the 100 rex dollars; and at these prizes wee parted with them.' On delivery, 865½ rials were found deficient in weight, and 24 were missing. The latter may have been due to coins slipping out through the seams of the chests, after the bags had rotted away. A remedy would be to cover the bags with skins, which 'by this country people is familiarly practised'. In the rix dollars 77½ were wanting in weight and 1½ in number, while three were brass ones. 'Gold, since the Dutch have not these two or three late passed yeares brought any from China, is againe become well requested; insoemuch that the Venetian is worth 9 m[ahmūdī]s and better, when formerly it hath bin sold for 8½, 2, 3, or 4 pice over. And ratably heereto are all other gold coynes vallued. Soe that, if through the late enhansment of the Spanish monies you bee not futurely soe well provided, or that they turne not to soe good accoumpt, you may supply that defect by sending forth some quaintities of gold, which wee doubt not but will proove more advantageous to you.' Of lead from four to six hundred 'great piggs' will sell here annually. The *Seaflower* was unable to dispose of any of her Canary wine at Mozambique, which had already been supplied sufficiently by two caravels on their way from Lisbon to Goa. Her other goods were also in small demand, as will be seen from the accounts sent herewith. Cannot decide what to do with the wine. They thought of sending it to Bantam, to be sold at Batavia, but are informed that the sale of wine there is a monopoly of the Dutch Company; while 'the Portugalls are soe base and beggerly that they will not at such cost meddle with such a comodity'. Beg the Company to resume the former practice of sending out Canary and French wine annually for the use of the factors. Advice as to the quantity and colours of broadcloth required for India and Persia. Knives and satins needed for presents; also some rich velvet for supply to the Emperor, patterns of which have been delivered to Fremlen. Dispute with Vīrjī Vōra over the quality of the coral brought by the 1642 ships, with the result that the price of part had to be considerably reduced. There is still a remainder on hand of that consignment, besides what came in the last ships. Quantity to be sent in future. Have just heard that Thomas Derham was alive at the time when the *Advice* was dispeeded from Bantam, and was then on board of her; will write accordingly to that place. Send a list of commodities likely to sell here. Among these they specially commend to the Company's attention elephants' teeth; 'and if such might bee accquired, and any your Indian or other cuntryes commodities sold at Gueney [Guinea], the course Mr. Courtyn tooke in designeing the *Planter* thither would (if at least it bee to you, as to him, equally faecible) in appearance proove advantageous to you.' For details of the disposal of their ships they refer to the transcript of Fremlen's journal [*not extant*] sent herewith. The *Supply*, dispatched from this port for Persia in company with the *Discovery*, remained at Gombroon until March 6 and returned to Swally on March 25, bringing horses and rosewater for the Company's account, besides passengers and freight goods. On April 23 she sailed for Achin, with a cargo consisting chiefly of freight goods. She called at Cochin on May 3, to take in some more freight, and reached her destination on the 25th. 'There they found six of the Esquire Courtyns people, deepe in debt, yett doeing nothing.' 'The concurse of many vessells to Achyn rendred the marketts more dull then usuall'; but a fair proportion of the cargo was sold and the proceeds reinvested. The Company is to receive from the freighters 25 per cent. of the value of the goods returned. 'The shipp came thence full, and yett left of yours and the fraughters goods, in charge of Maximilian Bowman, Thomas Fitch, and Francis Scattergood, as many as amounts to m[ahmūdīs] 50,000 . . . for whose bringing thence being obliged to the fraughters, and findeing that the trade in probability will become very advantageous to you, wee have resolved to send the *Hinde* this voyage for your owne accompt.' The *Supply* left Achin on October 20 and, after calling at Cochin, reached this port on December 11 [*sic*]. Clark, her master, died suddenly a few days later; and thereupon Lee was placed in charge of her. She is at present under orders for the Red Sea. The *Francis* reached Mokha on April 15, 1643, left again on August 17, and on September 2 reached Damān, whence after some delay she came to this port, in company with the *Dolphin* and *Hind*. She brought goods and money to the value of 47,644 rials 32[d.], besides a trifling amount of freight. She is now to accompany the

Supply. As the *Discovery*, which arrived on November 3, brought only a little pepper from the Malabar coast, the *Dolphin* was dispatched thither on the 13th to procure cardamoms and borax at Rājāpur and cinnamon at Goa. She arrived at the latter port on November 20, 'without speakeing with the Dutch, though they shott at her'; left again on December 4; anchored at Rājāpur two days later; and got back here on the 23rd. She is now fully laden for England; and 'on her your late President, William Fremlen, commands and takes his passage.' With her goes the *Discovery*, both being expressly enjoined to keep together on the voyage. The *Hind* was sent to 'Scinda' on October 25 and arrived there November 7. She sailed again a fortnight later, reaching Swally at the beginning of December, with 136 bales of piece-goods, which had cost 27,784 rupees 58 pice. She is now taking in freight goods for Persia. The *Seaflower* stayed at 'Bombaien' from the 5th to the 25th September, and did not arrive at this port until the 28th. She sailed for Gombroon on October 25; anchored there November 12; left on the 22nd; and got back to Swally on December 2. She is now to accompany the *Hind* on a fresh voyage to Persia; and later on she will be sent to Bantam. Lee's place as master has been taken by Gardner, the late master of the *Expedition*. Intend to ask the President and Council at Bantam to keep the *Seaflower*, as being more suitable for service in those parts, and to send the *Swan* or *Hopewell* to Surat in her place. The *Discovery* reached Gombroon on February 18, 1643, and remained there till March 14. She anchored at Mokha on April 27; careened at Assab; took in a freight for Cochin, and departed on August 10; and arrived at Cochin on September 5. Fifteen days later she proceeded to 'Purcutt', where a quantity of pepper was embarked; she then left on October 14 and got back to Swally on November 3. The *Expedition* sailed from Bantam on July 22 and arrived here on November 11. Upon examination it was found that she was unfit for further service and so she is to be broken up. The *Seahorse*, in her voyage to Basrā, called at Gombroon and then at 'Catteife [*see* p. 100], there to l[and] this King[s] goods and servants, sent purposely to buy horses with there proceeds.' Leaving that place on May 24, she reached Basrā on June 20; stayed there till September 20; anchored at 'Catteife' on the 27th, and, after embarking eight horses 'for accompt of this King', left on October 5; got to Gombroon nine days later; sailed on the 20th, with Messrs. Adler, Hall, and Wheeler on board; and arrived at Swally on November 7. She brought from Basrā, in goods and money, 29,489 rials, and from Gombroon 122,672 shāhīs, besides a certain amount received for freight. She has now been sent to Bassein to fetch some great guns 'made there for a new junck built in this river for the Princesses[1] accompt'; and later she will be dispeeded to 'Scinda' with tobacco. On her return she will go again to Basrā. Probably the *Prosperous* will then accompany her. Of Courteen's ships sent to the East last year, two, they hear, went to Achin, whence one of them was dispatched to England little more than half full. The *Advice* brought news that the *Bonaventura* had been wrecked at Mauritius. The *Bona Speranza* went to the Malabar Coast and there bartered brimstone and Biscay iron for cinnamon. She was then freighted by the Portuguese for China, but was captured by the Dutch and taken to Malacca. This has frustrated 'Captain Blackmans hope of like employment for shipp *William*'; 'with which shipp the *Planter* is alsoe arrived and returned for England, laden in the greatest part (as reported) with saltpeeter; nor indeed can wee thinke that her carga[zoon] imported any considerable summ, since in Goa they are enforced to empawne such goods as they cannot vend, though profferred at most despicable rates to raise monies to stopp there clamorous creditors mouthes at Rawbaag. In Achyn they are alike necessiated, for they borrow monies to buy pepper and, the covenanted time for payment being before there supplies arrived, they [are?] againe forced to sell there pepper to pay there creditors. Nor doth Captaine Blackman well know what to doe with his shipp *William*; yett some say hee hath agreede to take a fraught at Rajapore for Persia.' However, they will now 'leave them wrangling with and menaceing the Dutch, for dareing to shoote at His Majesties shipp and coulors (for that is the usuall appellacion whereby they distinguish yours from there shipping), and address ourselves to treate of the Hollanders; whose Hogen Mogen[2] Generall haveing the passed yeare purposely

---

[1] Probably the Princess Jahānārā, the favourite daughter of Shāh Jahān. Her trading operations are referred to on p. 256 of the *Dagh-Register*, 1644-45.
[2] 'Hunne Hoogmogenden' (i.e. the High and Mighty) was a title applied to the

(as published) sent one Pettr Borell[1], with the title of Commissary, to Goa to treat and conclude articles of peace with the V[ice] Roy &c., and (it seemes) ordered formerly there people on Coast Choromandell, Seiloan, and this part of India to proclaime the same with more then common ceremony; and that this Borrell had dureing the treaty received as much honor, respect, and noble entertainement as could possibly bee contrived. Yett his propositions were soe unreasonable and evilly disgested by the Portugalls that, it being feared the people would have offered some indignity to him, and findeing with him and his bounded commission an appeareing improbability of agreeing, the V[ice] Roy &c. determined to write there resolves to the Generall, and soe dismissed the Commissary; which suddainely after they put in practice, for, attending and accompanying him to the V[ice] Royes gallies with some of the best quallified persons in Goa, they gave him a ceremoniall farwell, sending after him all the furniture which, for use an[d] ornament, had served in the house appointed for his entertainement; which, consisting of a great quain[ti]ty of plate and rich carpetts, did (as some of the Jesuitt Padres advised us) amount to upwards of 50,000 xera[fins]; which comeing to the Admirall was not refused by the Commissary, although upon his owne comeing on board hee imediately put out his bloody ensigne. In imitation of his discretion the rest of the skippers did the like; and soe, his limitted time of stay being expired, hee sett saile for Ceiloan, and there began to show the effect of his intentions; but hee was well beaten in a skirmish for it, and soe returneing by Pollycatt to Battavia, dyed there[2] suddainely, leaveing the Portugalls infinitely distracted with his abrupt parting from Goa; for the former publicacion of peace had invited the Portugalls in generall againe to fall to tradeing, and thereupon divers vessells were sett forth to Melinda, Mocambique,

States-General of Holland. Here, of course, the reference is to the Governor-General at Batavia.

[1] For Boreel's mission see *ante*, p. 100; also the *Hague Transcripts*, series i. vol. xiii. nos. 410, 420, 422, &c.; and *Dagh-Register*, 1643-44, p. 186, &c. The Portuguese account of the negotiations will be found in the *Lisbon Transcripts* (India Office): *Doc. Remett.*, book 48, f. 149, &c.

[2] Boreel died at Pulicat on July 1 (N. S.), nine days after his arrival (*Hague Transcripts*, series i, vol. xiii. no. 410; *Dagh-Register*, 1643-44, p. 272). His tomb is still to be seen in the Dutch cemetery there (J. J. Cotton's *Madras Monuments*, p. 196).

China, and other places, which are now left to there fortunes. And yett wee doe not heare that they [i. e. the Dutch] have this yeare on this coast surprised any, but have rather bin loosers: whilst there shipp *Pas* [*Pauw*], commanded by Willibrant Gelemensen [*see* p. 114], there late President (as they tearmed him) in Persia, passing thence to Battavia with more then 400 bales of silke, was enforced (if not invited, in hopes of peace twixt them and the Portugalls) to shelter himselfe from a most violent storme, which tooke him neare Cape Commerin, as hee thought in a freinds port. But hee was noe sooner entred Mormagon then all was ceized on, inventorized, and finally landed and housed; whereof the V[ice] Roy kept one, Willibrant the other key; unto whome and his company untill the entry of September was affoarded as much liberty as the towne permitted, delivering up into the saide Willibrants possession whatever as his proper goods hee pretended unto; but when the time of there shipps comeing as accustomary, they were then jointly enclosed in a monastery and a guard sett over them; where at your shippe *Dolphins* comeing thence they were [conti]nued; and are like to remaine in such durance untill they are enfranchised [in lieu?] of others or a confirmed peace concluded.'[1] Three Dutch ships (one of them, the *Elephant*, being reported to be of a thousand tons burden) have visited Swally and have landed vast quantities of Southern commodities, which have been sold (especially the spices) at very great prices. Three ships have been sent to Persia and one to Goa and the Malabar Coast; while one is expected from Bantam [Batavia?] and two from China. The latter two are expected to bring a great mass of treasure, for those hitherto arrived had but a very small number of rials. They intend to dispatch a vessel to Mokha this year, but they declare that she is to be sent rather to fetch away their people than for purposes of trade. As regards 'the still unfortunate Portugalls, a very [fine?] galleon, called *St. Bento*, setting saile from Portugall in Aprill, 1642, spent eight months time ere shee attained Mosambique, rather a place within a small distance from Mosambique, where shee soe came on ground that, though the goods and men were in the great part saved, yett the land rather then water saint could not preserve his

---

[1] *Hague Transcripts*, series i. vol. xiii. no. 417; *Dagh-Register*, 1643-44, p. 187, &c. See also *Lisbon Transcripts: Doc. Remett.*, book 48, f. 268.

namesake from perishing.[1] Two caravells alsoe, which wintered at Mosambique and could not in May attaine Goa, arrived thither about the entry of September, and brought tydeings of [ ] galleons preparednesse to follow; but the time is not, it seemes, knowne when, for yett none appeares, and now untill the next yeare the Portugalls despaire to see [them?]. In Seiloan they have of the Dutch regained Negombo and manfully beate them in a land skirmish, wherein some say 700, some 500, but none report that fewer then 300 Hollanders were slaine. And yett they would, even upon any indifferent tearmes accept, if not begg, a cessation of armes of the Hollanders, who since the middle of September have not had less then five shipps at anchor before Goa, and whose commanders brought a pretended power to establish such peace twixt both nations as was ratified in Europe, but then the Portugalls must submitt to part with Ceiloan; otherwise the propositions falls, and with it all hopes of reconcilliacion. Upon these tearmes the affaires of both nations in these parts subsists: the Portugalls will not leave Seiloan, nor will the Hollanders leave the roade of Goa free from disturbance, its merchants freede of that distraction, which not only afflicts them but becomes common and distributive to as many ports and places as are commanded by them. And yett the earnest desire the Dutch had to enforce your shipp *Dolphin* to anchor by them at her returneing from Goa invited them to moor there shipps as farr to the norwards as before they ridd to the southwards of Goa; whereby they gave the Portugalls a very faire opportunity, with helpe of a darke night, to steale a passage for a caravell which, the day before your shipp *Dolphin* left Goa, was by the V[ice] Roy &c. dispatched for there country [2]—the rediculous issue of there mountainous determinacion to lade home there monstrous carracke and galleon, which, being advanced to the usuall randevouz for embarquing of goods, are now retired and will in probabillity remaine for ever in there rotting residence. With this people in generall, according to Your Worshipps injunctions, wee labour by all convenient meanes to continuate our wonted freindly correspondence.' One result is an annual request for the convey-

---

[1] The *Dagh-Register*, 1643-44 (pp. 53, 227) mentions the loss of this vessel and the arrival of the two caravels at Goa. See also *Hague Transcripts* series i. vol. xiii. p. 425.
[2] *Hague Transcripts*, series i. vol. xiii. no. 410.

ance to Europe of Portuguese passengers; and two have now been allowed to embark on the *Discovery*. Find that some of the goods allotted to the ships have had to be left out and others substituted; refer to the invoices for details. Have been obliged to agree with Vīrjī Vōra to pay him $\frac{1}{16}$ per cent. higher interest than formerly. 'Your Worshipps in former missives from this Presidency have bin advised [see the 1637–41 *volume*, p. 122] that it was noe lesse necessary in respect of her selfe as becomeing the honor of our religion and nacion that the daughter of John Leechland should bee sent to her kindred in England; for which alsoe wee remember that her uncle, Mr. William Leechland, petitioned and obtained your consents; which though you were then pleased to grant, yett upon arriveall of your pleasures therein, her mother being with the daughter retired to Barroach and Brodera, and soe missing that yeares passage, nor one nor the other were after that time thought on, untill May or June last passed, when from the mother was presented a petition to your President and Councell for leave to marry her daughter unto one William Appelton, a taylor and attendance [*sic*] at Surratt; whereof wee had duely considered, though wee found it a new thing never before desired or granted, yett withall it was apprehended a necessary meanes to preserve her honor and honesty unteinted, which till then, though shee wanted not provocations enough from her mother to tempt her to prostitution, was almost miraculously preserved; besides which the remembrance of your former grant for her comeing to England in your shipps, and her uncles charitable inclination towards her, invited us to gratiffie her desires. Soe that they were by our minister, Mr. Andrew Baines, solemn[l]y married, and have since (susteined by the charitie of your servants) poorely yett honestly and decently subsisted. Yett there maine comforts depending on your favors and the hopes they have to bee releived by Mr. William Leechland and the hopes they have in a peticion directed to Your Worshipps emplored your consent that whatsoever shalbee found due to John Leechland upon his accompt of wagis, if not already otherwaies disposed off, may (as upon his death bedd hee desired) bee sent them, that soe, whether you please to license there returnes from, or continuance in, India, soe much may at least bee added towards their sustenance and future subsistance.' A number of lazy or incapable seamen have

THE ENGLISH FACTORIES 153

been sent home in these ships. On inquiry they find that Saker died while the *Crispiana* was at Masulipatam and left no estate. A missing bale of cinnamon to be inquired about. Writings entrusted to Fremlen for delivery to the Company. Dutch letters enclosed for transmission to Holland. List of jewels found among John Wylde's goods. (*Copy. 36 pp.*)

EXTRACTS FROM JOHN PROUD'S ACCOUNT OF THE HOMEWARD VOYAGE OF THE *DOLPHIN* (*O.C.* 1857 [1]).

1644, *January* 26. Went into the outer road [of Swally]. *January* 29. Sailed. *February* 20. Crossed the Line. It was decided by consultation to make for Mauritius, as the *Discovery* was getting short of water. *March* 9. Reached the shoals of ' Malha ' [*see* p. 109]. Then determined to stand to the northwards and eastwards. *March* 24. A strong gale forced the *Dolphin* to take down most of her sails. The *Discovery* was then a mile or two astern. As night came on, the storm increased in violence. *March* 25. Early in the morning it was found that they had four feet of water in the hold; and as ' our poore ship lay all downe upon the side and never seemed to ease herselfe ', it was decided to cut away the mainmast. Upon this she righted herself, but was still swept by the waves, and was only kept afloat by constant pumping and bailing. However, the violence of the wind now rapidly abated, though the sea was still very high, and the ship was leaking badly. *March* 28. They got up a jury mast. *March* 30. It was decided to make for Mauritius to refit and to meet the *Discovery*. *April* 2. Passed Rodriguez. *April* 5. Sighted Mauritius. *April* 6. Anchored there ' in the bay by us called Carpenters Bay and by the Dutch Peeter Butts Bay '. A few hours later they discovered the *Hopewell* riding in ' the N.Wt. harbor '.[2] (2¾ *pp.*)

---

[1] A second copy will be found in *O.C.* 1856, and a third among the *O.C. Duplicates.*

[2] The story is continued in *O.C.* 1856, which is a collection of papers forwarded to Bantam, dealing mainly with the perilous voyage of the *Hopewell* from that port to Mauritius, her meeting with the *Dolphin*, the measures taken to repair both vessels (with the aid of the Dutch), and their preparations for their departure for Madagascar. An interesting account is given of the Dutch settlement in Mauritius. Duplicates of some of the documents will be found under *O.C.* 1860, 1861, 1869, 1870, 1893.

FRANCIS DAY AND GEORGE TRAVELL AT FORT ST. GEORGE TO THE PRESIDENT AND COUNCIL AT BANTAM, JANUARY 28, 1644 (*O.C.* 1859).

Wrote last on October 4, by a Dutch conveyance. Letters from Masulipatam, dated November 18, intimated that the factors had been able to make but small investments, 'the Dutch abounding soe with meanes and haveing given out such great quantities to merchants and weavers that little or nothing is procurable there, they keepeing a strict watch over those whom they have soe preimployed that nothing can pass them.' As here the position is as bad or worse, it is feared that the returns for Bantam will fall far short of what was intended. 'How for to remedy these evells and others of that nature is past our skill. Nay, such a storme is prepareing for us that tis to bee feared will even whorle us from this coast. Our neighbours the Dutch have bine longe a projecting and now they have wrought it that Mollay, their merchant, is like to bee as powerfull with this King as the Serkayle is att Gulcundah; and, to ingratiate him throughly into his favour, they have assisted Mollay with men and gunns for the subdueing of castles of our Nague for the King, or rather their owne use; by which meanes our Nague is casherd and hee substituted, and is allso made his Treasurer and dus even in a manner command all. And tis very probable that hee will governe all the sea ports even to the very verges of Cealon; and what this may come to in a short time is noe hard matter to judge of.[1] Beleive itt, tis not for naught that the Dutch assist him in this manner, for their ayme is to have the sole trade of the coast; and if you doe not sett to the helping hand, and that suddenly, adue to all.' It is useless to appeal to England, for 'there hath binn so many complaints of this coast that all that goes from hence meets naught butt disrespectts, soe odious and deformed have our actions bin made.' This is 'an accusative age', and so much has been said

---

[1] A Dutch letter from Pulicat of rather later date (May 4, 1644, N. S.) says that Chinnana (Malaya) by lavish presents, amounting to about 80,000 pardaos, had regained the favour of the King and had been by him appointed governor of the district round Pulicat; but that, on fresh accusations being brought against him of conspiring with the Nāyak of Gingī, the King had since deprived him of his post and ordered him to be imprisoned (*Hague Transcripts*, series i. vol. xiv. no. 429; *Dagh-Register*, 1643-44, p. 291).

against the Coast factors by those who have thus sought to ingratiate themselves that the Company has been altogether disheartened, 'which hath occasioned these parts to bee soe neglected'. Refer to a letter received from home by the *Dolphin* (via Surat). 'Towoards the foote thereof is a passion of unmeritted egreadiences. Wee are to give accompt of our actions to you; wee desire to know wherein wee have offended to merritt such invectives (wee meane sence Clarke and Hudsons dayes), and doe willingly submitt to your doome.' It cannot be denied that they have forwarded their accounts annually, and that in these 'there is nomination of all our remaines; yett you complayne to Europe for want of returnes, and our masters of their large resendments and want of fruits, and are doubtfull that much thereof are converted to private uses, when for many years together those that have had the managery thereof have bine forst to putt in practice many dishonorable shifts for procurement of money to feede themselves, and most commonly for two thirds of each yeare they have bin soe necessitated.' This has been again and again represented, and it has also been pointed out that 'by occasion of our deepe ingagements, the interest thereof takes a quarter partt of the large resendments; then the charge of shipping, &c., tryming of old, rotten, leaky, unproffitable vessels, added to our other charges of presents, dyett, &c., which being congregated will appeare no dispiseable some.' Regret that 'there is such facillitie and delight in frameing and makeing complaints', but console themselves with the thought that such treatment is 'in a manner hereaditure to the Coast factors, for these many yeares never any from hence could give content'. It would be far better to lay aside disputes and consult how best to save the Coast trade from disaster. The Dutch are certainly aiming at a monopoly, there 'never being such possibillities as at present. For the Portugalls, they play least in sight; nay, tis to bee dubitated whether they will have any abideing place in these parts within this few months, for the Dutch gives itt out that they intend to take St. Thomay at the returne of their fleete from Goa. And as for the Danes, hee is in as bad or worse condition; and tis very probable wee may bee in the same predicament in a short time.' Suggest that the Bantam President should visit the Coast to examine into the state of affairs. If the Dutch succeed in securing control of the coast line from Pulicat to Ceylon, they will quickly oust the English from trade in the Golconda parts by outbidding them for piece-goods; 'for rather then they will faile in its performance, they will hazard the loss of one eye to putt out both ours. Wee have in a former clause made nomination of Mollay. Wee are sorry wee have occasion to treate of him farther. Some few daies sence hee made demande to have the govermentt of this place and all the profetts to himselfe; which is contrary to those cowles of the former King and our Nagues, for by those the goverment is given to us, with halfe its proffitt; which if wee should yeeld thereto, by surrendering our previledge, the towne would bee suddenly ruinated by the raiseing of the customes; for therein they [i.e. the Dutch] ground theire pollice to worke us the mischeife. But wee intend not soe easily to part with our emunities; and if hee shall any way mollest us, if opportunity presents for a retalliation, wee shall make the best use thereof.' Believe that they could soon frighten him, if they had a small armed vessel to lie in wait for some of his. As regards the proceedings of the Danes, 'the 20th September last arived in this road a couple of vessells from Tranggabar; one being the juncke they tooke formerly from the Moores in Bangalla, and in her the old President; the other, called the *Christianhaven*, arived lately from Europe with a particular commander, though dispeeded from Denmarke in company of the *Golden Sonne* some four yeares sence, haveing bin imployed in the Kings of Spaine service for a longe time and there disposed or rather spent all their carga[zoon] except 300 candy of lead and a few broadcloths.[1] The 23th they sett saile for Messulapatan, and within three or four daies after arivall there to Emaldee; where laying their jonke on ground to trymme, by a southerly wind she was made unservicable, her maine timbers giving way.[2] . . . The prime November the President arived here in a smale boate with some 16 or 17 white men; and that in good season, for itt began to blow fresh that nyght [to?] have indaingered a better vessell then his was. The 20th ditto hee sett sayle for Triggambarr. With him wee sent an English man to advise us of the Presidents proceedings and to press him to performance; for att his being heere hee made offer to us [of?] the

---

[1] See *Dagh-Register*, 1643-44, p. 281. The 'old President' was Barent Pessaert, for whom see the last volume, p. 44.
[2] *Hague Transcripts*, series i. vol. xiv. no. 427; *Dagh-Register*, 1643-44, p. 286.

benifitt of his port and his best industry for investing whatt wee should desire, and to imploye his owne money to the amount of four thousand ryalls of eight, provided hee might bee repaid sometime in January.' They advanced him 500 rials, and were very glad of his offer, as there was so little opportunity for investment either here or at Masulipatam. On December 19 Greenhill was dispeeded to Tranquebar 'in our jallia' [see p. 133], with 3,500 rials in money and coral to be invested against the arrival of the *Advice*. With him went Robert Wright, a merchant born at Bristol of good parentage, who has spent many years in foreign parts. He came here in the *Christianhaven*, having joined her at the Canaries on the strength of promises which have not been fulfilled. He was very sick at his arrival, but has since recovered. They recommend him for employment, especially as Day, Peniston, Greenhill, and others are determined to go home next year. The goods laden here on the pinnace *Advice* are good, if few in number. The deficiency is due to the late arrival of the *Hart*,' the greate and lasting quantities of raynes', and 'some hinderances of Mollayes'. Should the calicoes to be procured at Tranquebar prove satisfactory, they will endeavour to obtain a further supply. ' Wee shall now treat somewhatt of this fortt erectition [*sic*], which hath indured maney batteries (and groundless ones), and endeavor to putt a period to all such vaine and unproffitable attempts; which may with facillitie bee effected if the Worshipfull Presidentt would bee pleased to sett to his helping hand and reflex upon the Armagon prizes, compareing them with these of this place. Indeed, if hee pleases to undertake it (as wee are confidentt hee will, being zealous of our masters good) and advise thus much for Eu[rop]e, wee shall not doubt then of a thriveing issue. For t[hos]e sorts as wee here pay 7, 7½, and 8 pago[das] wee did there pay 10, day [*sic*. ? nay] 11, 12 pago[das], and soe accordingly. This wee neede nott insert or nominate, being they are soe well knowne to the President and the bookes are yett extant which acknowledges as much; which dus not a little comforte us when wee cogitate thereon, and hope by his meanes this place, the Coast, and factors may bee better esteemed with our masters; for at present their factors are weary of their unthankefull employment, and most of [them?] doe desire a releasement; for poverty with content is better then abundance with discontent.' The gunner of the *Hart* was to have made trial of the gunpowder produced here, but was prevented by the sudden departure of the ship; it is therefore suggested that this should be done at Bantam instead. Some of the powder now sent is finer than the last; but the price will be the same, and they have agreed with the maker 'to have itt all of that goodness'. Could supply a larger quantity, if furnished with casks. Advices from Surat. It seems that the *Expedition* had not then arrived there; but they hear from Masulipatam that she passed Goa in September last. 'The 8th current here happened a most unfortunate accident, made soe by the success and nott the intent . . . our serg[ean]t, Jeffery Broadford, being the unfortunate man and theame for this inlargement, by killing of one of these natives. Hee, haveing licence to lye at his house, found a man at a most unseasonable tyme hid there. Hee by accident finding of him hid soe, and in the darke seizing on him, and the other strugling for an escape, which the sargant doubting, drew out his knife (not haveing his sword about him) and cutt him over the arme, soe for to give him a marke for to discover and knowe him the next day. And indeed itt proved soe that the man was easily to bee found; for whatt with timerousness and neglect to have his blood stincht, hee proved a corpes. Wee, haveing notice of the disaster the next morning, and being dubious that our masters might suffer somewhat, first sent our chirurgeon to see whatt wounds; which was fruitless, for his parents had intered him early in the morning, being ashamed of the act (for such ware his words). And not onely then but [on?] a generall conventing of ourselves and the most substantiallest merchants and committees[1] of this place, the father did there confess that his sonn received a just guerdon for his offence; which was averd and confermed by the abovesaid marchants and committees that such was the law and custome of the country; of which the father hath given under his hand, and testified by the said merchants, &c. Notwithstanding, wee intended his [i.e. Broadford's] mission to you; and would soe, if wee could by any meanes have found in one weake and disordered company a fitt man to have seated in his office; but tis our unhappiness that wee are totally unprovided of such, as will allwaes bee in that manner soe longe as wee are to bee supplied by the discretion of masters of shipps. Wee have allready said that the

[1] Kōmati, a merchant: see the 1630–33 volume, p. 183.

success and not the intent made itt unfortunate; for itt tis confest una vose by the inhabitants of the towne that saw him eare his interring that hee had noe other wound but onely on the armes; which confirmes that there was noe intent to take his life.' Will defer action for a time, to see whether any further question will be raised; but they believe the matter will drop. On Greenhill's return, however, they will draw both a consultation and an attestation, and send them to Bantam; and meanwhile ' our gunner hath undertaken, body for body, that the serjant shall not make any escape.' If he be ordered to Bantam, some 'man of goverment' should be sent to take his place. The *Advice* left Masulipatam on January 13 and arrived here on the 27th. This day she sails again, and is to call at Tranquebar for the goods being provided there. The gunpowder mentioned in the invoice was refused admission to the ship, ' pretending much daingers in regard of iron hoopes'. The necessary adjustment will be made in the accounts. (*Copy.* 11 *pp.*)

PRESIDENT BRETON AND MESSRS. MERRY, THURSTON, AND FITCH AT SWALLY MARINE TO THE COMPANY, FEBRUARY [7[1]], 1644 (*O.C.* 1862).

This letter is entrusted to Duarte Fernandez, who is bound on the *Supply* for Gombroon, and thence overland to Venice. Fremlen sailed on January 29 with the *Dolphin* and *Discovery*, carrying cargoes amounting to 931,000 mahmūdīs. The *Hind, Supply*, and *Seaflower* have now been laden for Gombroon with freight goods, pepper, &c. The *Seaflower*, on her return, will be sent to Bantam to replace the *Expedition*; and the *Hind* will follow her next year. Forgot to mention in their previous letters that, ' whilest your late President was yet in place, it was thought no less then absolutely requisite that our nation and your servants (almost forgotten at this Kings court) should by a vallid present to himself and sonnes become better known; that thereby we might if possible acquire satisfaccion for Raja Chuttersals[2] and others debts long owing, and as long by other means in vain sought after; wherby we also hope to purchase unto you large immunities in matter of your customes

---
[1] The date is supplied from another copy preserved among the *O.C. Duplicates.*
[2] Rājā Chhatarsāl of Būndī: see the 1634-36 volume, p. xxvi, &c.

and rhawdaries [*rāhdārī*, a transit duty], as the Dutch did the passed year[1] by the same means, the King having graunted them his firmaen to this Governor and Customers that their goods shalbe cleared at the rates themselves pretend they cost in Agra, with addition of 20 per cent. for charges, on Ahmuda[bad] goods 10 per cent., and Brodra and Burroach goods as they cost in those places; wheras Your Worshipps pay upon Agra goods 40, Ahmuda[bad] 25, and upon Brodra and Burroach 12 per cent. more then their cost, besides their exactions, even upon their first cost also.' The presents given by the Dutch are detailed in the enclosed list [*missing*]. Those to be offered by the English consist of the following: to the King broadcloths, satins, 'bayes', a very large looking-glass, and two Arab horses, costing in all 5,555 rupees; to Prince 'Darasacore[2]' one Arab horse, broadcloths, satins, a 'cabinet and looking-glass', a case of barbers' instruments, and an embroidered 'sweet bagg', at a cost of 2,334 rupees; and to Prince 'Morad Bux[3]' broadcloths, velvets, and a young Arab colt, at a cost of 1,100 rupees. In addition to these it has been decided that 'Assalam Caun[4] (in whose hands is the whole management of the Court affaires) should be presented with somthing worthy his acceptance'; the details are left to Turner's discretion. 'Mirza Jam Cully Beag[5], lately Governor of this place, our exceeding good friend, being called by the King to officiate som office in court, left this place the 24th December last; and we embraced that opportunity to remit unto Agra under his convoy, recommended to his care, such things as were destined for presents; he having made us large and (we are confident) reall promises to be very helpfull to our Agra friends, not only in procuring acceptance of what sent but also of what in our letters to the King and Prince (sent also by him) we demand.' The result they hope to announce in their next letters. The *Seahorse* arrived from Bassein on January 19, and was thereupon

---

[1] For the mission of Cornelis Weijland to the Great Mogul in 1642 see *Dagh-Register*, 1641-42, p. 193, and 1643-44, p. 163; also *Corpus Diplomaticum*, p. 388.

[2] Dārā Shikoh, the eldest son of Shāh Jahān. He was Viceroy of Sind, and so his favour was particularly necessary (p. 163).

[3] Murād Bakhsh, fourth son of the Mogul.

[4] Islām Khān Mashhadi, the Wazir.

[5] According to the *Dagh-Register*, 1643-44 (p. 196) he was succeeded by Sharafuddīn Husain, who had previously been Kotwāl of Agra.

ordered to 'Scinda', to carry thither some tobacco and bring back 'cussumba' [*see* p. 136] for Achin and piece-goods for Basrā. The tobacco, however, could not be procured in time, and so her voyage has been countermanded, for fear she might be forced to winter there, as was the case with the *Diamond* in 1640. She will therefore be sent to Rājāpur for 'cussumba', which can be bought at Rāybāg very cheap and in large quantities. The *Francis* will not be dispatched to the Red Sea, as formerly intended, but will accompany the *Seahorse* to Basrā. *PS.*—A mistake found in the account of the pepper brought by the *Expedition*. (4½ *pp*. Received overland *February* 20, 1645.)

INSTRUCTIONS FROM THE PRESIDENT AND COUNCIL AT SURAT TO PETER HERBERT, PROCEEDING TO MOKHA, MARCH 23, 1644 (*O.C.* 1863).

Had intended to embark the goods consigned to Mokha on the Dutch ship *Valkenburg*, whose commander, 'Paul Crooque', had agreed to receive them on freight terms (as he had also done in the case of the goods of several native merchants); but now, at the last moment, a Dutch vessel having arrived from Vengurla with pepper, he has refused to take any freight goods at all. Have therefore arranged, 'upon easy fraught and ensurance'[1], to send them on the *Salāmatī*, belonging to 'Hodgee Zaud Beague' [Hājī Zāhid Beg]; and Herbert is to take his passage in her, accompanied by Thomas Cogan and a broker, Somajī Pārak, who has previously served him at Mokha. On arrival Herbert is to deliver to the Governor the letters and present provided; then he is to take a suitable house and endeavour to sell his goods. 'You cannot ignore the injustice and violence the passed yeare was used unto Robert Cranmer in Judda, when the Governor enforced from him 2,000 ryalls upon Mr. Wyldes death, to secure (as hee pretended) the Companies estate, which by his decease in Moha would have bin forfeited in Judda to those Sheriffs [Sharīfs]; of which injury Mr. Oxenden complained to the Moha Governor, desyring his lycense that hee might in satisfaction thereof make ceizure upon such vessels that

[1] A list of the goods thus sent will be found in *Factory Records, Egypt and Red Sea*, vol. i. They were insured at five per cent. of their value.

usually arrive from Judda to Moha; whereunto hee would not assent, but promised, both verbally and by his letter to the President, that restitution should be made; wherof you shall not onely put him in minde but with all befitting importunity sollicite the same; assureing him that, notwithstanding wee would not willingly displease him (from whom our nacion hath received many favours), yet in discharge of our duties wee nor may nor will omit the recovery of it by some other means the next ensueing yeare, if hee please not to redress our masters wrongs and remit by you unto us.' Herbert is, however, to settle the matter by fair means, if possible. Directions for the purchase of 'mirh Hobsee' [Arabic *Habashī*, 'Abyssinian'], olibanum, and aloes Socotrina. With these goods he is to return on the Dutch ship, if he can arrange suitable terms; if not, on a 'Moores junke'. A debt to be recovered from Mahmūd Husain. A 'faire and civill comportment amongst those people' is enjoined; also daily prayer. Warn him to be frugal in his expenses. *PS.*—A debt to be recovered from Mahmūd Zamān. As the Governor will require a large present on account of the ship, 'and that, as accustomary, must be raised upon her carga[zoon]', they have agreed to contribute 1½ per cent. on the value of the Company's goods, as rated in the Mokha customhouse. (*Copy.* 4 *pp.*)

PRESIDENT BRETON AND MESSRS. MERRY, THURSTON, AND FITCH AT SWALLY MARINE TO THE COMPANY, MARCH 26, 1644 (*O.C.* 1864).

Wrote last by the *Hind*, which, accompanied by the *Supply* and *Seaflower*, sailed on February 8 for Gombroon. A letter received from Agra states that the factors have already in hand 700 bales of indigo and do not doubt to make up the number to 1,000, as ordered. The presents sent from Surat for the King and the princes have been duly delivered; 'which hath found such favourable and fortunate acceptance that Mr. Turner advizeth that hee nothing doubts thereby to purchase the accomplishment of our desires. And Mirza Jam Cullebeag, from whom the President hath allso received a letter, affirmeth that the King hath allready remitted unto us the excess of customs which wee paid more then the Dutch, and that in all other our demands hee is very confident wee shall be gratifyed. The Prince Darashacore, to whom Tuttah belongeth, hath allso multiplyed promises of favors towards your servants and affaires in that place. So that wee are in good hopes to reap the fruits of those large summs in presents (wee hope seasonably) disboursed.' Some indigo already received from Agra (part of which is intended for Basrā) proves to be both pure and of a rich colour. A further quantity is on its way, together with a consignment of piece-goods, and has probably reached Broach. It was dispatched from Ahmadābād on March 12, 'having at Montella, 80 course from thence, escaped a most eminent danger in being assaulted by a nomber of Coolies[1], who gained from the conductours three laden carts, and were carrying them away, untill those to whom they were entrusted, resolved either to dye or redeeme them, pursued the theives, and with most incredible vallour so acted their parts that they recovered the carts without loss of any goods; in which conflict Ebraim [Ibrāhīm], the conductour, and six others were slaine and twelve dangerously wounded. Those able to travail accompany the goods hither (although they are not hyred farther then Ahmadavad) to receive a gratuity for their good service, which they have very well deserved.' At Tatta piece-goods have lately risen in price, owing to large investments for Basrā, but they are expected to be cheap again shortly, and it is not likely that there will be any difficulty in procuring the quantities wanted for England. 'Scandara[2]' and 'Derbella' recently furnished a supply of 'narrow joories extraordinary in goodness and resonably bought, but become deare by an excessive custom exacted at Multan, which wee nothing doubt but the Prince will remit unto us. Indico of those parts continueth scearce and deare, not any having bin sold (though mixt indico) under 55 rupees per maund of that place, which farr exceeds in price the round sort made in Ahmada[bad], although (we beleive) it doth not at all excell it in goodness.' Have therefore reduced their demand for Sind indigo to a few bales, unless Spiller, who is going in May to 'Sevestan', finds better encouragement there. At Ahmadābād indigo is far from plentiful, 'although of late much bettered in its making'. Tash estimates the production this year at

---

[1] Kolis: see the 1634-36 volume, pp. 257, 293.
[2] Elsewhere 'Ckandara'. Kandiāro, about eight miles north-east of Darbēlo, is apparently meant.

6,000 maunds, of which the local dyers will require one-sixth. The Dutch have bought 500 bales; and orders have been given to the English factors to secure 1,200 maunds 'of the round sort'. Half this quantity they have already purchased at $18\frac{7}{8}$ rupees per maund; the rest will be obtained later, unless Dutch competition forces them to take immediate action. 'Saltpeter we have this yeare enordered to be bought in Malpore[1] raw or unrefined, and so brought from thence to Ahmada[bad], where it shall be refined in your owne howse; by which means wee hope to render it better and much better cheap unto you then the passed yeare.' Piece-goods procured at Ahmadābād, and ' brown cloth ' in Agra. ' In Brodera, Burroach, and Nunsarree [Nosārī] you have not any of your servants constantly resident; yet the investment of narrow baftaes are by the brokers continued and, as quantities are gott togither, are viewed and received by some one appointed therunto; of which so many as wee can procure at present wee cause to be dyed for Achyn, where they are very vendible. They continue yet something deare, but will (wee conceive) now suddainly decline, the heat of buying being over and cottonwooll fallen from 10 and 12 to 4 and 5 ma[hmūdīs] per maund. These investments we intend to continue, in regard that (if your occasions want not them for England) Bantam, Bussora, and Achyn may thereby be accommodated.' The factors in Persia have been directed to inform the Company direct concerning the state of affairs in that country. As regards the Coast, the last letters received from Fort St. George were dated October 20, 1643, though letters from Masulipatam of January 24 enclosed a transcript of one from Madraspatam of November 24. From these they ' perceive the estate of your affaires to be much altered since the time your servants generall complaints were they could not procure goods for want of monies; who now cannot procure goods for monies, but are enforced to pay their debts with such as they had reserved for investments; the Dutch, who are provided ever, having upon all occasions furnished the artificers and thereby so obleiged them to them that they remain totally at their disposure.' The *Advice* left Masulipatam on January 13 with goods costing 4,588 pagodas. Cannot dispose of the coral remaining at Surat, as Vīrjī Vōra, ' our allmost onely merchant ', has a large stock on hand

[1] Mālpur, a small state in Mahī Kāntha, about fifty miles north-east of Ahmadābād.

and is unwilling to take more, unless at very low prices. Quantity to be sent in future; also of broadcloth. The tortoise-shells from Bantam 'are not yet cleared from the customhowse (so insufferable are their delaies)'; but they will vend readily when received. 'In November last, when newes arrived that the Dutch in the Streights of Mallacca had surprized Mr. Courtyns *Bona Esperance*, bound for China laden with Portugals goods (which the Portugals did not think they durst attempt), and that then they [i.e. the Portuguese] had no means left to drive that trade, being that from Europe there was no directions given for cessation of the differences twixt the Dutch and Portugals, which being likely to continue, your President (who hath ever minded his obligacion to Your Worships), being desyrous to tender you some fruits of his endeavours, adventured a few lines to the V[ice] Roy, presenting unto him the impossibility that the Portugals should at present benefit themselves by that trade, as allso the many services your shipping and servants have done that State, and desyred him that hee would pleas to gratify you in his license that a ship of yours might for your proper accompt, soly laden with your goods (without being obleiged to carry ought for himselfe or any other Portugals), voyage to Maccaw; whereunto hee readily gave his assent. Yet, being doubtfull what might be the event, it remained silenced until the V[ice] Royes reply returned; which was received but two daies before your late Presidents departure, who, being made acquainted with the business, approved thereof. Since when wee have unanimously resolved that the *Hind* shall undertake the employment, and carry with her in mony, druggs, &c. . . . to the amount of 45,000 rupees; which, with the profit the druggs may produce, we esteem a competency to relade her back with China ware and China roots, and other things such as may most conduce to your advantage; and for management of this affair Mr. William Thurston, John Stanford, Joseph Cross, and John Goodyear are appointed. In the next place wee shall acquaint Your Worships that a voyage [is?] designed to your pinnace *Seahorse* to which wee have as yet ben greater strangers then the former, the Maniellies [i.e. the Philippines], whither wee are invited by many fair hopes of rendering it unto you as profitable a trade in the future as it hath in former times ben unto the Portugals, who inriched themselves thereby; and if wee err not in our judgments, wee may have fairer oppertunities then ever the Portugals yet had, being at present the onely nation that may commerce with the Spaniards. The doubt will be whither or not they may be trusted; wherof wee have seriously considered, and cannot conceive any vallid reasons why a nation with whom wee have peace and amity, who are exceedingly distressed for want of such things as wee shall supply them with, should not give us respective and curteous enterteinment; whereof, if wee will give credit to a Portuguez, one Jos. de Brito, that hath lived long amongst the Spaniards in that place and the passed yeare arrived from thence, wee may be confidently assured. But that which hath chiefly wrought upon our resolutions to experiment that place and trade are the profits which may be raised upon all sorts of clothing, vizt. two, three, wee dare not say upon some four, for one, although wee have it many waies affirmed for a certain truth; nor is it unknown to some of your servants that in Macassier (the onely place from whence they are at present supplyed with cloth) at what deare rates they that buy there purchase it, and yet are exceeding great gainers in its revend. So that wee hope you will not be displeased if wee have thought fit to venture a little, in hopes to gain unto you much; being resolved (as preintimated) to send the *Seahorse* thither with a carga[zoon] which may import 50,000 rupees, of severall sorts of clothing.' . . . And for disposure of this affaire wee have designed Edward Pearce, Thomas Breton, Thomas Reynardson, and John Mantell; and for their assistance have enterteined the forementioned Portuguez (or rather meistizo [half caste]) Jos. de Brito (whose family lives in Goa), of whom wee have received a very faire character, yet shall not credit him fur[ther] then reason directeth. In these our intended designes wee find all obstackles almost vanquished, only the Dutches discurtesies, which wee may expect to meet with in the Streights of Mallacca; where, however, we beleive they will not dare to molest your ships navigating, whilest for ought we know the seas ought to be as open for them as theirs. However, such fears must not deterr us from exerciseing our duties; nor would you, we beleive, that they should make us desist from prosecuting these designes, so long as we shall be carefull not to give them any advantage against us, by shipping either amunition or provisions. . . . Your seamen (at least those in these parts) being altogither strangers to the forementioned voyages, we were not a little perplexed where to be provided of an able pylott; when one [*blank*] tendered his service, a man that hath spent 30 yeares in those seaes and exhibited pregnant testimonies of his abillities in that profession, besides divers certificates hee hath of very good service done both the Portugals and the Spaniards in pilotting their galleons; him wee have enterteined at 800 rupees for the voyage; who obleigeth himselfe to harbour the *Seahorse* first in the Maneilles, and so proceed in the *Hind* for China.' The *Seahorse* sailed on February 14 for Rājāpur and Goa. At the former place she is to land a broker, who is to go up to Rāybāg to purchase 'cussumba' for Achin and 'uploat[1]' for China. She is then to proceed to Goa, carrying Thomas Breton (who was there recently with Thurston) to bring away such writings as are expected from the Viceroy and buy some cairo. [*Here two or more pages are missing.*] On the 19th [March?] arrived the Dutch *Waterhond* from Taiwan [Formosa]. She has landed 153 chests of silver of 2,500 rupees each, 40,000 rials, and some alum and china ware; but the bulk of her cargo is still on board and is destined for Persia, whither she is to sail immediately. She was convoyed up the coast by the *Hemskerk*, which touched at Vengurla and brought thence a quantity of pepper, which has been transhipped into the *Valkenburg*. The latter sailed on the 24th for Mokha; while the *Hemskerk* is to return to Goa with some piece-goods. 'Wee understand they have lost two ships in China: the *Flying Hart*, which perrished in a storm near Tywan, and the *Weedens*, which, being admirall of three ships, was fyred in fight with 60 and odd gallies on the coast of Cochyn China; in which the *Waterhound* was allso engaged and with much difficulty escaped. . . . The Dutch are very vi[o]lent in prosecution of the warr against the Portugalls in those parts, especially upon Ceiloan, where lately arrived a fleet of 16 sailes, which brought with them and landed 2,000 men, who have bin encountred by the Portugalls, but [we] cannot hear the Dutch boast of any great victory; yet they pretend the Portugalls had the worst of the day. However, they find them so strong that they despair of obteining their ends in gaining Columba; which they no

---

[1] Gujarāti *upaleṭa*, the fragrant root (*costus*) which forms the basis of the Chinese josssticks. It is also known as *puchok*; see the 1630–33 volume, p. 161.

sooner approached but were enforced to retire, finding it (as themselves say) too hott service for their undertaking.' As regards 'the Courtinians', their ship *William*, under Captain Blackman, was at Diu early in February, trying in vain to dispose of English commodities. 'From thence hee returned to Rajapore, very sick (as we heare) of his Indian employment.' Their *Bona Speranza* has been confiscated by the Dutch, and now forms part of the fleet employed at Ceylon. *PS.*—Received last evening from Madraspatam transcript of a letter sent thence to Bantam by the *Advice*, dated January 28 [*see* p. 154]. This is now enclosed. (10 *pp.*)

INSTRUCTIONS FROM PRESIDENT BRETON AND COUNCIL TO ROBERT CRANMER AND OTHERS, PROCEEDING TO BASRĀ, MARCH 26, 1644 (*O.C.* 1865).[1]

Although totally unacquainted with Basrā, Cranmer is appointed to the direction of a venture thither, on the strength of his nine years' experience in the Company's service, particularly at Mokha and Jiddah, where he has acquired 'the Arabian languadge'. He is to be assisted by John Rymell, Nicholas Buckeridge, and 'our broaker Sunker' [Sankar]. The goods provided have more than filled the *Francis*; and, as the *Seahorse* is now designed for another employment, it has been decided to embark the surplus in the *Salāmatī*, a pinnace recently bought of Duarte Fernandez [Correa] by 'Asavora' [Āsā Vōra], and 'fitted after the Christian manner'. After unlading her cargo at Basrā, the *Francis* is to be sent back to Gombroon to fetch thence some pepper and gum-lac intended for the former place but sent to the latter in the *Hind*, *Supply*, and *Seaflower*, which sailed on February 8. On arrival at their destination the factors should present 'our letters' to the Bāshā and Shāhbandar, and take a suitable house, preferably that occupied by Mr. Pearce 'at his last being there'. In disposing of their goods they should not 'refuse the first marketts, which commonly proves the best'. Their departure should not be delayed beyond December 15. Any small quantity of goods remaining may be entrusted to 'Moha Naran' [Mohan Nārāyan], the broker's kinsman; but if the quantity be large, they should leave the broker

---

[1] There is a second copy among the *O.C. Duplicates.*

himself behind to dispose of them. On quitting Basrā, Cherry, the master of the *Francis*, has directions to call at Gombroon for letters &c., and then proceed to 'Scinda', to embark whatever commodities Spiller and the other factors have provided. Goods may be accepted on freight from Basrā to that port. While at Basrā Cranmer and his associates must be careful to treat the people there 'courteously and respectively'; and they must not neglect their religious duties. Fresh meat to be provided for the crew of the *Francis*, 'according to custome', during their stay in port. In their own expenses the factors are not to 'exceede modesty and reason'. *PS.*—Of the accompanying packets, one should be dispatched to the Company via Aleppo immediately on arrival at Basrā, and the other six or eight weeks later. With each the factors should send advice of the state of their business. Goods to be sold on behalf of 'Mirza Arrab, our Customer' [*see* p. 23], and 'Myr Mahmud Amy [Mīr Muhammad Amīn]'. (*Copy.* 4¾ *pp.*)

WILLIAM PITT AT GOMBROON TO THE COMPANY, MARCH 27, 1644 (*O.C.* 1867).

About 612 tūmāns received last year as the English share of the customs at Gombroon. Adler and others proceeded to Ispahān on April 29, 1643, arriving May 29. They experienced great difficulty in selling their broadcloth, owing to its poor condition and want of variety. Part, belonging to the First General Voyage, is still remaining there under the charge of Thomas Codrington. While at Ispahān Pitt and his colleagues vainly attempted to procure a confirmation of the four farmāns obtained from the late King, especially those that permitted the English to keep a guard at the Gombroon customhouse and freed them from paying the usual duty of one per cent. at the sale of their goods. They were told by the Itimād-uddaula that the former privilege would only lead to disputes with the King's soldiers, and moreover was unnecessary, as order would be given that the English should not be defrauded of their share of the customs; while the duty of one per cent. would not be remitted, 'by reason (as hee said) this kingdome is not enriched by us, whereas formerlie wee bought the Kings silke [and?] such priviledges were allowed us; to which wee replied wee knew hee had heard of the distraction our kingdome was in, and that that comoditie was become of disesteem in Europe.' Thereupon, he promised to do something for them later; but such privileges are not to be gained except by giving large presents, and then they can only be maintained by further donations, both at court and at Gombroon. The factors left Ispahān on November 21 and arrived here on December 14. The *Seahorse* and the *Seaflower* had recently visited the port. Advice as to the colours of broadcloth suitable for Persia. Arrival of the *Hind*, *Supply*, and *Seaflower* on [March] 3. The Shāhbandar did not appear until the 16th. He pretended that he was delayed by much business, but probably his object was to defraud the Company of its dues, as in the interval many goods were carried away without paying customs. The accounts of the First General Voyage will be closed as directed, and the books sent home. Some goods suitable for presents should be sent, since a yearly visit to court is necessary. Debts of Merry and Willoughby. No money will be taken up at interest. The three bales of 'baies' are unsaleable here and will be sent to Basrā. 'The Dutch comaundor, Charles Constant, hath caryed himselfe soe imperious at court that the conceipt of his greate power and commaund hath almost made him loose himselfe, insomuch that hee hath bin infinitelie slighted by the King and Ettamen Dowlett [Itimad-uddaula] at the solliciting his Company affaires, beeing commaunded (as said) by his Generall to acquaint Ettamen Dowlett of their forces and that, if they had not kind useage, they would ruinate this bundar [port]; which in fine cost them greate presents, with submission, before their peace could bee made. Besides, they paid 900 tem[aun]ds custome for passed yeares, and forced to take 200 loades of silke at 50 tem[aun]ds per load. Few daies before this contract was made, the comaundor without license would have departed Spahaun. The daie appointed, his acquainteance (amongst the rest Phillip Wyld) came to bring him out of towne. Hee was stopped in the streete by Ettamen Dowletts commaund and desired by faire meanes to retourne to his house; in fine, by promises to those officers, was suffred to proceed till hee came out of towne about a mile; afterwards pursued by horsemen, that did not onelie bring backe but drubbe him &c. Dutch before hee was censeable of his disgrace; afterwards forced him into his house, and there certaine dayes was a strict watch kept within his house by Ettamen Dowlett his commaund. This proud comaundore persists to doe us all the disgrace lieth in his power, as Ettamen Dowlett informeth us; who at his first arrivall reported that our King and country was nothing in respect to theirs, and that, whereas formerlie wee were something strong, now altogeither become poore and weake, haveing not shippeing or ought elce to subsist the continuance of trade. William Pitt answered that, although they had falce and disgracefully abused us, wee scorned to relate anie thing of them, more then that His Majesties embassadours [1] (wee made noe quaestion) had informed the truth of all things, and therefore desired hee would bee refferred unto their relacion. This answer pleased Ettamen Dowlett soe well that hee presentlie rayled against the Dutch, sayeing it was alwaies their custome to abuse us secretlie, and that wee had alwaies honour and respect from his King for takeing Ormus.' Further purchases of silk by the Dutch. *PS.*[2] (*May* 15)—The foregoing is copy of a letter sent overland by Duarte Fernandez [Correa], who left Gombroon on March 30 for Ispahān and Aleppo. The Shāhbandar has not yet accounted to them for the English share of the customs this year; but they have received on account 300 tūmāns. (6 *pp.*)

THE COMPANY TO THE PRESIDENT AND COUNCIL AT SURAT, MARCH 29, 1644 (*Factory Records, Miscellaneous*, vol. xii. p. 117).

Forward a transcript of their previous letter [*see* p. 121], sent by the *Endeavour.* Owing to 'being here at home in disturbance and troubles amongst ourselves and most forraigne states in little better condition, the marketts in all places are much declined and commodities much fallen in their wonted prize and reputation'; and so they hardly know what to do. They are desirous, however, that 'the trade may be continued and not be lost; and also that the use and sales of commodities from India, as indicoes, callicoes, &c., with all kind of druggs may not be here out of request or sought from forraigne parts, as it would come to passe if wee should lay downe this our Indian trade. Wee have therefore taken this

[1] The reference is to Persian ambassadors, of whom several had visited England or Holland.
[2] Signed also by Philip Wylde.

resolucion yet further to prosecute this trade of India, that it may not fall to the ground; and although wee have not wanted oppositions and discouragements enough, both here at home by those that have and others that now would presse to be interlopers into our trade, with whome wee have had noe small contest.' Continuing the previous letter, they are glad to announce that the turmeric has now been sold, though the Roman vitriol has not yet found a customer. Trust that the account of the Third Joint Stock has been closed, and that satisfaction has been obtained for the losses in Persia on account of shortage of silk and the Gombroon customs. Sanction is given to the return of Adler, Hall, and Wheeler; and also to the re-engagement of Codrington at an increased salary. Cannot approve the use of force to obtain redress for the wrongs received at Gombroon, as to do so would be to hazard the trade; nor would it be safe to force the merchants resorting thither to pay the English share of the customs aboard their junks. The sorts and quantities of India goods desired for England have been sufficiently advised in the previous letter; but special care is enjoined regarding the quality of all goods returned. Defects in those last received. Some of the calicoes pilfered. Note with regret the disputes between Surat and Bantam, but hope that, now both Presidents have been changed, the differences will cease. Knipe's success on the Malabar Coast in the previous voyage has induced them to engage him again, and to instruct him to go in the *John* to that Coast on his way to Surat. The stock sent in that vessel and the *Crispiana* is not so large as was hoped, for lead is not to be had at a reasonable rate, owing to 'the stopp of that commodity in coming from the mines in Darbyshire'; broadcloth and other woollen manufactures are likewise scarce; while money, 'the life of trade', is hard to get. Would gladly have extinguished the debt at Surat; but 'the aversenes of the tymes' will not permit of this, and so they must put up with the loss caused by 'that devouring canker of interest'. Note the goods exchanged between Surat and Bantam; and trust that the *Expedition* has been sent back to the latter port and the *Discovery* dispeeded for England. The voyage of the *Hopewell* was so arranged as to give the factors on the Coromandel Coast all the time they said was necessary to provide piece-goods of satisfactory quality and at reasonable rates; if, therefore, they now fail, no credence will be given to their letters in future. In spite of the supplies sent to that coast from Bantam, Surat, and England, 'wee have not in the space of five yeares received but only one bale of thinn long cloth (which came by your conveighance), although wee have yeerly desired some for the keping of that clothing in use and to make it further desired here; but hetherto our labours and desires have bin prolonged with delayes, and the monies (wee fear) imployed in those new fortifications, of which charge wee would willingly have the certaine knowledge.' Note the employment of the *Hopewell* to Persia. Will not dissuade Fremlen from returning, as he wishes to do so, though they would have been glad to see him retain his post for a longer period. Approve Breton's succession as President, and trust that his ability and honesty will give cause 'to ranke him in our estimations with his predicessors'. Merry will doubtless prove 'a fitting man to be second in Surratt'. In response to their demand for small shipping, a vessel called the *Endeavour* has been built and dispatched to the Coast on her way to Surat. 'For our Persian affaires, wee must leave them unto you.' Bornford has arrived, but no explanation can be got from him regarding the three bales of earth found among the Lahore indigo. Fresh complaints have been received of the bad quality of that consignment and, unless more care is taken in future, 'indico will find but cold enterteynement here'. 'Wee see that fraighted ships are neither wellcome unto you nor here much acceptable unto us; but wee could not well avoyd the making triall of some without aspertions which would have bin cast upon us; which being now done, wee shall hereafter make use of our owne, which are cheaper unto us then fraited shipps.' Drugs and surgical instruments sent; also two pipes of Canary wine and two butts of strong beer. Regret the indebtedness at Surat; 'if it shall please God once to send us better times and a setled reiglement in our East India affaires, to keepe out all interlopers from frequenting those parts, wee [will] then (God willing) use our best endeavours to have you double stockt, that you may take all opportunities to make use of the best and most profitable marketts.' The letters from the Viceroy and others were duly delivered to the Portuguese Ambassador. 'And concerning the peace formerly made there betweene the Conde de Linharrees and Mr. Methwold, wee for our parts are resolved to continue that league still, and wee doe injoyne unto you the observacion thereof, since the Portugalls themselves are so willing thereunto. Therefore make use of that treaty; but be as cautious to keepe yourselves and our estates from danger as you may.' The diamond ring entrusted to Knipe has been duly delivered. Wonder that the rials should be found 'short in tale', and suspect some trickery on the part of the shroffs. 'Our casheires here doe avouch that the rialls went from hence in their full numbers; for they do not only tell them twise over but doe exactly waigh over every parcell, so that by this meanes none can be wanting but the scale would discover the same.' The factors ought themselves to 'tell them out', and not trust to others. The complaints of want of weight and of the coarseness of silver are also evidently 'abuses which your monychangers put upon you', to gain some abatement. The money now sent must be well looked to, for 'if the times should continue as now they are, wee know not how to furnish you with rialls or silver almost att any rate.' The cause of the want of sale of the broadcloth was not so much its coarseness as the competition of that brought by private traders; and the names of the latter ought to have been furnished, in order that the Company might call them to account, since the factors will not do so. However, a smaller quantity of broadcloth is now forwarded, so as not to 'oppresse' the market. As the 'grezio' coral is principally in demand, they will take care to send most of that sort in future. The present stock is intended chiefly for Knipe to sell on the Malabar Coast. Remarks on the other goods sent. Approve the measures taken to employ the smaller shipping. Regret the mortality among the factors. Note that three young men were taken ashore from the *Crispiana* to supply the vacancies. Do not object to Pynn, who was a purser's mate; but cannot see that John Mantell, who was only an attendant, and Richard Clark, one of the gunner's crew at 14$s.$ a month, can be fit for such employment; besides, the Company have no security for their good behaviour. Forbear, therefore, to sanction any wages for them until a report is made of their 'faculties' and security given. No thanks are due to those who employed them, as it is feared that this was done 'for favour more then ability'. Again acknowledge the receipt overland of the Surat letter of March 20, 1643. The ships now sent are the *Crispiana*, with William Bayley as master, and the *John*, under John Mucknell. The arrangements for their voyage detailed. Account of the cargoes of the two ships, amounting to 54,982*l*. 12*s*. 3*d*., including 46,635*l*. 12*s*. 10*d*. in silver, and 6,836*l*. 17*s*. in coral. The following factors come in them:— Edward Knipe at 200*l*. per annum; Henry Garry, a bred merchant and skilful in accounts and languages, engaged for seven years at a salary of 40*l*., with 10*l*. increase yearly; John Burnell, entertained for a like period at 30*l*.; Henry Hunt, at 13*l*. 6*s*. 8*d*.; Richard Davidge, experienced in the linen trade, both here and in France, and now engaged for six years, at 70*l*., with 10*l*. a year increase; Hugh Fenn, 'a Hamborough [Hamburg] merchant', for seven years at the same rate; Thomas Andrews, for seven years at a uniform salary of 30*l*.; John Lewis, at 30*l*. for each of the first five years and then 40*l*. and 50*l*. for the other two; Gilbert Harrison, at 20*l*. for the first five years, and then 30*l*. and 40*l*.; and Joshua Blackwell, on the same terms as Harrison. 'Their severall rankings and imployments' are left to the President and Council. As regards shipping to be sent back, 'wee desire but one shipp to be retourned us yeerly, for these reasons: first, because wee had rather have small retournes and a stock left in the country to bee profittably imployed and take off all interest then to have large retournes and remaine indebted; secondly, aboundance of East India commodities make them disesteemed and undervalued; thirdly, our marketts here being dead and quantity of East India goods coming will make them be sold farre under valew.' Presume that the *Discovery* was dispatched for England about the beginning of this year. Possibly the *Dolphin* accompanied her; but if not, she must be the ship to come home this time, and the *Crispiana* and *John* must both be employed in the East, though the former vessel should not 'winter out if it may be otherwise disposed.' Goods to be sent home in this year's ship. Of saltpetre 20 or 25 tons should be included 'for kintlage'; but it must be well refined, and this should be done 'wher it is bought, be [it] in Agra or Amadavad, for in Surratt wee understand there is noe peterhowse.' Of the silver now forwarded, the Spanish rials of eight are worth 5*s*. per ounce; the ducatoons, 5*s*. 4*d*. each or 5*s*. 1$\frac{2}{5}$*d*. per ounce;

the 'crosse dollers' [*see the* 1634–36 *volume*, p. 225], 4s. 3d. each or 4s. 9d. per ounce; and the silver bars cost 5s. 4¼d. per ounce. Piece-goods to be supplied to Bantam. 'The trouble hath bin extrordinary which wee have had in attending the Parliament to oppose Mr. Corteene and others with Captaine Bond from going for India and planting att Madagascar; and the busines is not yet concluded, and therfore wee may doubt that in the interim of this dispute their ships now ready may slip away on their intended designes. The ships are five in number, vizt. the *Sunne*, *Hester*, *James*, *Thomas and John*, and the *Loyalty*. The three former are said to be under Capt. Bonds command, to erect a new commonwealth in Madagascar, and therfore they shall export men, women, &c., and wee know not what. The two latter are said to be fore Mr. Curteenes accompt and commanded by one [ ] Earle and John Durston. These two are cleared in our custome house and not one pennyworth of marchandize or monies, but victualls with pouder and shott. These and the former have such a crew in them that, although they pretend planting and marchandizing, yet wee feare they intend to fly at all, if they can meet with good game, either on the coast of India or in the Reed Sea, where best purchase may be had. And to these wee may [add] that wee [are] informed that there is a French shipp of Dieeppe gone also that way. Wee suppose you know her errand and what marketts shee will make, if she can meet with chapmen accordingly. It will be therfore fitt that you should send a ship to the Reed Sea for trade, to waite upon those marchants, least they shall take more then ever they intend to pay for; and also to give notice to the marchants of your towne and others thereabout residing, that if their men and vessells and goods be mett withall, let them take notice from you who are the most likeliest to be the actors.' Urge a further effort to recover the money due on Sir Francis Crane's tapestry. Wine sent on the *John* for sale. Knipe has in his custody a bundle of letters for the Viceroy and others, received from the Portuguese Ambassador. The remains of the First General Voyage to be cleared. Have considered Merry's letter of January 17, 1643, and are willing to accept the proceeds of his rhubarb in part payment of his debt. He must, however, pay the remainder, together with interest, and they regret that he should set so ill an example. (*Copy.* .32½ *pp.*)

INSTRUCTIONS FROM THE COMPANY TO EDWARD KNIPE AND HENRY GARRY, APRIL 1, 1644 (*Factory Records, Miscellaneous*, vol. xii. p. 111).

Garry is joined with Knipe to help him and to take charge in case of his death. Have also sent in this ship (the *John*) as assistants John Burnell, a bred merchant, and Henry Hunt, a young man of not much experience. An account of the voyage to be kept. Private trade to be suppressed, and any found aboard to be seized. After leaving Madagascar, if there is time, they may call at Mozambique to trade, and then proceed to the Comoros. They are next to sail to the Malabar Coast, and sell their coral, &c. in any port between Cape Comorin and Surat, investing the proceeds in cinnamon, pepper, cardamoms, or other suitable commodities. Certain butts of wine to be sold for the benefit of the owners and the money to be paid into the Company's cash at Surat.[1] Care must be taken to reach that port by December 10 at the latest. No Roman vitriol should be bought. On arrival at Surat an account of their proceedings is to be given to the President and Council; their commission is to be surrendered; and Knipe is to take up his employment there according to agreement. The extra provisions put on board are not to be riotously consumed, as they are intended 'for the gratifying of freinds and for intertaynement of such of the cheife of the Portugalls as may come abord.' Any remainder is to be given up at Surat. (*Copy.* 6 *pp.*)

[EDWARD KNIPE] ABOARD THE *JOHN*[2] TO THE COMPANY, APRIL 18, 1644 (*Factory Records, Miscellaneous*, vol. xii. p. 109).

They sailed from Dover Roads on April 6, in company with the *Crispiana* and *Blessing*, and forty other ships. In 48° they met with stormy weather, in which the *John* behaved very well. As the slow sailing of the *Blessing* much hindered the other two, a consultation was called, at which it was decided 'when once past the Canaries if betwixt this and then the *Blessing* mend not her pace, to bid her

---
[1] This was a private venture of some of the Committees: see the Court Minutes of February 16, 21, and 23, 1644.
[2] They were then in lat. 37° N., i.e. near the Azores.

company adieu and betake ourselves to the perfection of our voyadge.' (*Copy.* 1¾ *pp*)

EDWARD KNIPE TO RICHARD SWINGLEHURST, SECRETARY TO THE COMPANY [APRIL 18, 1644][1] (*Factory Records, Miscellaneous*, vol. xii. p. 85).

Entreats him to believe that he is not ungrateful for past favours, and declares his intention of procuring for him the goods Swinglehurst has desired a third party to obtain for him at Cochin. Forgot to acquaint him with an incident which occurred during his last voyage, and which may possibly be brought up in his absence by letters from Surat. This happened at Goa, where Knipe employed a Portuguese named 'Lewis Robeiro' to buy for him a parcel of bezoar. Robeiro cheated him therein to the extent of about 300 pardaos; and so, when he came aboard to buy coral, Knipe taxed him with his deceit, with the result that he gave him 'a diamond ring off his finger in recompence'. Knipe then sold him part of the Company's coral at nearly 100 per cent. profit, taking bills on Cochin for the amount. 'At my coming to Surrat he had writt to the President that I had cheated him in five chests of corrall, by which hee was like to lose 1,300 pardos, and besides I carried away a ring of his he gave me in earnest for the corroll, worth 400 pardos.' Both statements were absolutely false. Mr. Millet can prove that Robeiro examined the coral closely before he bought it; while the contention that the ring was given 'in earnest', when the whole transaction was concluded within two hours, is absurd. Possibly Robeiro hoped to induce Knipe to do him a courtesy in the price to be paid for the coral; if so, 'I thinke I did him a sufficient one'. Commendations to Mr. and Mrs. Tomlins[2]. Should Thurston bring home any sweetmeats on Knipe's account, Tomlins is authorized to 'distribute them equally betwixt his wife and mine.' (*Copy.* 2¾ *pp*.)

---

[1] No indication is given of when or where this letter was written; but internal evidence suggests that it was penned on board the *John* at the same date as the letter to the Company.

[2] Thomas Tomlins had been purser in the *Crispiana*. In 1646 he became Clerk of Blackwall Yard.

THE SAME TO WILLIAM METHWOLD [APRIL 18, 1644]¹ (*Ibid.*, p. 88).

Regrets that he did not see Methwold before leaving London, and assures him of his deep gratitude for the many favours he has received from him. (*Copy.* 1 *p.*)

THE VOYAGE OF THE *HIND* FROM SWALLY TO MACAO AND BACK ² (*Marine Records*, vol. lxvi).

1644, *April* 26. Sailed. *May* 2. Anchored at Goa. *May* 5. Set sail; and in going out met the *Supply* and *Seahorse*. Between five and six o'clock at night they overtook a great junk. 'Shee tould us that shee beelonged to Cananore and cam from the Red Sea. Shee lowered all her sayles amayn. Mr. Lee sent his boot aboord and tooke two or three men from them. Next went our boote aboord of her; and beeing there, it seemed som of our men offered them som violenc, which made the Malabares to ryse up in armes and chaced our men overboord and killed on man out right and 5 or 6 men they wonded. Imediatly they hoysed up theyr sayles and thought to run away; but wee could keepe them way. Wee shot divers shot to them from the three shipes. At length wee shot her mayne yard in two. Wee kep by her all that night, and the next morning shee ran ashore into a sandy bay caled Colio; but the men ran ashore (but three or four). Wee went aboord of her with our bootes and had som moneyes; and finding her halfe full of water wee set her afier.' *May* 23. The *Supply* parted company for Achin. *June* 13. Anchored off 'Poolagare³', and procured wood and water. Sailed again. *June* 16. Two Dutch ships met them and accompanied them to Malacca.⁴ *June* 18. Anchored in that port. 'Our marchantes had good quarter. The Governour sent a bote aboord to take in our empty caske to fill them with water. Moreover, hee sent us beeves and duckes and henes; but provigon is very deere heere.' *June* 21. The ships departed. *June* 27. Got clear of the

¹ Undated, but apparently written at the same time as the foregoing.
² A journal kept by Richard Matthews. It contains a number of rough sketches of the coast and islands passed.
³ Pulo Jarak, in the middle of the Malacca Strait, and not far from the Sembilan Islands.
⁴ See the *Dagh-Register*, 1643-44, p. 127.

Straits of Singapore. *July* 1. Anchored at 'Poolatimong[1]', where some provisions and water were procured. *July* 3. Sailed. *July* 16. Saw the island of 'Mindoro' [one of the Philippines]. *July* 20. The *Seahorse* departed for Manilla. *August* 4. Met a boat with Chinamen, who agreed to pilot the ship to Macao. *August* 7. Anchored at Macao. ' Mr. Blakeman[2] cam aboord of us and towld us that hee had good quarter. The sam day in the afternoone our marchantes went ashore and spoke with the Governour and weere kindly entertayned.' *August* 8. Oxen and hogs were sent on board. *August* 12. Weighed and 'went beetweene the ilands of Don John to winter.' Courteen's *William* was then riding there. The *Hind* was now unladen, hauled ashore, and repaired. *September* 10. She was got afloat again. *October* 31. The *William* departed from Macao. *November* 4. The *Hind* returned to Macao. *November* 19. She sailed. *November* 27. Saw ' Poolacondore[3] '. *December* 1. Anchored at ' Poolatimong'. *December* 12. A 'proo' brought a note aboard from Mr. Tyndall, apprising them that the *Seahorse* was at anchor off the NW. part of the island. *December* 13. She joined the *Hind*. *December* 15. Both ships departed. *December* 17. Entered ' the new straytes' [of Singapore]. *December* 20. Anchored off Malacca. *December* 21. Departed, but were stopped by four Dutch ships and induced to return. *December* 22. Anchored at Malacca again. Mr. Thurston went ashore to speak with the Governor. *December* 25. The merchants, &c. came on board and the ships sailed. 1645, *January* 5. Passed ' the iland of Nicobar '. *January* 12. Saw Ceylon. *January* 13. Passed Point de Galle. A boat from the Dutch fort brought a message that there were three English merchants on shore, ' but wee gave noe great credit to them'. *January* 20. Passed Colombo. *January* 24. Sighted Cape Comorin. *January* 30. Passed Cochin. *February* 1. Saw ' the rocke caled the Sacrificing Rocke[4] '. *February* 6. Met a Dutch ship from Surat, which gave the intelligence ' that this yeeare was com from England seven shipes '. (*The journal ends abruptly on February* 8. 40 *pp.*)

[1] Pulo Tioman, off the south-east coast of the Malay Peninsula.
[2] Blackman, the commander of Courteen's ship, the *William*.
[3] Pulo Condore, off the Mekong estuary in Cochin China. The East India Company established a settlement there in 1702, but the settlers were massacred three years later.
[4] Still called Sacrifice Rock. It is twenty miles north-west of Calicut. See the references to it by Fryer and Hamilton.

ANOTHER ACCOUNT (*Marine Records*, vol. lxv. p. 61).

1644, *April* 26. Departed from Swally Hole. *May* 2. Anchored off Goa. *May* 5. Departed, and were joined by the *Seahorse* and *Supply*. Chased a great Malabar junk. 'Presently wee sent our longboat aboard of hir with 27 men in her, whereof they wounded and killed one out right, he being a quartermaster named Charles Scott. All this tyme our longboat lying closs by their side, we tumbled one atop of another, they cuting our men worst of all going over the side, they pressed out soe thick on us, they being in number neare upon two hundred. All the tyme we lay by the jouncks side they hove over great stones and bruised sum of our men, but not very much. At length we got of and got aboard of the *Supply*; and then our ship edging to them we plyed our great ordnance upon them all night, they shouting but litle at the *Suply* or *Seahorse*, but only at us; we still following them, she stering away NE. into the shore.' *May* 6. 'This morning our boat came from the *Suply* with all our men (save four very much wounded). We tacked and stood after her, she standing into a bay caled Dewua, sum 12 lea. to the southward of Goa. . . . In this bay she run aground betwene eight and nine in the morning, and we stood in after her. . . . Wee presently maned boeth our boats, and the *Suply* and *Seahorse* maned there boats, and clapped her aboard. And there were sum five Malibars, besids the master of the vessell, and they shot at our boats; but our men entred and killed them; at the which tyme our longboat, lying by the side, was sunck; the which we lost. . . . Betwene four and five afternoone the *Seahorses* boat was apointed to set the vessell afire, which they did, and before we could get out of sight of her she was burned downe to the water, she being 500 tunns.' *May* 23. The *Supply* departed. *June* 18. The *Hind* and *Seahorse* anchored off Malacca. *June* 21. Sailed again. (*The copy ends abruptly on June* 22. 14 *pp.*)

ROBERT BOWEN, HENRY OLTON, AND HUMPHREY PINSON [IN ST. AUGUSTINE'S BAY] TO THE COMMANDERS OF SUBSEQUENT SHIPS, MAY 15, 1644 (*Factory Records, Miscellaneous,* vol. xii. p. 150).

The *Endeavour* set sail from the Cape on March 28 last, but owing to contrary winds did not reach this place until May 7. Next day came a boat from the shore with a number of men in Courteen's service, who had lost their ship, the *William*, on an island to the eastwards of the Cape, but had managed to reach Madagascar in their longboat. Have taken them on board, to the number of seventeen English and four French. Their boat has been broken up as unfit for further service. 'In the same distresse found wee some 250 Duchmen in Saldania Bay, who in faire weather runne themselves ashoare.[1] They, according to their owne relation, saved their carga[zoon]; but for their shipp, named the *Mauritius Iland*, burthen 12 hundred tonns, [it] is irrecoverably lost. Beefe may be bought on the other side of the river for 10 rangoes a beefe, or 8 rangoes and 20 samma sammas[2]; but cheaper if your rangoes be cleare and without flawes. At your coming in, if you give any to the blacks, let them be of the worser sorte; for they are growne so cunning that, if they know you have better, they will sell you noe beefes for the worser sort.' Obtained themselves a plentiful supply. Intend to depart this night for Johanna. (*Copy.* 1 *p.*)

THOMAS COX AND THOMAS HILL, ABOARD THE *ENDEAVOUR* [IN ST. AUGUSTINE'S BAY], TO THE COMMANDER OF ANY OF COURTEEN'S SHIPS, MAY 16, 1644 (*Factory Records, Miscellaneous*, vol. xii. p. 151).

'The *William* of London, in the service of the Worshippfull William Corteene, Esquire, Mr. Thomas Cox of Rediriffe commander, being lost the 18th of June, 1643, by distresse of wheather betweene two small ilands distant from the Cape Bona Speransa on this side 140 leagues, but by Gods great mercy saving all our lives and the Esquires carg[azoon] of mony, wee made meanes upon one of the ilands to build our long boat bigger with peeces of our shipp, and therin having past many dangers, keeping along the shoare 14 dayes, afterwards putting to sea, after 16 dayes tyme wee arrived the last of August all of us att this place, with very little trade to maintayne us, living among these people almost nine months. The 7th present here arrived the *Endeavour*, Mr. Bowen commander,

---

[1] See Capt. Minors' account in *O.C.* 1868; also the *Dagh-Register*, 1643-44, pp. 79, 81.
[2] *Samisamy* is Malagasy for some kind of bead; while *rango* ('long') probably indicates the long beads which were in special demand (see the 1630-33 volume, p. 42). Lockyer (1706) mentions 'beads and rangos' among articles suitable for sale at the Cape.

belonging to the East India Companie, by whom wee understood of the troubles in England; also that there was four shipps for the Esquire to come out, and ready before them, but that they were stopt by the Parliament and all the men discharged, and they could not say whether they would come out this yeere or noe.' Have now, for the safeguard of their lives and the Esquire's money, accepted Bowen's offer to carry them to the Comoros, where they will await 'your coming'. Have found this place very unhealthy, having lost twelve of their number. Advice as to the purchase of cattle. (*Copy.* 1¼ *pp.*)

THOMAS GEE AND RICHARD WOTTON[1] AT SEA NEAR DARTMOUTH TO THE COMPANY, JUNE 17, 1644 (*Brit. Mus. Egerton MS.* 2086, f. 147).

All on board are well. Have been troubled with contrary winds ever since leaving the Downs, but are doing their best to pursue their voyage. (1 *p. Seal.*)

ABSTRACT FROM MICHAEL YATES'S JOURNAL OF THE VOYAGE OF THE *HOPEWELL* FROM MAURITIUS TO SURAT (*O.C.* 1861).

1644, *June* 22. Sailed from Mauritius, in company with the *Dolphin*. *June* 23. Lost sight of her. *June* 24. Saw 'Domas Masearenos' [Réunion]. *July* 4. Found the forepeak full of water, but baled it out. Discovered that the leak was due to an auger hole left unstopped. *July* 7. Reached St. Augustine's Bay, and found there the *Dolphin*, which had arrived that morning. *July* 26. They sailed for Johanna, and there awaited the ships from England. *August* 9. The *Crispiana* came in, commanded by William Bayley. *August* 11. The *Loyally* arrived, under Mr. Durson. *August* 17. The *Hopewell*, *Dolphin*, and *Crispiana* sailed for Surat. *August* 20. Another leak was found and stopped with ' collow [i.e. coal-dust] and coales '. *September* 16. Saw the coast of India in about 20°. *September* 18. Reached Swally Bar. *September* 19. Went into the Road. (1 *p.*)

---

[1] Gee was master of the Company's ship *William*, bound for Bantam; while Wotton was a factor on board her.

THOMAS COX AND THOMAS HILL [AT FORT ST. GEORGE] TO THE AGENT AND COUNCIL THERE, JULY 5, 1644 (*O.C.* 1874).

Request protection and advice as to the disposal of the money saved from the wreck of their ship and now brought hither in the *Endeavour*. Their orders were to deliver it to Courteen's factors at Achin; but they cannot tell how to do this without difficulty and danger. (*Copy*. ¾ *p*.)

REPLY OF THE AGENT AND COUNCIL [JULY 5, 1644] (*O.C.* 1874).

Cannot suggest any method of remitting the money to Achin, 'here not being any shipping belonging to this port that voyages it thither. And touching protection of you from the dainger of theis natives, tis such, by reason of the warrs of theis parts, wee cannot secure our one people.' (*Copy*. ¼ *p*.)

THOMAS COX AND THOMAS HILL TO THE AGENT AND COUNCIL, JULY 5, 1644 (*O.C.* 1874).

Request that they will continue to take charge of the money, on the understanding that the amount will be repaid in England by the Company to 'the Esquire Courteene', together with such 'lawfull consideration' for its use as shall be determined 'by equall parties on both sides'. They make this offer because they see no means of delivering the gold to any of Courteen's factories, and 'here wee knowe not how to secure it from our owne shipps company.' (*Copy*. ½ *p*.)

REPLY OF THE AGENT AND COUNCIL [JULY 5, 1644] (*O.C.* 1874).

They are ready to redeliver the gold, and certainly cannot accept it on the conditions mentioned. 'Yourselves are not ignorant of the great troubles and broyles of theis parts, both homebred and forreigne, and how our neighbours the Dutch are beseeged in their castle of Pollicatt by the Moores [*see note on p.* 193]; and for any thing wee knowe wee may bee in the same predicament in few dayes.' (*Copy*. ½ *p*.)

THOMAS COX AND THOMAS HILL TO THE AGENT AND COUNCIL, JULY 6, 1644 (*O.C.* 1874).[1]

Desire them to retain the money and leave the question of its repayment to be settled at home between Courteen and the East India Company. (*Copy.* ½ *p.*)

THE REPLY OF THE AGENT AND COUNCIL [JULY 6, 1644?] (*O.C.* 1874).

Agree to this request, and will advise the Company at the earliest opportunity. (*Copy.* ¼ *p.*)

THOMAS GODFREY'S ACCOUNT OF THE VOYAGE OF THE *HART* FROM BANTAM TO SWALLY (*O.C.* 1875).

1644, *July* 12. Sailed. *August* 6. 'Came upe with the Chagues' [i. e. Chagos]. *August* 30. Saw 'the maine land'. *September* 24. Were NE. of Sanjān. *September* 28. Anchored in Swally Hole. (*Abstract.* 1¼ *pp.*)

ROBERT BOWEN, ABOARD THE *ENDEAVOUR* IN MASULIPATAM ROAD, TO PRESIDENT BRETON AT SURAT, JULY 13, 1644 (*O.C.* 1876).

Left the Downs on January 10, 1644; crossed the Equator February 14; and reached the Cape March 25, where they found the Dutch ship *Mauritius Island* cast away, and 250 or 300 of her crew on land, whom they supplied with provisions. Sailed again on March 29, and anchored in St. Augustine's Bay on May 7. There they took in the master (Cox) and sixteen of the crew of the *William*, of 140 tons, freighted by Courteen for Barbary and thence to Achin, but wrecked 150 leagues to the eastward of the Cape, on a small island three leagues from the main. The survivors had with them in Barbary gold about 4,500*l.*, besides two small brass guns; all which have been delivered to the Agent at Fort St. George. Left Madagascar on May 16; got to Johanna May 24;

[1] This letter and its reply were printed in John Darell's pamphlet entitled *Mr. Courtens Catastrophe* (London, 1652). In this it is stated that Cox died on the way home, and that Hill on his arrival in England ' obscured himselfe '.

sailed on the 29th; and arrived at Madras July 2. Departed on July 10 and reached Masulipatam two days later. 'From whence wee are consigned for Gingerly and into Bengala for a fraight for Persia; whence I hope to bring you the bravest ship of hir burthen as ever came to Surratt; for shee sayleth better then any Dutch ship that ever wee mett (which doth anger them much) and workes very well.' (*Copy.* 1 *p.*)

ROBERT CRANMER AND JOHN RYMELL AT BASRĀ TO THE COMPANY, JULY 16, 1644 (*O.C.* 1880).

Enclose a packet from Surat, which doubtless relates all that passed prior to their departure from Swally on March 31. Off Gandevi River they met the *Seaflower*, returning from Gombroon. She had lost company with her consort, the *Hind*, the night before. The *Supply* had been left at Gombroon, but was to follow in a few days. The *Francis* had a tedious passage to Gombroon and did not arrive till May 11. Sailing again on the 16th, they procured a pilot at 'Carracke[1]' on June 5, and reached Basrā on the 23rd. The Bāshā was absent; but they visited the Shāhbandar and were courteously received. Set to work at once to unlade the *Francis,* and were surprised to find the cargo considerably damaged; in consequence it was July 7 before she was dispatched to Gombroon for the rest of the consignment. The enclosed copy of a letter to Surat [2] will show what goods have been sold here and also the current prices. Arrival of a Cambay junk, which they passed on the way. Other vessels are expected; and so there is little likelihood of much freight being forthcoming for India. Some money sent in the *Francis* to 'Congo' [Kung] on freight. Have just received letters from Peter Herbert, &c.,[3] who set sail from Swally on March 24 in a junk for Mokha, but after spending seventy days at sea were forced to bear up for Gombroon, where they arrived on June 5. It is hoped that their goods will be brought to Basrā by the *Francis*. The gum-lac, &c.

[1] Khargu Island (see the previous volume, p. 245).
[2] *O.C.* 1873. It adds nothing of importance.
[3] See *O.C.* 1872. The reply will be found under *O.C.* 1878; while the letters dispatched at the same time to the factors at Gombroon and to Robert Cherry, the master of the *Francis*, form *O.C.* 1879 and 1877 respectively. They only deal with the lading of the *Francis* and similar topics.

formerly intended to be forwarded from Gombroon to this place have been countermanded, as they are not vendible to profit here. Will write again about the end of August. (3½ *pp*. *Received February* 20, 1645.)

WILLIAM FREMLEN AND JOHN PROUD, ABOARD THE *DOLPHIN* [AT ST. AUGUSTINE'S BAY], TO THE COMMANDERS OF SUBSEQUENT SHIPS, JULY [25?], 1644 [1] (*Factory Records, Miscellaneous*, vol. xii. p. 155.)

The *Dolphin* and *Discovery* sailed in company for England from Swally on January 29 last and crossed the Line on February 20. Then, finding themselves belated and in need of supplies, they resolved to make for Mauritius. On March 9 they reached the shoal of 'Malha' [*see* p. 109], and it was thereupon thought advisable to stand to the eastwards for six days to weather the shoal. On March 24 came on a most violent hurricane, which separated the two ships. The *Dolphin*, owing to a leak in her stern, and to shipping several seas, had 4½ feet of water in her hold and 'laid alongst for more then an howers tyme without righting'. The mainmast was cut away and the ship then righted and was pumped dry. The hurricane having passed, they refitted her as far as they could, and on April 6 reached Mauritius. They anchored at first off Carpenters Bay, but on learning that the *Hopewell* was lying in Coopers Bay, they removed thither. Stayed until June 22, and with the assistance of the Dutch set up a new mainmast. The two ships sailed together, but the *Hopewell* lost company the day after leaving Mauritius. The *Dolphin* met with much foul weather in rounding the head of Madagascar, and did not reach this place until July 7. Received the enclosed letters from 'Andre Peela', with whom this is now left. Obtained a good supply of cattle and oranges at the usual rates. Having now waited some time for the ships from Europe and conceiving that they must have passed on to the Comoros, it has been determined to follow them thither to-morrow.[2] *PS.*—Have decided to leave the letters in 'Andre Manfecks' charge. The *Hopewell* was in sight of this road before the *Dolphin*

[1] Enclosed in their subsequent letter of August 17, and received with it by Knipe at Johanna.
[2] For the consultation at which this decision was reached see *O.C.* 1881.

arrived, but could not get in until the 8th. The two ships are now sailing together. (*Copy.* 3 *pp.*)

CONSULTATION HELD ABOARD THE *DOLPHIN* AT JOHANNA BY WILLIAM FREMLEN, THOMAS ADLER, JOHN PROUD, &C., AUGUST 16, 1644 (*O.C.* 1883).

They have met to decide as to the disposal of the *Dolphin*. From the *Crispiana* they have learnt 'the condicion and estate of our miserable country, finding the distractions, together with the Kings forces of shipping on the west part of England, dayly to encrease, so that Scilly, Famouth, Dartmouth, Waymouth, Bristow, and other considerable ports and places of England were (when the *Crispin* came thence) under His Majesties goverment and in his servants possession: that Plymouth also was beseiged: that his protection was withdrawn from his subjects, and they thereby left as a spoile and pray to our owne and other nations, and the west parts of England in generall infected with rovers, both English, Dunkerkers, and others, that little safety for a single ship (but even by accident) could be expected; insomuch [th]at our Honourable Employers, this and the passed yeares, would not but in joint company dismiss their outward bound shipping, though designed and readied for severall voiages.' It will therefore be unsafe for the *Dolphin*, having lost company with the *Discovery*, to proceed alone. Further, she is much weakened by the storm she passed through, and her cargo has suffered so much damage that a large part will probably not be worth freight and customs. It is therefore agreed that the wisest course is to return to Surat.[1] (*Copy.* 1¼ *pp.*)

WILLIAM BAYLEY AND OTHERS[2] ABOARD THE *CRISPIANA* AT JOHANNA TO THE COMMANDERS OF SUBSEQUENT SHIPS, AUGUST 17, 1644 (*Factory Records, Miscellaneous*, vol. xii. p. 150).

They lost sight of England on April 8 and arrived at St. Augustine's Bay on July 27 and this island on August 9. Here they found the *Dolphin*, bound from Surat to England, but forced hither

[1] The commanders of the *Crispiana* and *Hopewell* both concurred in this decision (*O.C.* 1882).

[2] John Pearson, Richard Davidge, Hugh Fenn, John Lewis, and Thomas Methwold. This and the succeeding letter were found by the *John* at Johanna on August 25.'

'by violence of a Harry Cane'; also the *Hopewell*, homeward bound from Bantam, but likewise obliged to take shelter from bad weather. All three are about to depart for Surat. (*Copy.* ½ *p*.)

WILLIAM FREMLEN, THOMAS ADLER, AND JOHN PROUD, ABOARD THE *DOLPHIN* [AT JOHANNA], TO THE COMMANDERS OF SUBSEQUENT SHIPS, AUGUST 17, 1644[1] (*Factory Records, Miscellaneous*, vol. xii. p. 153).

Left St. Augustine's Bay on July 26, and reached this road on August 3. The *Crispiana* arrived on the 9th, and two days later came in the *Loyalty*, a ship of nearly 300 tons, freighted by Esquire Courteen. The *John* had parted with the *Crispiana* near the Equator. Are now about to sail for Surat, in company with the latter vessel and the *Hopewell*. From a private letter they understand that the *Endeavour* left Madagascar on May 16, reached Johanna on May 24, and departed on [June] 8 for the Coast of Coromandel. If this letter is received by those on the *John*, they are entreated to procure a mainmast for the *Dolphin* at some port on the Malabar Coast and bring it to Surat. Believe that there are two at Goa belonging to the Company. (*Copy.* 2 *pp*.)

THOMAS IVY, HENRY GREENHILL, AND GEORGE TRAVELL AT FORT ST. GEORGE TO THE COMPANY, SEPTEMBER 8, 1644[2] (*O.C.* 1885).

Cogan sailed in the *Hopewell* on August 27, 1643, for Bantam, leaving Francis Day in charge here. The *Hart* arrived on September 23; the disposal of her cargo has been already advised. The *Endeavour* anchored in the roads on July 2 last, bringing sufficient money to pay all their debts. At St. Augustine's Bay she picked up some survivors of Courteen's ship *William*, who had managed to save two brass guns and gold to the value of 9,000 ducats. These have now been handed over to the Agent for the use of the Company, who are to give satisfaction for the same to Courteen at home, the gold being reckoned as 4,500*l*. The *Swan* reached this place from Bantam on August 4, bringing Thomas Ivy

---

[1] Found at Johanna by the *John* on August 25.
[2] For an abstract of part of this letter see *O.C.* 1884.

as Agent, and Thomas Winter. The cargo was invoiced at 9,458 rials of eight, in addition to which the remains left by Day were 106,126 rials. Refer to the enclosed consultations for the disposal of the *Swan* and *Endeavour*. The latter brought letters from the Company dated November 27, 1643, to which they now reply. The failure to send sample bales of piece-goods was partly due to the absorption of their funds in paying interest on their debts; but now that they are free from that 'eateing ulcer', they hope to give better satisfaction. At present they can only send a bale of 'morees'; and as the *Swan* is to leave Masulipatam for Bantam by October 5 at the latest, while the *Endeavour* cannot be back so soon from the Bay of Bengal, nothing more can be provided till the next shipping. Refer to Cogan for information as to the estate of Thomas Rogers. Yard's *Endeavour* is still lying on the beach, and is worth little or nothing; they trust he has given satisfaction at home for his proceedings in the matter. Have sold five chests of coral at 115 pagodas per maund, and could dispose of 4,000 lb. yearly; the 'grezio' is the sort required. Messrs. Olton, Methwold, and Isaacson duly arrived in the *Endeavour*. The last-named went on in her to Masulipatam on July 9, and died there on August 2. Olton has been appointed to take charge in Bengal, as Hatch desires to be relieved. He has been instructed to send samples of all sorts and to make an investment in ginghams, &c. for England. Methwold is to be second to Winter at Vīravāsaram. 'The Fort St. George hath allready cost in building 2,294*l*. 17*s*. 2½*d*., as by the abstract of the charges [*missing*] which accompanieth this appeareth; and to finish the rest and to compleate it according to the worke begune, with warehouse roome, lodging for factors and souldiers, with other needfull additions of building, and soe fortified as fame reporteth it is (though not soe), it cannot cost less then 2,000*l*. more. Notwithstanding three of the foure quadrangle points bee finished, yett the other point, with the three walls betweene the three points which are finished, with lodging and warehouse roome, will cost full as much as the sume aforementioned. And the monthly charge which wee are at now for fiftie men is 54*l*. 6*s*. 6*d*., as by the abstract [*not extant*] of the perticulers of mens names and wages appeareth; soe that, when it is compleated, there cannot bee less then 100 souldiers; which will double the charge. What ammunitions ettc.

is at present in the Fort [by?] the perticuler list hereinclosed [*missing*] will appeare; which is as much as nothing for the defence of such a place, the gunns excepted; but when it is finished and 100 souldiers for the defence of it, wee need not feare any inland enemy neare unto us in these parts. But how this poore trade heere will mainetaine the charge cannot bee apprehended by the former [*sic*] of us; for the Dutch are growne soe potent that they have allmost gotten the whole Coast trade into their owne possession, and have soe dispersed their moneyes in all parts that wee cannot gett cloth for our money. Soe that the tymes are turned upp syde downe; for formerly they [i.e. previous factors] complained for money and now wee know not how to lay out that litle remaineing stocke wee have, unless wee will take such trash as hath allwayes bin sent from hence to Bantam, which is noe course for us to stopp the Presidents complaints. But in course of tyme they may bee brought to make better cloath; for they seeme to bee acting [i.e. active] people and willing to indeavour any thing that is by us desired.' The orders for sending the *Endeavour* to Persia will be duly carried out; at present she has gone (July 23) from Masulipatam to Bengal with a small freight. Would much prefer to see the Company's ships employed in carrying its own goods. Commodities to be carried to Persia by the *Endeavour*. Ivy found on his arrival the Coast remains reckoned at 66,328 new pagodas, but from this must be deducted 10,925 pagodas for desperate debts at Masulipatam brought forward from the Armagon books. The remainder was distributed as follows: in Fort St. George, 48,952 rials; in Masulipatam, 31,184 rials; in Bengal, 8,510 rials[1]; while in addition the *Swan*'s cargo from Bantam was 9,458 rials, making 98,104 rials in all. If this does not agree with the home accounts, the difference must be explained by Cogan, who has probably arrived in England, and Day, who proceeds to Bantam on the *Swan*. That vessel carries hence goods to the value of 6,063 pagodas for the General Voyage, and they have instructed the factors at Masulipatam 'to compleate that accompt and sett a period thereunto'. Cannot commend the quality of the calico put aboard the *Swan*, but trust to send better in future. Have also laden in her some indigo, bought here at 24 pagodas per candy; and some gunpowder costing 22

---

[1] The rial of eight appears to be taken at 5*s*. and the pagoda at 8*s*.

pagodas per candy. Have already intimated their dislike of 'the letting out of the Companies shipps from the Coast to bee pack horses for other men in that unproffittable Persian trade'; but, as it is the Company's wish, the *Endeavour* shall be duly sent thither. Had they had a free hand, they would rather have invested the 5,000*l.* assigned for that purpose in piece-goods, which, if transported from Bantam to the Manillas, would have produced 'three for one proffitt in fowre months'. Now, however, the 'President of Surratt hath gotten the honnour and start of our President of Bantam, by whome this voyage hath bin long in agitacion, but could never as yett bee perform'd, in regard the President of Surratt [? doth en]gross upp all the small shipping, soe that they at Bantam have their hands tyed behind them for want of meanes and shipping. This Maneela voyage, to the Agents knowledg, is the best and proffittablest in these parts of the world; whose experience taught him when hee lived at Maccassar, where the Maneela merchants hath annually recourse and doth give there 150 per cent. proffitt for the foure sorts of white cloath aforesaid; and pepper to our knowledge, if to the quantitie of one hundred tonns per annum, will sell there for 15 rialls of eight the pecull. And wee are certaine that Surratt cloth will not sell for halfe the proffitt as the Coast cloth, nor halfe the quantitie. And now in regard the Spaniards hath warrs with the Dutch and Portugalls, the latter which formerly supply'd them with cloth from Maccasser and these parts, of boath which they are now debarr'd, therefore wee well know that if the President of Bantam had but a shipp and meanes, they might sell every yeare in Coast cloath and pepper to the amount of 100,000 rialls of eight at the Maneelas, and at noe less gaine then 2½ or 3 per cent. proffitt; which wee will maintaine'. Moreover, the expense and risk would be only half that incurred in making the voyage from Surat, seeing that the distance from Bantam is so much shorter and there is no danger to be feared from such enemies as 'the desperate Mallabarrs'. An additional reason is that, 'if the Maneela trade, or some other, bee not followed from the Southward, wee shall have but litle trade heere; for noe comodities will sell heere for any considerable proffitt, and rialls are of soe litle vallue that wee cannot putt them of at the prime cost. Soe there is nothing like gould for the provideing of goods and constant proffitt. Soe if the Maneela trade were followed from Bantam, wee might out of a small stocke every yeare from hence bee supplyed from the Maneelaes and Macaw per via Bantam with 50,000 rialls of eight in gould; and in two yeares tyme wee will undertake that the Company need send noe more stocke hether, but wee should bee suffitiently supplyed from Bantam; provided they bee supplyed with twoe shipps, each of 200 tonns burthen, which would supply this place and the Maneelaes under one.' Although all European commodities (coral excepted) are in little demand, yet, in hopes of better times, they would be glad to receive the quantities specified of coral, broadcloth, and lead for sale; mirrors and knives for presents; and a stock of money, mostly in gold. The Company's servants now on the Coast are:— at Fort St. George, Messrs. Ivy, Greenhill, and Travell, factors, with Martin Bradgate and Walter Robins as assistants; in Masulipatam, Thomas Peniston and John Brown, factors, with Hercules Heywood, Edward Winter, and Thomas Perks as assistants; in Vīravāsaram, Thomas Winter and William Methwold, factors, and William Minn, assistant; in Bengal, Henry Olton and William Gurney, factors, and William Netlam, assistant. The names of all the English soldiers will be found in a list enclosed [*missing*]. Disposal of the twenty-one men belonging to Courteen's *William*: two are dead; two are at Masulipatam at their own charge; William Hill has gone thither to get a passage to Achin; Thomas Cox and five others proceed to Bantam in the *Swan*; seven have joined the garrison here; and three are employed in the *Endeavour*. Money lent to Cox and Hill, to be repaid in England; their maintenance referred to the Company's consideration. The wars in these parts made them glad to entertain some of these men as soldiers; 'for the Moores but five weekes past had advanced with there armes within three myles of Pullicatt, and sent unto the Duch Governour to surrender up there castle; and we did suddenly expect the same. But shortly after the Jentues came downe with a greate power, gave the Moores battle, rowted there armie, and put the Moores to flight beyond Armagon [1], where they are now agathering a head againe;

---

[1] The Dutch Governor of Pulicat, writing to Batavia some months later, reported that on reaching that fortress from Masulipatam on July 15 (N.S.) he found that the forces of the King of Golconda, under 'Casy Aly' [? Kāsim Alī], had subdued the whole of the neighbouring towns without opposition and were demanding the submission of Pulicat itself, promising at the same time that the Dutch should retain all their privileges. Of this

soe the dainger that we live in is yet unknowne,' Geoffrey Bradford [*see* p. 158], 'who was shipped out corprall of the *Discoverie*, 1632, at 25*s*. per month and taken ashore at Armagon the same yeare, hath liv'd there and here since as serjant of the souldiers'; now upon his petition he has been allowed forty rials of eight per annum for apparel. On re-examining the accounts, they find that out of the 98,104 rials mentioned earlier no less than 22,455 represent dead stock and bad debts; so the effective stock on this Coast is only 75,649 rials, from which goods to the value of 20,000 rials have now been laden on the *Swan* for Bantam. The *Seaflower* is to be sent hither from that place in April next, coming by way of the Straits of Malacca direct to Bengal and so to Masulipatam and Fort St. George; 'by which ship we doubt not to cleare the Coast of all the remaineing stocke.' Accounts sent to Bantam. Hercules Heywood, having served at Masulipatam as a writer for five years at 18*l*. per annum, has been re-engaged for three years at 30*l*., subject to the Company's approval. (*Copy. Damaged.* 9 *pp. Received December* 8.)

EDWARD KNIPE, HENRY GARRY, JOHN BURNELL, AND HENRY HUNT AT JOHANNA TO THE COMPANY, SEPTEMBER 11, 1644 (*O.C.* 1886).[1]

Account of the voyage of the *John*. In May they spoke Courteen's *Loyalty*, commanded by Captain Durson, bound for Mozambique and Kārwār. In order to anticipate her, it was decided to go on ahead of the *Crispiana* (which sailed more slowly than the *John*) and to proceed straight to Mozambique without calling at Madagascar, the two ships meeting again at Johanna. As soon as the vessels parted, Mucknell, the master of the *John*, who had been an eager advocate of the separation, began 'his drunken and debauscht courses, callinge into his roundhousse the most debauscht

---

demand no notice was taken, and the invaders, finding the fortress amply equipped, contented themselves with a demonstration at a safe distance. The Nāyak of Gingī, who was then in rebellion against Srī Ranga, advanced with the intention of joining the Golconda army; whereupon the King recalled Kistappa Nāyak, who was operating againest the Gingī chief, and restored Chinnana to favour. Kistappa fell unexpectedly on the Moors and completely routed them, killing their commander and several other men of importance (*Hague Transcripts*, series i. vol. xiv. no. 431; *Dagh-Register*, 1644-45, p. 325).

[1] For another copy see *O.C.* 1890.

ungodly people in the shipp.' In the end he pretended to desire a reconciliation, promising 'reformacion of his liffe and conversacion; and to that purpose invited all of us with all his officers on shore the 29th August; when after dinner he most villanously stole aboard, wrought with his rogues on board to cutt cables in the halss, cutt loose sayles, and stood away for the offine, and left us miserably heere on this unhealthy island.' No provocation had been given him by Knipe, who confined himself to urging the chief officers of the ship to remonstrate with the master on his evil courses; with the result that these officers have likewise been left on shore. Could not take any steps to secure the ship, as the sailors were completely under Mucknell's influence. The latter showed great unwillingness to come to Johanna and meet the *Crispiana*; and when the factors sent him a written remonstrance, 'hee spent most parte of that night in vilifyinge us and indeavouringe to stirr upp his menn to mischeefe us.' They should have mentioned earlier that at Mozambique, where they arrived on August 11, they were disappointed in selling their wine, a large stock having been brought thither from Lisbon a short time before. They accordingly departed on August 21, carrying letters from the Governor to the Viceroy of Goa, and also, at the request of the former, one Senhor 'Joan da Maya Caldera', Agent for the King of Portugal at Mozambique, who was desirous of a passage to India for himself and his family. He brought on board upwards of thirty persons, and gave Mucknell 200 rials of eight for the use of his roundhouse. He, with his wife and most of his servants, is now proceeding in a boat to Mohilla, in hopes of meeting some vessel of Mozambique; and to his care these letters are entrusted. If they arrive in good time, the Company may be able to intercept the *John*; but possibly this may be effected here, for Knipe has written to the Governor of Mozambique, begging him to send a vessel of some force for that purpose[1], and it is their intention to embark in her and search all these islands and the coast of Madagascar, for the *John* 'cannot yet depart to pass the Cape this two mounths'. If they meet her they can probably master her, as she has many sick on board, besides those of her crew who were unwillingly drawn into the design and others who by this time have repented of their action. It is estimated that the active mutineers

[1] For copies see *O.C.* 1888 and 1890.

cannot number more than thirty, while 'wee on shoare here are 21 persons, and those the principall officers of the shipp'. It is the more likely that the Portuguese will lend assistance, in that Senhor Caldeira claims to have lost in the *John* to the value of 17,000 xerafins. Lest he should make any demands on the Company, they have procured from him a certificate that he did not acquaint them of any goods he brought on board (except provisions) or arrange with them for freight. Letters[1] are being sent to Mohilla for any homeward-bound ship that may arrive there; and they are hopeful that before long some vessel will come from Surat in quest of them. (*Copy*. 5¼ *pp*.)

A NARRATIVE OF MUCKNELL'S TREACHERY [2] (*O.C.* 1887).

Mucknell having left them on the island of Johanna and run away with his ship, they have drawn up this account 'for mortallity sake' and to clear themselves from all complicity in his crime. His dissolute behaviour described; also his threats against Knipe, who had merely let him know, by means of others, 'that if his cariage did not alter, he [Knipe] did intend, when God shold blesse him safe to the coast of India, there to secure the Companies goods and write to Surratt for other ships, and have nothing to doe with him.' On August 24, fearing that he intended to pass by Johanna, the factors sent him a written order to put in there; whereupon he violently railed against them, 'saying that hee wold not be ordered by Jacke Straw and Watt Tyler.' However, after their arrival at Johanna, Mucknell professed to be anxious for a reconciliation, and besought the minister [3] to make peace between him and Knipe. To this end, on August 29 all went ashore, 'hopeing to make it a day of Jubilee'; but after dinner Mucknell privately stole away and got on board. The rest waited for him until sunset, and then went down

---

[1] For copies see *O.C.* 1889 and 1890.

[2] Enclosed in the foregoing. It is signed by the four who signed the letter, and also by Henry Tyrrell and Henry Wheatley (master's mates), the Rev. William Isaacson, and fourteen of the crew. For other copies of this document see *O.C.* 1890 and the *O.C. Duplicates*.

[3] The Rev. William Isaacson, son of Deputy Isaacson, was chosen to go as minister to Surat in the *John* on Feb. 16, 1644. He was afterwards the first resident chaplain at Fort St. George (see Penny's *Church in Madras*, p. 661). A brief account by Isaacson of Mucknell's employment of him as a peacemaker will be found under *O.C.* 1890.

to the shore to return to the ship. There they perceived the latter making ready to sail; and presently two of the quartermasters came ashore in the 'jelliwatt[1]', having hazarded their lives rather than join in the plot. They related that Mucknell, 'as soone as hee came aboard the ship in the afternoone, went into the great cabbin and, calling the whole ships crew to him, spake thus unto them . . . There is a difference betweene Mr. Knipe and myselfe, and the reason is because I have given you too much sacke, and more then I can answer when I come to Surratt; so that when I shall arive thither, he threatens to turne me out of my ship. I have allwayes found you able and honest fellowes and men that have stucke by me. I hope therefore that you will not now see me disgrac't. I here declare myselfe for the King. I have had an intent that way from the beginning of the voyage, but cold never find a fitt oportunity untill now. Wee will first steere our course toward the Red Sea and gett what wee can there; and at the beginning of the yeare returne for England. Wee have Famouth, Dartmouth, or Bristoll to goe to, where we shalbe wellcome. You that are for the King, and will agree to this motion, hold up your hands. Upon which they all cry'd: One and all; except [*here follow eighteen names*], all which were violently detained on shipboard.' The accusation against Knipe of interfering in regard to the amount of drink consumed on board is entirely false. List of the ten ringleaders in this outbreak. (3 *pp.*)

ROBERT CRANMER, JOHN RYMELL, AND NICHOLAS BUCKE-
RIDGE AT BASRĀ TO THE COMPANY, SEPTEMBER 17, 1644 (*O.C.*
1891).

The *Francis* arrived from Gombroon on August 20. List of her cargo. The boat sent from here with letters to Herbert, &c., at Gombroon was met by the *Francis* at Khargu. Many of their goods here remain unsold, but they have disposed of the gum-lac and pepper brought from Gombroon. Deficiency in the weight of the latter. 'Dulka longhees' [Dholka *lungīs*, or loincloths] sold at unexpected rates, being usually only vendible at Red Sea ports. Cannot get any freight yet for India. The Dutch *Waterhond*,

---

[1] On this word, and its connexion with 'jolly-boat', see *Hobson-Jobson, s. v.* Gallevat.

which left Gombroon on May 15, is said to have been cast away near Muskat with a cargo worth ten lakhs of rupees.[1] It is also reported that the Dutch have not received a single bale of silk from Persia for two years. Hope to leave this place on October 15. (2½ pp. *Received March* 4, 1645.)

EDWARD KNIPE, HENRY GARRY, JOHN BURNELL, AND HENRY HUNT AT JOHANNA TO THE COMMANDER, ETC., OF THE NEXT ENGLISH SHIP, SEPTEMBER 20, 1644 (*O.C.* 1892).[2]

The enclosed papers[3] will relate the treacherous proceedings of Mucknell, the master of the *John*. That vessel was met three days ago about the latitude of Juan de Nova by the *Thomas and John* (commanded by Earl) which arrived here this morning. Mucknell pretended that he had met at Johanna the *Dolphin*, proceeding to England; and that, as the latter was unseaworthy, her cargo had been transferred to the *John*, which was then sent back home. By offering to take letters to England, he enticed on board many of the officers and men of the *Thomas and John*; whereupon he secured them and threatened to proceed to violence unless he was supplied with what he needed. By these means he forced from them gunpowder, match, candles, 'and their Kings coulours'. He also detained three of their trumpeters, and released two of his own men who were unwilling to remain with him. He declared to several who went on board 'that before his departure from England hee sent the King 100 p[ounds?] with promiss ere longe to bringe him a good shipp; and that his intencions were from the first of the voiage to runn to the Kinge, and never could have oportunity before his puttinge it in practice.[4] His resolucion was to direct his

[1] This was untrue: see p. 218.
[2] For a copy see *O.C.* 1890.
[3] Copies of the documents given on pp. 194 and 196 were left with this letter.
[4] In *O.C.* 1890 will be found a copy of a letter said to have been written by Mucknell after his departure to some of those left ashore, in which he avers that this had been his resolution from the commencement of the voyage. See also in the same collection a declaration by Richard Lawrence and a narrative by Anthony Archer, who commanded the boat which was sent aboard the *John* when she was met by Courteen's ship on September 15. He bears testimony to Mucknell's excited and truculent behaviour, and adds: 'After hee had his demaunds, he would have the Kings colors, which was then aloft; but could not have it graunted: soe hee had the Jack. In our former discourse he told me he lost 500*l*. per anum by goeinge to the Kinge and, though it were more, his desire was soe

ymediate courss for St. Hellena, and thence for the Coiba [1] Islands, and there to gather tydings concerninge the affaires of England; yf the difference should still remayne betwixt Kinge and Parliament, then for Bristoll or some other the Kings ports. Butt still our hopes are, either by mutiny amongue his menn, or by the Parliaments shipps or other occasion, our masters may againe injoy their shipp and goods; which God graunt. Amen.' As it is useless to pursue the *John*, even if a Portuguese vessel arrives from Mozambique, they have arranged to embark in the *Thomas and John*, which is bound for Rājāpur. They are all in good health, and have been well treated during their stay in the island, especially by the Queen, who has provided them with all necessaries. Being unable themselves to make any return, they entreat any of the Company's servants into whose hands this letter may fall to offer her some recompense; also to carry the letter to England, leaving a copy for the next ships. (*Copy.* 1½ *pp.*)

JOHN YARD AT SURAT TO THE COMPANY, NOVEMBER 20, 1644 (*O.C.* 1898).

Wrote last from Mauritius, describing his voyage from Bantam. Now entreats the Company to withhold its decision on the charges made against him until he has an opportunity of vindicating himself in person. (1 *p.*)

PRESIDENT BRETON, THOMAS MERRY, AND RICHARD FITCH AT SWALLY MARINE TO THE COMPANY, NOVEMBER 28, 1644 (*O.C.* 1901).

Will relate in its due place the return to this port of the *Dolphin*, the landing of her damaged goods, and their replacement by others, in readiness for her second attempt to get to England. Trust that her

---

much bent to goe to His Majestic, by reason of an abuse he received of the Parlament, now last being at home, that he would be contented to loose it to goe to the Kinge, for then he was in hopes ere longe to have the cuttinge in peeces of some that now are burgeses in the Parliament.' The *Thomas and John* was wearing the King's colours by virtue of the royal grants to Weddell and Courteen (see *Court Minutes of the East India Company*, 1635-39, pp. 129, 275).

[1] Apparently this is an error for Caribbee, i.e. the West Indies (cf. *O.C.* 1914). Brewster (p. 240) specifies St. Christopher's Island as the point to be made for.

consort, the *Discovery*, has safely reached home, but until they hear, 'her unknown fortunes will posess us with feares and hopes equall.' Wrote last, by way of Basrā, on March 26. Account of the voyage of the *Francis* to that place, where the markets were found tolerably good. Acknowledge the receipt of the Company's letters of November 27, 1643, and March 29, 1644. Account of the voyage of the *Endeavour*, the wreck of the *Mauritius Island*, and the rescue of the survivors of the *William*. The *Endeavour* likewise took off at St. Augustine's Bay 'four Frenchmen, who had travailed 150 leagues by land from a fort they have upon that island [1], presenting themselves, implored the[ir] passage and release from thence.' On July 2 the *Endeavour* reached Fort St. George [2], whence the Company's letters were sent overland to Surat, arriving August 18. The *Crispiana*, *John*, and *Blessing* left England together on April 8, and continued in company until May 3, when the *Blessing* was left behind, 'by reason of her bad sailing.' They met again on May 16, and next day encountered Courteen's *Loyalty*, bound for Mozambique. Knipe, fearing to be anticipated there, desired that the *John* should go ahead of her consorts; and this was agreed to. She separated on May 20; the *Blessing* lost company on the 22nd; and on the 30th the *Loyalty* departed. The *Crispiana* now continued her voyage alone, and on July 27 reached St. Augustine's Bay, where letters were found, notifying that the *Dolphin* and *Hopewell* had departed for Johanna the day before. On August 2 the *Crispiana* followed, and a week later anchored at Johanna, where she found the other two. They were soon joined by the *Loyalty*, but could hear no tidings of the *John*. The three ships sailed together on August 17 and reached Swally on September 18. Now reply to the letters thus received, commencing with that sent by the *Endeavour*. As already advised, the promise made by the Bantam factors of sending hither the *Expedition* was not fulfilled; nevertheless the *Seaflower*, returning from Gombroon on March 29, was on April 20 dispeeded for Bantam with a cargo amounting to 128,925 mahmūdīs, and reached that port on June 4. Explanations regarding certain baftas alleged

---

[1] At the Bay of Santa Lucia, on the south-eastern coast of Madagascar (see the narrative of François Cauche in *Relations Veritables et Curieuses de l'Isle de Madagascar*, Paris, 1651).
[2] *Dagh-Register*, 1644-45, p. 331.

to be missing from her cargo. Willingly agree to 'what you have been pleased to command touching a friendly correspondence betwixt this and the Bantam residency and mutuall assistance of each other.' It is their intention accordingly to send a cargo yearly to Bantam, and they are promised in return pepper and other suitable goods. The *Hart* sailed from that port on July 12 and reached Swally on September 28, bringing pepper, tortoise-shells, cubebs, and 'two noories [Malay *nūri*, a parrot] desired by us for this Governor'. She came round by way of 'the Chawges' [Chagos], for fear of the Malabars. The resultant loss of time might be avoided if the Company would supply a vessel of greater force for this service. Most of the *Hart's* crew are now up country, employed in convoying money to Ahmadābād and bringing down the goods ready for England. Rejoice at the safe arrival home of the *Crispiana* and *Aleppo Merchant*. Note the complaints that some of the goods had been pilfered, but cannot see how to prevent this 'whilest your goods must be brought from such remote parts, and entrusted to the convoy of these people'. However, they will do their best to stop such practices in future. Find no encouragement to buy Persian silk, 'in regard that from the King it cannot be purchased under the excessive rate of 50 tomaens per load; and, if bought of particular men, the King (as the Dutch have experimented) exacts such excessive customes, payment wherof we may not hope to avoid, notwithstanding your right and priviledges due (to so despicable a condition are your affaires there at present declined), that although in its first cost it appear reasonable, yet in conclusion becomes as dear as the other. So that the Dutch now deal almost only with the King, of whom the passed year at that unreasonable price they bought 450 bales, and have again this year contracted for 550 bales more; which pennyworthes we nothing grutch them, since the proceed of such goods as we send thither, being returned in monies, may to your much greater advantage be here employed.' They will therefore refrain from further purchases until instructions arrive from England. Regret that the Biāna and Sarkhej indigo found 'such despicable declined markets' at home, and that amongst the former a quantity of dirt was discovered to have been substituted for indigo. Similar complaints have been made by the Dutch and other purchasers, and they suspect that the fraud has been perpetrated between Rānder and Swally. Will do their best to detect the guilty parties. Have passed on to the factors up country the Company's complaints of the poor quality of the Biāna indigo, and trust that an improvement will result; but the 'unseasonableness of some years renders the very best but bad'. Details of the indigo procured this year for England, Basrā, and Mokha. By buying in partnership with the Dutch, the price has been brought down to from 26 to 31½ rupees the maund, though the indigo is stated to be of the best quality. 'From Agra we have lately been advized that, for want of rain and by reason of the small quantity of seed sowed this year (occationed by the mean price that indico hath in Agra been sold for the two passed yeares, at which rates people under so great taxations cannot subsist) there will not be above half or two-thirds so much as used to be [in] former years.' However, they are confident of procuring at least 500 bales for next year, and they hope to get another hundred from Sind, 'which sort the last year you much desired.' The Company's instructions that the Sarkhej indigo should be 'made flat, according to its pristine auncient form', shall be obeyed in future years; but they came too late to affect the purchases for the present season, which are nearly all of the round sort. Since then the price at Ahmadābād has risen by three or four rupees per maund, though the indigo is inferior in quality to that of former years, owing to adulteration. This they impute chiefly to the reckless way in which the Dutch last year bought all they could get, bad as well as good, which encouraged the manufacturers 'to debase the comodity exceedingly in goodnes'. Will be mindful to send home some indigo unmixed with sand; 'yet the long-continued custome and practice of these people induce us to believe that their experience hath found it to preserve the indico, being tender and flat, from breaking, by filling the vacuous places betwixt the pieces, as the bales are upon any occation removed.' Moreover, the sand is not included in the weight, but added afterwards, 'by guess, about 10 or 12 sear' to each bag. As for the Company's market being spoiled by the quantity of indigo brought home as private trade, they are 'wonderstrook and silent in admiration at the undertakers boldnes', and at the same time unhappy at having fallen under the Company's censure themselves. Promise to do their best to prevent such abuses in future. Regarding the complaints made of 'the Scinda or Nusserpore joories', they explain that 'the make of all sorts of cloth in that place doth much degenerate from former times, and yearly declines, by reason of the ready vend it findes at Bussora, which occations many buyers, in so much that narrow baftaes of all sorts are lately risen 5 and 6 rupees per corge, and yet made worse then ever, the Derbella and Ckandara cloth being now no better then the Nusserpore; wherof Mr. Spiller hath had this year some experience, he having by our order spent the passed raines, from May to September, in those upper countries of Sehwan or Seuestan and the adjacent places; whither he was sent chiefly to make a full discovery of what indico those parts may produce, as also to buy 200 f[ardle]s, if they had been procurable; but the people are so exceedingly opprest and kept so miserably poor that, notwithstanding the soil is fertile and propper and would produce large quantities of good indicoes, they have neither will nor means to manure and sow the ground; so that the small quantity the country produced, not exceeding 400 maunds double (which is scarcely sufficient for the expence of those parts), rendered the commodity very dear, far beyond 40 rupees, the price we had limited. Yet were there no other buyers then the Tuttha dyers, which paid 41½ rupees, besides 3 rupees per maund other charges.' Spiller bought, therefore, but a trifling quantity; 'yet is he of opinion that the next year, if a man continue there, to encourage the people by impresting 800 or 1,000 rupees in small sumes, that upwards of 100 f[ardle]s may be procured at reasonable prizes: which we intend, God willing, to experiment; and the rather, because Derbella and Ckandara are not far distant from thence, where we intend a residence; and if they can procure the cloth to be well made, we have given directions for the buying of 10,000 peeces against the next year.' Spiller also, when at 'Sehwan', gave the weavers instructions as to the dimensions of the cloth, and left a broker with 1,000 rupees to follow the investment. Intend in addition to buy there a quantity of goods for Persia or Basrā. The goods procured in Sind last season, viz. about 7,000 pieces of narrow 'joories', with a little saltpetre and indigo, will be embarked upon the *Crispiana*. No 'eckbaries' sent home this year; while the 'mercoles' forwarded cannot be commended. For the carelessness with which the latter have been bought, the Agra factors have been severely reprimanded, and ordered to buy none in future less than fifteen yards long and one yard wide. The 'Dereabads' are, 'for their sorts, the best made of any cloth comes from thence.' They have bought nearly 30,000 pieces, and will send home about half, keeping the rest for Mokha and Basrā. As desired by the Company, these cloths have been bleached 'at Lucknow, the place where they are made'; but since the former orders have now been cancelled, they intend in future to have the bleaching done at Broach or Baroda, as in former times. 'Semana cloth you have been formerly advized is not procurable at any reasonable rates', though they expect one bale from Agra before long. Details of 'Agra clothing' ordered for next year, part of which will be 'brought brown to Ahmuda[bad], and there converted into such sorts of blew cloth, pintadoes, &c., as will be wanting for Bantam and other investments; besides which we have here seen baftaes which come from Matchawara[1], 200 course [*kos*] beyond Agra, both broads and narrowes, which both for size and making of the cloth we believe will very well like you.' Have already dispatched thither 'a trusty experienced Banian' and, if his report be favourable, an Englishman will be sent to make an investment. Nosārī and Surat narrow baftas, on account of their goodness, are as much esteemed here as in England, and are very vendible at Achin. Will send home 8,000 pieces, bought, it is true, at rather dear rates, yet as cheaply as possible. The broad baftas are also good but expensive. Baftas and Guinea stuffs obtained at Baroda. 'Buroach, which hath formerly been the most eminent place in these parts for baftaes, is now become of all other the worst, the making, both of broad and narrowes, being so exceedingly declined, and the prices so unreasonably raised, that we have not been encouraged to buy any of either sorts since our Acheen investment (wherunto we were then necessitated in regard of the shortnes of time).' Finding evidences of fraud on the part of 'Dew Docee' [Deodāsī], the Company's broker there, they seized and imprisoned him, until Vīrjī Vōra became his surety and promised to see them righted. The broker has undertaken to pay a fine of 12,000 mahmūdīs, but has nevertheless been dismissed from the Company's service. This will be a salutary warning to other brokers. Quilts and 'chints' pro-

---

[1] Māchhīwāra, 27 miles east of Ludhiāna, in the Punjab.

cured from Ahmadābād, made in accordance with the Company's wishes. A quantity of cotton yarn now sent; more will follow by the *Crispiana*. 'Saltpeter was the passed year procured in Ahmuda[bad] with so much difficulty that, in hopes to be better and cheaper furnished, we were induced to send and buy it this year at Malpore [*see* p. 164], where it is digged, and cost raw no more then 4 and 4½ rupees for 5 double maunds. But before its arivall at Ahmuda[bad] the excessive charges more then doubled the prime cost; and then refining it to that height and purenes you desire, notwithstanding it was done in your house at Ahmuda[bad] and all frugality that might be therin used, yet it comes to cost you no less then [*blank*] rupees the small maund before it be embarqued on board; which far exceedeth our estimate.' Desire to know whether the Company wish to have future consignments refined to the same degree, in view of the high cost. Will buy no more until that expected from Tatta has been received and examined. The 'muttutta' [*see* p. 86] was only sent home after they had tried in vain to sell it at Gombroon and Basrā. Of 'tincall or borax' they are sending 34 jars, and have yet on hand a large quantity which cannot be cleansed in time for dispatch this year. All concerned have been warned that this commodity is reserved for the Company. The missing jar of borax must have been purloined on board ship. Were unable to procure any suitable gum-lac; but they send some olibanum, myrrh, and aloes socotrina. Pepper and cardamoms obtained at Rāybāg, and to be brought from thence by the *John*. The ships are not to touch at Madagascar (unless they leave this place later than is expected), and therefore it will not be necessary to furnish them with many beads; nor will any be sent to England. Cinnamon purchased at Rājāpur from 'Lewis Riberio', who had brought it thither from Ceylon in order to export it unmolested. 'Fifty-eight quint[als] are in Lewis Riberioes custody, since received of the Vice Roy in truck of damar; besides which we long since desired him to buy of particular merchants 200 quent[als], and entreated the Vice Royes license for its exportation; who could not consent therunto, by reason of the strickt inhibition received from Portugal not to alianate any of that specie,[1] yet is content, for

---

[1] In the spring of 1644 the King of Portugal wrote to the Viceroy, warning him to prevent the sale of cinnamon and other spices to the English—a prohibition which he repeated

the respect he bears unto you, to connive therat.' Still, it is doubtful whether the desired quantity can be obtained. Francis de Brito, of Cochin, made offer to put a consignment on board an English ship at his own risk, and was told in reply to communicate with the commander of the *John* on her arrival on the Malabar coast. That the dry ginger formerly sent home found so bad a market may have been due to its poor quality. The quantity left behind, after being vainly offered for sale at Gombroon and Mokha, was finally disposed of at a considerable loss. Note the poor prices obtained for sugar and turmeric, and will observe the Company's directions not to send home any more. Regret the loss sustained in the sale of the latter commodity; 'but that it should be charged to the buyers accompt, because you did not require it, might stagger our resolutions in many things we undertake without your order, did we not know that the distance of place admits not of your frequent direccions, and that you have been pleased to approve of such undertakings whilest your benefit is therin chiefly aimed at (as it was then; at least we know no other inducement that should occation its sending). But the chief agent therin [i.e. Fremlen] going towards you, (without staynong his worth by any addition our pen may blot in his commendations) we refer him unto (which we are confident he cannot want) your more courteous reception and enterteinment.' Refer the Company to Robinson for an explanation of the shortness of some of the baftas sent in the *London*. The *Endeavour*, which is said to be a very serviceable vessel, left Fort St. George on July 10, reached Masulipatam two days later, and on the 23rd sailed for Bengal. On her way she was 'to land John Brown and Edward Winter at Jerreleene[1] with a chest of rials, which is enordered to be invested

in the two following years (*Lisbon Transcripts* at I.O.: *Doc. Remett.*, book 48, f. 309, book 55, f. 31, book 56, ff. 125, 138). The trade in Indian commodities (cinnamon excepted) had been thrown open to all Portuguese subjects by a royal decree of December, 1642; and this made it all the more necessary to maintain, for revenue purposes, a strict monopoly of the traffic in cinnamon.

[1] From p. 186 it is clear that 'Gingerly' is intended. That word was sometimes written 'Gergelin' (see *Hobson-Jobson*, s.v. 'Gingerly'). A Dutch letter from Masulipatam (*Hague Transcripts*, series i, vol. xiv. no. 437; *Dagh-Register*, 1644-45, p. 321) says that the factors were landed at 'Sicacol', i.e. Chicacole. It adds that they lost their chest of rials through the upsetting of their boat, and that the local governor forbade the weavers and merchants to sell any goods to the English without his consent. It was anticipated, therefore, that the attempt to settle a factory there would be abandoned.

into beeteles and long cloth for Persia. For Bengala they have also sent one chest of rials, and enordered to be provided for Persia 150 bales of sugar, 10 or 12 bales of gurras, and the like quantity of course sannas. Mr. Netland was the year before sent thither, with more monies then they computated might discharge those debts; which overplus, as also what will remain of the 4,000 rials sent upon the *Endeavour*, Mr. Hatch &c. are enordered to invest into ginghams, sannas, cossaes, and hummanees propper for England, intended to be sent unto you as a testimony what cheap and well made cloth those parts affoards.' Investments for Persia were also being made at Madraspatam and Masulipatam. News has reached Fort St. George that the *Endeavour* had arrived in the Bay, but in passing the bar at Balasore she 'lost an anchor, beat off her rudder and some of her sheathing'; these damages, however, can be easily repaired. Did their best to remit funds to the Coast from Surat, as ordered, to provide an investment for Persia, but found they could not get bills of exchange on Golconda except at 8 per cent. loss; so in lieu thereof they prevailed upon 'Ckyratt Ckaun' [Khairāt Khān] to transfer to Surat the liability of the Coast factors' debt to him. The money sent to the Coast upon the *Endeavour* was sufficient to pay all the sums owing there. Arrival of the *Swan* on the Coast, and her departure from Masulipatam for Bantam on October 8. The 'Serkail' [Sar-i-Khail: *see the* 1634-36 *volume*, p. 325] sends yearly from the Coast to Persia a large quantity of goods, 'which, under pretence that they belong unto the King of Golconda, [he] expects should be landed free of custome, inasmuch as concernes your proportion therof, in retaliation of the immunities you receive in his country; but whether they be propperly the Kings or Serkailes, it is not much materiall, since the Serkaile governes the King and consequently the country. In which requests of his, our Coast friends will not for any consideration that we give him any denyall; nor indeed do we think it fit, since it might occation unto them much trouble, and is unto you very little losse, so long as you receive not your due proportion of customes, but must take what they please to allot you.' List of the goods thus passed at Gombroon custom-free. If this practice be continued, 'the customes of your goods at the Coast (except your trade were greater) wilbe more then sufficiently paid for, whilest in appearance you are therfrom exempted.' The factors in Persia have doubtless advised the Company fully of the state of trade in that country. Difficulty experienced in disposing of broadcloth there. The Company's share of the Gombroon customs declines annually, and is likely to be 'much less this year then ever, notwithstanding that by more then ordinary presents Mr. Pitt &c. were licensed to insinuate themselves with the Sultan and Shawbunder; in liew wherof, they received nothing but disrespect and affronts, it now being publiquely told them that it is honour enough for you to have a name of being the Kings partners. Besides, the better sort of goods are either not brought at all to the customhouse, or carryed away at their pleasures and customed publickly in other places, wher your servants are not suffered to come. And so by degrees they are rooting you out; wherunto a very few years more will give a conclusion. In the interim yours and the nations honour payes dearly for the poor pittance you receive.' Indian cloth sold at Gombroon. The *Francis* arrived there on July 18, and eleven days later sailed on her return voyage to Basrā, which was reached on August 20. Good sales at that place. 'The trade of Gomroon we cannot much commend unto you, since no great profit may be expected whilest so many Moores and other shipping so frequently resort thither, by which means a comodity can no sooner be in any request but such vast quantities are sudainly sent that it becomes of no esteem. The like is it with Mocha. So that Bussora is yet the place that produceth you most profit; and will so continue untill the trade be open to the Dutch, who will quickly be the ruin therof, as they are of all others.' However, as it is necessary 'to keep your shipping in action', they intend to make investments for all these places. For Mokha goods are being provided at Ahmadābād and Cambay to the value of 50,000 rupees, besides an investment of 20,000 rupees at Agra. For Persia about 100 bales of cloth from Sind will suffice, in addition to what the *Endeavour* will carry thither from the Coast. As regards Basrā, the return of the factors from thence will be awaited before any orders are given; but as far back as last May they dispatched two brokers to Golconda and Daulatābād respectively, to provide certain sorts of piece-goods which 'will require most time'. Will reply by the *Crispiana* to the letter brought in that vessel. As regards her cargo, there is a fair

THE ENGLISH FACTORIES

demand for the broadcloth, though the greens are rather 'too sad'; but private traders must be prevented from dealing in this commodity if the sales are to be satisfactory. The 'baies' are in no demand, except the scarlet ones. Resent the imputation that they do not attend properly to the weighing and counting of the money received. 'It is a busines that passeth not in private, but is constantly done in your warehouse, wher your rials &c. are first told and then weighed; wherupon two or three of your servants are constantly attendant, wherof your Accomptant is usually one, or (if he be upon any occation absent) some one of Councel or of trust is entrusted therwith.' Have previously complained of the lightness and coarseness of the rials sent; and now find the last consignment much worse than any before received. The proportion brought to Surat contained 'only 560 Civill [Seville] or of the best sort: 14,727 Mexico: and 3,333 of the course or new sort' ['Peru' *in margin*]. The two former kinds were sold at the usual rates; but the third they are keeping for some other occasion, rather than part with them at 208¼ rupees [per hundred], which is the highest price offered, either here or at Ahmadābād. 'The duckatoons and cross doll[ars], being new species, we have with all possible industry endeavoured to raise in price; and have sold the former at 258 rupees the hundred (delivered by tale without weighing), which produced 5*s*. 9⅝*d*. per piece[1]; and cross doll[ars] at 207 rupees (by tale also), which we find to amount unto 4*s*. 7⅞ pence per piece. By these latter the sheroffs complain to be loosers, in regard they hould not out in weight as they expected of them. There are not any lacking in tale; but of the duckatoons two are wanting. In the ingots of silver there were 12 ingots inferiour in goodness unto the rest ⅛ ma[hmūdī] per tola, but were not discovered by the sherofs when we sold them, not any happening amongst the musters we gave them for tryall. So that we disposed of them at one rupee per tola, as the same sort of silver was sold in anno 1636; only we have now procured 10 rupees per ingot more, and (upon allowance of ½ tola per ingot in weight) they were delivered as they weighed in England and were invoyced, accompting 2 tolaes 19 vals [*see the 1624–29 volume*, p. 156] to the ounce, which we find to be the exact weight. About the courser sort we had afterwards some trouble

---
[1] Taking the rupee at 2*s*. 3*d*.

with the sheroffs, but dismist them without any allowance. The chest of rex doll[ars] were sold at the usuall rates of 216 rupees and 16 p[ice][1]; only, by reason of some emulation amongst the sherofs, we procured upon the whole an overplus of 25 rupees, which, however, is not usually atteyned.' Part of the treasure was reserved for Ahmadābād, and, together with 'as many rupees as raised the whole sum to 180,000', was sent thither under the escort of thirty-two Englishmen. The fine broadcloth and knives will be very useful for presents. Much of the writing-paper sent was damaged on the voyage by wet. A supply of the same kind as that whereon the present letter is written would be of service 'in our correspondency with the Portugals, who (how mean soever the import of their letters be) are very curious in their paper.' Thank the Company for sending them 'two pipes of Canary, an antidote against, and a chest of chyrurgery, a remedy for malladies.' 'If you please to encrease the quantity of the former, it would be but necessary. This Governor, and the better sort of this people with whom our busines lyeth, being fallen into a vain of drinking, often importune us to supply them; which we may not refuse. Our Portugall friends also (as accustomed) expect to be therwith gratified.' The chest of 'chyrurgery' has been examined by the surgeons here, who have pronounced the medicines tolerably good; as, however, many are superfluous (being either useless or procurable in India), a list is sent of what should be provided in future. Regret the non-appearance of the *John*, whose coral would have sold readily at Rāybāg, and now, it is feared, the Portuguese may have supplied those markets, for 'three galleoons arived in September last from Portugal, and are (for fear of the Dutch) harboured in Bombaien; but what they have brought, more then store of men, we cannot yet receive any certain newes of.' Most of the coral that came in the *Dolphin* and *Hind* was sold to 'your sheroff Tulcidas', the 'gretzo' at $9\frac{1}{8}$ rupees per seer and the 'teraglia' at 40 and 45 rupees per maund. Of the 'gretzo', however, two chests were reserved and sent to Macao in the *Hind*. The 'recaduty' of the same consignment, and the coarse coral brought from Mokha by the *Discovery*, were sold to Vīrjī Vōra at $6\frac{1}{4}$ rupees per seer and $36\frac{1}{2}$ rupees per maund respectively. The coral beads from Mokha

---

[1] Per hundred: cf. the 1634-36 volume, p. 68.

they sent to Golconda by their broker 'Dewcurn' [Deo Karan], but he reports that there is no demand for them. Have also on hand here some coral returned from Cochin. The tortoise-shells received from Bantam sold at 110 rupees 'per maund of 40 sear, 20 pice weight.' Small demand for lead; 'yet if you shall continue to send as accustomary, the Governor (it being the Kings comodity) will not fail to take it at the usuall price; but if you abstein from sending some time, it may happely also be raised in price, wherin we shall not be wanting to lay hold of all opportunities.' 'Ellephants teeth' are now in good demand, and it may therefore be worth while to dispatch some from England. As regards money, it is most profitable to send 'ducatoons', if procurable, and next to them cross dollars. Of the disaster to the *Dolphin* the Company will receive full accounts from her commander and her master, 'whose sence of their sufferings will dictate unto them more lively and propper expressions.' Briefly narrate, however, the voyage, the storm, the arrival of the vessel at Mauritius 'with the help of a jooree mast', her meeting with the *Hopewell*, and their joint voyage to Surat, where both were unladen. The enclosed paper will show what goods were taken out of the *Dolphin*, what were left on board, and what have since been embarked. Account of the miserable state of the *Hopewell's* cargo and the measures taken to dry and dispose of it. That vessel has been surveyed by the masters and carpenters here, but they could not find any defect likely to occasion the damage. The master (Yates) goes home in the *Dolphin*, and doubtless the matter will be further examined on his arrival. The *Crispiana* sailed on October 23 for 'Scinda', carrying some of the pepper taken out of the *Hopewell*; part of this is to be sold there, and the rest sent in the *Francis* to Gombroon. The *Crispiana* is to bring back the goods provided at Tatta for England; also the factors and their money, &c., expected from Basrā by the *Francis*. On her return the former vessel will start for England (it is hoped some time in December). The *Hind* got back from Persia on March 30, bringing three horses, with some fruit and rosewater. At the same time arrived the *Seahorse* from Rājāpur and Goa. In her voyage to the latter place, she '(besides the two Mallavars she surprized near Rajapore) also encountred two more not far from Goa, took one of them, and chased the other untill for refuge she got amongst the Dutch, then riding before Goa, who protected her from us. So that, having taken what they found of vallue out of her they surprized, they sunck the vessell with the rest of her lading and left the men to shift for themselves in their boats, and so entred into Goa; from whence we received by her 19 pipes of Portugez wine (bought for and since sent to Maccaw and the Manielies), 27 candies of cairo, 92 bales of cussumba from Rajapore (provided for Acheen), and (that which we most desired) the Vice Royes lysence for the *Hyndes* voiaging unto China, with his recommendatory letters, wherin he freely and nobly gratified us; as also in the liberty of an orankay [1] of Acheen, who had been long prisoner in Goa, a man of very great quallity and esteem amongst the Acheeners, whose Queen, having fruitlesly long laboured for his enlargement, desired our assistance therin, making mountainous promises of immunities she would bestow on you, if we could procure his liberty; which we happely effected, and are in expectation shortly by the *Supply* to hear of her performances.' On April 26 the *Hind* sailed for Macao, with a cargo invoiced at nearly 140,000 mahmūdīs, entrusted to William Thurston, George Oxenden, &c. In five days she reached Goa, 'where their busines was only to receive on board the promised Acheen orankay, and to get cancelled an obligation wherin Lewis Riberio had voluntarily, without any directions from us, in our behalf engaged himself unto the Vice Roy that the *Hynd* should bring from Maccaw for the Kings accompt a quantity of copper which was there remaning; wherunto we might not for any considerations submit; for which we exhibited such reasons that he sudainly gratified us. So that in 24 howers the business being effected, and the Acheener on board, the following day Mr. Broadbent sailed off and anchored in the outward road before Goa, where he was enordered to expect the *Supply* and *Seahorse*; which not appearing, the 8th May he weighed anchor and set sail from thence, rather (we suppose) making choice to touch at Acheen, there to land the orankay, then to abide any longer upon that coast in that late season.' On April 29 the *Supply* and the *Seahorse* were dispeeded in company, the former for Achin with a cargo invoiced at over 127,000 mahmūdīs, the latter for the Manillas with goods &c. to the value of about 110,000 mahmūdīs, entrusted to Edward

[1] Malay *orang kāya*, a person of importance.

Pearce, Thomas Breton, &c. Nothing was heard of them until June 9, when 'Lewis Riberio from Goa advized us how two of your pynnaces, bound down the coast to the southwards of Goa, encountred a very great and rich Mallavar jounk belonging to Cannanore, which set sail from Mocha about the time your ship *Discovery* left that place, but lost her voiage, wintered at Shear [Shehr], and then happely fell upon that coast, was taken and carryed off to sea by your said pynaces, which we suppose were the *Supply* and *Seahorse*. Not many daies after, the same pleasing newes was confirmed by letters Virge Vora received from Mallavar, whose relacion saith that she was worth 900,000 fanams (which is accompted 200,000 rupees[1]), that she had in her 500 men and made very strong resistance, so that 250 of them and 40 English were slain in the conflict. And this is all we yet hear of the busines; only we are enformed that the Mallavars are preparing what strength possibly they may to be revenged; which, by Gods permission and blessing, we shall the best we can provide for, aswell in an offensive as defensive way.' For this purpose they intend to dispatch the *John*, *Francis*, *Prosperous*, and *Kit* to the Red Sea to intercept the Malabar traders, the *Francis* and *Prosperous* lying off Aden while the other two 'keep the Bab' [i.e. the Straits of Bābu-l-mandab]. 'And so we have fair hopes yet further to chasetize those villaines, since there were of them last year four sail at Mocha and three at Aden, in both which places they have left upwards of 20 people to make sale of such goods as would not vend during the time their ships continued there, and will undoubtedly again return this year. And if you enquire why we will venture your estate upon a ship designed to such an employment, or doubt that, having surprized any Mallavars, it should disturb your trade in Mocha, be pleased to take notice that in the former there is not any danger, they being open vessels and, though full of men, not able against such a ship to make any resistance; and for the latter, we have often declared our resolutions to that Governor, who hath nothing to say therunto, provided we disturb not the peace of his port within the Bab. This busines being over, if your people we shall send to Mocha find the relations true which we have thence received, that by arrivall of a new Bashaw at Savakan [Suakin] (one very desirous of trade and

---

[1] Taking the fanam at 6*d.* and the rupee at 2*s.* 3*d.*

that gives great encouragement to merchants) the trade be open and that goods sell at extraordinary prizes, as it is reported, your pynnace[s] *Francis* and *Prosperous* are intended to voiage thither, laden with pepper and such course goods as are propper for that place ; from whence being returned to Mocha, and that the season of the year will not longer admit of the *John* and *Francis* stay in those parts, the *John* shall return for Suratt, pynace *Francis* take a fraight for Persia, and the *Prosperous* and *Kitt* we intend to make sale of at Mocha, they being propper for those parts, to go betwixt Mocha and Judda, but altogither unfit for your service here.' The *Hopewell* being found, though old, yet strong and capable, has been bought for the Joint Stock from the General Voyage for 405*l*. Having been trimmed and placed under the command of Edward Lock, second mate of the *Crispiana*, with a crew of 45 men, she sailed on November 7 for Cochin, there to await the return of the *Supply* from Achin and escort her back to Surat lest she should be attacked by the Malabars. The *Supply* is expected here by the middle of December, and will then be sent on a voyage to Persia. Afterwards she may go to the Manillas (should the first venture prove successful) or else to Achin. The *Hind* on her return will make a voyage to Persia and thence to Bantam. The *Seahorse* and the *Endeavour* are destined for Basrā. The *Hopewell*, after a voyage to Persia, will be resheathed in the river here. The damaged pepper in the *Dolphin* has been replaced from the *Hart's* cargo. Disposal of the remainder of the latter. The pepper obtained in the Deccan is 'extraordinary good, and bought cheaper by 25 per cent. then we have at any time known it.' The cubebs fetched 12 mahmūdīs per maund. 'The passed year we advized you of a large present given this King and two of his sonnes; which hath been very well accepted by them and wrought desired effects ; the King having been pleased to gratify us with his firmaen for reducing in this customhouse the rates of Ahmuda[bad], Agra, and Brodra goods, the first from 25 to 5, the second from 40 to 20, and the last from 12½ per cent. (that they were used to exact more then the cost of the goods where they were bought) to nothing ; which will in short time reimburse you of what was given, besides many other conveniencies we find therby.[1] The elder Prince, Darasacore

[1] See the *Dagh-Register*, 1644-45, p. 227.

[Dārā Shikoh], hath also exprest how acceptably he esteemed what given him, in wryting a courteous letter to your President and retributing a jewel of dyamonds and rubies, vallued at 1000 rupees; but the latter we have not yet received. If it come in time, it shalbe sent you by the *Crispino*. He hath also been pleased to graunt us severall neshans [*nishān*, an order] or letters in your favour for Tuttha, that customhouse and country belonging unto him. In June last, after too long patience, we were necessitated to dispence with Mr. Tash his absence in Ahmuda[bad] and send him for Agra, to enquire into the state of your affaires there and take charge of them, since Mr. Turner, strangely infatuated, had silensed his pen and from August (that the *Seaflower* arived) to that time did not reply one word to any of our generall letters; yet bought such goods as were inlisted and at several times enordered to be provided, dispeeded severall caphilaes [*qāfila*, a caravan] in October, December, January, April, and May, but without invoyce or any word of advice; so that often the goods arived before we knew of their dispeed, except the Dutch gave us notice therof; which we might no longer endure; so called him from thence, to give a reason of such his remiss and negligent abearance, and are now in expectation to hear of his departure thence. In the interim the care of your busines in Ahmuda[bad] is left unto Robert Heynes, who was then second to Mr. Tash, and hath since his departure carefully and honestly discharged the trust we reposed in him. Your auncient Agra broker, Dongee [Dhanjī], for his negligence in your busines, disrespective abearance formerly towards Mr. Turner &c. English and to Mr. Tash since his arivall in Agra, but chiefly for endeavouring to distroy Mr. Turner by sorcery, we have dismist your service. Since when some accions of dishonesty have been objected against him, but are not yet proved; wherinto we have expressly enordered Mr. Tash &c. to make diligent enquiry and, if he therin be found culpable, he shall (God willing) be made to suffer the deserved guerdon of his demerits.' Have related in a previous letter how the Dutch broke their promise to carry a quantity of broadcloth to Mokha for the English, and how in consequence it became necessary to embark the goods in a junk bound for that port. The vessel sailed on March 23, but met with such adverse winds that she could not reach the Arabian coast and at last put into Gombroon, where the two English factors on board her landed their goods and took steps to dispose of them. Of the Dutch *Valkenburg*, which was to have carried them, nothing has been heard since she left Mokha three months ago [1]; so perhaps this was 'the Almighties providence to preserve your servants and goods from a greater disaster.' A quantity of tobacco sent to 'Scinda' in a frigate belonging to 'Derge Saw' [? Dhairya Sāhū] has been lost, owing to the vessel being cast away 'near unto Jagatt [2]'. 'However, we having ensured them, you wilbe no great loosers therby. Yet shall we not hereafter expose your goods to the like hazard.' Adjustment of the accounts of the First General Voyage. As letters recently received from Goa brought no news of the arrival of the *John* on that coast, it has now been determined to send the *Hart* to Rājāpur to fetch the pepper and cardamoms waiting there, as these are wanted for lading the *Crispiana*. They greatly need cordage, tar, and other ship's stores, especially casks. The masters reserve the best for themselves and land only the bad ones; and they do the same with the seamen, keeping all those likely to be of service and handing over, for employment here, the 'rascallity'. The result is that 'the masters of your pynnaces rather desire these laskars then such English as are left for them; to prevent which in the future we earnestly entreat you that such men as you intend unto us may by name be inlisted, and they obliged to serve three or four years (or as many as you shall think fitting) in the country; which will avoid much trouble, and by this meanes your small shipping wilbe better manned and your estate secured.' President Breton thanks the Company for his appointment, and assures them of his zealous and faithful service. 'What disaster befell one of Mr. Courteens *Williams* near the Cape we have already related unto you. The other, Capt. Blackman commander, set sail from Goa the 6 April for Maccaw in China, by letters from the King, their constant importunity, but we rather believe by undertaking privately to serve the Portugals, having obteyned the

---

[1] She was delayed by contrary winds and did not reach Swally till the end of January, 1645 (see p. 249, and *Dagh-Register*, 1644-45, pp. 231, 238).

[2] Jākhau, in Cutch. Baffin's map of India (1619) shows it as 'Jaqueta'. Just below, in the same map, is 'Gigat', which is probably a duplication. Below that again is 'Por', i. e. Porbandar; this explains the reference to a port of 'Pore' on p. 302 of the 1634-36 volume.

THE ENGLISH FACTORIES 217

Vice Royes license.[1] Her lading for Mr. Courteen &c. accompt (as we are informed) consists of 90 candies uploat [see p. 167], 30 candies olibanum, 15 pipes of Portugez wine, 16 candies cotta[2], 120 maunds rosamalla [see p. 61], 4,000 zera[fins] in ruff amber (which they brought from England), 15 maunds small coral, 10 pieces of stamel cloth, 4 pieces ditto black, 10 corge zarasses[3], 22 almodes[4] of oil, 30 maunds of renoceroes hornes, 13 maunds [of] points of elephants teeth, and 2,000 rials in plate [i. e. silver]; all importing about 6,500*l*. sterling. The purchasing wherof, and other their engagements, have disabled Mr. Ferrar, their Agent, from buying any goods the vacant time of raines; so that they have passed the winter in Goa idly, and still continue in the same condition, the *Loialty* not having brought them any means to put them in accion. So that how they will return those two ships administers unto us occation of wonder, and raiseth in us no less fear that their necessities may prompt them to perpetrate some hostile unlawfull act, either upon yours or the shipping of this country, the *Loialty* being designed from Rajapore to Gomroon with 100 tonns of fraight goods only. In Acheen their people (as Mr. Bowman adviseth) are in as bad or worse predicament, being deeply indebted at excessive interest, and not any means to defray ordinary expences. In May last arived at Goa from Portugal two galleons, having spent 14 months in the voiage; which brought them for supplies 1000 men, great quantity of provisions, some treasure, 280 maunds of ruff corall of severall sorts, 200 peeces of stamel cloth, and 50 barrels of quicksilver. The 12th of August also arived a small caravell, which came in company of another that went for Ceiloan with advices only; and besides two other galleons forementioned, which arived at Bombaien in September last. The Dutch in these parts only prosper and flourish; who by their industry, patience, and infatigable paines and unalterable resolutions purchase [i. e. obtain] what they please; by which meanes they have now added to their other spices half the cinamon upon Ceiloan. Upon the 19th ultimo here arived from Battavia

---

[1] See the *Dagh-Register*, 1643-44, p. 241.
[2] Probably cutch or catechu (Hind. *kattha*): see the 1634-36 volume, p. 228.
[3] Or *sarasses*, a kind of piece-goods.
[4] An *almude* is a Portuguese measure for wine or oil, equivalent to about four gallons. Fryer says that at Goa 'one barrel is six almoodaes'.

two ships, the *Weesel* and *Overskay*. The former continueth still in this road; out of which have been landed good quantities of cloves, nutmegs, mace, sappon and sandall, copper, jussett[1], and elephants teeth. The other with her entire carga[zoon] was the 23 following dispeeded for Gomroon. These brought newes that nine sail more were gone for Goa, with a commisary, to endeavour a reconciliation of the differences between them and the Portugez; which the 1st of November was concluded of, the *Pao* with her lading of silk being restored to the Dutch and they allowing to the Portugals 23,000 rials for what was surprized in the *Boa Esperanca* (said to be worth 80,000). The cinamon of Ceiloan is to be equally reparted betwixt them, untill the business shalbe determined in Europe; only in the interim the Dutch must deposit so much mony as their shares may import. Upon the 21th here also arived the *Nassaw* and *Waterhound*, and upon the 24th current came the *Arrendt*; but what they have brought, or whither from hence designed, we cannot yet learn. The Portugals, having now an open trade, are resolved towards the fine of December to dispeed for Portugal two galleons and a pynnace. So that we believe in the future, as cinamon will not be here procurable, so your desires of any quantities will seace.' Messrs. Fremlen and Adler were last year granted 1,500 mahmūdīs for their ' sea provisions '. A similar sum has now been paid them on demand for the same purpose; but it is left to the Company to decide whether this is to be treated as a gift or a loan. ' Seriaes' supplied to the *Dolphin* to be made into sails if necessary. The Dutch have just informed them that the *Hind* and *Seahorse* have passed the Straits of Malacca in safety. (32½ *pp*. Received *July* 27, 1645.)

EDWARD PEARCE, THOMAS BRETON, AND JOHN MANTELL, ABOARD THE *SEAHORSE* IN MANILLA BAY, DECEMBER 1, 1644 (*O.C.* 1902).

Wrote by the *Supply*, and also by Dutch conveyance from Malacca, narrating the taking of the Malabar junk and ' what pas'd betwixt us and the Hollanders in the Streights of Mallacca '. Will now relate what has happened since they parted ,with the *Hind* on

---

[1] Hind. *jast*, tutenague or pewter (see the 1624-29 volume, p. 360).'

July 20 'off the island Cabritoll[1]'. On the 22nd they anchored in the Bay of Manilla, two leagues from 'Cavitte[2]' and (as directed) sent Joseph de Brito to Manilla to obtain permission for their landing. He returned with a message that the Governor would not receive them, because they brought no iron or saltpetre for the King of Spain. However, the same evening a gentleman came aboard 'in the Kings barge of state with a white flagg', and on behalf of the Governor invited them on shore; 'telling of us also that the Governor tooke it unkindly that, having white men of our owne nacion on board shipp, we wold send a Portugall negro to treat with him about trade; for De Brito, so soone as he had admittance unto the Governor, told him that he was sent from Surratt by the President of the English nacion as an embassador, with comiscion to treate with him about a free trade: that he had the sole mannagement of the Companies busines: and that he had brought an English shipp by virtue of an agreement made by Don Joan Lopis and Captain Weddall att Micaio [Macao] and the Governors warrant given him when he was last heare for bringing a ship unto Mainela. Theis speeches of his put the Governor into a jelousy that wee weare laiden with Portugalls goods, and that wee, to coulour the busines, weare com with three or fowre English men. Therfore in great displeasure (that espetially a negro shold be sent unto him) he answered De Brito that Don Joan Lopis invited the English unto his port of Mainella uppon condicion that they shold furnish the King of Spaine with iron and saltpeeter, and if wee had brought any such, and complyed with the contract, wee weare welcome and he wold receive us; otherwise wee might retorne from whence we came, or awaite the new Governors arrivall. And so dismis'd him, not suffering him to go into any howse or speake with any freind, but sent a soldier to put him out of the towne.' The factors were much astonished to hear that De Brito had so far exceeded his commission; but this proved only a foretaste of 'his knavery and insuffitiency in this employment.' However, 'Edward Pearce and Thomas Breton, accompained with De Brito, embarqued themselves in the Kings barge and went to the towne of Cavitte, where we weare entertained by the Governor of that place and

---

[1] Cabra or Goat Island, near the entrance to Manilla Bay.
[2] Kavite, on the eastern shore of the Bay, is still the port and marine arsenal of Manilla.

lodged that night in his howse. The next morning we went to Mainela; wheare so soone as wee weare arrived we had admittance too and was received by the Governor, Don Sabastian Hurtatho Querqero Mendoso. We deliverd him the Presidents letter, and withall acquainted him with the long continewed and earnest desires you had that the same freindly correspondency and free trade practized in Europe betweene the two nacions might be extended to theise remoter parts. The Governor replyed that, in respect wee came not in the tyme of his governement, he had no power to receive us; but if we wold awaite the coming of his successour, who was daily expected, he wold do us as much good as possible he was able. And so dismissed us, and order given to Don Francisco de Figuroo, Serjant Major, to give us entertainment in his howse; where we continewed awayting the new Governors[1] coming to towne, which was not untill the 12 August; whom we went twice to vissit and cold not be admitted to speak with him. The third tyme we weare sent for into his chamber; where wee made knowne unto him how long it was since our arrivall in this port, that wee feared much damage had befallen our goods, by reason of extraordinary fowle weather we encountred in our voyage hither, our ship being very leake. We therfore desired him we might have licence for the landing and selling our goods before the New Spaines ships departed; withall we deliverd him a wrytinge ... wherin we largly declared to him our minds; which at his better leisure we desired him to peruse. He told us our busines shold have a quick dispatch, and dismissed us. The 19 ditto the Governor referred our busines unto the High Court of Chancery; where the Kings Fiscall thought it not convenient we shold have a free trade in theis parts: first, because theis islands are not included in the artickles of peace betweene the two Kings of England and Spaine: secondly, that they might suspect that, under covert of the English, the Portugalls (rebbells to the crowne of Spaine) had mannadgd this designe to worck their further einds: and thirdly, that without supplying this place with ammunicion of warr, as iron, saltpeeter, musketts, brass, tynn, anchours, cables, &c., wee weare of no use to the King; as for other commodities, they had no need of us, being plentifully supplyed by the Chynas; wheruppon issued out

[1] Don Diego Faxardo.

THE ENGLISH FACTORIES

an order of court that wee shold depart, having supplyed ourselves with what was necessary for our voyage back, and that we shold not retorne againe hither untill the King of Spaine had so determined.' They were now at a loss what to do, especially as the westerly monsoon made it almost impossible for them to get to Macassar; while the voyage to Macao was equally dangerous, their goods were unsuitable for that place, and their reception was doubtful, as the license obtained from the Viceroy mentioned only the *Hind*. They therefore petitioned, first for leave to sell their whole cargo, and then (on that being refused) for permission to dispose of enough to realize 10,000 rials of eight, to pay their expenses. This also was rejected; but on their representing that they could not leave until the monsoon changed, and that they would be unable to do so then, unless they were allowed to raise money by selling to the extent already mentioned, their request was at last granted. On September 2 they repaired to 'the Cavitte', and took a house to sell their goods in. A present to the Royal Treasurer induced him to take only three per cent. customs, 'wheras we shold have paid six per cent., as the Portugalls did when they traded to theis parts'; and in addition he favoured them by examining the goods in their own house, thus saving them the expense of carrying them 'unto the Kings almazeenes' [Sp. *almacen*, a storehouse]. They were and still are generally suspected of being spies, acting in the interests of the Dutch, if not actually Dutchmen disguised as English; while others declared them to be pirates, intending on their putting to sea to 'take their China vessells and spoyle their trade'. Petitions were daily presented to the Governor, urging that the English should be detained until the end of the monsoon to prevent this. Fearing the effect of such representations on the Governor, the factors proposed to him that they should themselves remain and send back their ships to Surat, carrying letters from him asking for a supply of iron and saltpetre; but they stipulated that, if this supply could not be made for fear of the Dutch, a ship should be allowed to come from Surat with a cargo of merchandise and sell it here, and that they should be allowed to return in her. This overture was rejected, so far as the bringing of merchandise was concerned, in spite of the fact that 'we, in selling our small quantity of goods, have brought downe the price of all China cotton cloathinge 25 per cent.' Thereupon the factors presented a petition for leave to depart at once; 'which was graunted by the Royall Acquerdo [*Acuerdo*, Council] and referred to the Governor as Captaine Gennerall to give order to the Castilliano[1] (under whose commaund our ship lay) that we might quiettly depart without being molested by any. A petticion we also made unto the Governor, which desired a quick dispatch; to which he gave no answer; which was caused by many petticions made to him, both by the cittizens of this place and China merchants, that, if he suffered us to depart theis fowre monthes untill the vessells weare all com in, we wold spoile the trade of all theis parts by taking what vessells we mett withall. The Governor was troubled on both sides. Unwilling at first coming he was to displease the townesmen; and as loath he was to detaine us against reason. But our oppositts carryed the bell away, and we condemned to stay we cannot tell how long.' They waited upon the Governor and remonstrated; whereupon he advised them 'to present unto him our last petticion denyed by the Royall Aquerdo, for our stayinge heare uppon our owne condicions, and he, as he was Governor [and] Captaine Generall, would graunt our request, and wold also wryte unto you for iron and saltpeeter; which if you did not send, you shold send a shipp the next yeare uppon what tearmes you pleased.' This was accordingly done, and they now enclose the Governor's letter[2]. The arrangement is in their opinion a good one; 'for now, if you can contrive a way (through the Streights of Sunday or otherwise) to send them a small quantity of iron and saltpeeter, though they wryte for greate quantities, yett any thing will serve their tournes. However, they will receive a ship the next yeare uppon what condicions you pleas; which if shee arrives any tyme in July, before the New Spaine ships depart, the Companie will make an extraordinary good voyage of it, and very likely wee shall cleare two for one. The trade in this place is very much decayed since the Portegues left it, and the cittizens mightely impoverished; yet will their prowd hearts heardly acknowledge it. Every yeare they send one or two gallioones to Nova Spaina a quarter laiden with wax,

---

[1] The *castellano* or captain of the fort at Kavite.
[2] The original (damaged) forms O.C. 1894, while a copy will be found under O.C. 1895. See also O.C. 1899 and 1900 for related documents.

China silcks, and Coast cloathing (when they can gett any from Macasser, which hath beene in very small quantities since the Portegues are bannished Manilla). Theis gallions retorne hither the same yeare with nothing but provicions to supply this place and rials [of] eight to defray the extraordinary charge the King is at; for theis islands yeild him little or no proffitt more then his customs, which is but a small matter towards his extraordinary expences. The natives of this country are gennerally as lazy as the Spanniards are prowd; and weare it not for the great nomber of Chinas that lives amongst them, which manures [i.e. cultivates] their grownd and feedes them with rice, fish, and flesh, and brings them provicions out of their owne countrey, they wold starve, for they are not able to live of themselves. The commodities these Phillipine Islands yeilds is only suger and logwood. The former is at present so deare that nothing can be gott by it in Surratt. Of the latter we have sent you 362 peeces for want of other laiding. Som gold they have which they procure from the natives mountiners (their enimies); which the late Governor engrossed, and hath made it so extraordinary deare that wee dare not deale in it at present. As we make money and find its price to fall, wee shall bring the Companies estate into as little bulck as we can possibly contrive against the next yeare. Their trade to Macasser and Comboja is so little as not worth mencioninge. Once in a yeare, or once in two yeares, it may be, they send a small vessell to Macassar to buy Coast cloathing; and the like they do to Camboja, and bring from thence bees wax. The only traders to this place are the Chinas, which furnish the Spanniard with raw silcks and silck stuffs of all sorts, lynnen cloth, cotton clothing of the same lengths and breadths as your narrow baftes are in India; which they bring browne and dy them heare black to make womens mantles and mustezees [*see* p. 166] cloakes, which are worth aboute 4 m[ahmūdīs] per peec in Surratt; which they sold heare before we came for 20 single ryals the peec.' The 'clothing' brought by the English came to a good market. The rest of their goods have been registered by the King's Treasurer, but not yet valued; it is hoped to sell them at double their invoiced cost. 'Goods most propper for this place are all sorts of Mesulapatam or Coast clothing, as long cloth, morees, sallampores, homoomies, salooes, serasses, &c. Theis people are not accustomed to clothing made up after the Indian manner; your dutties and other sorts of broad clothing wold have beene worth 20 per cent. more then they now are, if they had not beene stiffned and foulded up in papers; for theis merchants give it a bad report, saying it is made up with lyme and gum, which decayes the cloth, and if itt shold ly uppon their hands but one twelve month, it wold be rotten. . . . Therfore pray what you send hearafter, lett it be packt up as itt comes from the washers, without paper or stifninge, only smoothed out like unto the Coast long cloth; and lett the length of the baile be the breadth of the cloth.' Send a list of what would be a suitable consignment next year, to which should be added some iron and saltpetre. They would then hope to clear two for one, and bring back a lading of sugar and cowries. 'This commoditie requires a months tyme to gather and ly in the sun to rott the fish that is in them. But theise cowrees are speckled ith outside, and we know not whether they will sell so well in Surratt as the white ones.' Did their best to 'corrupt both the Kings Fitscall and Ovedores [Port. *Ouvidor*, a magistrate]' with offers of money to procure leave to sell their goods this year and depart; but these officers were afraid to accept any bribes, because the Governor himself refused to take the present brought by the English. They were willing to buy goods at half their value; 'but like ungratefull people they have never don us any good for our curtesies. Every one is our freind at hom in their howses; but in court, I thinck, they are all our enemies. Very desirous weare they to have made prize of us, to which purpose they called two councells of warre, because this yeare newes came that in West India rove more then 100 sailes of Englishmen, which doth mischeive the Spanniards very much; but in respect we came into the bay with a white flagg and was received with the like by the former Governor, they thought it best to lett us alone.' They were urged to enter into an agreement to bring ammunition yearly; but this they could not do, being expressly forbidden in their commission. Then it was proposed that they should leave their goods here and sail for Macao to convey the Governor's ambassador thither, after which they might go on to Surat; but no merchandise was to be brought the following year, unless accompanied by iron, &c.; 'which they so much want that they are enforced to breake up one vessell to make another serviceable to saile unto West India. They wold willingly make peace with the Portegues att Micaw and give them free liberty to trade into theis parts, if they wold furnish them with ammunicions. The force the King of Spaine hath belonging to theise Phillipine Islands and the Malucoes is only six gallioones and one gally; two of the which went this yeare to Nova Spaina, two more they have rydinge heare (one of which is to be broaken up), and the other two lyeth som 40 leagues from hence, so old that they dare not adventure them to sea. They are very desirous to build new shippinge, to which purpose they have caused much tymber to be cutt; but as yett they know not wheare to gett iron, for in all the Kings almazins their is not five pecoes [pikuls]. Their goes uppon the *Seahorse* an old Fleminge, named Captaine Wm. Cheloan, mencioned in the Governours and Officers Royall letters, sent by them purposely to see whether we have enfourm'd them the truth concerninge the Dutch at Mallacca. They will not believe that they can hinder us from furnishing this place with iron, &c.; neither will they believe that they have shippinge and a factory att Surratt, but have sent this man purposly to be an ey wittnes therof, and to see what possibillity there is in supplying them with what they want. You may pleas to entertaine Capt. Cheloan as one that hath don the Companie very good service since our coming hither, being better acquainted with the customs of this place then him wee brought with us. He hath order from the Governor to carry himself very privatly, that he be not discover'd by the Portuges and the Dutch, and that by his meanes the Governor loose not his much desired supply of iron, &c.' The Governor's chamberlain, Daniel Jones (an Englishman, but passing here as a Fleming), has written on behalf of his master for a supply from Surat of beaver hats, knives, &c. The Governor will insist on paying for these, 'for such is his good disposicion that he will not receive any thing as a guift'. His wishes should be complied with, and at the same time some similar articles should be supplied for use as presents to others. Jones, who has been very helpful to the factors, has asked them to forward a small quantity of gold for him to Surat, for investment in cinnamon or other goods likely to yield profit here. They accordingly send the gold, which is valued at '12 rials of eight the taie (one taie is $2\frac{13}{18}$ tolaes of Surratt waight)'. Would be glad of an opinion as to the desirability of buying some next year. 'When we came first to this place, and doubted not of a free trade, wee enquired after this comoditie, but then it was worth 13½ and 14 ryals [of] eight the taye; but now, since the late Governor, Don Sabastian, is imprisoned for robbinge the Kings coffers, his estate is seized on and the goods and monies they have taken from him vallewed att more then three millions. Hearuppon the price of gold began to fall, and is now com to the vallew above said; but now it is too late for us to looke after any.' Have borrowed, and now send, all the silver they could procure, in order ' to cleare as much of the Companies estate from this place as possible we cold.' Desire an opinion on the value of the silver, which is of various kinds. The Portuguese always allowed six per cent. more for bullion than for rials. ' The 26 peeces made up tryangle wise is called virgin silver, the purest sort that is brought to theis parts. The like, we believe, weare never seene in Surratt, for there is no mixture of any other mettell in it, and very little loss in the melting therof.' Trouble caused by the fact that they had two Dutchmen among their sailors; no more should be sent, 'nor Dutch built vessells, although they have certificat from Dunkerk that they weare bought there.' Enclose accounts of sales, &c. Their household expenses will appear heavy; but at Basrā 'a better howse may be kept for four larees a day then we can with our good husbandry contrive it heare for 3½ rials and 4 rials [of] eight per day.' Desire a supply of wheat, candles, arrack, and other provisions; also a little sack, 'for this is a very unwholsom place.' The cost of victualling the ship has been heavy. While here, the sailors had three 'beeves' [oxen] a week. The ship's bread, provided at Surat, was very bad. The Governor desires that the accompanying letters may be forwarded to the King of Spain. Particulars of money found in the possession of sundry men, and evidently taken out of the Malabar prize; advise a strict investigation on the arrival of the ship at Surat. (*Copy.* 11½ *pp.*)

[   ] AT GOA TO [   ], DECEMBER 10, 1644 (*O.C.* 1904).

'Had your currall come with these shipping, it had produced good proffitt; nor can it faile whensoever [it] arrives in these parts.

So great a quantity cannott bee procured in Europe yearely as would vend here. Indeed, it is the onely comodity certainely in esteem; cloth, lead, or what els sent, findes not present sale, nor in the like demaund. Genoa pepper[1], if lar[ge] and good, 20 or 30 bales may sell yearely; as also as many peeces [of] perpetuanoes, greenes and red[s], with some olive colours.' (*Extract.* ¼ *p.*)

PRESIDENT BRETON AND THOMAS MERRY AT SWALLY MARINE TO THE COMPANY, JANUARY 3, 1645 (*O.C.* 1905).

Now answer the Company's letter of March 29, 1644. Regret the troubles and distractions in Europe. The factors in Persia have abandoned all hopes of obtaining what is due from the King for shortage of silk, and have written off the amount (141,646 shāhīs) as irrecoverable. The other injuries suffered in that country must be patiently endured, since such is the pleasure of the Company; and in any case no force can be used with the means now at their disposal. Pitt writes from Gombroon that, contrary to expectation, the customs will amount for the year to as much as 616½ tūmāns. Anticipate no difficulty in sending home the goods prescribed, except perhaps as regards indigo from Agra, where some trouble has been experienced, owing to the small quantity produced this year and the competition of the Dutch. On the other hand, the cotton cloth of that part is now more reasonable in price, in consequence of 'its disesteeme in Persia'. The instructions as to the dimensions, &c., of calicoes will be duly followed. Supply from Tatta of cotton goods and indigo; but the six bales received thence of the latter commodity and now sent home are much poorer in quality than previous consignments. Will continue a friendly correspondence with the Bantam factors, 'although on there parts they deale very injuriously and disrespectively with us, not only in reproveinge us for disposeinge of your shippinge for China and unto the Maniliaes without their leaves, because they pretend those places have a nearer relation to that residency then this (although wee know not for what reason), but by resolvinge, before they know what will bee the successe and event of our undertakeings, to bee our rivalls; to which purpose Mr. Ivy adviseth (although the

---
[1] Perhaps a copyist's error for velvet.

Bantam President conseale it from us) that the *Michaell* is prepareinge to send to the Manillias with a qualifyed person to capitulate with that Governour touchinge a future free commerce.' Believe that the Company will not approve this action. Note that Ivy, in his letter of September 8 [p. 192], speaks of such a venture having been long contemplated at Bantam; but they cannot find any proof of this. Combat the arguments advanced against the trade with Manilla being conducted from Surat. It will be easy to procure Coast goods; while, as for danger from the Malabars, ' it is not to be esteemed great, since the Portingalls, now that they have peace with the Dutch, must necessaryly take some coaurse to curbe them, that their smal vessels may trade freely and in safety; or, if they should not, wee must send such shippinge as may not feare their attempts.' Moreover, some of the goods specially in demand at Manilla can best be procured here; while the returns of sugar and sappan-wood will at this place and in Persia produce nearly treble their cost. Have already advised their disappointment in the trade on the Malabar Coast. Knipe's lavish commendations induced them to send Thurston thither last year and to counsel the Company to dispatch a ship direct to those parts, with the result that the *John* was instructed to call there on her way. Had she obeyed instructions and kept with the *Crispiana* as far as the Comoros, the worst that could have happened would have been the loss of a small amount of time. Now, however, it is impossible to say what damage has been caused to the Company, for nothing has yet been heard of the ship and the best that can be hoped for is that she has merely lost her voyage. Even that is a great trial for them, as they exceedingly need both the ship and the means she was bringing. Note that the Company could not this year supply them with sufficient money to discharge their debts; so they wait in patience, relying on the Company's promise to relieve them as soon as possible. Their indebtedness has hitherto prevented them from making any investment on the Coromandel Coast. Concerning affairs in those parts the Company have doubtless received full information from Day, Cogan, &c. The goods sent home in the *Hopewell* from Bantam would have given very good content, had the voyage been completed. Have now washed and bleached all the cloth taken out of her; but it is in bad condition, 'and they propose to send it all back to Bantam in the *Hart* to be disposed of there. A bale of 'pantadoes' has been found uninvoiced, probably laden in lieu of some 'comitters' that are missing. Fremlen's experiences in the unfortunate voyage in the *Dolphin* are narrated in the accompanying papers, which are sent in case the *Crispiana* should arrive before that vessel. Breton acknowledges with gratitude the favour shown him by the Company in appointing him President, and promises to deserve their good opinion. Merry also expresses his thanks for the post of Second in Council and Accountant. The President and Council are grateful for the *Endeavour*, and would be glad to receive two or three more of the same build, but of a burden not less than 250 or 300 tons. They could then part with some of their smaller vessels 'unto our Coast freinds, which may from thence be very well imployed to the Bay, Pegoo, Denaceree [Tenasserim], and other places, from whence, were those trades experimented, might be derived competent gaines.' Fear, however, that they may be forced to lay up some of them for want of stores. Enclose a list [see *O.C.* 1884] of the most urgent of these needs, and beg that they may be supplied. As regards Persian affairs they refer to the factors' letters, &c. Note the dispatch of Knipe and regret his non-arrival. Cannot defend Bornford in the matter of the indigo, but will do their best to prevent such deficiencies in future. Rejoice that the Company have resolved not to employ any more freighted ships. Have already forwarded a list of medicines yearly required; now beg that these may be 'somethinge encreased in the quantity, by reason th'expence thereof wilbee enlarged something beyond our expectations for the ensueing reasons. Assalaut Ckaune[1], a very great Umbra[2], gratious with the King and our very good freind, haveing long importuned us to supply him with [a] chirurgeon, wee consideringe how advantageous itt may be unto you, and haveinge a fitt oportunity, one Gabriel Boughten, late chirurgeon of the *Hopewell*, being thereunto very well qualifyed and being willinge to stay, wee have thought fittinge to designe him to that service; wherewith Assal[aut] Ckaune is soe

[1] Mīr Abdul Hādī, to whom the title of Asālat Khān had been given. He had succeeded Salābat Khān as Mīr Bakhshī (Paymaster-General), when that official was stabbed to death, in the presence of the Emperor, by Amar Singh on July 25, 1644 (*Dagh-Register*, 1644–45, p. 332).

[2] *Umarā* (really the plural of *amīr*), a noble.

well pleased that lately, when Mr. Turner was to leave Agra, he accompanyed Mr. Tash and Mr. Turner to the King, who honord them more then ordinary in a long conference he held with them, dismissing them with vests, and sending unto the President a firman and dagger; which not being yett received, wee know not what the former may import or the latters valew, but shall hereafter advise; and if the dagger be of any considerable worth, it shall be sent you, with the jewell we foreadvised the Prince lately sentt unto the President, both expected by Mr. Turner.'[1] Cannot express the many advantages that will result from paying off their debt, should the Company be able to furnish them with funds for that purpose. Have advised the Portuguese Viceroy of the delivery of his letters. 'Your pleasures also touchinge continuance of the league and amity with that nation we take notice of; which according to your directions wee shal with befittinge caution be very carefull to preserve. Nor is there any doubt but itt wilbee inviolately observed on their parts, that mutyall freindly correspondency formerly practiced beeing still continued betwixt us reciprocally on both partes.' Must still maintain that the want of sale of broadcloth was due chiefly to its poor quality, and in proof of this they refer to letters from the Persia factors. 'The greenes also this yeare received are of sad and dull colours, not soe pleasing to these people as bright grasse greenes and popingiaes.' Have as yet sold only two pieces, at eight rupees the 'covid'. Two more pieces were opened and found to be very spotted and stained; the rest are in the custody of the Governor, to whom it is hoped to sell them. Approve the Company's intention to send in future only the larger sort of coral. Had the parcel laden in the *John* arrived seasonably, it might have been sold at Rāybāg to great profit; 'but now the Portingales have peace and an open trade, wee may not expect the like oportunity, since they will undoubtedly aboundantly supply

---

[1] 'On February 7 [N.S.] Mr. Turner, the late chief at Agra, arrived in Surat, bringing (in return for the great present already mentioned) a present from King Shāh Jahān to President Breton, consisting of a "chinder" [Hind. *khanjar*, a dagger] with a gold hilt, set with diamonds, rubies, and emeralds, and also a medal of the same, set with diamonds, the former being valued at 2,000 and the latter at 1,500 R⁸ [? rupees]' (*Dagh-Register*, 1644–45, p. 244). The medal, which was apparently the 'jewel' presented by Dārā Shikoh (p. 215), was sent home early in 1646, but the dagger was retained at Surat, on the plea that 'it may, upon some occation or other, happely be usefull here' (*O.C.* 1976).

those marketts in the future. Nor may wee encouradge you to designe any other ship hereafter (as the *John* now was) to Cocheene or the Coast of Mallabar, being it is most certaine that neither pepper nor cinamon wilbe acquirable.' Two chests of the coral received last year were found to be very inferior to the rest: samples from these are now sent. Lead is in no great demand, as 'the contry is soe plentifully stored'; it would be well, therefore, to abstain from sending any for another year. Are glad that the Company approve their employment of their small shipping. If the Manilla trade proves favourable, the *Dolphin* would be a suitable vessel to send thither. Deprecate the Company's displeasure at their taking men ashore to fill vacancies, and declare that they 'know not of any in Indya that by favour or any sinister meanes purchasd their continuance in the contry, or that any have been taken ashoare which were not quallifyed to doe you service.' Will refrain in future from any such action; and now return Richard Clark. Mantell would have been sent also, but he is absent on the Manilla voyage. Commend Clark, who has served for sixteen months very ably and honestly as steward of the Surat factory, and has since voyaged to Achin in the *Supply*. Of the factors that came in the *Crispiana*, Fenn and Harrison proceeded by that vessel to 'Synda', to assist Spiller there; Davidge and Blackwell will start shortly for Agra, and with them Andrews will go to Ahmadābād; while Lewis is employed in the office at Surat. In obedience to the Company's orders, they will only return one ship each year. This time it is the *Crispiana*, the cargo of which does not differ much from the list sent by the Company. Have done their best to prevent any private trade being embarked to their employers' detriment. Will also send yearly to Bantam a cargo of the goods demanded from thence; but they must look to the Company to provide means for this, as the returns from Bantam are usually not half the value of the goods sent thither, and consist chiefly of pepper, which is shot loose among the bales in the homeward-bound ship, and does not in any way reduce the quantity of goods to be provided here. 'Off the shipps intended into these partes by Mr. Courteene and Capt. Bond, wee doe not heare of any arrived but the *Loyalty*, comanded by Mr. Dearson, who spends his time in voyadginge betweene Goa and Rajapore, but finds not any ladeinge to returne this yeare for England; nor can wee imagine how or when they wilbe able to send backe hir and the *William*, which now they shortly expect from China; haveinge neither goods nor meanes and (which is worse) beinge very deeply indebted both in Decan, Goa, and Acheene. Soe that wee are very doubtfull their necessityes may induce them to undertake some illegall enterprises, wherein God grant you suffer not as you did for Cobb, or in some of your owne shippinge; both which wee shall the best wee may studdy how to prevent. Wee doe not hear of any French shipp seene in these parts; soe that we beleive that of Deepe you speake of is gonne for the backeside of Madagascar, where they have a fort and plantation, if they have not left it lately.' The business of Crane's tapestry was included in the petition they presented to the King, but nothing resulted, the Rājā pleading poverty and inability to pay; so they are now offering to sell the debt to the King, and hope 'by Ilausatt[1] Ckauns meanes' to obtain for it two-thirds or three-quarters of the amount. This will at all events reimburse the Company for all that has been spent in the matter. The Spanish wine sent in the *John* may perhaps be disposed of at Manilla, should a second voyage thither be thought advisable. The winding-up of the First General Voyage and the Third Joint Stock has been delayed by the non-arrival of accounts from Persia and from Agra. The former stock has been credited with the proceeds of the damaged pepper taken out of the *Hopewell*, and also with the value of that ship; the Voyage is therefore to be regarded as interested to that amount in the cargo of the *Crispiana*. Adjustment of the sum due from Thomas Merry. Regret that this ship has been detained beyond the date fixed. Particulars of her cargo. Of Agra indigo they send more than was asked for, and yet have a quantity over. This was due to orders given before the Company's letter was received; but the indigo has been bought at a very moderate price and, though not so good in quality as could be wished, is the best the country affords. The Ahmadābād indigo was also purchased at much less than the present rate, and they do not doubt their ability to dispose at a profit of any left over. The indigo from Tatta is very poor. The saltpetre, they fear, will not come up to expectation in goodness and will moreover be deemed dear, occasioned partly by the cost of

[1] Probably a slip for 'Isaulatt', i.e. Asālat.

refining and partly by 'his ignorance that bought itt raw at Malpore'. However, they intend to persevere, and to send thither in future some able, experienced person. Two of the saltpetre bales missing, for which the master of the ship is blamed. The 'deriabades' sent were bought and 'cured' in Lucknow; desire to know 'whether that or Barroach whiteing please you best'. The narrow baftas from Surat, Nosārī, and Gandevī may be judged dear, but they are as cheap as could be obtained, and are at all events good. Of these they could furnish 10,000 or 12,000 pieces yearly. The remaining narrow cloths are from Nasarpur and 'Kandiera'. Particulars of the 'mercules' and broad baftas sent. Forward also five bales of 'chints', six of quilts, one of 'tappiceels', and four of 'guldars and sallows provided in Gulcondah and Decan'. A bale of 'Samana cloth', of various prices, has been provided. Have not been able to procure much cinnamon; that obtained by 'Lewis Robero' from the Viceroy is still in the custody of the former. Only six bales of cotton yarn sent, 'roome being wantinge for the rest'. Regret that out of the 645 maunds of 'tincall' bought last season in Agra, they can at present lade only 34 'duppers' [leathern jars: Hind. *dabbah*], containing 236 maunds. The remainder only arrived at Ahmadābād recently, and is being cleansed there, 'in regard itt may there be done in a month or six weekes times, and cannot here be effected in treble soe much, nor for almost double the charge. If hereafter you desire any quantity of this specie, it will be very necessary you send caske for itts reception, duppers being subject to leake and spoile what lyeth neare them. Besides, losse of the oyle [1] spoyleth the comodity it selfe.' Could not put the present consignment into casks, for they are wholly destitute of any. Regret that they cannot send the promised quantity of 'Gunny [i.e. Guinea] stuffes', as all but three bales of those provided are still at Broach. Bought a quantity of cardamoms, but cannot find room for them in the ship. Aloes, olibanum, and myrrh sent; also some gum-lac procured from Agra. In the box of 'writeinges' will be found a small parcel of seed pearl, taken by the *Seahorse* from the Malabars. Forward some amber, musk, and rings belonging to the late Walter

---

[1] In Johan van Twist's *Generale Beschrijvinge van Indien* (1648), it is stated that borax was usually packed in a pouch of sheepskin, which was filled with oil for its better preservation (p. 65).

Clark, whose account is not yet cleared. Will send Wylde's account when perfected. Yard goes home in this ship, taking with him some bales of cloth belonging to him, referred to in the Bantam letter [p. 126]. Bear witness to his very civil and commendable deportment while here; and testify that, as regards the dispute over his purchase of the *Endeavour*, he has now satisfied them that he had ample warrant for his action. Humphrey Weston, who also goes home in the *Crispiana*, is commended for his services. To both him and Yard advances have been made of 300 mahmūdīs to purchase provisions for the voyage, it being left to the Company to decide whether these sums should be recovered or remitted. To John Stanford, who returns on account of ill health, a similar allowance of 200 mahmūdīs has been granted; while half that amount has been advanced to [Richard] Clark. Account of pepper laden in this ship. Letters from Masulipatam announce that Roger Adams, a master's mate who had been lent to the 'Cirkaile' to pilot his junk to Mokha, died during the voyage. His ready money, amounting to 700 rials, has been received from the nākhudā and should be paid over to his mother; the rest of his estate has not yet been realized. Regret to learn that Peter Herbert died on October 8 last at Gombroon. Quicksilver and vermilion have risen in price very much; suggest the dispatch of a supply of each. The *Hopewell* brought seven seamen formerly in Courteen's service, six of whom came in her from Bantam and the seventh was found at Mauritius. All have been engaged for the Company, and three are now going home. If any ships be sent out for service in these parts, they recommend for employment John Pearson, the chief mate of the *Crispiana*. The *Dolphin* sailed from Swally for England on November 29, calling at Damān, as she passed, for a supply of arrack. Before she was out of sight the *Crispiana* appeared, returning from Tatta with cloth, indigo, saltpetre, and other goods. As she had seen nothing of the *Francis*, the *Hart* was dispatched on December 2 to meet and escort that vessel to Swally. Have since heard that the *Francis* reached Gombroon from Basrā on October 31, and sailed for Sind on November 5. Letters from Tatta mention her arrival at that place; so they are in hourly expectation of seeing her and the *Hart*, which will then be dispeeded for Bantam. As the absence of the *John* will frustrate the intended expedition to the Red Sea against the Malabars, they will send the *Francis* to Basrā instead with Sind calico and pepper. From that port she will proceed to Mokha, 'to meete the ship which wee send from hence with the goods provided for that place; and if at Mocho they heare of good markets att Sanakain [Suakin], she may voyadge thither to experiment the trade of that place. If nott, she shall be returned from Mocho to Persia with fraight goods; there encounter the pinnace, which in March shall from hence saile for Bassora, in hir returne accomp[anying] hir thither [hither?].' The *Supply* arrived here from Achin on December 8, and reported bad markets and poor sales at that place. 'Our great hopes of the rich Mallabar prize is also become nothing, notwithstanding she was encountred out of sight of land by your three pinnaces, the *Hind*, *Supply*, and *Seahorse*; to whom without any resistance shee strucke not only hir sailes but yards upon the deck; insoemuch that Mr. Lee in the *Supply*, being nearest, sent his boat on board and brought away three of the most quallifyed persons, who desired favour and acknowledged themselves lawfull purchase. In which interim the *Hinds* boat went on board with an unruly crew, who presently began to pillage, cut and slash the Mallabarrs; whereupon suddainly they betooke themselves to their armes, slew two, and endangered the rest of those that were on board, who to save themselves were forced to leape, some into the sea, others into the boat; and soe in an instant hoysed their yards, sett their sales, and stoode in for the shoare, maintaineing skirmish all night; and the next day ran on ground, where, after all the people had left hir, six men excepted, they very valiantly fired hir, enjoyinge only [*blank*] rials, which they found on the upper decke; dishonourably looseing unto you a rich prize, and therein to the nation much honour.' Letters received from the factors on the *Hind*, dated in Malacca Road June 20, report the arrival there of the two ships. They 'were by the Dutch respectively used, and then in readines to prosecute their voyadge.' Certain bales of cinnamon sent home to be disposed of on behalf of 'Lewis Robero'. Some silk which came on the *Hopewell* has been washed and is now forwarded. Have just heard from Chaul that the *John* has been at Mozambique, and sailed thence four days before the galleons that arrived in 'Bombaia' on September 26; this makes them fear that some accident has befallen her. Merry apologizes for the imperfect state of the Fourth Joint Stock accounts now sent home, and promises to send a more complete statement by way of Basrā. The non-arrival of the factors in the *John* has made it necessary to take on shore Thomas Methwold[1]; trust that the Company will approve this, and also the detention of the steward's mate of the *Crispiana*, Gregory Downs, who has been made steward of Surat factory. Last year William Pearce, 'chirurgion of our house', was allowed to go home, and John Tindall was taken ashore from the *Dolphin* to supply his place; now Tindall proceeds to England in the *Crispiana*, and John Anthony is entertained instead. Reiterate their request for the names of all seamen sent out for service in the East, as the commanders will not willingly give up men that are useful. Also urge the dispatch of ships' stores, which are much needed here. They are about to send the *Supply* to Gombroon with freight goods and pepper. Enclose a valuation of the goods landed from the *Dolphin*. A packet of letters forwarded, which the Dutch chief at Surat desires to have delivered to the Dutch Company's agent in London.[2] (*Copy.* 21¼ *pp.*)

JOHN FARREN, JOHN DARELL, AND ABRAHAM HUNT[3] AT GOA TO THE PRESIDENT AND COUNCIL AT SURAT, JANUARY 10, 1645 (*O.C.* 1907).

Trust that their letter of December 26 has been received and will be promptly answered. Their demands appear to them so just that they are confident of their being granted. The injury of which they

[1] Purser of the *Crispiana*. He was probably the late President's second son.
[2] This letter is followed by a list (*O.C.* 1906) of the writings sent home in the *Crispiana*, including accounts from Surat, Ahmadābād, Tatta, Fort St. George, and 'Nassapore' [Nasarpur]: copies of consultations and of letters to and from various factories: papers relating to the *Dolphin* and *Hopewell*, &c.
[3] These were factors for Courteen's Association. The letter here given and the previous one of December 26 (which was signed also by Thomas Billidge) were printed by John Darell in 1652 in his pamphlet entitled *Mr. Courten's Catastrophe and Adieu to East India*. The demand was for the money saved from the wreck of the *Little William* and paid into the Company's treasury at Madras. No satisfaction having been received, in February, 1645, a protest was drawn up at Goa, alleging that great losses had been caused to their employers by the detention of this money and by the capture of the Cannanore junk, which had led to reprisals being threatened by the Malabars against Courteen's settlements, particularly that at Kārwār. The junk, by the way, is stated to have belonged to 'Mamula Croe, King of Cannanore', a personage who may be identified with Mammāli Koya, the local Māppilla chief (Logan's *Malabar*, vol. i. p. 360). Darell adds that Courteen's ship,

complain 'was contrived in England (as wee understand) and effected at Madrasapatam'; and it is rendered worse by being 'accompanied in all parts and places with aspersions, detractions, and damageable defamacions.' Cannot find any justification for these, especially as the imputation of complicity with Cobb and Ayres has been disproved 'before supream authoritie'. Desire to be informed wherein they have wronged the East India Company or its servants; and await satisfaction of their demands, 'to prevent further and future proceedings.' (*Copy.* 1 *p.*)

THOMAS MERRY IN SURAT TO JEREMY SAMBROOKE IN LONDON, JANUARY 12, 1645 (*O.C.* 1908).

Wrote briefly by the *Crispiana*, apologizing for the unbalanced state of the accounts sent home by that ship. Now, having had time to examine the invoice of the cargo, he finds that he must also implore favour for many errors therein, due to the negligence of others and his own preoccupation. Encloses a fresh invoice, and points out the differences. (1¼ *pp.*)

EDWARD KNIPE, JOHN BURNELL, AND HENRY HUNT, ABOARD THE *VALKENBURG* [AT SWALLY, TO THE PRESIDENT AND COUNCIL AT SURAT[1]], JANUARY 28, 1644 (*O.C.* 1912).

Regret to 'bee the intelligencers of such woefull tydings' as are given in the enclosed paper.[2] They left Johanna on September 20 in Courteen's ship, the *Thomas and John*, bound for Kārwār; but easterly winds forced them to the Arabian coast, which was reached on November 3. Having watered and refreshed at 'Cusheene' [Kishin], they put to sea again, but it was December 12 before they sighted 'Dofarr' [*see the* 1637-41 *volume*, p. 210]. Two days later they found at 'Moorbad[3]' this Dutch ship, which had left

the *Loyalty*, was sent after the Company's *Endeavour*, with orders to capture her, but failed to effect this; also that the protest was sent home by the *Thomas and John* in October, 1645, and was pleaded at the bar of the House of Lords in the spring of 1647.

[1] The letter is endorsed as received at Surat on the same day as it was written.

[2] Now *O.C.* 1890. It contains copies of the narrative of Mucknell's proceedings already given (p. 196), of the letter to the Company (p. 194), of that of September 20 (p. 198), and various connected papers. It has also a copy of the letter given above.

[3] Murbāt. In the Dutch records it is styled 'Moerabath' (*Dagh-Register*, 1644-45, p. 244).

Mokha for Surat on August 24. Though short of provisions himself, her commander courteously offered them a passage, which they gladly accepted. Sailing on December 16, the vessel reached 'St. Johns' [Sanjān] on January 25. The *Thomas and John* departed at the same time from Murbāt, promising to take their letters for Surat and England, but she kept at such a distance that they could not send them aboard before she parted company on the 18th. Earl, her master, died on November 30 and was buried next day on the coast of Arabia. Their misery has been much aggravated by the mutinous behaviour of Henry Tyrrell, Henry Wheatley, and Richard Clark, who are believed to have belonged to Mucknell's faction and to have been left on shore unwillingly.[1] Henry Garry is also accused by some of having encouraged Mucknell in his treachery.[2] Knipe conceives himself bound to report these facts, because on the departure of the *John* he was elected commander of those left ashore.[3] He was much troubled by the behaviour of the persons named; the rest 'shewed themselves very cyvill and well govern'd people'. Two of the party died on board the *Thomas and John*; the others are all in good health. (1¼ *pp.*)

HENRY BREWSTER'S[4] NARRATIVE OF THE BETRAYAL OF THE *JOHN*, FEBRUARY 14, 1645 (*O.C.* 1917).

The *John* being a better sailer than the *Crispiana* and having also to call at Mozambique, it was agreed that she should go on ahead, rejoining her consort at Johanna, at which place the latter

[1] Details of the charges will be found under *O.C.* 1890 and 1911. Their answers constitute nos. 1914, 1915, and 1916.
[2] The charges against him are given in *O.C.* 1890 and 1910. The latter contains also Garry's answers. The nature of the charges is sufficiently indicated by the documents calendared later.
[3] The original agreement to this effect forms *O.C.* 1909. There is a copy under *O.C.* 1890.
[4] Brewster, who was a midshipman on board the *John*, was the first to bring to London the news of Mucknell's treachery and the arrival of the vessel at Bristol. At a Court of Committees held on January 24, 1645, he gave a full account of the matter and was rewarded with 5*l.* and a promise of further consideration. A week later he was instructed to put his narrative into writing, but his request for employment as a master's mate was refused, on the ground that there was no vacancy. In March he was discharged from the Company's service, as it was reported that he had been sent to London by Mucknell to advise the latter's wife to join him; but hopes were held out that he would be employed again the following year. This does not appear to have been done.

was to await her until August 25. The *John* reached Mozambique on the 11th of that month and remained there until the 22nd, the merchants meanwhile trading with the Portuguese. Before sailing they took on board a Portuguese, his wife, and about fifty other passengers. The Portuguese agreed to pay Mucknell 200 rials of eight for the use of the roundhouse as far as Cochin or Goa; and the first falling out of Mucknell and Knipe was over the payment of this money. The former told Garry that he would not take Knipe's word for it, but would have the money paid down on the quarterdeck table next day, or he would turn the Portuguese out of the cabin; whereupon Garry offered to pay the amount himself in English gold. The second cause of disagreement was a note sent to the master by Knipe, Garry, Burnell, and Hunt, requiring him to put into Johanna; 'as soone as Mucknell read itt over he fell a swaring and asked whether itt was a consoltattion or a muteny, for he had ordered his matts, before the noatt came, to shape ther course for Johan[na] and to putt in there.' The *John* reached that island on Sunday, August 25, and Mucknell and the merchants went ashore. They heard that the *Dolphin, Hopewell,* and *Crispiana* had started for Surat eight days before: that the *Dolphin* had 'spent her mast' and her cargo was damaged by water: and that the *Hopewell* was too leaky to continue her homeward voyage. There was a letter concerning the *Discovery,* but Brewster could not learn its contents, though he heard Mucknell 'pittie the men much and saie iff there was noe newes of her att St. Helena that she was loast.' Nothing was heard of her at that island when the *John* was returning. Between Mozambique and Johanna Mucknell plotted to invite the four merchants, three of his mates, the minister, the surgeon, the boatswain, the carpenter and the gunner on shore, under pretence of being reconciled to Knipe. 'Soe they had a great dele of good cheare provided for them abord and itt was carried ashore to be eatten.' It happened that Edward Stannyon and the cooper, having quarrelled, had taken swords with them, intending to fight; and this was reported by Richard Low to Mucknell, who thereupon rose up and said he would see the two men into the boat. Thus leaving the company he went down to the shore and, meeting the cooper, thrust him into the boat and bade the sailors pull for the ship. When he came aboard he ordered the boatswain to 'call all hands aloft';

whereupon they all assembled in the great cabin. Mucknell then 'caled for a cup of wine and dranke. When hee had druncke, he stands up. Ses hee: Genttillmen, I have somthinge to say, and I will be breefe (ses Mucknell). Mr. Knipe has threattned to turne me outt of the ship when he comes to Sirratte; butt I hope that I have nott behaved myselfe soe that you will se me turned outt; to which they answered and said that they would nott soe longue a[s] life lasted. He hearinge them say soe, ses Mucknell: Heare I sese uppon the ship *John* for the Kinge (this was upon the 29th day of Augst): and tomorrow, as soone as we are of the ilande, every man of yow shall have a 100 riales of eight apece; and as soone as we are cleare of this iland we will breacke open the Portingalles chest and the marchants chests and se whatt moneye or moneys worth is in the ship. Yow shall have ⅔ and the King ⅓ and the ship. And we will set these blackes ashoare att Comorow, and then we will awaie to the mouth of the Read Seas and see whatt purchas [i.e. booty] wee can take ther amoungst the junckes. Then wee will awaie for St. Kittes and heare whatt newes ther. Then we will goe for Ingland. Looke, what monie or moneys worth we take yow shall have ⅔ and the King ⅓ and the ship; and I will bee the man that shall answaire for you all and suffer death for yow all.' Thereupon John Pearce and Richard Clark desired leave to go ashore, but Mucknell called them 'roundhed doges' and threatened to cut off their heads if they spoke 'such another word'. He further declared that 'if hee saw two men talking together, he swoare that he would cutt of the head of one of them; and kept us under soe that we could nott speacke one with another to know one anothers mind; and we had noe weapons to withstand them, for all those that he had acquainted with his ploatt had armes, and all the rest of the armes in the ship was maid fast with wiar.' The Portuguese passengers were now put into the 'jellowatt', and Pearce and Clark were ordered to row them ashore. Brewster begged in vain for permission to go with them; but Mucknell promised to set him ashore at St. Kitts and to give him a note to say that he had been kept aboard by force. The boat was so full that those in it cried out that they would be drowned; whereupon Mucknell threatened to shoot them if they did not put off. He then cut the cables and let the ship drive, fearing lest, if he stayed to weigh the anchors, the seamen might change their minds 'and putt hime by his prettence'. The weather being calm, the *John* lay in sight of Johanna for more than twenty hours. The following day the chests belonging to the Portuguese were broken open. Mucknell gave away the clothes found therein, but put the money and gold into a box, which was sealed up. 'An invoice was taken of itt; soe there was aboutt 70*l*., and that was the most itt could bee. Itt was nott waied, butt by peaseing [1] of itt.' Next Mucknell made all the crew 'sett there hands to the bringin of the ship home to the Kinge'. When they made Comoro, Mucknell abandoned the idea of going to the Red Sea, 'becaues hee did nott knowe all his mens minds; butt he would keepe the blackes and stronge watters and cloath and sell them att St. Christovers and soe load her with tobackow for Ingland.' Plying to windward to reach St. Augustine's Bay, they met the *Thomas and John*, belonging to Courteen and commanded by Earl. The latter, being very sick, sent his mate Archer on board, accompanied by two merchants. Mucknell told them that he had seized the *John* for the King and had left twenty-three of his company at Johanna, two letters for whom he handed to the new-comers. He then demanded to be supplied with 'two barells of powder, 12 canes of mach, som candells, and the Kinges coulers'. He was asked for his commission. ' He drew his cuttan [2] and tould hime there was his commishtion : and if he had nott those things within a glase that he would be aboard of him.' The things were sent; whereupon Mucknell returned one of the powder barrels, with some olives and sweetmeats. Thus they parted, being then in the latitude of 16° S. On reaching St. Helena, a letter was found that had been left there by the *Mary*, announcing that she 'was gon for Asention to turtell'. While riding at St. Helena, Mucknell was told that three men were conspiring 'to cutt hime and his partie of and soe a brought the ship into the Downes againe'. Thereupon he sent ashore for one of them, William Poynter, and on his coming abord 'seasede [i.e. fastened] his hands to the maine halerds and caused one of the blackes to cutt of one of his eares'; and this he did without examining Poynter as to the truth of the report. Next Mucknell sent for the other two, and would have treated them in

---

[1] Weighing in the hand.
[2] Sword (Japanese *katana*).

a similar fashion, had not so many of the crew begged him on their knees to be content with leaving the offenders ashore. 'He answered them never a worde; butt went into the roundhouse and tooke a pistole that was charged with a brase of buletts in itt and fired itt att his owne brest; and itt would nott goe of and, as he was a cockinge of itt againe, Edward Owen brack into the roundhouse and stayed his hand, or ells hee had kilde himselfe. Att St. Helena he left six English men and one Japane[1] and all the blacke women and children ashore; for his mind was changed that he wolde nott goe soe far to the westward as St. Kitts.' The wind holding to the eastward, they could not fetch Fayal, and so they came on to England without meeting a sail after leaving Ascension. Mucknell had intended to make for Falmouth, but the wind was SSE. and they could not weather Scilly. No one would undertake to pilot the ship to Bristol, and during the night she drove between Lundy Island and the mainland without seeing the shore. By the next morning they were off Barnstaple Bay; 'then we had one that did undertake to carrie the ship within the Holmens[2].' That night (January 15) they anchored against 'Hartlie Poyntt', out of command of the fort; and Mucknell sent Edward Owen and the boat's crew ashore for news. They were detained on shore that night, it being thought that the *John* must have been forced in by foul weather. Next day Captain Salter came aboard and carried the ship into 'Kinroade[3]'. Mucknell sent word to Sir John Pennington[4] that, if he had not such quarter for his men as he had promised them, he would blow up the ship. Sir John replied that the men should have what had been promised them; and he sent the King's broad seal aboard to show his authority. Brewster heard Mucknell say that he would have a free pardon in the King's own hand for what he had done. When he went on shore he instructed his mate, Howard, to let nothing be removed from the ship till he heard from him. Seven guns were fired on his leaving the vessel; and that night he went to Bristol. What entertainment he had there Brew-

---

[1] Called a Chinaman on p. 264. According to *O.C.* 1934 he was really a 'China mestizo' (half-caste). He, the six Englishmen, five black women, and nine children were brought on to England by the *Dolphin* and *Crispiana* (see p. 260).
[2] Flat Holme and Steep Holme, two small islands at the mouth of the Severn.
[3] King Road, at the mouth of the Avon.
[4] The royalist admiral.

ster cannot tell, as he himself left that city early next morning. (*Appended are the names of thirteen men who were confederates of Mucknell in his plot. 6½ pp. in all.*)

DECLARATION BY HENRY GARRY AT SURAT, FEBRUARY 20, 1645 (*O.C.* 1918).[1]

Thinks it advisable to place on record his account of what happened on board the *John*, with especial reference to the charges made against him by Knipe, which he answered a week ago before the President and Council here. Until they parted company with the *Crispiana*, Mucknell's behaviour gave no cause for complaint; but from that time onwards a change took place in his demeanour, probably owing to the disputes that occurred between him and Knipe. Relates instances of the latter's unkind and arrogant treatment both of himself and of Mucknell, to the great grief of both. The master showed great dejection, saying that 'he would rather dye then endure such chubbings' [*see* p. 64]. Account of events at Mozambique and the embarkation of the Portuguese, which brought on further disputes as to the payment of the passage money. Another quarrel led to Knipe's threatening publicly to send to Surat for other ships, and to his saying that he would not make a further voyage in the *John* while Mucknell commanded her. Proceedings at Johanna. Garry was sick on August 29, ' the appointed day for peace', and would have remained on board had not the master sent for him. Mucknell got away on the pretext of looking after the cooper, who had come ashore to fight a duel. On finding themselves deserted, they elected Knipe as their commander; and while going back to the town to look for lodgings, they met Richard Clark and John Pearce, whom Mucknell had sent on shore with the Portuguese passengers. Garry blamed Knipe for quarrelling with the master; whereupon he replied that, had he known Mucknell was such a rogue, he would have behaved differently. Knipe said moreover that it had been his intention, if he found the *Crispiana* at Johanna, to transfer to her the goods and money in the *John*; 'speakeing likewise of the brave voyage that hee intended to have made to China.' Knipe also showed some uneasiness lest Mucknell

[1] Copies will be found among the *O.C. Duplicates* and *Triplicates*.

should proceed to Surat and lay complaints against him. On September 11 the Portuguese departed, carrying letters to be forwarded to the Company. Eight days later a sail was seen, which all hoped would prove to be the *John* returning; and Knipe expressed his willingness in that case to forget the past. However, it turned out next day that the vessel was the *Thomas and John*, which had met with Mucknell's ship and now brought a letter from him. From the time the party embarked in the *Thomas and John*, Knipe began to vilify Garry, striving to make him odious to the rest. William Tomblings died October 8, and Henry Flanner on the 27th of the same month. Three days later Knipe called upon the rest to sign a document he had drawn up, and they did so. Garry and others attempted to read it, but were induced by Isaacson to forbear, he assuring them that it was identical with a paper they had signed at Johanna. This afterwards led Garry to fear that there was some trickery involved. On November 3 they reached the coast of Arabia near a town called 'Herig' [Harāik?], but could get nothing there, and were directed to Kishin Bay, where they bought a supply of water. On November 30 William Earl died. A Dutch ship was found at anchor on December 13, and next day they went on board her; she sailed on the 16th, and reached Swally on January 26. Garry has since discovered that his suspicion was correct and that the narrative he was induced to sign had been altered by Knipe from the form originally agreed upon. (14½ *pp.*)

EDWARD KNIPE'S ANSWER TO GARRY'S DECLARATION, SURAT, MARCH 11, 1645 (*O.C.* 1920).[1]

As Garry's 'brainesick story' contradicts the previous joint report signed by every man left ashore (himself included), and as moreover 'he cannot find any of his delinquent party so much Knight of the Post[2] as himselfe to confirme any whitt of his riblerable', Knipe cannot imagine 'why his prittle-prattle shold be minded'; since, however, the President and Council desire him to reply he will deal with 'what (in his Irish Italianated language) my capacity can make sense of.' He maintains, and is ready to prove, that it was Garry who revealed to Mucknell what Knipe had

---

[1] A copy will be found among the *O.C. Duplicates.*
[2] An old term for one who gained a livelihood by giving false evidence.

privately said to the other factors as to his intentions of securing the Company's estate on the reaching India. 'And for the affronts put uppon Mr. Garry (as he is pleas'd to terme them) I confess that whilst Mr. Bailey, my selfe, and others weare civilly in discource, he wold often fly out into such bawling manner of singinge, with many other foolish and ridiculous antique postures, to the disturbance of our society; insomuch that I checkt him for it, and withall acquainted him that manner of carriage did rather become a fidler then a merchant; uppon which, it seemes, he tooke such snuff that he hath not yett blowne it out.' As for any unkindness shown by him to Mucknell, Knipe appeals, not only to the testimony of others, but also to the evidence of a previous letter [*see* p. 194] which Garry himself signed. Though the latter was named by the Company in the commission for the voyage, yet the Governor himself told Knipe that this was done 'for no other respect then mortallity sake'; it seems, however, to have given Garry the idea that he was not sent out as an ordinary factor, thus increasing his 'extraordinary conceipt and opinion of him selfe'. Admits that he warned Hunt and Burnell against playing for money, but denies that he said that Garry had cheated them at cards. The allegation that Knipe's unkindness moved Mucknell to tears was borrowed from Tyrrell; such behaviour was not uncommon with the master when he was 'mawdlin drunck', and he has often on such occasions 'fallen into straing raptures, saying why might not he com to be Lord Admirall of England, with aboundance of such idle foolish exprescions'. The responsibility for the separation of the two ships rests with Bayley, whom the Company had placed in charge of both. Garry's account of the proceedings thereon is false in many particulars. Admits that he spoke sharply to Garry on one occasion, when the latter disparaged London, 'saying it did more abownd with whores then Venice, and many other disgracefull speeches used concerning cittizens wives'; but it is not true that he called him 'sonn of a curtizan'. However, 'as I spoake nothinge in prejudice of his birth, so will I say as little in defence of it; because the party in England that told me he was borne in Venice, his father an Irishman, his mother a Venetian [1], did not acquaint

---

[1] This identifies Garry with the Captain Henry Garry or Gary who was Governor of Bombay (for the Crown) from May, 1667, to September, 1668, when the island was handed

me they weare lawfully marryed; and nothing makes me more suspect his legitimacie then excepcion taken when no cause given, because the proverb saith: A galled horse will soone winch [1].' Knipe narrates some trifling disagreements he had with Mucknell, but denies many of Garry's assertions concerning them. Explains his reference to demanding another ship from Surat. Accuses Garry of incensing Mucknell against him, by reporting, in an aggravated form, various expressions he had used. The master was so enraged that one night he came creeping to the cabin door, with the intention, as Knipe believes, of murdering him in his sleep, had the door been (as usual) unfastened. Mucknell, when seeking reconciliation, promised to tell Knipe something which would make one whom he took for a friend ashamed; and this points clearly to Garry. Pearce is ready to testify that the latter told the master that 'there was no hopes of reconsiliacion; and who can tell whether that was the chiefe cause or not that made Mucknell runn into desperacion?' Controverts Garry's account of what was said at Johanna. Declares that the two papers signed, the one at Johanna and the other later, differed only in the wording, as now explained in detail. The fact that Garry signed without objection the general narrative should prevent much credit being given to his subsequent contradictions. His great intimacy with Mucknell leads to a suspicion that he knew of the latter's designs. Knipe cannot tell whether the two plotted to poison him ('according to the Itallian manner'); but, on pretence of killing rats, the master 'was earnest with Mr. Low for poyson'. As for Garry's veracity, written testimony is produced of his having forsworn himself, and of his having brought false charges against divers men. Garry's insinuations against others are also refuted. *Annexed*:—Written testimonies

over to the Company's representatives. Fryer, who voyaged with him from Goa to Kārwār, says of him:—'He is a person of a mercurial brain, a better merchant than soldier, is skill'd in most of the languages of the country, and is now writing a piece in Arabick, which he dedicates to the Viceroy, with whom he is in great esteem. He lived at Achein, and was created a noble by that Queen: was born a Venetian, but of English parents: by which means he understands Italian, Portugueze, and Latin perfectly, and is an accomplished courtier' (*New Account*, p. 157).

Garry was elected a factor on December 8, 1643 (see *Court Minutes of the East India Company*, 1640–43, p. 367).

[1] This saying (made familiar by *Hamlet*) appears in a letter of Kerridge's from Surat in August, 1616, under the form of 'A galled jade will winch.'

by Isaacson, Hunt, Burnell, and others, in support of Knipe's statements. (*In all* 18½ *pp.*)

THOMAS MERRY AT SURAT TO [ONE OF THE COMMITTEES IN LONDON?], MARCH 23, 1645 (*O.C.* 1921).

Explains why he has not answered earlier his correspondent's two letters. His wishes regarding his rhubarb detained by the Company. Has learnt with regret the disturbance caused by the civil war to the trade of the Company, but trusts that these troubles will soon come to an end. Courteen's interference has much injured the trade here; however, his affairs are in a bad way and it is likely that 'his action will extinguish of itself'. The Company's credit here has suffered by the loss of the *John*, the uncertainty as to the fate of the *Discovery*, &c., but has been revived to some extent by the success of the China and Manilla ventures and of the local trade. They are much hampered by the heavy debt, and also by the want of small vessels to replace those worn out. Factors also needed; for want of them too much has been entrusted to others, to the Company's loss. These views might be communicated to Messrs. Burnell [1] and Methwold, who will doubtless assist the Governor to devise remedies. Refers to his private dealings with Thomas Skinner [2]. Trusts that news will be received of the safety of the *Discovery*. All the shipping employed last year from Surat in voyages in these seas have safely returned to port. *PS.*—Sends salutations to Methwold and apologizes for not writing to him. (4 *pp. Much damaged.*)

PRESIDENT BRETON AND MESSRS. MERRY, KNIPE, THURSTON, AND FITCH AT SWALLY MARINE TO THE COMPANY, MARCH 31, 1645 (*O.C.* 1922).

Refer to previous letters sent by the *Dolphin* and *Crispiana*, which sailed on November 28 and January 3 respectively. Now write by 'land conveighance' to advise what has happened since.

---

[1] Thomas Burnell, one of the Committees. Methwold was Deputy-Governor.
[2] Secretary to the Merchant Adventurers. There are several references in the Court Minutes to his receiving money and goods on behalf of Merry.

The *Hart* returned from 'Scinda' on January 15, bringing with her the *Francis*; 'wherein the Mallabars mallice was happily prevented, who, had the *Francis* bine alone, would undoubtedly have assaulted her, they encountering neare unto Due Head 16 sayle, which came within shott of them, and [it] being calme continued surrounding them the space of six howres, but proceeded not to any further attempt. Soe that (the Almighty be praysed) wee received in safety from Bussora 61,902 r[ials] of eight, the product of such goods as were there disposed of, besides 4,000 r[ials] left by our directions with Mr. Spiller at Scinda; which voyage hath produced unto you neare upon 70,000 m[ahmūdī]s gaines, customes and all other concomitant charges discompted; which encouraged us againe to provide for continuance of that trade.' On January 25 the *Hopewell* returned from her coasting voyage, bringing a lading of 'catches' from Ceylon, cinnamon from Goa, pepper from Rājāpur, and some cardamoms, cotton yarn, and gunny. It was then determined to send her to Mokha, 'and to that purpose wee caused her the 5th February to be grounded upon Swally Sands, with an intent to chenam[1] her, as wee had lately done the *Supply*, it being an extraordinary preservative against the worme'; but the weather turning bad, she was so beaten against the sands that she became leaky. She was taken, therefore, into Surat River and examined, with the result that she was declared to be 'defective in hold'. During the next rains she will be thoroughly repaired, if the carpenters consider that the result will be worth the expense. In her voyage down the coast she had a skirmish on November 20 with a fleet of Malabar boats, and four days later captured one containing a few things of small value. On January 28 the *Hart* sailed for Bantam and the *Supply* for Persia, the former carrying goods to the value of 181,217 mahmūdīs, and the latter a cargo worth 50,618 mahmūdīs, besides freight goods producing 15,666 mahmūdīs. By the Dutch *Wezel*, which arrived here on the 14th current, advice was received that the *Supply* had reached Gombroon on February 19.

[1] Mr. T. Avery, Chief Constructor at the Bombay Dockyard, has obligingly informed me that the practice of daubing *chunam* or lime on the bottoms of wooden vessels is still in general use on the western coast. The lime is mixed with gingelly oil and gum sundarac, and then smeared thinly over the planks. 'It hardens well in a day and becomes ultimately like stone; thereby preventing the *toredo navalis* getting at the wood and boring holes in it.'

The Dutch *Valkenburg* anchored here on January 28 and to the general amazement brought Knipe, Isaacson, and nineteen others belonging to the *John*. Refer to the enclosed papers narrating Mucknell's villany in running away with that ship. Knipe has since brought charges against Garry, Tyrrell, Wheatley, and Clark who, after examination, have been suspended and will be returned to England by the next ship. Knipe is going to Agra to take charge there, accompanied by Burnell; Tash, on being relieved, will return to his former post at Ahmadābād. Isaacson is now on board the *Hind*, while the seamen have been assigned to various ships. Caldeira, the Portuguese who embarked at Mozambique in the *John*, pretended at Johanna that his losses amounted to 17,000 rupees; and since then a claim has come to hand from the Goa Viceroy for 20,854 xerafins received by the said Caldeira in Mozambique. An answer was returned which will, they hope, satisfy the Viceroy, though not, perhaps, the claimants; and, according to promise, they now send home the documents received, in case the *John* be recaptured. 'Wee cannot in words express how prejuditiall the *John*[s] loss hath been to your affaires in these parts, besides what you loose by and upon her; your creditts, which untill the newes thereof continued reasonable good, in expectation of large supplyes by her, being at that very instant totally ruined, in soe much that neither in Surratt nor Ahmudabad for many dayes could wee procure 100 rupees; which much retarded the Bussora investment and enforced us, with unparraleld patience and no less shame, to submit unto the continued exclamations of those wee were endebted unto by exchange, having noe meanes left us to give them satisfaction. Many of our creditors, unto whome wee were also engaged at interest, required (as they still continue to doe) theire monies. Virgee Vora also begins to appeare very doubtfull of us; all of them directly or by consequense letting us understand that theire expectations (pardon, wee entreate, the expression, being it is not ours) have been so long deluded that they will no longer trust us; which in theire accions they make good, for indeede noe sooner doe any monies arrive from any parts but, before wee can gett them coyned, they throng to share it. Indeede, our predicament was much worse then these lines can represent unto you, untill it pleased the Almighty the 4th current to releive us by bringing in safety the *Hinde* from Maccaw and *Seahorse* from the

Manielies [1]; whose voyages (praysed be God) have proved reasonable prosperous, although short of our expectations. However, this benefitt wee have already found that our clamorous creditors are thereby something pacified, peradventure in hopes of payment; but whether they will soe continue when they receive not satisfaction, wee are as doubtfull as wee are fearefull that this theame may prove displeasing unto you.' Could not, however, in duty refrain from representing their need of funds. 'By the books of accompts received of the China voyage, wee finde the reprizall monies taken from the Mallabars encreased to 6,926 r[ials], which helped well to defray the excessive charges of Maccaw; whither your ship *Hinde*, haveing accompanied the *Seahorse* neare unto the Manielies, prosecuting her voyage without [the?] sholdes, arrived the 7th August; where Mr. Thurston &c. received respective enterteinement from the Portugalls at theire first landing, but afterwards were by them and the Chinezes injuriously exacted upon, and that principally in measuring the ship, for which they paid 3,500 r[ials], whereas there due in reason should not have been above 800 r[ials], nor so much in proportion to the *London*, which paid but 1,400. But that which rendered the voyage much less proffitable then it might have proved is the extreame poverty of the place, not appearing the same it was at the *Londons* being there; rendered soe by the loss of theire former trades to Japon and the Manielies; the former of which they lately attempted to recover by sending a pynnace into those parts, but had theire people which voyaged thither all cutt off. And now lately (which makes them more miserable) China is wholly imbroyled in warrs. One of the cheife mandereens, being risen in rebellion, is growne soe powerfull that he possesseth a greate part of the kingdome and is likely to be owner of it all; the King, after he had slaine [his] wife and two of his childeren, haveing hanged himselfe, for feare of falling into his hands [2]; which disturbances, with the Portugalls poverty, have left Macchaw destitute of all sorts of comodities, there not being to be bought in the citty either silkes raw or wrought, China rootes (other then what were old and rotten), nor indeed anything

[1] See the *Dagh-Register*, 1644-45 (p. 244) for the arrival of these vessels and a brief account of their experiences.
[2] This refers to the rebellion of Li Tsze-cheng against Tsung-cheng, the last Emperor of the Ming dynasty. Li succeeded in capturing Peking, whereupon the Emperor committed suicide in despair.

but China ware, which is the bulke of the *Hinds* lading, the rest being brought in gold. Nor could anything at all, dureing the shipps stay there, be procured from Cantam [Canton]. However, wee doubt not but by her returne to double the principall of what sent from hence.' The Manilla letter will relate ' what unexpected difficulties your servants imployed thither encountered in theire enterteinement, occasioned in part by the interregnum which happened just at theire arrivall in the change of governours. Also what jealousies and suspitions were enterteyned of them; [which] with patience and industry haveing vanquished, they were afterwards with exceeding greate courtesy received; and soe continue there resident, that Governour (whose letters unto us accompanies these) haveing sent upon the *Seahorse* one Captain Chaloan, a Fleming by nation, to treate with us about supplying that place with iron and saltpeeter, whereof they are in exceeding greate want; and if wee could therein comply with his desires, wee might obteine from them what lyberties and priviledges wee please, and thereby settle unto you the most proffitable trade that you ever yet in any parts enjoyed; the place being nothing inferiour for proffitt unto what wee formerly heard and related unto you. But it will be impossible unto us to furnish them with the prementioned species, such vigilant eyes have the Dutch over our accions; and without that, wee feare they will not desire our returne thither more then this voyage. And although the bussiness might possibly be effected through the Streights of Sunda [and] that the proffitt which those species might produce, and other conveniencies which infallibly would accrew thereby, are powerfull inducements to invite us to its undertaking, yet without your possitive order will wee not hazard your shipping and meanes to so eminent a danger, but rather propound unto you the obteyning from the King of Spaine his consent and lysence for an open and free comerce betwixt us. In the interim wee shall not be wanting on our parts by befitting insinuations, if possible wee may, to procure continuance of this new begun correspondency. The cure of this country cloathing with cange [Tamil *kanjī*], or rice water, dislikes those people; and yet Mr. Pearce &c. advize they doubt not to double the principall, all charges discounted, for what wee sent upon the *Seahorse*.' The cargo intended to be dispatched thither this year is shown in the enclosed list. Were the trade constant, they are confident they could prepare a yearly consignment that would treble its cost. Should the Spanish King's licence be procured, the Company must send out two or three good ships of 300 tons or upwards, of good strength. The *Seahorse* brought back from Manilla rials, bullion, and sappanwood to the value of 29,522 rials of eight; 'the bulloin the finest that ever yet [was] seene in these parts, and indeede so fine that wee shall be enforced to melt it and mix it with the r[ials] to make it of a fitt alloi for these sheroffs, who will not exceede a rupee the tola in price. The sappon wood will here yeild three times its cost'; while Manilla sugar (of which only samples were received) will give cent. per cent. profit. Forward two packets from the Governor of Manilla for transmission to the King of Spain. As the *Hopewell* was found unfit for the service, the *Hind* and *Francis* were on March 26 dispeeded to Mokha, carrying (besides freight goods) a cargo costing 224,877 mahmūdīs. George Oxenden is chief and Joseph Cross second; while Rymell, Hunt, and Goodyear have been sent as assistants. 'The *Hinde* from Mocha wee have designed to sayle unto Tuttacoreen, whither Mr. Oxenden is enordered to send upon her 15,000 r[ials] of eight, which against her arrivall wee hope to have invested in catches (a sort of cloth very vendible in the Manielaes and all parts), cinamon, and pepper; wee intending to send thither Bennidas, your broker (who the passed yeare was employed att Raybag), to make provision of the same. The *Francis* wee would willingly should have voyaged to Sauakann [Suakin] to have experimented those marketts, which are said since enterance of a new Bashaw to be very good; but her late departure hath declyned for this yeare these resolutions. Soe that she is appointed to attend Mr. Oxendens &c. commands in Mocha Road, to bring them back with the returne of the cargazoones proceede and such druggs, mirh, allois, and olibanum as wee have directed them to buy against your next shipps returne for England. However, wee have enordered your factours to informe themselves well touching that trade; that, if it prove answerable to report, wee may send thither the ensueing yeare. The *Seahorse* being now full laden for Bussora, here yet remaineth large quantities of goods for your accompt proper for that place; whereat you may happily wonder, findeing that wee have enterteyned 38 bales of freight goods; which wee professe and intreate you to beleive was much contrary to our desires; but this Governour (lately arrived[1]) would not be denyed transport of the Kings goods, in regard former Governours have been gratified in the like nature. The rest belong unto Virgee Vora and other our eminent creditours whome wee may not displease; this being the least of many inconveniencies which frequently wee experiment attends our being soe deepely engaged.' Enclose an abstract of her cargo, which is consigned to Robert Cranmer as chief, Revett Walwyn as second, and Thomas Cogan and William Weale as assistants, with 'Suncker' as broker. Cranmer last year gave ample testimony of his ability and carefulness; so they have every confidence in his management. A letter received from Masulipatam on February 28 advised that the *Endeavour* reached that port from the Bay on November 23 last, ' and was againe dispeeded from [? for] Madraspatam the 23 December, with a carga[zoon] from that place importing 7,458 pagodes, besides wee know not what goods provided by Browne at Jenjerlee [see p. 206] (whereof Mr. Penniston could gett noe invoice nor accompt) and others brought from the Bay by Mr. Hatch'. Brown and Hatch embarked on her. Later letters from Madraspatam state that she passed by that place without stopping; but this is explained by letters from Gombroon, announcing her arrival there and saying that she had found it impossible to touch at Madraspatam owing to foul weather; Hatch and the rest had therefore been landed at 'Ponte de Galle' in Ceylon, to make their way thence to the Coast. The *Supply* and *Endeavour* are hourly expected from Gombroon, and the latter will probably then be sent to Basrā with the goods left behind by the *Seahorse*. The *Supply* it is proposed to dispatch to Achin and Manilla. No goods will be sent to the former place, but Turner will be left on shore 'to cleare that bussiness'; and on her way back from Manilla the *Supply* will take in at Achin the produce of the stock now there. As she will probably then be very rich, either a ship will be sent to meet her and protect her from the Malabars, or else she will be ordered to go direct to Gombroon and so get back to Surat by about March 20. The pinnace *Seaflower* arrived at Masulipatam

---

[1] We owe to the Dutch records (*Dagh-Register*, 1644-45, p. 245) the intelligence that a new governor, by name 'Miersia Amijna' [Mirzā Amīn?], reached Surat in February, 1645; also that Shāh Jahān had appointed his third son (Aurangzīb) to be Viceroy of Gujarāt, Surat excepted.

from Bantam on January 6, having lost her voyage through bad weather. It was decided that it was too late for her to go on to the Bay of Bengal, and so on January 18 she sailed for Madraspatam, where she will remain until the end of April, and then return to Bantam.[1] At Surat they hope to have a ship's lading for England ready by next December. It will be very similar to the cargo of the *Crispiana*, with perhaps a larger quantity of cinnamon. Agra calicoes are cheaper; but the indigo, both of that place and of Ahmadābād, is much increased in price.[2] Tash has bought 500 bales of Agra indigo at from 37 to 40 rupees per maund; and they have on hand here 69 bales of last year's purchases. In addition, 100 bales, which have been sent to Mokha, may possibly come back unsold. At Ahmadābād the price is 23 and 25 rupees per bale, and so they will not attempt to buy any. They have on hand a quantity of Deccan pepper, and some tincal from Ahmadābād; myrrh, aloes, and olibanum they expect from Mokha. 'Ship *William*, belonging unto Mr. Courteene, arrived from China unto Goa the 5th January, haveing touched at Acheene and Columba upon Seilon in her returne[3]; and at Columba Mr. Blackman (as Lewis Ribero adviseth us) had conference with Don Phillipo do Mascarenas, who is to succeede V[ice] Roy; with whome he hath made a contract to bring him shott and divers other things, to be repaid in cynamon, but wee cannot yet learne at what prizes. Wee beleive he hath noe greate reason to boast of his gaines in his Chyna voyage, his carga[zoon] thither importing no more then 7,000*l*. starling, returned in 1,800 peculls suger, 1,000 peculls of tuttanager, 150 peculls of defective Chyna rootes, 100 loaves of gold, 14 tubs Chyna ware, 5 peculls of raw silke; which must defray customes, the charges of his ship, and 8,000 ryalls paid the Chynezes for her measuring and other duties; which unreasonable exactions of the Chynezes (wherein you have shared deepely) were in revenge of the injuries they received from Captain Weddall, as you may please to read in the Captain-Generall of Maccau and Citty Councells letters[4] to the President herewith sent you. Towards the beginning of this month Captain

---

[1] *Dagh-Register*, 1644–45, pp. 344, 350.
[2] See the *Dagh-Register*, 1644–45, p. 245.
[3] *Ibid.*, p. 283.
[4] Copies of these letters (in Portuguese) form *O.C.* 1896, 1897.

THE ENGLISH FACTORIES

Blackman was in Goa Road, makeing sale of his suger and other goods, intending with his gold to discharge his ingagements in Rajapore (for monies taken up at his departure for Chyna); where it is said the *William* and *Thomas and John* shall lade saltpeeter, pepper, and turmerick, and soe sometime in Aprill sett sayle for England; but wee cannot easily creditt that part of the story touching the *Thomas and Johns* returne, they being already indebted in Raybag &c. upwards of 20,000 pag[odas][1] and are fallen into soe much discreditt by the arrival of the *Loyalty* and *Thomas and John* without meanes that they cannot upon trust procure any goods; nor, when Mr. Durston tendered his ship to freight for Gombroone at Rajapore, although there were many merchants, not any of them would entrust theire estates on board him, soe jelous and doubtfull are people gennerally of them. Indeede, theire predicament is such that wee dare not this yeare (as wee did the passed) send to make any investment in Raybag or those parts of Decan, though goods are procurable at very easy rates, for feare your estates should be ceized on to satisfie theire engagements. In transcript of a letter [2] (lately received from Lewis Ribero) herewith sent, you may please to take notice of a protest [3] Mr. Farren &c. have made in Goa against wee know not whome, touching the Mallabar jounke which the *Hinde, Supply,* and *Seahorse* fyred the passed yeare goeing downe the coast; which protest they intend to remitt unto England upon the *William*; whereunto wee conceive wee shall not neede to send any other reply then the said letter, which exhibbitts the unreasonableness and unjustness of theire pretence. The Dutch only florish in these parts; who are furnished with large supplies of goods and monies at pleasure to purchase what they desire; which hath this yeare been encreased by the returne of what theire goods sold in Persia produced; hither in monies they haveing drawne from thence as much of theire estate as they could, on purpose to put in practice theire designe against Ormos; whither they are lately from Ceilon gon with ten sayle of shipps, which carry (besides seamen) 1,500 souldiers, and in each ship a frigatt ready to sett up; commanded by Cornelius Bloocq, who intends first to fortifie upon Kish-

---

[1] The *Dagh-Register*, 1644–45 (p. 305), says 14,000 to 15,000.
[2] A certified copy of this letter (in Portuguese) forms *O.C.* 1919.
[3] See a note on p. 236.

mee and then doubts not at pleasure to possess Ormoos. Nor is there any great question to be made thereof, it being very meanely provided; soe that what will become of your long since declyning proportion of customes for the future wee may easily imagine, although wee know noe right they have thereunto, notwithstanding they gaine the place. However, it shall not be lost for want of requireing; and if wee cannot by that meanes obteyne your right, wee shall protest against them, and soe leave the business referred to your farther resolutions. In the interim wee have enordered Mr. Pitts &c., when the King and Ettomon Dowletts passions shall be over for the loss of the place to treat with them that wee may have a continued residence and free trade in theire country; wherein wee doubt not but they will readily gratifie them, and then, whilest the Dutch enforce all sorts of Moores shipping unto Ormoos and endeavour to make that the mart as formerly, wee, in transporting your goods imediately unto some port of theires within the Gulfe, doubt not to obteine unto you a very proffitable trade.' *PS.*—The *Hopewell* has now been pronounced past repair [1]. (7¾ *pp.*[2])

PRESIDENT BRETON AND MESSRS. MERRY, KNIPE, AND THURSTON [AT SWALLY MARINE] TO THE COMPANY, [MARCH 31, 1645] (*O.C.* 1923).

Have already intimated in the general letter their views on the Manilla trade, but now desire to suggest in a more private manner that, if the Company decide to follow up the matter and can obtain the King of Spain's assent, a small vessel should be sent thither direct from England, by way of the Sunda Straits. Though no great profit would be obtained on the iron and gunpowder, the obligation would be such that 'other important conveniencies' might issue therefrom. As an alternative, since iron and saltpetre are much cheaper in India than in England, a vessel might be sent from Surat to Manilla with such secrecy that the Dutch would not know of it in time to intercept her. Something of the kind is

---

[1] See a note to this effect, signed by Bartholomew Austin and John Privett, under *O.C.* 1927.

[2] *O.C.* 1926 is a copy of the list of packets dispatched with this letter. It contains nothing worthy of special notice.

necessary, if the trade is to be maintained, for the Spaniards will expect to 'have their occations accommodated.'[1] (1 *p.*)

President Breton and Council at Swally Marine to William Pitt, etc., at Gombroon, March 31, 1645 (*O.C.* 1924).[2]

Since writing on February 5 ('by Hadgee Zahads jounke the *Mahmudy*'), they have received three letters from Gombroon by three Dutch vessels. Commend their prudence in refusing to accept the unreasonable farmān 'touching the customes' offered them by the Itimād-uddaula. The Dutch scheme they mention for attacking Ormus is now being put into execution, a fleet of ten sail having been dispeeded with 15,000 [*sic in both copies*] soldiers and a double proportion of seamen. They carry with them frigates ready to be set up on arrival; also materials for fortifying on Kishm. No doubt the Dutch will succeed, and this will put an end to the factors' negotiations for further farmāns. Have no intention, however, of forgoing the Company's claim to share the customs, and so the factors must protest against the Dutch for any damages resulting from the action of the latter. It will then be necessary for Pitt and the rest to repair to Ispahān, 'to acquit the Company and yourselves of haveing any notice or knowledge of theire designes, and to answer all invectives and reproaches which Ettamon Dowlatt &c. in theire passions will be ready to express, laying the blame upon us; who will undoubtedly pretend that, had wee not been obliged to defend the port, themselves would have taken more care for its security; but that will be easily answered, whilest they are not ignorant how they have enfringed theire contract, and how impossible it was, with that poore pittance of customes they pleased to allow the Company, that they should mainteyne any competent force for the same; whereas, had they dealt equally with us and suffered us to have had men in garrison according to contract, the Dutch would not have dared the undertaking thereof.' The factors may then represent that the Company is desirous of continuing friendly relations with Persia, and that, if granted the same immunities as before from customs duties, 'wee shall continue to frequent theire

---

[1] Attached to *O.C.* 1925 is a short extract from a private letter to Methwold, referring to this letter and urging the expediency of a further voyage to Manila.

[2] There is a second copy among the *O.C. Duplicates.*

ports'. Should Gombroon be ruined by the Dutch (as is likely), 'then our shipping shall fraequent Rashear [1], or some other port that shall be thought most fitting, up higher in the Gulfe.' In the event of the factors finding, on their return to Gombroon, the Dutch in possession of Ormus, a written demand should be made upon them for 'the moiety of customes and castle'; and, failing satisfaction, a protest should be recorded. Rejoice that the English merchants escaped, when the Dutch and others suffered, in 'Gombroones disasters by the earthquake'. The goods received in the *Wezel* have been sent to Mokha. Movements of shipping. (*Copy.* 2 *pp.*)

HENRY GARRY AT SURAT TO THE COMPANY, MARCH 31, 1645 (*O.C.* 1925).

Relates briefly the betrayal of the *John* and the subsequent experiences of those left ashore by Mucknell at Johanna. On their reaching Surat, Garry was charged by Knipe with being confederate with Mucknell; whereupon he was imprisoned on board the *Hopewell* for fourteen days and afterwards at Surat. Protests his innocence and begs that judgement may be suspended until he has been heard in self-defence. Meanwhile he has answered in writing the accusations made against him and has shown that his 'chiefe accuser hath bene the greatest occationer of this prejudice to Your Worships'. Tyrrell, Wheatley, and Clark have been similarly attacked, but the accusers are men who have sinister ends of their own. (1½ *pp. Received via Aleppo, November* 24, 1645.)

ADAM BOWEN [2] AT DEAL TO THE PRESIDENT AND COUNCIL AT SURAT, APRIL 1, 1645 (*Factory Records, Miscellaneous*, vol. xxiv. p. 63).

Has been directed to advise them that there are aboard the *Eagle* four pieces of brass ordnance, which they are at liberty to sell to the Portuguese; 'but lett it be done with as much secrecy as may bee.'

[1] Reshire, close to Bushire. The Portuguese at one time had a fort there, but lost it after the capture of Ormus; to-day there is only an insignificant village on the site.

[2] He was employed by the Company as writer and 'register' of letters to foreign parts and keeper of the calico warehouse, and had been sent to see the coral and money put aboard the outgoing ships in the Downs (see *Court Minutes of the East India Company*, 1644-49, p. 79).

Warns them that a quantity of coral belonging to private traders has been smuggled aboard the *Eagle* in the Downs; this should be seized upon arrival at Surat, and the owners' names notified to the Company. (*Copy.* 2 *pp.*)

EDWARD KNIPE AT SURAT TO THE COMPANY, APRIL 2, 1645 (*O.C.* 1928).

Trusts that no credence will be given to any accusations against him. So far from quarrelling with Mucknell, he did his best to avoid giving him offence, and it was only in private that he remonstrated with him on his drunkenness and evil behaviour. Bayley promised that the *Crispiana* should wait for the *John* at Johanna until August 26, and had he kept his word Mucknell would not have had an opportunity of carrying out his design. Refers to the accompanying papers for his disputes with Garry and others. Since he has been prevented from serving the Company in the manner intended, he has placed himself at the disposal of the President and Council; and 'Agra being in a manner destitute, by reason of Mr. Turners being called downe (Mr. Tash only supplying his vacancy), that imployment being proffer'd mee, I willingly embraced'. Though his contract was only to stay one year in the country, he now proposes to remain longer, in order to do the Company acceptable service. Assures them that, however 'lyable (as well as the meanest) to imperfection of judgement', his sole aim has been their benefit. *PS.*—When he wrote his answer to Garry, he was not aware that it would be sent home, and now he has no time to re-write it in a style more suitable 'for veiw of so grave an assembly'; craves their pardon, therefore, for its imperfections in this respect. (3 *pp.*)

[WILLIAM FREMLEN AND JOHN PROUD?] ON BOARD THE *DOLPHIN* AT ST. HELENA TO THE COMPANY, APRIL 14, 1645 (*O.C.* 1929).

Narrate their former disastrous voyage as far as Mauritius, their meeting with the *Hopewell*, and their proceeding with her to St. Augustine's Bay. There they found letters left by the *Endeavour*, giving an account of her taking off the survivors of Courteen's *William* and four Frenchmen who had come across Madagascar from a French settlement on the east coast; also of the wreck of the Dutch ship *Mauritius Island* at the Cape. Voyage of the *Dolphin* and *Hopewell* to Joanna, and thence, in company with the *Crispiana*, to Swally. There the *Dolphin* was emptied, her goods dried and repacked, and her hull repaired. She sailed once more for England on November 29, 1644, and reached the Comoros on December 31. After watering, she departed on January 3, but owing to contrary winds and calms did not sight Cape Agulhas until February 16. Stormy weather forced her round the Cape without being able to enter Table Bay; whereupon it was resolved to proceed to St. Helena, which was reached on March 11. There they found at anchor the Dutch *Orangia*, which had been driven away from the Cape with the loss of three anchors. A messenger sent on board for news of the English ships expected from Bantam came back without any, but 'to our no less grief then amazement' brought with him three of the crew of the *John*, from whom was obtained the enclosed narrative [*missing*] of the 'miscarage' of that vessel. On March 12 another Dutch ship, the *Malacca*, arrived, having likewise been forced away from the Cape. Nine days later came in three more, the *Olifant, Zeeland*, and *Delft*. These could give no intelligence of the *Discovery*, but related that three English ships (afterwards found to have been the *Sun, James*, and *Hester*) had passed the Cape, bound for Madagascar, 'to found a plantation' there. On April 6 the *Crispiana* arrived from Surat, followed four days later by the Dutch *Haarlem* and *Banda*. These brought news that the Bantam ships might soon be expected; whereupon it was decided that the *Dolphin* and *Crispiana* should wait for them. The seven Dutch ships, commanded by Paulus Croocq ('late Commandore at Surratt'), are now about to sail, their departure having been hastened by the *Haarlem* having been blown to sea last night. This letter is sent by them.[1] (*Copy.* 3¼ *pp.*)

---

[1] The story is continued in *O.C.* 1931, which is a consultation held on board the *Dolphin* on April 30, deciding to await the coming of the Bantam ships until May 8. A further consultation was held on May 7, when it was decided to take on board 'the English and blacks left here by John Mucknell' (*O.C.* 1934). The two ships reached England in July, 1645.

A letter in the *Cape Town Monitor*, Sept. 3, 1855, refers to a rock inscription at St. Helena which seems to relate to this visit of the *Dolphin*.

BARTHOLOMEW HOWARD'S [1] ACCOUNT OF THE BETRAYAL OF THE *JOHN*, APRIL 28, 1645 (*O.C.* 1930).

At Mozambique there was 'a grudging' between Knipe and Mucknell, because the ship was detained there to so little purpose; and Mucknell further resented the large number of Portuguese passengers (forty or more) brought on board against his will. As soon as they were at sea, he demanded the immediate payment of the money due for his cabin, but the Portuguese told him it would be paid at Goa. To this the master refused to agree; nor would he accept Knipe's guarantee of the payment. Thereupon Garry 'brought the money to him, which likewise bred a hatred betweene Mr. Knipe and hee'. Mucknell was further angered by receiving a note from Knipe and the other factors, ordering him not to fail to put into Johanna. At that place, however, there was a seeming reconciliation, and Mucknell invited the merchants and others to breakfast on shore. Howard remained on board to see the water-casks stowed in the hold, and he was surprised when the master came off and ordered him to call up the men. When they were all on deck, Mucknell led them into the great cabin and addressed them, declaring that his differences with Knipe had been mostly for their sakes, and asking whether they would stand by him. 'They made answeare that they would soe farre as their lives would goe. Why, saith hee, then I am for the King, and wee will goe for the King home. They made answeare: Wee will spend our lives for him. Then said hee: Those that are for the King and mee, hold upp their hands; which they did. Then hee tooke a cupp of wyne and dranke to them the Kings health; and soe bid every man fetch a sword out of the gunne roome'. Howard remonstrated, but was ordered with threats to his cabin. After the ship had set sail, Mucknell told him 'that hee was now captaine and I should bee master; but I told him I had rather remaine in the condition I was

---

[1] Howard was one of the master's mates of the *John*. He was imprisoned in the Poultry Compter and was now endeavouring to convince the Company that he had been an unwilling participator in Mucknell's crime. He appears to have been kept in prison until the following November, when, as the sailors brought back from St. Helena gave testimony in his favour, the Company decided to permit his release (*Court Minutes*, 1644-49, pp. 84, 110).

in before, and went downe againe. And some two dayes after hee told mee that, if I would not consent and bee maister, hee would sett mee ashoare on some island. Well then, said I, to save my life it must bee soe; hee intending then to have gone for India to have seene what hee could have gott, but after altered his resolution and would goe for England.' They went straight to St. Helena, where Howard spent several days hunting with the men, until recalled by Mucknell, who declared that he had discovered a plot on board. He cut off one man's ear and put him ashore, and would have served others in the same way, but was persuaded to be satisfied with landing them. The *John* then proceeded to Ascension and so for England. Howard would have been glad to escape from Mucknell at Bristol, but 'hee would needs have mee lodge in the house of a strong Malignant, where hee alsoe lay himselfe'. By threats Mucknell got him on board again, when the ship was ready to sail on a fresh cruise; but 'the next day morning, before hee was upp, I gott on shoare and then made all the dispatch I could away, being as fearfull of Sir John Pennington as of him, in regard I had received a commission from him to goe out as leiutennant in the *John*.' Beseeches the Company to believe that this is the truth, and that he acted only under compulsion. 'If I had not beene questioned by the Committee of Parlyament, I would have come and committed myselfe to Your Worshipps mercies.' (2½ *pp.*)

ANOTHER ACCOUNT BY THOMAS BUCKINGHAM [APRIL, 1645?] (*O.C.* 1932).

Believes that Mucknell's reasons for acting as he did were the following. 'The first was (as I have heard him say) hee had some frends that were merry in his house at Wapping, and some of them in their discourse called the Parliament "Roundheaded divills"; for which hee was putt in prison and cost him 4 *li.* and odd pound to bee released.' The second was that he fancied the Company mistrusted him; the third that Knipe had threatened to get him turned out of the ship on arrival at Surat; and the fourth '(as hee pretended) out of conscience and loyalty to the King'. Disagreements first arose between Knipe and Mucknell owing to the former reproving the latter for calling ordinary seamen into the roundhouse to drink and gossip with him. Then Knipe and Garry 'fell at differ-

THE ENGLISH FACTORIES 263

rence, and it was reported by some that wayted in the great cabbon that Mr. Gary sided with John Mucknell and revealed many secret passages and intencions of Mr. Knipes [unto?] him, which in the opinion of manie agravated the quarrell.' Believes that Mucknell intended to have carried out his plot at Mozambique, but was afraid to do so because the ship was anchored under the guns of the castle. The embarkation of the Portuguese passengers there was a further cause of quarrel, and on the way to Johanna Mucknell ' incensed the seamen against Mr. Knipe for bringing those blaks into the shipp, and telling them they would bee all poisned if they stayd long abord.' Buckingham was dangerously sick at Johanna and unable to go on land. Mucknell invited the merchants and others ashore when the ship was ready to sail, and then stole on board himself. ' First hee called all hands aloft uppon the decke and commaunds some of his plott to arme themselves with musqueots, halfe pikes, and swords, and to make the gun roome sure. Then hee comaunded the boat to bee manned and some of the armed men to fetch the Portingalls wife out of the round house and putt her into the boate, shee and as many of her servants and slaves as the boate could hold. Those sudden strange accions amazed some that were in health as well as those that were sick, knowing nothing what the meaning of it might bee. Then hee declared to the whole companie that hee had seized on the ship for the King and drew his sword and sayd hee would mainteyne with his life what hee had done, and whosoever durst oppose him in it hee threatned to cutt his head off or fling him overboard; and if any man did offer to swim ashore or goe into the boate, hee comaunded they should shoote him.' The two who were to row the boat were the only ones allowed to go on land. Then the cables were cut and the ship sailed; whereupon Mucknell ' fell to drinking of healths and promising the seamen that all the riches and goods should bee theirs that was in the ship '. Fresh officers were appointed; the chests of the Portuguese and of those left ashore were broken open and distributed, except the money and jewellery; and it was declared that any one found conspiring against the King or the captain would be thrown overboard. Finding mention made in Knipe's papers of a large quantity of gold, which was not forthcoming, Mucknell made every one on board swear on the Bible that he knew nothing of it. Account of the meeting with the *Thomas and John*. Those who came on board from the latter were plied with drink and were then told by Mucknell that he had seized the *John* for the King 'and that hee would have them to goe along with him'. They objected and declared that 'if they were abord their owne ship they would not take those affronts of him'. Hereupon Mucknell in a rage ordered the guns to be run out ready for action. 'This putt the Squires men in some feare' and induced them to promise to supply any stores Mucknell might require. He had some gunpowder, &c., and kept also three of their men who were drunk and had fallen asleep. The *John* then proceeded round the Cape to St. Helena. There Mucknell declared that he had discovered a plot to betray him and carry the ship to the Company. Those implicated were set ashore ; also a Chinaman and about twelve black women. Three days were spent at Ascension. 'John Mucnell went ashore and many more with him, and hee told them that hee might doe the Companie as good service discovering what was on the island to succeeding mariners as hee had prejudiced them in carrying the ship from them to the King. Upon this island wee found nothing but some few goats, quails, and infinite number of sea fowle (which are soe tame you may ketch them in your hand), and great store of fish to bee taken there and sea turtles ; but on the iland there is noe inhabitant but what I have mencioned. There is not any wood nor spring of fresh water that wee could find ; but tis all over as if it had bin burnt with fire. In sircumferance wee commend it to bee twenty miles.' They next made their way to Bristol and anchored in King Road. Mucknell was invited to go on shore to speak with Sir John Pennington, who 'made him very wellcome and gave him thanks for the good service done to the King'. Pennington had already received from the purser (with whom Mucknell had quarrelled) a full account of the vessel's lading ; 'which prevented John Mucnell, insoemuch hee could not conseale any thing that was not made knowne ; soe all was rendred into Sir Johns hands. Moreover, John Mucknell told him if hee might have leave to goe agayne to the Indies, hee would bee out but 16 or 18 months and for every day that hee was out hee would bring to the King a thousand pounds per day. Sir John wondred why hee desired to goe to the Indies agayne, for (sayd hee) if the Companies shipps take you, you are a lost man for ever ; and besides the King hath more need of you at home, uppon the English cost. Then hee answered: as pleased the King to dispose of him, hee would venter his life to the uttermost. The next day Sir John sent a dispatch to Oxford to the King to lett him know what an act of worth and loyalty Capt. John Mucknell had done for His Majestie and that hee deserved honnour and reward, and the companie to have 11 months pay and 13 months gratuity, which made twoe yeares pay; and when it pleased God to send him to his right agayne, hee would reward everyone according to his desert.[1] The seamen were all payd in peeces of eight, the Companies o[w]n moneys that was sent out in the shipp. Three of the chests I saw broke open; what was done with the rest I know not. And every man had two yards and a halfe of redd, and as much of grey, to make two suites apeece. This hee gave to engage them in the robbery as well as himselfe; for afterwards hee would often say: Nay, Gentlemen, looke to your selves, for you are all as deepe in as I am.' Will now take leave of ' Sir John Mucknell [2] ', by describing his manner of life while homeward bound. He would spend some time in reading books, but soon fell to drinking, first with his officers and then with the ordinary seamen. ' Threescore houres (hee would bragg) hee could sitt and drink and not bee sleepy. And when hee was in his cupps hee would say: I am a prince at sea. I am the proudest man uppon the face of the earth. I am an English man and, were I to bee borne againe, I would bee borne an English man. I am a Cockny: thats my glory.' He often threatened to cut off Buckingham's head or throw him overboard.[3] (10½ *pp.*)

WILLIAM PITT AND PHILIP WYLDE AT GOMBROON TO THE COMPANY, MAY 16, 1645 (*O.C.* 1937).[4]

Wrote on March 27, 1644, and sent a transcript by the *Francis*, which reached this place on May 11 and sailed for Basrā five days later. They then proceeded to claim from the Shāhbandar the Company's share of the customs, amounting to 132,067 shāhīs,

[1] This seems to be really part of the King's answer.
[2] This was either a mistake or an anticipation that was never realized, for there is no evidence that Mucknell was knighted.
[3] The succeeding paper (*O.C.* 1933) contains notes of charges against certain men implicated in Mucknell's treachery.
[4] For another copy see the *O.C. Duplicates*.

but could only get from him 616½ tūmāns[1]. Leaving the money in the care of the Dutch, the factors set out for Ispahān, where they arrived June 22. Though they gave valuable presents to the King and his nobles, they were unable to obtain any satisfactory answer regarding the renewal of their privileges; but the Itimād-uddaula promised a farmān ordering the Shāhbandar to deal fairly with them about the English share of the customs. Pitt left Ispahān on September 18 and arrived at Gombroon on October 13. Here he found Thomas Cogan, who had been sent from Surat on a junk, together with Peter Herbert. Their destination was Mokha, but contrary winds and want of water forced the junk to this port, where she arrived on May 29. Herbert died on October 9. The goods they brought remain still unsold, and are now to be sent to Basrā. The *Francis* came in from that port on October 31, and proceeded to Sind on November 4. Note the Company's orders regarding silk. There is no chance of recovering the amount said to be due from the King. Salary of Thomas Codrington. It is impossible to force merchants to pay customs before their goods are landed, except at the risk of losing the Company's trade in these parts and endangering the lives of their servants. The prospects of the English are much brighter at present, owing to the Dutch having quarrelled with the Persians. Constant, the Dutch chief, has agreed to pay the King 50 tūmāns per load for silk. Codrington, who was left at Ispahān, has since advised that he had refused to accept the promised farmān, as it ordered the Shāhbandar to 'pay us yearelie soe much and noe more than wee received last yeare'. 'The 4th January last, about half an houre before breake of day, it pleased God to punish this bundar with a fearefull earthquake, which ceased not altogether till about a month since. The first shake lasted about a quarter of an houre; soe terrible that it hath made a lamentable spectacle here, for it hath throwne down all the houses in this citty and destroyed whole families in an instant. The Sultan [i.e. the Governor] here was at the same time in his hommom or hott house, which, with part of another wall, fell upon him and buryed him soe deepe under the earth that it was an houre ere hee could see any light or that any man knew whither hee was

---

[1] The tūmān was worth about 3*l*. 6*s*. 8*d*. and the shāhi 4*d*. The claim, therefore, was for just over 2,200*l*., and the amount received 2,055*l*.

liveing or dead; and when (after much rummageing) his head appeared and gave testimony that hee was liveing, it was yett $2\frac{1}{2}$ houres more before hee could bee taken out of the same place. Then hee was found somewhat bruised in his face and with a great skarre[1] in one of his feet, which to all mens thinkeing was not dangerous; yett of the same hee died the 14th ditto month. About two dayes after this mischaunce befell him, finding himselfe ill, [hee] sent for the Governour of Laure [Lar], who very fortunately arrived here the day before hee died and saved this citty from plundering by its owne souldiers. The Hollanders by the fall of theyr howse had two of their young scrivauns[2] slaine and had like to have lost four more, had not God most miraculously delivered them, for they were soe decpe buryed under the ruines of their house that it was four houres before they could bee found and taken out from the place they lay in. For ourselves and servants wee cannot sufficiently praise the Almightie for His mercifull protecting of us; for, although the fall of our house was equall or rather greater than any other, wee haveing onely bare walls standing and not a safe roome to shelter our heads in, yett it hath pleased Him of His infinite mercy to preserve us from any hurt, for which His blessed name bee ever praised. The Dutch Commaundor Constant, with all his people, when they were ashoare here, not dareing to adventure themselves in their tottering ruinated house, had theyr habitation on the sands in tents and smale houses they built of bamboes, and wee, for want of tents, live at present in kedjans [palm-leaf: *kajan*] houses built in the middle of the yaerde of our house.' On January 21 arrived a new Shāhbandar, who speedily proved as bad as his predecessor, 'for this hath alreadie found the waye to steale goods out of the customehouse in the night and dispatch them privately out of our sight, on purpose to deceive Your Worships of your rights.' For these abuses force is the only remedy. On February 19 the *Supply* came in from Surat, bringing (besides passengers and freight) a cargo amounting to 161,979 shahīs in broadcloth, calicoes, pepper, cardamoms, &c. The calicoes and pepper have been sold at a profit of 32 per cent.; while the broadcloth, though in very poor condition, has made a gain of about 26 per cent. The profit in

---

[1] An old word (distinct from 'scar', a cicatrix) meaning a cut or incision.
[2] Writers (Port. *escrivão*). For particulars see the *Dagh-Register*, 1644-45, p. 251.

these cases may appear small, but it must be remembered that their orders are to enter the cargoes received at the rate of 3⅕ shāhīs to the mahmūdī, whereas the latter is only really worth 3 shāhīs. Similarly, as regards the goods from Masulipatam the pagoda is reckoned at 32 shāhīs, though it is only equivalent to 28. 'This wee thought good to intimate unto you, that Your Worships may perceive that this factory, though of late much despised, is not altogeither soe unproffitable as it seemes to bee.' On March 11 the pinnace *Endeavour* brought from Masulipatam passengers, freight goods, and a consignment of calicoes &c. amounting to 372,509 shāhīs.[1] Some of the goods were shipped to Surat in the *Supply*, and the bulk of the remainder sold at a profit of 39 per cent. There is now small chance of further sales, as all the merchants have already 'retired themselves out of these heatts'; so it has been decided to send the rest of the goods to Basrā. Have forwarded the proceeds of the sales to Surat by the *Supply* and *Endeavour*, which sailed in company on March 20. Any further money received will be remitted by exchange to Ispahān. 'Our newes at present is that here are eight Hollanders shipps of warre rideing now at an anchor in this roade, which came in at severall times in severall fleets. On one of the two first that came hither arrived one Commaundore Nicholas Block, who is both Gennerall and Commissary of the whole fleete. At his first comeing ashoare hee gave out that hee came as an embassadour unto this King; upon which the Governour and Shawbundar here enterteyned him very courteously and forthwith dispeeded an expresse unto the King with newes of his arrivall, and proffred the Commissary or Embassadour (as hee first tearmed himselfe) that, if hee would goe up unto the King, hee should have the best accomodacions this country affords, and that they would send some of their cheifest men to accompany him up; which hee refused, and onely sent up a petition unto the King, the contents whereof (as wee heare) were as followeth: First, hee demaunds restitution of the 4,900 tem[aun]ds forced from them by Ettam[on] Dowlett at severall times. Next, hee desired the priviledge to buy silk where and from whome they pleased in this Kings dominions. Thirdly, that they may land their goods custome free. And lastly, that in case at any time they should have

[1] Cf. *Dagh-Register*, 1644-45, p. 253.

any difference with this country people, that not any but the King should call them to quaestion or meddle with them.[1] Wee heare also that they have proffred the King, if hee will lett them have the half of the customes here, they will defend this port from any enemy shall come against it; but this last wee beleeve is a fable, because wee know it lieth not in theyr powers to make such conditions on a suddaine before they have leave for the same out of Holland. Before this petition was dispeeded, the aforesaid Commaundor Block and Commaundor Constant, the cheife that resided here on shoare, threatned the Governour and Shawbundar here that, if they received not the better answer from the King or graunt of their requires, that they would ruine this port or bundar; which words affrighted the Governour and Shawbundar exceedingly, and made them forthwith take care to provide for them, not onely in theyr castles but of souldiers to defend this citty or bundar; of which (by report) here are already, beside what are in the castles, about 1,500 musketteeres, and more daily expected; which the two Comaundors heareing of, and feareing least they should bee incompassed and layed hold of in the night, day after day sent their goods aboard, keepeing not soe much as a chest on shoare; which done, the 13th Aprill they imbarqued themselves with all their people aboard their shipps, where they have remeyned ever since, and have sent unto the merchants here ashoare to come aboard theyr shipps to buy theyr sugar and other goods; but they will not adventure aboard, and if they would, they could not buy any of theyr goods, beeing forbidden by the Shawbundar to buy any thing of them. And yett the Governour here suffred them to come on shoare to fetch fresh provissions till the 19th ditto that they ceazed on a Surratt juncke that was comeing in here with store of Persian passengers and goods. The passengers they suffred to come on shoare, but the junck and goods they kept in their possession till yesterday, when they released both on the payementt of 100 tem[aun]ds for custome; which mony they have promised to restore back againe, if they make a peace with these Persians. Soe soone as wee had newes that they had taken the aforesaid junck and demaunded custome for the goods, wee sent Samuell Wilton unto them, to know the reason of

---

[1] For an account of the grievances of the Dutch see the *Dagh-Register*, 1644-45, p. 246. Blocq's proceedings on his arrival are detailed at p. 253 of the same volume.

their thus proceeding and hindring Your Worships from your shares of custome; to which they retourned answer that they must looke after theyr owne rights from theese Persians, whome wherever they meete with them they would ceaze on them and their goods, although they bee aboard Your Worships shipps; by which you may please to take notice how wee are like to bee troubled with them. The 22th ditto they sent ashoare one of their young men, who speaks good Persian, unto this Governour, to desire, or rather require, fresh water and other provissions, and to know what was become of their caphila of silk and two of their people that came with it from Spahaun; to which the Governour replied that for their people hee knew nothing of them; but for fresh provissions, hee sayd, if Commaundor Constant (who was cheife here) would come ashoare and live freindly, he should not want for anything this cittie affords; but since hee soe abruptly tooke his leave of him and now keepes aboard altogeither a proffessed enemy, there is noe reason hee should furnish him with fresh provissions; whereupon the scrivan tould him that, if hee would not send their silk and people aboard, they would come ashoare and fetch them; at which the Governour, being extraordinarily vexed, wished the scrivan to goe aboard, and come ashoare noe more, for if hee did hée would kill him; and had hee not imbarqued himselfe the same instant as hee did, not onely hee but the whole boats crewe (though well armed) had bin ceazed on and peradventure lost their lives; for presently there came to the waterside a greate quantity of souldiers, both foot and horse, in pursuite of them. This passed the 22th ditto. The followeing morneing, about eight of the clock, came the Hollanders two greate boates, well armed with souldiers, very neare the shoare before the custome house; which the Banians and other poore people perceaveing, and not suspecting any hurt, according to their usueall custome flocked togeither to the waterside; when the Hollanders, observeing their time, discharged their smale peeces they had in their boates head, togeither with their musketts, upon them and killed five men outright and maimed about 20 more, and forthwith put of their boate againe; yett not soe soone but that they were overtaken with a greate valley of shott from the shoare, which wee beeleeve made them censible of their presumption in approaching soe neare in that manner as they did; of which had theese people in the least suspected, they might very well have bin cutt off all. And yett wee think they had their payment, for from our house wee could see the smale shott from this shoare fall thick in the water very neare about their boates, which being as full of souldiers as they could well stand one by the other, it is impossible they could escape without much hurt. Their boates had not gotten halfway on board but the two castles here ashoare began to shute at their shipps; which presently answered in the like language and soe continued the whole day, the shipps plieing their shott on this towne and the castles at the shipps. Whither or not they hitt them wee cannot tell; but five or six of the shotts from the castles lighted very neare them, and others fell not in the water as wee could perceive, which makes us beeleeve they lighted in the shipps. All this passed before they receivd any answer of their petition from the King; which arrived not here till the first Maye. Then they received the Kings firmaund, which gave them little or noe satisfaction unto what they required, for it onely invited the two Commaundores to goe up to the King, with fayre promises that they should bee kindly used and receive content to their owne desires. But it seemes all this would not satisfie the two Commaundores, who presently wrote a letter to the Governour of this citty and required from him the particulars mentioned in their petition aforesaid, with an addition that the King would doe them justice for the wrongs Commaundore Wilbrent [see p. 114] and Commaundore Charles Constant suffred here in their persons; [and] also demaunded 8 tem[aun]ds on a loade for all the silke they bought here theese 12 or 14 yeares at 50 tem[aun]ds per loade, with the interest of the said mony; all which if the King would not condescend unto, they could not come to any peace with him; which demaund of theirs is soe unreasonable that wee thinke the King will never yeald unto it.' Will advise further developments from Ispahān, whither they are now proceeding. Cannot yet tell what the English share of customs will come to this year, but expect it will be rather more than last year. Wish that they had authority to buy silk, for it is likely to be cheap, owing to the quarrel between the King and the Dutch. 'Wee heare that S[igno]r Bastian [1], the

---

[1] Valentyn, who calls him 'Willem Basting de Oude', prints his itinerary (vol. v. p. 245). In the Dutch records he is styled 'Bastinck'.

second of the Dutch, and another Dutchman which is with him are stopt with their caphila of 35 loads silke at Jeroome [1], where they have bin beaten and threatned to have their heads cutt off, on purpose to make them confesse what the Gennerall entends to doe this yeare with so many shipps heere in this roade. Some report that S[igno]r Bastian is sent for (by the King) up to Spahaun. The most part of this manzoone three friggotts of the Portugalls have frequented this Gulfe and sometimes anckored in this roade, on purpose to watch for Surratt juncks and others to force them to Congo [2] to make them pay custome there; whether they have carryed one Dabull junck, and had carryed two more, had they not escaped from them after that they thought they were sure of them.' The *Seahorse* arrived here on the 11th instant and brought instructions from Surat to protest against the Dutch ' for disturbing your port'; this was done yesterday, and copies of the protest and of the reply are enclosed.[3] According to the advices from Surat there are yet two Dutch ships to come. ' This evening here arrived seven Portugall frigotts, which anckored in this roade by the Hollanders, and wee beeleeve to joine with them against theese Persians.' (*Copy*. 14½ *pp.*)

ADAM LEE AND THOMAS WHATMORE, ABOARD THE *SUPPLY* IN MALACCA ROAD, TO [THE PRESIDENT AND COUNCIL AT SURAT], JUNE 30, 1645 (*O.C.* 1941).[4]

Narrate their proceedings since leaving Swally.[5] Reached Achin on May 20 and sailed again nine days later. All the merchants there were in good health. On June 7 they met the Dutch *Ackersloot*, bound for Achin under Commissary Arnold 'Vallanicke'.[6] When approaching Malacca, on June 24, five Dutch men-of-war were encountered. Escorted by these ships, the *Supply* two days later

[1] Jahrum, about halfway between Shīrāz and Lār.
[2] Kung (see p. 244 of the previous volume).
[3] See *O.C.* 1935 and 1936. The Dutch reply is couched in conciliatory terms, but denies the right of the English to protest, as the port of Gombroon does not belong to them and the Dutch are only exercising the rights of war. The English are further warned not to assist the Persians by carrying goods or ammunition for them.
[4] There is another copy among the *O.C. Duplicates*.
[5] For a list of the cargo of the *Supply* see the *Dagh-Register*, 1644-45, p. 246.
[6] Valentyn calls him 'Arnold de Vlaming van Outshoorn'. In the *Dagh-Register*, 1643-44, he is termed 'Arnold de Vlamingh'.

anchored in Malacca Road. The Governor received them courteously, but intimated that their vessels must be searched. This was done accordingly on June 30, but in a perfunctory manner. The Dutch helped them to fetch wood and water, and the Governor presented them with a couple of 'beefes'. They have now taken leave of him. (*Copy.* 2 *pp.*)

ROBERT CRANMER, REVETT WALWYN, THOMAS COGAN, AND WILLIAM WEALE AT BASRĀ TO THE COMPANY, JULY 31, 1645 (*O.C.* 1943).[1]

Forward two packets from Surat. Sailed from that place on April 3, and reached Gombroon on May 11. 'Wee expected to have seene the Dutch at anchor under Ormoose, who (by report) were in beseige of that place; but till two dayes before wee left Bunder (or the 15th of this month May) they lay under the iland Larrack; when they all weighed, stood into the road of Gombroone, and anchored within Your Worships pynnace *Seahorse*.' The Gombroon factors have no doubt acquainted the Company of the differences between the Persians and the Dutch. The English factory being in ruins and the factors bound for Ispahān, it was decided to take to Basrā all the goods on hand at Gombroon; and, as the *Seahorse* was already full, these were put into three country boats. In company with these, the voyage was resumed on May 17, but the wind forced the boats to take shelter in 'Congoo' [*see* p. 272], where their goods were transferred to a 'greate tranka[2]', which sailed with the *Seahorse* on May 26, reached the island of 'Carrack' [*see* p. 186] on June 15, and Basrā on the 29th. 'Wee landed and vissited the Bashaw[3] and Shawbunder, who were very joyfull of our arrivall and gave us very courteous entertenment. Wee perceive that, by reason of the lateness of the yeare and the warrs twixt the Dutch and Persians, they doubted of our this years comeing to Bussora. Wee finde the merketts this monsoone in Bussora much inferiour to those of the passed yeare, both for quicknes of sale and shortenes in price; Spahan being so over-

[1] For the list of packet accompanying this letter see *O.C.* 1964.
[2] A kind of boat used in the Gulf of Persia. The derivation of the name is uncertain (see *Hobson-Jobson*, s.v. 'Trankey').
[3] Alī Bāshā (see the preceding volume, p. 245).

glutted with all sorts of cloathing that this yeare the greatest part of the goods in Gombroone were transported thence in small vessells for this port, insoemuch that the towne is now so full of cloathing that merchants dare not adventure to buy till the Portugalls armado or caphila be arrived, wherein is two jouncks of Hodgee Zahad Beagues, richly laden with all manner Agra, Guzuratt, and Decaun comodities, besides divers others from Dio, Cambay, Chowle, and Dabull, &c. There supply of Scinda comodities will this monzoone be wanting unto them, for by advice from Muskatt to these merchants five vessells, which were laden and ready to sett sayle out of that river over the barr, mett with such extraordinary greate seas that they were forced to returne to Bunder Larree, where they must winter till the fine [i.e. end of] September. This wee thought would have been some advancement to your business in the sale of Your Worships comodities, espetially in blew cloathing; but since, to our greate sorrow, the 19th present arrived two Dutch shipps [1], laden with severall sorts merchandize; whose very name hath so much dulled the merketts that since theire arrivall the sortements of goods with us have seldome been enquired for. At theire first comeing on shoare, for three dayes (till they were provided of a house) wee could not avoyd enterteyning them. Ever since till this day they have been contracting with the Bashaw and Shawbunder concerning customes and divers other articles; who hath promised them the very same as formerly agreed on by our nation, but no other; which they seeme to slight, pretending that they shall be much more benefitiall to the port then wee are; nominateing theire force in shipping, and that, if they would not graunt theire requests, they would sell theire goods in theire ships or [and?] depart; and upon some occasion gave many superbulous answers, when reply was given by this Governour.[2] (who is now Shawbunder) he admired they would leave theire antient port Gombroone; and, whither they came or not, theire goods was transported hether in small vessells; and that theire comeing was for theire owne benefitt and no advantage to him, neither did the King or he ever send for

[1] The *Delfshaven* and the *Schelvisch*: see the log of the expedition kept by Cornelis Roobacker and published (with notes and an introduction) by A. Hotz in the *Tijdschrift van het Koninklijk Nederlandsch Aardrijkskundig Genootschap*, series ii. part 24 (1907).
[2] Mahmūd Āghā (see later).

them; and if that they would not be content with the very same artickles as agreed on twixt the English and them (with whom [i. e. the English] for these seven yeares they never received the least discontent) that the river of Euphrates was broad enough : they might goe when they pleased. But since they have better considered, and this day begun to unlade theire shipps[1]. Wee understand by theire cheife factor, S[igno]r Seserious [Dirck Sarcerius] &c. that since our leaveing Gombroone they drew all theire force to the iland of Kishmee, where they landed 600 souldiers and brought theire ships very neare the shoare and made a battery against the castle, which (by theire report) with the expence of 3,000 greate shott dismounted all theire ordinance and put theire land forces to flight [2]. This they pretent was done only to make the Persian censible of what they can doe if occasion requires. Imediately after, upon receipt of a letter of promise for payment of theire demands sent from the King[3], Gennerall Block and Commandore Willibrant repaired on shoare, the former being gonn for Spahan and the latter now bussily imployd in building or repaireing a house for theire affaires in Gombroone.' On July 26 the *Endeavour* arrived, having left Swally on April 16 ; she is to remain until the middle of September and bring away the factors. The *Seahorse* is ordered to quit this place by the end of August and to proceed to Tuticorin, there to meet the *Hind* from Mokha and accompany her to Surat. Will endeavour to procure as much freight and as many passengers as possible, but have had no success at present. ' Our cheifest hope is of Congoo, where, by that Governours relation [at] the time of our being there, gave us hopes that good quantities

[1] From the report of the Dutch merchants themselves (*Hague Transcripts*, series i. vol. xv. nos. 473, 474) it appears that they behaved with considerable arrogance in these negotiations. They demanded complete freedom from customs duties, boasting of the power of the Hollanders and their ability to enrich the country by their trade, and belittling the commerce of the Portuguese and the English. The Āghā, however, while professing his readiness to treat them with all reasonable consideration, firmly refused to forgo the duties, urging that, if this were granted, other nations would claim similar privileges. Thereupon the Dutch, rather than return empty handed, decided to land some goods and try the markets. They describe the Āghā as very obstinate and autocratic, and say that he is all-powerful with the Bāshā.

[2] For an account of this abortive attempt see an extract from Gelijnszoon's journal in *Hague Transcripts*, series i. vol. xv (no. 478); also the *Dagh-Register*, 1644-45, p. 260.

See the *Dagh-Register*, 1644-45, p. 262; and *Hague Transcripts*, series i. vol. xv. no. 472.

of both speties would attend our ships comeing from Bussora.' Enclose copy of a letter sent recently to Surat, and other papers. These have been somewhat delayed by 'the extremity of heates and unwholsomeness of the climett this yeare'. There has been much sickness in consequence, both on shore and in the *Seahorse*. Three of her crew have died, and many are ill. Those on board the *Endeavour* 'begin to grow crazy'. 'The antientest liver in this towne cannot remember the like extremity of heats.' (*Copy. 3 pp.*)

WILLIAM PITT, PHILIP WYLDE, AND THOMAS CODRINGTON[1] AT ISPAHĀN TO [THE PRESIDENT AND COUNCIL AT SURAT], SEPTEMBER 7, 1645 (*O.C.* 1944).

Arrival of the *Seahorse* on May 11. As directed, they protested against the Dutch, whose reply has been forwarded to the Company. The *Seahorse* sailed on May 16 for Basrā, and next day Wylde and Wilton started for Ispahān. 'The 19 ditto arrived in Gombroone Capt. John Durson, with two marchants, on Esquire Courteens ship *Loyallty*[2], with a freight of Moores and Banian goods from Rajapore, and brought for their imployers accompt onely about 200 tem[aun]ds worth of sugar, some smal quantity of rice, plancke, and bamboos. At their first comeinge ashoare, they landed at and came directly to our house, where not finding soe good entertainement as peradventure they expected, the next day they hired a house of ther owne and pretended to stay there all the heates to make sale of ther goods; which William Pitts perceaveinge drew a protest against them for comeing to our Honorable Employers port and disturbeing ther trade; to which Capt. Durson [returned] a contraprotest, copy of which goeth hereinclosed to your perusall.[3] Before they came to

[1] The two latter sign only with reservations.
[2] Cf. the *Dagh-Register*, 1644-45, p. 264.
[3] Pitt's protest forms *O.C.* 1938, and Durson's answer *O.C.* 1939. With the latter was transmitted a document signed by Durson, Pr. Demasters, and Stephen Hill, and entitled 'a declaration or analysis of the two Companies, vizt. Courtenians and Cockenians' (*O.C.* 1940). In this Courteen's Association is alleged to be 'grounded upon supreame authoritie, by patent under the greate seale of England, justified in each particuler clause before a Parliament Comittee, legall, nationall, by Parliament allowable'; while the original Company is denounced as 'illegall, monopoliticall, by Parliament damnable; which, togeather with the dissolution of their Joint Stocke, declares them noe corporation or company at all.' Pitt's employers are declared to be a third body of 'Cockenians' (from the name of the Governor, William Cokayne), claiming without reason to be the East India Company, and their proceedings are roundly denounced. A claim is asserted to the English rights 'in the

an anker, William Pitt went to the Governour and Shabunder and acquainted them that the aforesaid ship belonged not to our Honorable Imployers, and that not any of the Esquires people or shipping ought to come where we are or have our residence; to which the Shabunder replyed that since they were come with marchants goods to his Kings port, he could not put them away till such time he heard from his Kinge; but said he would deale with them soe this yeare that they should have noe encouragement to come thither, againe; besids [he] promised to make them pay the full customes that other strangers pay, butt was not soe good as his word, for (as we are informed by our brokers) hee hath since remitted them the same; and they, haveinge sould off their sugar, are gone for Bussara. What project they have in their heads to come into these parts and to goe for Bussora we cannot certainely advice you. Their cheifest pretence at first was that they came only with freight goods, being (as they say) driven therunto by our Honorable Imployers, by deteineinge from them 5,000*l.*, which (as they say) Mr. Bowen forced from them and should have sett them about other imploymentt where they have ther residency. They enquired much after Mr. Bowen and complained that hee had done them much wronge. Besids, some of them reported that they are come out a wild goose chace; which, with their goeinge for Bussora, makes us to suspect they have noe good meaneinge unto our Honorable Imployers ships or estates there.' Have accordingly sent an express to the factors at Basrā, warning them of this.[1] After much wrangling with the Shāhbandar about the customs, he made up the amount to 615 tūmāns, 100 shāhīs, and this it was deemed prudent to accept. The money was remitted by exchange to Ispahān, where Pitt arrived on June 17. Sales of broadcloth &c. there. Interview with the Itimād-uddaula. As for the Dutch, 'about the begininge of June last they with seven shipps beleaguered the castle of Kishmee, on which they spent 2,000 shott, butt did little hurt, only brake downe the upper parts of the walls of itt. They had once landed four[2]

castle and customes of Ormos, as a flower belonging to the Crowne'; particularly as these rights were acquired in the first place by Captain Weddell.

[1] See *O.C.* 1942. That there were good grounds for the factors' fears is shown in a note on p. 236, *supra*.

[2] In the letter to Basrā (*O.C.* 1942) the number of guns landed is given as three. From Geleijnszoon's report this seems the correct number.

peices ordinance, but was soone forced to carry them abord againe by new forces of the Persians that the Shabunder sent over. This newes was carryed in five dayes up to the Kinge, who, beinge more feared then hurt, presently sent for S[igno]r Bastian, the second of the Dutch, and told him that, if Comander Blocke would cease from his warrs and come up unto him, he should have what justice and content himselfe should desire.' Thereupon Blocq set out for court and arrived here on July 16; but after being feasted by the Itimād-uddaula, 'his cold turneing unto a burninge feavour, and that encreasinge every day more and more on him, the 10th July [*should be* August] he died; and the next day, by order of Ettam[en] Dowlett, was accompanied to his grave by all the Armenians.' Since then the business of the Dutch has been at a standstill, awaiting intelligence from Gombroon. Now answer two letters received from Surat. Money missing from the chests sent in the *Supply*. Will see to the recovery of the value of the counterfeit &c. coin when next they are at Gombroon. The *Endeavour* reached that port on June 27. Have already mentioned the negotiations of the Dutch with the Persians; as nothing has been said to the factors on the point, they hope that the English rights will not be affected. The Mokha goods landed from the native vessel were sent on to Basrā, as previously advised. Intend to buy some horses for Surat at Shīrāz, where they are cheaper than at Ispahān. Trouble with their late broker. Their reasons for remitting their cash to Ispahān were that the Dutch at Gombroon refused to take charge of it and that they were afraid to send it to Surat, for fear of the Malabars. Goods sent in the *Supply*. Cause of the poor prices realized by the Masulipatam goods. Regret that the rosewater proved to be of bad quality. Will endeavour to supply the fruit, &c., desired. The money and goods for Surat are now being sent down to Gombroon for embarkation in the *Endeavour*; also their letters and accounts. 'Now you [may] please to take notice that soe soone as the King had received newes of the Hollanders assaulting Kishmee, Ettamen Dowlett paid backe, or willed the Duch to discount it upon accompt of silke, the [*blank*] tem[aun]ds which were forced from them; and it is not onely said by the Dutch themselves but by others that the King in his fir[maun]d to the Comander Block sent down promised to lett them have silke att the price they had in Shaw Abass time, which was (as weé heare) att 32 tem[aun]ds per load. How Ettam[en] Dowlett will performe the Kinges [promise?], now the aforesaid Blocke is dead, time must shew. The Dutch here report that they have already liberty [to buy?] where and of whom they please.' Codrington has been busy all the year in endeavouring to collect the outstanding debts, but there is no hope of recovering anything. Pitt is unable as yet to accompany Wylde to Gombroon, but will start as soon as he can take leave of the Itimād-uddaula. He reiterates his desire to be allowed to go to Surat by the first ship. Wylde also petitions for leave to return to India and thence to England, his covenanted time of service being nearly expired. (*Copy.* 8 *pp.*)

THOMAS IVY, HENRY GREENHILL, GEORGE TRAVELL, AND WILLIAM MINN AT FORT ST. GEORGE TO THE PRESIDENT AND COUNCIL AT SURAT, SEPTEMBER 8, 1645 (*O.C.* 1 45).

Wrote last on August 5 [*not extant*]. 'Wee have formerly advised you of the greate difference betwixt the Dutch and Molay, which now is fallen into open warrs. And 13th August there was a Dutch marchant going from St. Tome to Pullicatt, and within five miles of the place, at a little towne where lay 150 of Molays souldyers, was by them seased upon; which newes presently was carryed to Pullicatt; whereupon the Dutch Governour presently sent out 40 Dutch musketeirs and 150 blacke souldyers, with two brass guns, to rescue their marchant and to take him from Molayes souldyers perforce. But noe sooner the Dutch approached neare the towne where their marchant was, but the Gentues souldyers (being but 150, as aforesaid) plyed att them with ther small shott, and the Dutch answering them againe with there two brasse gunes, which they discharged at the Jentyues six or eight tymes, which noise drew more ayde unto the Jentues; which soone caused the Dutch to retreate to their fort, but was forced to leave their two brass gunes and their marchant behind them, to their great disgrace and shame[1]. The marchant is now in our fort, upon his ransome of 2,000 pag[o]ds, which the Agent hath, upon a letter from the Governour of Pullicate to him, ingaged himselfe unto Molay for the payment of the mony or the returne of his person dead or alive

---

[1] A brief account of this incident will be found in the *Dagh-Register* for 1644–45, p. 356.

uppon demand. Soe that it is come to such a passe, through Molayes meanes, who is in such favour with the King that he ruleth both King and contry, and hath prevailed soe farre with the King to send his mandates to all his governours throughout his kingdome to seaze uppon all the goods which is in any Jentues marchants hands belonginge unto the Dutch; and whosoever shalbe found to deny any of their goods, that party to be seazd upon and all his estate forfitted unto the Kinge. And it is not only the goods of the Dutch they seaze upon, but their persons also. Soe that they have in Allumbrough [Alamparai : *see the preceding volume*, p. 267] seazd upon two Dutchmen and taken 6,000 ryalls of eight in goods from them and put their men in irons; and here in these parts they have seazed upon neare 30,000 ryalls of eight more in goods. And most parte of the said goods are allready gott together by the Kings officers to a greatt towne [Punamallee?] some t[w]elve miles from our fort, where all the other goods must be brought, and there sould by the Kings Bramine and officers to those marchants that hath mony to buy them. Soe that what goods is already sould is bought by our marchants which are indebted unto our Company; which they have brought unto our fort for parte satisfacion of their debts. And soe soone as the rest of [the] goods are gott together, they intend to buy them alsoe and bring them unto us. Soe that within this 20 dayes we make noe question but they will bring us in to the amount of 30,000 ryals in very good cloth; soe that wee shalbe indebted unto them about 10,000 ryals, which we have ingaged ourselves to pay in 20 dayes, in regard the money is the Kinges. Therefore, to maintaine our marchants and our owne creditts, we have required Mr. Pennistonne to take up soe much mony at Meslapatam for three months tyme, and presently to remitt it unto us, in which we hope he will nott fayle us. Wee disputed amongst ourselves before wee received these goods of our marchants, beinge taken from the Dutch marchants by the Kinge and Molay as aforesaid, whether wee might in the least kind infringe the articles of peace betwixt [us] and the Dutch, or that they could in any kind have any pretence against us in this doeinge. Soe wee jointly and severally concluded that we might lawfully receave these goods of our marchants, they being ingaged to our Company and the goods in the open markett sould unto them by the Kings officers. ' Moreover, the Dutch had never possession of these goods, neither were they taken from them, but seized upon by the Kinge in the hands of his owne subjects; soe that noe man can justly say that they are the Dutch their goods. Neither as yett hath the Governour of Pullicatte protested against us for doeinge what we have done; which if he should, we would answere him as his predecessor did Mr. Cogan, when he went to Porta Nova to receave cloth their for which he had long before paid out the Companies money and was frighted from thence by the Dutch ther invention without receiveinge any cloth att all, and was glad he gott himselfe away safe from thence; when presently a Dutch ship afterwards came and carryed away all the cloth to Pullicatte [see p. 38]; soe all the satisfaccion that Mr. Cogan could gett from the Dutch Governour [was?] that he receaved the cloth of their marchants that were indebted to ther Company; which answere wee shall now returne unto them, if they att any time question us in this cause.' Yesterday the *Advice* returned from 'Townapa[tam]' [Tegnapatam], bringing goods to the value of 13,000 rials of eight. Hope, therefore, to dispeed her by the end of this month to Bantam with a good cargo, and to have ready a cargo for Persia by December 10. Will then, on hearing from Surat, prepare a lading of cloth to be sent to Bantam next April in the *Seaflower*. 'Soe, as it is our care in the provideing of these goods, we must beseech you and the President of Bantam to provide us with shippinge and monyes for the mainteininge of our creditte, which now lyeth att stake with our marchants, for, if we now fayle them, they wilbe utterly disparaged and we shamfully disgraced, even to the losse of the Companies trade in this Kings dominions, which is proferred wholly to us and that the Dutch shall never trade here againe, provided we have an annuall supply of 150,000 rials of eight; which we can easily invest here at the same charge as we now are att. And we are confident that our marchants will not fayle us in what they promise, in reguard the cheife [1] of them is Molay his bosome freind, whome he endeavoreth to make sole marchant in this Kings dominions, as himselfe was in a manner when he was with the Dutch.' As a vessel will be needed to send to Persia in December, they suggest the purchase of one which 'Molay' was preparing for a voyage to Achin, since abandoned

[1] Apparently this was Seshadri Chetti (see pp. 81, 294).

owing to the rupture with the Dutch. He asks 3,000 rials for her. Pollen, the master of the *Advice*, who saw her at Tegnapatam, considers her suitable. The manning of her is a difficulty, unless they take some soldiers out of the Fort (which will leave them 'miserably provided here') and fill up with 'Jentue saylors'. Lament that the Company 'will not afford us as much as a boate upon the Coast'; but it is useless to complain. Request instructions upon the point; also the speedy remittance of 20,000 rials without fail, to enable them to meet their engagements. (*Copy.* 3 *pp.*)

WILLIAM PITT AND THOMAS CODRINGTON AT ISPAHĀN TO THE PRESIDENT AND COUNCIL AT SURAT, SEPTEMBER 18, 1645 (*O.C.* 1946).

Wrote last on the 7th, on which date Philip Wylde set out for Gombroon. The Dutch here have been ordered to return to that place. They petitioned the Itimād-uddaula for the performance of the King's promises made in his recent farmān. 'He desired to know of them which way they could performe ther promise to his Kinge in bringinge more profitt to his port then the custome of their goods amounts unto; to which they replyed that they [would?] wright unto the marchants of Meslapatan, India, and Visapore [Bījāpur], and desire them to come unto Gombroone. Edmund [*sic*] Dowlett returned them answere againe that, when hee sees they can performe their promise, his King will not be backward to make good his firman, and to that purpose have [hath?] written unto the Generall of Batavia, and hath resolved to send a Persian and our quondam linquist Shavelle[1] unto him to treite about their bussinesses, or, if they cannot come to agreement with him theire, to desire him to send some understanding man hether to end theire differences here. In the meane time till the aforesaid messengers returnes from Batavia, they have leave to land and make sale of their goods and to buy silke where or of whom they please, without payinge custome for it. . . . The 4,900 tomands which was forced from them is not (as the second of the Dutch reported it was) returned to them, nor like to bee; for Edmund Dowlett in our presence made appeare unto them that the custome of their goods

[1] In *O.C.* 1944 he is termed 'Shavallee' and 'Shevallee'. He had recently quitted the English service for the Dutch. The name may be intended for Shāh Walī.

amounts to 30,000 tomands, of which his Kinge hath received noe more then the aforesaid 4,900 tomands; soe that there rests due from them 25,100 tomands, which the King hath now remitted unto them.' (*Copy.* 1¼ *pp.*)

ROBERT CRANMER, REVETT WALWYN, AND THOMAS COGAN AT BASRĀ TO THE PRESIDENT AND COUNCIL AT SURAT, SEPTEMBER 22, 1645 (*O.C.* 1947).[1]

Reached this place on June 29, and were well received. They found the city glutted with goods, owing to the stoppage of trade at Gombroon by the hostilities there. Two Dutch ships arrived here on July 19; 'but as yet have landed but little goods and sold but to the amount of 15 or 18,000 rials, for to receive which they were forced to stay there ship some 16 dayes longer then intended. One of them[2] some six dayes since sett sayle for Gombroone.' They have, however, spoiled the market for the English. The Dutch are generally hated here, and the Governor has several times told them that they can go when they pleased, if they are not satisfied to have the same privileges as the English. Deficiencies and defects in the *Seahorse*'s cargo. That vessel was dispatched to Tuticorin on August 28. Six of her crew died here. The *Endeavour* arrived July 26, but it was the end of August before they could house all the goods she brought. List of deficiencies in her cargo. 'Capt. John Durson, belonging to the Courteens Company, arrived here the 3d August with a poore carga[zoon], vizt. some 100 bags of pepper for accompt of theire Company, 40 loggs, as many plancks, and a parcell of bass to make roapes. He anchored some five dayes at Bunder Reack[3] and sold some of theire goods; but after the Persians repented theire bargaine, and he sayled from thence without any mony, but at parting brought from that place a slave woman and her child and forced from another Banyan a parcell of pearles worth some 10 or 15 tomands; but the owners of both were here before the ship to complayne. Wee advized the Governour &c. that they belonged not to our Company or ought to come where wee were; but here all companies have liberty to trade.

[1] Sent by the *Endeavour*. Another copy will be found among the *O.C. Duplicates*.
[2] The *Delfshaven*.
[3] Bandar Rig, a little to the north-west of Bushire.

Wee desire your instructions or advice by first ship what course wee shall take, if for future they come to this port.' The factors persuaded Durson to restore the slave woman and the pearls. The Governor of Kung promised to induce the merchants there to provide freight for the *Endeavour*; so Walwyn has been sent in her to look after this, and is to remain at Kung until fetched back. Forward a list of goods they would be glad to receive for sale here, though the markets are very dull at present. The vessel bringing them should arrive early in May. Hope that the experience of the Dutch this year will discourage them from coming again. The China ware brought by the *Seahorse* was much damaged. The largest sorts of dishes, bowls, and jars would sell well here. Have received 549 rials for freight of goods embarked in the *Endeavour*; and are sending in her 38,753¼ rials, as the result of their sales. The Bāshā is dispatching to the President an Arabian horse. Enclose a list of goods wanted for presents. 'The King, haveing been very sick this and the last yeare, would perswade his sonn, Hassan Beague, to be Bashaw, but he will not by any meanes accept of it; wherefore this day, with consent of all the Beagues in this country, have made his sonne second person in Councell and Governour of Bussora; and this day Mahmud Agga left of his place of goverment and remaines only Shaubunder; which is much better for our bussines. If Your Worships please to write two or three lines to Hassan Beague, it would be a great help to the Companies bussines, if at any time wee should want his assistance. The Dutch and Capt. Durson were very important [importunate] with the Shaubunder to goe and see theire ships; but (what his reason was wee know not) he would not goe to any of them, but invited himselfe and other cheife men aboard the *Endeavour* one morning by breake of day; when wee made them the best bankett wee could contrive, and presented them according to theire quallities.' Forward accounts and transcripts of letters, and desire a supply of provisions. Lee, the surgeon, desired to proceed to Surat in the *Endeavour*, but could not be spared, 'and the rather by reason that the Governours kinsman and Ally Agha were his patients.' *PS.—* Enclose letters for the President from the Bāshā and the Governor. (*Copy.* 3¼ *pp.*)

Notes of the Voyage of the *Falcon* (*Marine Records*, vol. lxv. p. 95).

1645, *September* 25. Anchored in Swally Road. *October* 28. Set sail. *November* 18. Anchored in 'the road of Sind'. List of goods embarked there, including 70 bales of private trade. *December* 7. Reached Swally, and disembarked the cargo. (¾ *p.*)

The King of Vijayanagar at 'Arlour[1]' to the Agent at Fort St. George, September 25, 1645 (*O.C.* 1948).[2]

'Zree Seringo Raylo, King of Kings, a God in his kingdome, in armes invincible, &c., unto the Captain of the English, these. The Hollanders, who have their residence in Pallacatt, not valuinge my letters, hath constrained mee to commence a warre against them, the charge whereof is committed unto Chenana Chety [Malaya: see p. 50], whom you are to assist therein with artillery, powder, shott, fireworks; and in soe doing you shall pleasure us. Whatever goods appertained unto the Hollanders in my kingdome I accompt it as my peculiar and proper wealth; which, being all come to Madrasapatam, wee will that you buy and pay monies for the same, proceeding therein as Chenana Chety and Seradra[3] shall prescribe, not failing at all in its performance. And whereas I am given to understand by Chenana Chety that you intend to send upp a man of quality unto us, [I] am very well pleased, for that you have allwaies esteemed my ordinances; and as Chenana Chety will advize, soe shall you bee sure to receive content; nor bee you induced to beleive the contrary, but confide upon our word and hast to visitt us by your second and whomsoever else you send along with him; for whose secure repayre unto our court this our firman shall suffice. As for other matters, Chinana Chety will advise you.' (*Copy.* ½ *p.*)

[1] Raya Elluru, now known as Vellore.
[2] A copy of a translated version enclosed in the Madras letter of October 1, 1645 (see p. 291). The copy was apparently made at Surat. What became of the original document is not known.
[3] An error for 'Sesadra', i.e. Seshadri Chetti.

Consultation held aboard the *Eagle* in Swally Hole by Messrs. Merry, Thurston, Tash, and Fitch, assisted by Thomas Stevens, Andrew Trumball, and Thomas Tomplins (Purser), September 29, 1645 (*O.C.* 1949).

The *Eagle*, *Falcon*, and *Lanneret* having arrived here, the President (who was himself too unwell to leave Surat) sent down the members of his Council to superintend the landing of their cargoes. Whilst thus employed, Courteen's ship *Hester*, commanded by Robert Hogg, anchored in the road, 'with the Union flagg in his mainetoppmasthead'. This intrusion into the Company's chief port, and 'his well knowne pyraticall practise by intercepting a small jounck or tawrin [1] belonging to the King of Cushan [2] haveing allreadie made him famous (rather infamous) amongst these people', it was deemed advisable to examine into his authority for such actions, and also to require him to take in his flag. As regards his coming to Surat, Hogg pretends that he was obliged to do so by the Governor of Mozambique, who required him to transport hither João da Maya Caldeira, the Portuguese left at Johanna by Mucknell; but it is believed that he really undertook to do this in order to ingratiate himself with the Portuguese. He declares that he will merely trim and provision his ship and then depart; but he refuses to enter into any obligation not to trade here. In consequence, with the assent of the President, orders are given not to permit him to land or embark any goods whatsoever. After several attempts at evasion, he produces his commission; but nothing can be found therein warranting either his coming to this port or capturing 'our freinds jounck'. As to the flag, he pretends that it was hoisted without his knowledge, but he refuses to take it in voluntarily; whereupon order is given that it shall be lowered. Understanding that Hogg intends to proceed to Surat, it is decided to rejoin the President there and further consider the matter. ($1\frac{1}{2}pp$.)

[1] See the preceding volume, p. 42.
[2] Kishin, in Southern Arabia. Regarding this capture see a Portuguese letter from the Captain of Bassein, which forms *O.C.* 1950.

MESSRS. IVY, GREENHILL, TRAVELL, AND MINN AT FORT ST.
GEORGE TO THE COMPANY, OCTOBER 1, 1645 (*O.C.* 1952).

Wrote last on September 7, 1644, by the *Swan*, which left Masulipatam on October 8 and reached Bantam December 26. During the twelvemonth that has elapsed since then, they have not received one word from the Company, and they can only conclude that 'you have totally forgotten us and doe intend to sett a period to this trade'. Meanwhile, they have provided cargoes for various vessels at a cost of over 102,000 rials of eight, viz. the *Swan* for Bantam (as aforesaid), 15,112 rials, 59*d*.: the *Endeavour*, which sailed for Persia on December 23, 1644, 23,650 rials, 33*d*.: the *Seaflower* for Bantam, May 5, 1645, 37,466 rials, 4*d*.: and the *Advice*, which has gone to Masulipatam to complete her lading for Bantam, about 26,000 rials. The enclosed abstract will show which of the goods were intended for Europe; trust that these will duly reach the Company, 'for wee have by Gods assistance and our indeavours mett with merchants that hath brought such a trade to your new Fort St. George that Bantam nor Surratt shall not want cloath, if they supply us with shipping for its transportation and some reasonable stocke for the maynetenance of the same.' Draw special attention to some samples of longcloth, indigo, and gunpowder; the last they believe is as good as any made in Europe. Have experimented with the manufacture here of all sorts of Surat cloth (except 'silke pattolas and tapichindas'); some specimens have been sent in the *Advice*, and they make no question of succeeding, if they can get from Surat 'a skillfull workeman for their well makeing upp and the glazeing of their heads'. 'For the prizes of the cloath, wee beleive they wilbee something cheaper then at Surratt; and indeede, if this place were well supplyed with stocke and shipping, wee neede not seeke further for any sort of goods, betteelaes and redd cloth excepted; which wee have now at last discovered by the falling out of the Dutch with Mollay, their cheife merchant and founder of their trade uppon this coast.' The *Advice* has orders not to leave Masulipatam for Bantam before November 2. Meanwhile she will ride at 'Emalldeene' [*see* p. 75], where she will be as safe as in the Thames; and it is found by experience that vessels leaving this coast in November get to Bantam as soon as those that start a month or more earlier. They have, either ready or in prospect, sufficient cloth to provide a cargo for Persia, if a ship and money be sent hither from Surat. This abundance of cloth is due to 'the difference betwixt the Dutch and Mollay, their quondom great merchant, which is now fallen out into open warrs, and ever since the 13th August Mollay, by order and leave of the Kinge, hath beseiged Pullecatt and by the same order and power hath seiz'd uppon all the goods in the Jentue merchants hands in this kingdome belonging unto the Dutch (for which they say they have given out money to these merchants, but never had possession nor made price of the goods), and taken three Dutchmen captives, one of which is in our fort, uppon ransome of 2,000 pagodaes, and the other two are prisoners at a sea port towne named Allumbrough. It is credibly reported that the Kinge is sending downe great ordinance and more power against Pullecatt to burne the towne and beate downe the fort. The former may bee done; but for the latter they will finde a hard taske to performe.' The Dutch lost two guns in attempting to rescue their merchant. The King is said to have 'vowed the distruction of Pullecatt and to turne all the Dutch men out of his cuntrey'. The origin of these differences will be found in the enclosed translation of a letter addressed by 'Mollay' to the Dutch 'Gennerall of Battavia'.[1] This will also show 'the Hollanders great tradeing and falce projects with Your Worships in this Kings territoryes'. The whole trade is now offered to the English: 'which wee could easilye maynetayne, if you pleas'd to shew us any reasonable countinance therein, which may bee done in continually keepeing on this coast of a pinnace of 80 tonns, and an annuall supply from Europe, Bantam, and Surratt [of] 150,000 royalls of eight, which is but from each place 50,000.' The goods seized by the King's officers as Dutch property have been sold to the merchants employed by the English and are now proferred by them to the factors in satisfaction of their engagements; but they

---

[1] Not now extant. There is, however, under *O.C.* 1884, an abstract of the covering letter, in which it is stated (apparently from the missing enclosure) that 'the occasion of the warr betweene Molay and the Dutch came by the Governours of Pullicate imprisoning of Mollays sonn, brother in law, and famillie and takeing awaie of Mollays goods, upon a pretence that he was indebted to the Dutch.' For these disputes see a letter from Pulicat (March, 1645) in *Hague Transcripts*, series i. vol. xiv (no. 432).

will not be accepted until the approbation of the Surat President has been received, as the Dutch threaten to search the English ships and confiscate any of these goods they may find. 'If Your Worships suffer these affronts, it wilbee noe less dishonnour unto our nation then disparradgement unto your servants.' Now that the *Advice* has departed, they have no vessel left on the coast. The Company's servants are as follows: In Fort St. George: Thomas Ivy, Henry Greenhill, George Travell, William Minn, and Thomas Jermyn, factors; and Martin Bradgate and Walter Robins, writers; together with the soldiers, &c., enumerated in the enclosed list [*missing*]. In Masulipatam, Vīravāsaram, and Petapoli: Thomas Peniston, Thomas Winter, Richard Hudson, William Methwold, William Gurney, Edmund Styles, and Christopher Yardly, factors; and Hercules Heywood and Edward Winter, writers. 'At Bengalla': Henry Olton and William Netlam. They are thus at present better supplied with merchants than with means; but 'in hopes of future imployments' they have prevailed upon four of these, whose periods of service have expired, to remain for three years longer from September 1. Greenhill, who has served fourteen years (the last six at 60*l.* per annum), has been re-engaged at 100*l.* 'Hee hath bin the Accomptant Gennerall on the Coast this foure yeares; whose honesty and abillityes hath bin soe well approv'd of that wee hould him worthy and deserveth the best imployment in your service, if occasion requireth.' Minn and Jermyn have been given 40*l.* per annum; while Robins, who has been a writer for over five years, has had his wages increased to 20*l.* Trust that these arrangements will be approved by the Company. 'Wee have bin often tymes sollicited by this Kinge to give him a vissitt, which never was yett done to him or his predecessours since our first arivall heere, which is now seven yeares allmost; soe, if wee any longer deny his reasonable request, wee may suddainely expect his just displeasure and peradventure have a seidge about us, as our neighbours the Hollanders of one syde and Portugalls of the other, which are seldome free, notwithstanding their great power and defence, who hath twenty for one more then wee; soe that, if the like should happen unto us, what can you expect of 50 well and sicke men to defend your estate and fort against the Kings power, when one of his merchants hath queld the Hollanders soe, that they dare not stirr out of their fort or putt their feete ashoare in this Kings dominion? And now the King himselfe hath taken it to hart, in the behalfe of Mollay, his cheife counceller, to comence warrs against the Hollanders. Tyme will produce the event thereof; for it is growne to that height that the Hollander must leave this Kings cuntry, or Mollay fall into utter distruction. Soe that wee have nothing more to trust unto then our civill comportment and respect to the Kinge and great ones, which hath hetherto prevayled before the Hollanders potencie; and at present are in such esteeme with the King and great ones that the whole trade of this kingdome is proffered unto the Honourable English East India Company. And for the mayntenance of the same and the Kings favour, wee are ... resolved within this few dayes to send upp Mr. Henry Greenhill[1], with foure other English souldiers for his attendance, for the reconfirmation of what was graunted unto Mr. Cogan by the Great Nague, under whose protection formerly wee liv'd, but now the Kinge hath taken his power and this cuntry from him; soe that his power and protection is of noe longer vallue. Soe now findeing a fitting oppertunity, wee doubt not but to have our old priviledges reconfirm'd, with the adition of a great many more, by this now reigneing   ing, which hath brought all his great lords unto his comand, which hath not bin this 40 yeares before. This by Mollayes assistance wee make noe question to obtayne. And another reason for the sending of Mr. Greenhill to the King is because that our powerfull freinds the Governour &c. of Pullecatt would make us beleive that Mollay is a villiane and a heighway robber and that wee, in receiveing those goods of our merchants which Mollay hath stollen and sould to them, are as bad as hee, and therefore will take those goods out of our shipps wheresoever they meete them, and to this effect hath given their commissions to all their comanders to search our shipps wheresoever they meete them; thinkeing thus to buncke us out of 400 bales of goods which our merchants hath in Fort St. George and at our washers in possession; soe should wee disapoint our Surratt President of his Mocho shipps ladeinge of goods (and better goods wee know hee cannot have for that place). Therefore, untill wee have

---

[1] In Bruce's *Annals* (vol. i. p. 415) Greenhill's mission is erroneously stated as having been to the King of Golconda.

his approbation, wee are resolved to our power to maynetayne our merchants in that just cause that wee well know they are in, in regard wee finde they doe truely indeavour your proffitt and their owne credditts; and for these goods, wee well knowe they have paid to the uttermost vallue of them, and soe must wee likewise. Therefore, because the Hollanders shall not say that wee are the receivers of stollen goods, wee doe send Mr. Greenhill and four other English men unto the Kinge, to beseech his hand and signett to testifie to the whole world that Mollay is noe villiane nor theife, and what warr is comenced against the Hollanders is by His Majesties command, as well as the goods taken from his subjects belonging to the Hollanders, sould by his officers with the same comand. Soe that when wee have this from the Kinge under his owne hand and signett, and that by his owne hand is delivered unto Mr. Greenhill, in presence of four other English men, wee hope, when wee shall have sent the coppie thereof to the Governour of Pullecatt, hee will noe longer threaten us for the receiveinge of stollen goods. This wee intend to doe before wee receive a peece of these 400 bales of cloath; and then in the future, if the Hollanders abuse and affront us, wee make noe question but you will maynetayne us in a right and just cause.' Information has been received from Bantam that the Company have ordered Ivy to repair to Bantam; though this is 'contrary to contract', he will obey and will depart by the next ship. He would have gone by the *Advice*, but it was the unanimous opinion of the factors that his so doing 'would have redownd unto your loss and hindrance of the Coast trade'. He thanks the Company for appointing him to be President at Bantam, but begs leave to return to England the following year, when his covenanted period will be nearly expired. *PS.*—'This instant wee received a letter from the King by two of our owne servants, whome wee sent to him for that purpose; which letter was deliverd unto our servants in the presence of the Kinge, who with his owne mouth bade them to deliver it unto the Agent. The translate of that letter out of Jentue into English [*see* p. 285] wee send unto you herewith for your perusall.' (*Copy.* 8½ *pp.*)

MESSRS. IVY, GREENHILL, TRAVELL, AND MINN AT FORT ST. GEORGE TO THE PRESIDENT AND COUNCIL AT SURAT, OCTOBER 1, 1645 (*O.C.* 1951).

The warfare between the Dutch and 'Molay' increases daily in intensity. Had meant to send the *Advice* direct to Bantam, but, owing to want of washers, they could not get their cloth ready in time; and so on September 22 they sent her to Masulipatam, to complete her lading there. None of the goods put into her at this place were from those taken by 'Molay' from the Dutch merchants, except perhaps three bales of white salampores received from 'Sesadra', and even these have no mark upon them that would identify them as Dutch property. These three bales are intended for Europe, and will, it is thought, prove a very profitable commodity. Enclose a copy of a letter received from the Dutch Governor of Pulicat, warning them not to buy any of the goods seized by 'Molay'[1], and notifying that instructions have been given to search all English ships 'and to take such goods out'. The *Advice* has passed by Pulicat without interference, and so the Dutch protest is looked upon as 'a scarecrow'. However, they have not yet bought any of the goods (except the salampores) purchased by their merchants from the King's officers; and they will await instructions from Surat before doing anything of the kind. Still, the dealers have been allowed to warehouse some of the goods in the Fort; and the factors intend 'to maintain our merchants in a true and just caus, as wee beleive they are in.' 'Molay' has full authority from the King for all his proceedings, as will be seen from the enclosed copy of a letter from him to the Governor-General at Batavia; and they look upon these goods as taken in war and therefore lawfully purchasable. That the hostilities were commenced by the King they will shortly be able to prove under his own hand. 'To that purpose wee are now sendinge Mr. Henry Greenhill unto him with four other English men, who shalbe testators of the same that what is donne against the Hollanders is by the Kings comaund and consent; and untill we have this under the Kings hand and signett, wee will not receive

[1] See the *Dagh-Register* for 1644-45, p. 356.

one piece of these goods, but keepe possession of it untill we heare from you.' Forward transcripts of their letter to the Company and other papers, with their books of accounts. *PS.*—The 'cossas' and ginghams taken out of the *Endeavour* at Surat were provided for England and should be sent thither. Enclose a translation of a letter just received from the King. (*Copy.* 3¾ *pp.*)

THE SAME TO THE PRESIDENT AND COUNCIL AT BANTAM, OCTOBER 1, 1645 (*O.C.* 1953).

Wrote last on July 31, by a Dutch conveyance, notifying the arrival of the *Advice.* Answer various points in the letter she brought. Bridgeman has been made purser of the *Advice* (as ordered) and returned to Bantam. William Brown has also been sent; but Jeremy Root was too ill to embark. Trust that the *Seaflower* will be dispatched to this place without fail, as they have plenty of goods for her, if means be sent for their purchase. Forward samples of cloths made here in imitation of those procurable at Surat. The deficiency in the sandalwood laden upon the *Seaflower* was caused by the use of the brass weights sent out by the Company in 1640, which are two per cent. too light. The wetting of that vessel's cargo was due to a leak; but the fine cloths have now been put up 'in wax rappers' to prevent a repetition. Have sent to 'Gingallee' [*see* p. 75] for the iron required for Macassar. Wish that the *Swan* had proceeded on the Manilla voyage in spite of the threats of the Dutch, which are nothing but 'scarecrows'. There is not a better market in the world; and Bantam, Jambi, &c., will not find vent for all the goods now sent or in preparation. 'Wee were in good hopes that you would againe have made triall with the *Seaflower* to obtaine Bengalla through the Streightes of Mallacca. But wee still meete with the Hollanders interpossitions by the way, which still are a hinderance to our masters just and lawfull trade; and ourselves not haveing any shipp or meanes to send thither, have obtain fraight for the Companies goods and Mr. Oltons passage from thence to Messulapatana, only leaveing Mr. Nettlam to looke unto the Companies howse. So that, if the next yeare wee are noe better supplyed with shipping and meanes then this, wee intend to dissolve that unproffittable factorie.

Mr. Olton wee intend, after Mr. Penistons repaire hither, to appointe cheeif at Verashroone, and Mr. Winter to succeed Mr. Peniston. Accordeing to your order and directions wee have likewise long since sent unto Mr. Olton the transcripts of Mr. Hatch his bookes of accompts &c., for his satisfaction and directions of him in that litle or noe bussiness which hee maketh such a stir aboute.' Hudson denies the truth of Gardner's accusations, and has consequently been permitted to retain his post. Request that certain deficiencies in the cargo of the *Advice* may be made good. The four 'lascars' have been sent to Masulipatam. As regards general news, the factors refer to their accompanying letter to the Company. Would be glad to have an opinion from Bantam as to the lawfulness of their receiving the goods taken from the Dutch. Forward (with a translation) a letter addressed by 'Mollay' to the 'Generall of Battavia'. This would have been sent by the *Seaflower*, but it arrived too late. Enclose also a correspondence with the Dutch at Pulicat, and request that all these papers may be transmitted to the Company after perusal. Their accounts have been sent by the *Advice*; also three bales of goods belonging to the son of 'Sessadra Nague, our cheif marchant' [*see* p. 281]. These should be sold and the proceeds returned by the next ship. *PS.*—'Att the sealeing upp hereof, we were pressented with a petition from the souldiers for the desireing of a minnister to be heere with them for the maintainance of their soules health; which petition goeth heerewith, beseecheing Your Wisdomes devote consideration therein.' *PPS.*— Enclose a translation of a letter just received from the King. (*Copy. 7 pp.*)

ROBERT CRANMER, THOMAS COGAN, AND WILLIAM WEALE AT BASRĀ TO THE PRESIDENT AND COUNCIL AT SURAT, OCTOBER 3, 1645 (*O.C.* 1954).

Avail themselves of an opportunity of sending a note 'per convoy of Hadgee Zahad Beagues jouncks'. Trade is very dead, both here and at Bagdad and Aleppo. Send a revised list of goods desired for next year. The town is so full of all sorts of commodities that prices have fallen considerably and they will have hard work to sell their stock before next monsoon. Enclose a list of the goods sold by the Dutch at this place, with the prices realized. If the latter promise more profit than the sorts already asked for, next season's consignment should be modified accordingly. Two small brass guns were bought from Capt. Durson for the use of the *Seahorse*, at Mr. Tindall's request. The purser of the *Endeavour* refuses to give any account of the way in which he disbursed the money advanced to him to provide necessaries. Some rule ought to be laid down as to fresh provisions for the ships. 'A quarter of a sheepe a mess use[d] to be the custome.' The Dutch report that they have taken Ormus, but there is no confirmation of this. The Portuguese have spread a story that 'the ensueing yeare they shall have warrs with us and the Vice King will not give lycence for our comeing more to Bussora; and this wee conceive is partly to feare the people not to send theire goods in the Companies vessels.' Request certain articles for presents. 'Chaires and cotts[1] of guilded Brodra [Baroda] worke are not here acceptable. Those now required of seesum[2] of 5½ rup[ees] price are of more vallue.' (*Copy.* 1¾ *pp.*)

THOMAS PENISTON, THOMAS WINTER, RICHARD HUDSON, WILLIAM GURNEY, AND EDMUND STYLES AT MASULIPATAM TO THE PRESIDENT AND COUNCIL AT BANTAM, OCTOBER 3, 1645 (*O.C.* 1955).

Received last night a letter from Pollen [master of the *Advice*], announcing his arrival at 'Hemaldeene' [*see* p. 75], and asking for a smith and caulkers. Conclude that he intends to repair his vessel there, before coming on to this place to embark the goods they have ready. Particulars of those she embarked at Fort St. George. (*Copy.* ¾ *p. Received 'per Dutch conveyance'*, November 6.)

ATTESTATION BY THOMAS STEVENS AND ANDREW TRUMBALL AT SURAT, OCTOBER 3, 1645 (*O.C.* 1956).

Testify that the trèasure brought from England this year arrived in bad condition. 'At its comeing into the warehouse, the chests were found most of them shaken, and soe oppen that a passage was left for the rials to run out. Further, at oppening many of them,

---

[1] Bedsteads. For an early example of this word see the 1622-23 volume, p. 125.
[2] *Shīsham* or *sīsū* wood, much used in India for making furniture.

the baggs were found rotten and torne by the nayles, the monies being scattered in the chests.' (½ *p.*)

WILLIAM PITT AND THOMAS CODRINGTON AT ISPAHĀN TO THE PRESIDENT AND COUNCIL AT SURAT, OCTOBER 6, 1645 (*O.C.* 1957).

Ten days ago they presented a petition to the Itimād-uddaula, complaining that their broker at Gombroon had been refused permission to attend at the customhouse (as usual) to note the issue of goods; whereupon he wrote an order for a farmān to be sent thither to remedy this and other abuses. 'Hee alsoe the same day graunted us two other peticions some few days before delivered unto him, vizt. one about the releasement of the Kings duties of one per cent., the other about our ruinated howse in Bunder [Gombroon], for which hee enordered wee should bee allowed for two years that wee had payed beeforehand. This passed the 24th ultimo. The 29th ditto hee sent both the cheife of the Dutch and us vests from the Kinge; before whom the next day, as hee sate in his mayalists [1], wee presented ourselv[e]s; and, after wee had eaten in his presents, tooke our leav[e]s of him. The followinge morneinge about breake of day (by whose order is not yett certainely knowne) Edamont Dowlett was killed in his owne hows by Jonne Ckaune [Jānī Khān] and five more great men, who cut his body all into peeces, to noe little joy to all in generall here, except the Queene Mother, who (as wee heare) doth much lament his death.[2] In his place the Kinge yesterday was pleased to establish Callosa[3] Sultan, who had the office once before, and that ten years togither, in the raigne of Shabas [Shāh Abbās], the grandfather of this Kinge. Hee is reported to bee a very honest man and a friend unto our nacion; soe that wee hope our Honourable Imployers businesse in these parts will in future prove better then formerly it hath been.' These troubles have delayed the promised farmāns; but to-morrow the factors will visit the new Itimād-uddaula and remind him of them.

---

[1] The *Majlis*, i.e. the court, is meant. The word has become familiar to newspaper-readers as the title of the Persian Parliament.

[2] Valentyn (*Oud en Nieuw Oost Indien*, vol. v. p. 247) says that the Queen Mother was a friend of Mirzā Taqī, the murdered Itimād-uddaula, and that it was at her instance that the Shāh punished the murderers.

[3] A copyist's error for Khalifa Sultān.

News from Basrā. Were surprised to learn that neither the *Seahorse* nor the *Endeavour* would call at Gombroon on the way to Surat. The money sent down from hence to the port will therefore have to remain there, until either it is fetched by some vessel from Surat or some Dutch conveyance is to be had. *PS.*—'This instant after the finishinge this letter, the Kinge here, to revenge the death of Ettam[on] Dowlett, who itt seems was murthered without his concent, ha[th] cut of the heads of three of thes dukes and three other great men, vizt., Jonne Ckaune Curchee Bashee, Nocoda Ckawne, Arab Ckawne, Abass Culle Beague, Byram Alle Beague Shechavand, Jebadar Basshee[1]; whose heads leyeth this instant in the Midan[2] before the Kings dore, with the bodys of the two former, whose heads being first cutt off was caused by the Kinge to be caried upon poles about the cittie, with these words proclaimed with it, that this is the punishment of all such as killeth any man without order from the Kinge. It is thought that more heads yett wilbe lost about this busines.'[3] (*Copy.* 2¼ *pp.*)

[1] These names and titles are: Jānī Khān, the *Qūrchī Bāshī* or commander of the Tartar cavalry, Naqdī (?) Khān, Arab Khān, Abbās Qulī Beg, Bairām Alī Beg Shaikhāvand, and possibly the *Jīlaudār Bāshī*, described by Tavernier as 'le chef des valets de pied'.

[2] The well-known Maidān or central square, on the western side of which is the royal palace.

[3] In a later letter from Pitt and his colleagues, dated at Gombroon May 9, 1646 (*O.C.* 1991), the following account is given of these events:—

'About breake of day newes was brought us that Ettam[en] Dowlett was slaine by Johnne Ckaun and five other nobles, whose lives hee intended to have taken away the very same morneing and neare about the same time; of which the aforesaid six nobles haveing intelligence, [they] mett the same morneing very early in the Midanne before the Kings house, where on a suddaine, as they satt on their horses, [they] tooke councell togeither and resolved to take away the life of Ettam[en] Dowlett first, although they were sure to live but a day after him; which accordingly they put in practice, for they had noe sooner entred his house and come where hee was (at prayer) but Johnne Ckaun told him hee had eaten the Kings bread undeservedly; upon which Nogdee Ckaun stucke him through the body with his dagger, and presently the other foure cutt him in peeces; which done, Johnnee Ckaun went unto the King and, holding his sword on his necke, acquainted him of what hee had done, sayeing, if hee had displeased His Majestic, hee was willing to suffer for it. The King for the present seemed glad, and commended him for his paines, desireing to know who were his fellow actors with him in the murther, and willed him to give him their names, for that hee would reward them for theyr good service; which being effected, the said Johnne Ckaun, haveing leave to depart, retourned to his house very joyfull; and soe continued with the rest of his freinds till the 6th October, when very early in the morneing, about breake of day, the King sent for him and Nogdee Ckaun, and caused both their heads to bee cutt off; and afterwards sent for the heads of the other four, vizt. of Arrab Ckaun, Abasse Culle Beage, Byram Alle Beague Shemvand, and Jebbidar Bashee;

PHILIP WYLDE AND SAMUEL WILTON AT GOMBROON TO [THE PRESIDENT AND COUNCIL AT SURAT], OCTOBER 12, 1645 (*O.C.* 1958).

Arrived here on the 10th current, and found in the road the *Endeavour*, which had arrived on the 7th. Have embarked in her their money, a chest of raisins, and one horse, received in part payment of a debt. Could not find at Shīrāz any horses worth buying, and have therefore advised the factors at Ispahān to purchase some there. Send an account of freight embarked in this ship. (*Copy.* 1 *p.*)

THE SAME TO [THE SAME], OCTOBER 14, 1645 (*O.C.* 1958).

Enclose a transcript of the preceding letter. Money advanced to Bowen for the purchase of provisions for the *Endeavour*. (*Copy.* ½ *p.* Received by a Dutch ship, November 11.)

DECLARATION BY JOÃO DA MAYA CALDEIRA, ABOARD THE *HESTER* AT SWALLY, OCTOBER $\frac{15}{25}$, 1645 (*O.C.* 1959).

Narrates his embarkation in the *John* at Mozambique, and the subsequent quarrels between Knipe and Mucknell, which resulted in his being left at Johanna. Claims compensation for his losses. (*Copy. Portuguese.* 2 *pp.*)

MESSRS. CRANMER, COGAN, AND WEALE AT BASRĀ TO THE COMPANY, OCTOBER 17, 1645 (*O.C.* 1960).

Wrote last on July 31. The *Seahorse* was dispatched on August 28, and the *Endeavour* on September 22.[1] 'Tradeing was all which were brought on the Midanne before the Kings house, where they remeyned till the sunne went downe. Soe soone as the former two heads were seperated from their bodies, they were put upon two pooles and carried about the Midanne with theese words proclaimed, that this is the punishment of all such as dare to kill men without order from the King. And yett it is credibly reported that the King, if hee did not comaund it to bee done, yett was very glad that hee was soe ridd of Ettam[en] Dowlett; and indeed soe were all his people in generall, many of them for five daies togeither makeing feasts for joy they were soe well ridd of such a divell. Since his death it is reported that hee conspired the death of the King and intended to settle his younger brother in his throne. It is likewise credibly reported that there came into the Kings treasure by the death of the aforesaid six men about 500,000 temaunds.'

[1] Roobacker (see p. 274) mentions the arrival on August 22 (O.S.) of an English pinnace named the *William*. Probably this was the one formerly belonging to Fremlen and employed by the factors for their private trade (see p. 31); if so, the reason for not saying anything about it in the present letter becomes at once apparent.

never deader and this place not knowne to be soe much overprest with goods as it hath been this monzoone'; with the result that their sales for the year amounted only to 44,318 rials of eight, and of this sum they could only get in sufficient to send 38,753¼ rials by the *Endeavour*. Enclose copies of their letters to Surat and other papers. Durson's proceedings here. 'At theire parteing hence, the 11th October, [they] made great preperations for the Dutch, &c. Robert Cranmer was invited, and must not deny them, but, foreknowing what might happen, prevented. Thomas Cogan was lycensed; when, being on board them, Mr. Durson and their merchant, Peeter de Masters, could not forbeare but expresse theire passion. Theire hopes were to have had Robert Cranmer. Some trechery was intended on him, but what wee know not. The thought of 5,000 pound sterling taken by Mr. Bowen lyes heavy at theire stomacks, pretending it hindered the *Loyaltyes* voyage this yeare for England. To Mr. Wallwin in Congoo and our freinds in Gombroone wee have given notice; who wee presume will not overcreditt them.' Death of Blocq at Ispahān. It is rumoured that at Gombroon 'Willibrant' has sold all his goods for some 15,000 tūmāns and, after shipping the money, together with 3,000 tūmāns received from the King, has withdrawn his people and 'proclamed warrs'; further, that the Dutch intend to take 'the Moores jouncks bound for Gombroone and they expect 10 or 15 sayle of ships more to take Ormooze and Kishmee.' This letter is sent by way of Aleppo, and the factors would be glad to receive a reply by the same route, 'for that wee remaine here the whole yeare'. They can forward any letters intended for Surat by way of Muskat and 'Scinda'. (*Copy*. 1¾ *pp*.)

EDWARD KNIPE AND WILLIAM JESSON AT AGRA TO THE PRESIDENT AND COUNCIL AT SURAT, NOVEMBER 12, 1645 (*O.C.* 1961).

Rejoice to learn the arrival of three ships from England. Note the instructions given for the purchase of goods. Have bought a parcel of 'guzzees', 'beeing a reasonable good sorte of cloth betwixt 10½ and 11½ gerraes broad. But wheras you are pleased to say that none must bee under 12 gerraes or 19 tusso, wee cannot tell whither you derive the gerraes from the tassooes or the tussaes from the gerraes; appeareing to us great disproporcion therin, for, uppon compareing a Surratt covett (which wee have in the howse) with our Agra covett, finde $10\frac{1}{2}$ gerraes Agra to agree with 19 tussaes Surratt.'[1] Enclose for comparison the length of the Agra 'covet', marked also with 'gerraes', and request instructions. Particulars of the 'guzzees' last sent to Surat. 'That sorte of cloth is made in Gocull[2], where, by residence of a trustie broker, might bee yearely large quanteties procurable. These people here wee finde them soe extraordinrilie full of deceipt as cannot by anie meanes urge us to put confidence in anie of them. Imployment for two or three honnest able brokers from Surratt would bee here both advantagious to themselves and usefull unto our masters; [wee?] haveing (as wee suppose) oftentimes diverse gainefull opertuneties which wee dare not make use of (in provission both of cloth and indico) for feare of beeing abused by them, haveing had, since Edward Knipes comeing hither, diverse experiments of their willingnes to defraud. But how to better ourselves wee know not; feareing, if wee showld discard theise now in our imployment, to have worse in their roomes. Itt may verie well bee answered thoes brokers in Surratt are as craftie knaves and have as nimble a facultie in deceipt as thoes here; which cann hardly bee denied, while they are amoung their owne tribe, with such able coadjutours to help them to binde upp the bundle of their falcities under a faire glosse hardly discerneable; but when hither transplanted, the soyle will not prove soe firtle to their fraudulent humors, when and where they will bee soe odious to theise people as not anie of their actions possible to bee obscured from our knowledge.' Have lately bought a quantity of a very good sort of cloth. 'Whether to call them guzzees or baftaes bee most propper wee cannot tell. They are made about Kerriabaud[3], where formerlie the Dutch have had residence in quest of this sorte of clotheing; which by reporte use[d] to stand them in (hither to Agra) 25 rupees per corge. Their dimencions are betwixt 18 and $18\frac{3}{4}$ Agra covetts long and full $\frac{3}{4}$ broad; which will stand us in nett under 20 rupees per corge.' Intend to dispeed

---

[1] By the 'covett' is meant the Indian *gaz*, which contained 16 *girās* or 24 *tasūs* Tavernier makes the Surat *gaz* four-fifths of that of Agra, and this agrees fairly well with the calculation in the text.

[2] Gokul, a village near Mahāban, in Muttra district, about twenty miles north-west of Agra.

[3] Khairābād, in Sitāpur district, about forty miles north of Lucknow.

these and the 'guzzees' previously bought to Ahmadābād as soon as possible, as they think it better to send off their goods whenever they have got together a reasonable quantity than to wait and send them all together. Knipe notices 'the Companies slight esteeme of his service', but is comforted by the knowledge of his innocence of the charges against him. These (as he understands from friends in England) are that he took 100*l.* from one Buckner for bringing out his son, and that he had 1,100*l.* in English gold with him in the *John*.[1] As regards the first, he acknowledges that such an agreement was made, but declares that Buckner has failed to pay more than a part of the money; while, as for the other charge, if any one can prove that he had even 15*l.* aboard in English gold, he will forfeit all claim to salary and confess himself unworthy of any future favours. He admits that ('by reason of the troubles in England, not knoweing where to leave anie thing safe') he brought out a certain sum (far less than that reported) in foreign gold, jewels, &c., intending to employ it at interest in Surat; but that he had no design of private trade will appear from his strictness at Mozambique in this respect. He thanks the President and Council for their defence of him, and promises to deserve their good opinion. Davidge was dispeeded to 'Matchewarra' [*see* p. 204] on October 29, and a copy of the Surat letter has now been sent to him as a guide in his investments. Jesson will start for 'Lucknoo' in time to arrive by the end of this month. In case he cannot there obtain the desired 'eckbarres', his broker has been sent in advance to 'Jellelpore[2], where Mr. Jesson saith hee cannot deceive if hee would, because what there bought is registred by the towne broker.' Blackwell, upon Knipe's arrival, was appointed house steward and cannot be spared; so Burnell is to be sent with Jesson in his place. Knipe was not aware of the custom of transmitting monthly a statement of household expenses, but in future will punctually observe this practice, and now sends the accounts from June to September. 'Six daies before Mr. Davidges departure hence, came Allebux [Allah-Bakhsh], whoe brought us noe comfortable tydeings of Chittersalls bussnes [*see* p. 159], telling us of the little probabillitie

---

[1] See *Court Minutes of the East India Company*, 1644–49, p. 76, &c.
[2] Jalālpur, a cotton-weaving centre in Fyzābād District (Oudh). For an earlier reference see p. 178 of the 1618–21 volume.

of effecting ought therin till the Kings retourne for Agra, beeing soe intent uppon his designe on the Tarters[1] as will incline his eare to no other storie but what may induce to their overthrow. Assulett Ckaune hee reportes not to bee taken prisoner; onely had lost some of his men, beeing outed by the Tarters of a hould formerlie taken by the Kings forces. The King sent for him to Lahoar, where by this tyme wee may guesse hee is with him; but how long his stay may bee in the Kings presence is uncerteine, because (itt is reported) the King doth dayly place and displace his umrawes [see p. 229]. Soe that wee cannot affoard you anie comfort att all in that bussnes. Notwithstanding have retourned Allebux againe to Lahoare with the trumpeter, whoe departed hence in company of Mr. Davidge; and have urged him, if hee finde Assulett Ckaune with the King, to move with what possible dilligence hee may in the bussnes. Wee have not omitted wryteing to Assulett Ckaune, imploreing his assistance therin.' Have also instructed Allah-Bakhsh to press 'Zeruffden Hussen' [Sharafuddīn Husain: see p. 160] for payment of his debt; but the bills have been retained here, owing to a rumour that he has been appointed Kotwāl of Agra. Note that their proposal, to use up the inferior indigo 'in cureing cloth for our owne occasions', is disapproved at Surat. Express their thanks for the strong waters, sword-blades, and other goods intended for presents; also 'for the sack and sallett oyle you have bynn pleased to limitt us'. Knipe hopes that he may without offence claim the greatest share of the sack, 'to ballance his smallest proporcion of comfort.' Disposal of damaged broadcloth. 'The byrams, allthough expressed under the title of amberties in invoice, yett are of a different makeing up, beeing slenderly beaten; as wee conceive, propper for England.' Request an opinion on the suitability of these and of the various sorts of 'Derriabauds'. Have examined every piece and returned those torn or stained. No more broadcloth should be sent up at present. Wrote on October 19 to Heynes and the rest at Ahmadābād, giving them notice of the dispeed of the caravan and requesting a supply of money. As none has been received, they have now taken up 10,000 rupees on a bill of exchange drawn upon Surat at $4\frac{3}{8}$ per cent. loss. With this money they will commence their indigo investment. Since Knipe's

[1] The reference is to the campaign against the Uzbeks in Balkh and Badakhshān.

THE ENGLISH FACTORIES

taking charge, the interest on debts to the extent of 12,000 rupees has been reduced from one to three-quarters per cent. per month, and no fresh debts have been incurred at a higher rate than seven-eighths per cent. There are three principal creditors to whom the factors owe 57,000 rupees, and in these cases the interest is still one per cent. ; but they hope to secure a reduction before long. 'Thoes that are greate monied men here in the towne, and live onely uppon interest, receive from the sherroffs noe more then $\frac{5}{8}$ per cent. per moneth. The sherroffs they dispose of itt to others [at] from 1 to $2\frac{1}{2}$ per cent., running some hazzard for the same, and that is their gaines. Now when a sherroffe (for lucre) hath disposed of great sommes to persons of qualletie att greate rates, not suddenly to bee call'd in to serve his occasions, then beginn his creditours (as in other partes of the world) like sheepe one to runn over the neck of another, and quite stifle his reputacion. Thus, very opertunely to our purpose hath two famous sherroffs bynn served within a moneth, one of which faileing for above three lack of rupees, diverse men have lost great somes and others totally undonne therby; which hath caused men of late to bee verie timerous of putting their monies into sherroffs hands. Therfore wee say att this present had wee monies to make use of this opertunety by sending the same to our creditours howses, [wee] doe verilie beleive, rather then they would accept therof, [they] might bee brought downe to our owne rates; to accomplish which, wee desire att once to have speedilie remitted us att least 80,000 rupees; by which meanes wee have some confidence to wipe the name of one per cent. cleane out of our bookes. By reporte of all men that have bynn uppon the indico imployment, thoes that are the owners therof will not bee brought to anie reasonable price for their comodity till necessety forceth them to sell; and wee have heard itt by English and Dutch spoken that they have not, uppon their comeing to Byana, bought one seare of indico in a moneth after, the sellers beeing soe extra-ordnary unreasonable in their demands. Then how is itt possible wee showld advise of the rates therof before wee have beate a bargaine? For allthough about Coria [Koriā] and other partes where English and Dutch useth not to goe to make their owne investments, the price is comonly broken by Mogulls and Armenians; but in Byana, Hendowne [Hindaun], and thoes partes adjacent, no

Mogull or Armenian can breake price there, because their whole dependance is uppon our two nacions; and in tyme when they have bynn att varience with ech other, striveing whoe showld give most for the comodity, then hath bynn the sellers harvest. Wee, to prevent this inconveniencie, findeing Signor Van Burgh [1] a rationall honnest man, have soe accorded as not one to out vie the others, conceiveing a sufficient proporcion for both parties. Now, soe long as the Hollanders shall walke with us upprightely, wee intend our correspondencie shall admitt of noe exception ; but if once wee finde them fallter, will use them according.' Their agents in 'Coria' have sent word that the price there is 33 rupees per maund, 'not fully dry.' Will let them go on buying small parcels, until the factors are sure of getting all they want at Biāna and Hindaun, and then they will be stopped. The investments here (in indigo) may be computed at 80,000 rupees; at 'Lucknoo', 32,000; at 'Matchawarra', about 16,000 ; and the debts here about 110,000 ; total, 238,000 rupees. Towards this, they desire (as already stated) an immediate remittance of 80,000 rupees. The reduction of the rate of interest will not only save money but will improve the factors' credit. The Dutch start for Biāna to-morrow, and Jesson will accompany them to commence the investment. Knipe will relieve him there as soon as he has dispatched the calico from this place. Have sent specimens of 'the new sorte of baftaes ' by ' Signor Byars, a Dutchman bound to Surratt.' Last night they received the President and Council's letter of October 18, but cannot find time to answer it fully now. Arrangements made for the charge of the caravan. Hill left for Surat on October 27, with permission either to accompany the carts or push on ahead. 'Uppon dispeede of our caphilla wee had notice of a Rajahs sonne which lay robbing on the way betwixt Mogullka Surah and Mirta [2]; which caused us to enterteine for defence of our goods ten men more then ordinarie.' May possibly draw on Surat from Biāna for 7,0c0 or 8,000 rupees. Note the protest received from João da Maya Caldeira, and the answer returned. Knipe will speak for himself as soon as he gets

[1] Nikolaas van der Burgh is mentioned in the *Dagh-Register*, 1643-44, pp. 172, 193, as a Dutch merchant at Agra.
[2] Mughalkasarāī was a well-known halting-place about twelve miles north of Sironj, and is probably the place referred to on p. 135 of the 1630-33 volume. No place called Mirta is to be found in the neighbourhood.

leisure; meanwhile he desires that the enclosed note may be forwarded to the Senhor. Witnesses can be produced from among the *John's* company that at Johanna Caldeira declared that Knipe was 'innocent in knowledge of what hee brought aboard'; and Burnell testifies to this effect in the accompanying certificate. Will do their best to reduce the price of the indigo, and will buy only that of really good quality. *PS.*—Their need for cash will probably induce the 'money mungers' to demand a high rate of interest; if so, they will give bills on Surat instead. (7½ *pp. Received December* 6.)

THE GRANT FROM SRĪ RANGA RĀYALU REGARDING MADRAS [1].

A. THE CONTEMPORARY VERSION (*O.C.* 1696 [2]).

'In the yeare Parteewa, the month Cartida, the moone in the wane [3], the King over all Kings the Colliest [Holiest] and amongst all cavileers the greatest, Zree Renga Raga, the mighty King God, give[s] this cowle unto Agent Thomas Ivie, cheife captain of the English, and the Company of that nation.

For as much as you have left Armagon and are come to Zree Renga Ragapatam [4], my towne, at first but of small esteeme, and have there built a fort and brought trade to that port: therefore, that you may bee the better incuraged to prosecute the same and amplifie the towne which beares our name, we doe freely release you of all customes or duties upon whatsoever goods bought or sould in that place appertaininge to your Company. Also we graunt unto your Company halfe of all the customes or duties which shalbe received at that port; and the rents of the ground about the village Madraspatam, as also the Jaccall ground [5], wee

[1] This grant was the outcome of Greenhill's mission, referred to on p. 290.

[2] Endorsed by the copyist: 'Coppie [of] Kings cowle given to the Agent concerning privilidges reconfirmd.' I am inclined to think that it was copied at Madras. There are two other transcripts at the India Office, viz. *O.C.* 1697 and no. 1696 in the *Duplicate O.C.* series; but both are copies made at Surat and sent home from thence in 1646. The second o fthese has been printed in *The Founding of Fort St. George* (p. 32). All three versions are practically identical.

[3] I.e. the second half of the month *Karttika*, in the year *Parthiva*. This agrees with the date in the later version (November 15), except that in that the year is, by a slip, given as 1643 instead of 1645.

[4] 'Zerec Renga Rayapatam' and 'Zree Renga Rayapatan' in the other two copies.

[5] Possibly the 'jackal-ground' was a waste piece of land between the Fort and Madraspatam.

give you towards your charges, by way of piscash. Moreover, for the better mannaging your bussines, we surrender the government and justice of the towne into your hands. And if any of your neighbours of Pundamolee [Punamallee] shall injure you, we promise you our reddy assistance. And for what provissions shalbe brought out of that cuntry, we will that noe junckan [toll: Tamil *chungam*] be taken thereon. If it fortune that any of your Companies shipps shall by accident of weather or otherwise be driven ashoore at that port, whatsoever can be saved shall remaine your owne. And the like touching all merchants that trade at that port, if the owners come to demand it; but if the owner be not to bee found, then our officers shall seize on the same to our behoofe. Wee alsoe promise still to retayne the towne in our protection and not to subject it to the government of Pundamolee or any other Nague. And whatsoever marchandizes of yours that shall pass through the cuntry of Pundamolee to pay but halfe custome. In confidence of this our cowle, you may cheerfully proceede in your affairs; wherein if any of our people shall mollest you, wee give you our faith to take your cause into our owne hands to doe you right and assist you against them; that your port and this our cowle may stand firme as longe as the sunn and moone endureth.

ZREE RAMA.'

B. A LATER VERSION (*Treaties*, vol. iii, p. 117).[1]

'Translation of a cowle given by Steeranga Railo to Agent Ivie, dated 15th November, 1643.[2]

You have left the place called Armagon, and are come now to one of my new towns called Steeranga-Rayapatnam, where you are making a fort and bulwarks and to do your merchandize and trade; to which purpose I give you this cowle with the following contents, vizt.: Touching your Company's merchandize, they shall pay no

---

[1] Transcribed at the East India House (about 1812) from a book (no longer extant) of *Letters From Fort William*, 1713-14. It is evidently derived from an independent translation. Further copies (identical in wording) will be found in *Treaties*, vol. ii (p. 1) and vol. ix (p. 141).

In *Factory Records, Miscellaneous*, vol. xxiv (p. 103), will be found a copy of a letter from Madras to Bengal, dated Oct. 23, 1711, giving a brief account of the first settlement at Fort St. George, and of the privileges subsequently obtained. It is probable that this translation of the 1645 grant was forwarded at the same time.

[2] An error for 1645.

custom, neither for importing nor exporting any of their goods. And all what shall come in for custom of the said town, the half shall be for your Company and the other half for the Divan. And besides this, I do freely give to the Company the town called Madrassapatam, and all the ground belongeth to it, at their disposure; and all the government and justice of the said town shall be executed by you. And if any person should wrong you in any part of my country or in the said town, in your merchandize or in any other matters, I shall take care to do you justice and right. Also no people belonging to the Governor of Pundamalee, nor of its country, shall come nor have any thing to do in your town; neither shall you pay any juncan for what provisions shall be brought for your Fort's use. If any of your ships should be cast ashore, you shall take all the things that shall be saved. And if any other ships, belonging to any other strangers, should [be] cast ashore: if there be no owners for it, then all them things that shall be saved shall be for the Divan's account. And besides, the said town shall never be under the government [*sic*] of Pundamalle's country, nor shall be given to any other government, but shall remain clear under the Divan. Seeing I have given you the like cowle concerning the said town and merchandize, I shall take care that you shall in no ways be molested by no person; to which you' may trust to my feet[1] and do your merchandize without any kind of fear.'

PHILIP WYLDE AND SAMUEL WILTON AT GOMBROON TO THE PRESIDENT AND COUNCIL AT SURAT, NOVEMBER 16, 1645 (*O.C.* 1962).

Acknowledge the receipt of a letter of October 13. Enclose advices from Pitt regarding the proceedings of the Dutch, &c. 'The late news is: the Kings firmaund[2], here arrived, confirmed a peace with the Holanders for two years ensueinge, giveinge them such libertie and license of trade accordinge to their owne demaunds, payinge not any duties and buyinge silke of whome and where they

---

[1] This word is queried in the MS.; the original probably had 'faith'.
[2] For a Dutch version of this document see *Hague Transcripts*, series i. vol. xv. no. 476. A letter from the King to the Dutch chief forms no. 481; and the reply will be found under the same number.

please; articles of which and others of the like nature are sent by Comandore Wilbrent to Spahan, there to bee confirmed.[1] Thus with a great deale of facilitie the Dutch are like to have theire trade and proceedings established, to their employers benefitt and their nacions honor; putinge the Pertians rather in feare of what they intended then as yett any thinge accomplished, haveinge nither taken townes or chastles; only they beleagered that of Kishme, spendinge shott without execucion, and burninge their lathers (as they say) in sight of the castle by reason they were to short to scale the walls; afterwards retired abord the shipps, wastinge more shott at a marke unknowne more then the noys of their ordenance; which terified the Pertians and brought them to this subjeccion. [This?] causes the Dutch to bee transported with soe much pride of theire valor that if possible they possesse these sillie people they are able to encounter with the whol world, promiseinge to deffend this port against all nations. Nay, Commandore Wilbrent hath tould us here hee will doe it against the Portugalls, as alsoe to other nacions soe far as his gunns will reach; to which was answered little, least wee should publish our oune shame of doeinge that which reason invites, when the materialls are knowne to bee wanting. Your desires are to bee further informed concerning Bunder Sware[2]; to which wee cannot say more then what our informacions formerly assertained; beinge here now, on a second inquirie, informed by them that have traded in those parts, giveinge it a good comendacions for the vendinge such goods as our list preintemated. From thence here hath lately arrived about 300 chists [of] shuggar. It being a reasonable good sorte, sould at 13 lar[res] per maund of 33 lb., which hath caused the quantitie the Dutch hath to decline much in price; whose currentt rates is 12 lar[res] per maund, when not longe since sould for 15 lar[res] per maund. The said place is

[1] See nos. 476 and 477 in the same series.
[2] This form of the name leaves it doubtful whether the place intended is Sūr or Suhār, both being ports of Omān, the former being SE. and the latter NW. of Muskat. When, however, in January, 1646, the *Lanneret* proceeded thither, the Portuguese at Muskat protested against English interference, declaring that the port was within their sphere, 'allthough of late expelled from thence' (*O.C.* 1978). This would be true of Sūr, but not of Suhār, which was retained by the Portuguese until a later date (Badger's *Imāms and Seyyids of Omān*, pp. xxv, 69).
It appears from *O.C.* 1970 that the English had been invited in 1645 to trade at this port by the then Imām (Nāsir-bin-Murshid).

said to afford great quantities annually; whose current rates there is 11 larres per maund.' Broadcloth has long been 'a drugg in these parts', especially at Ispahān. 'This country affords more lead then can finde vend, brought from Cremon[1]; whose currentt price is 16 sha[hees] per maund of 33 lb.' Enclose a list of goods and their prices. Note what has been done at Surat about Hogg, the commander of the *Hester*. Pitt did the like at Gombroon upon the arrival of Durson with the *Loyalty*; 'who voyaged from hence to Bussora, and returned into this roade the 30th October, comeinge onley for freight. When at his arrivall hee vizited the Sultan, beinge kindly enterteined and promised curteous usage, not only for the present but likewise for the future, although the Sultan was suffitiently enformed from us how unwarantable it was for him to come into this porte and, if hee received any fraight, our Company was clere from all clamors that was like to ensue. However, Durson prevailed and gott some few passengers with their goods and monies, the greatest parts beinge merchants hee brought hither from Rajapore. The 4th currentt hee departed at [? mid]night, leaveinge behind him his broker, passengers, and one English boy. At news thereof the Sultan suposed his new enterteined friend was noe better then a piratt, beinge noe less suspected by his passengers, &c. But it pleased God three days after hee mett with a storme in the Gulph which brought him back to Larrack; when some good angell inspired him to send his boate ashore for his passengers (but supposed rather for his mates sonne, the boy). But after arrivall many revileinge words the Sultan gave, and profered the passengers, if they pleased, he would deteine the whole boats crew of English till their goods were brought ashore from the shipp; but, like a company of silly fools, they perswaded the Sultan to the contrary and desired boats to carry them abord, that they might take their passage to Rajapore; whereupon hee declared thei had licence, but hee was free from giveinge them any such councell; and soe they departed.' Indigo now commands a good price, being very scarce here. The commodities of 'Scind', such as 'meanaes, udpotaes, cuds Meirzaie, alejaes Bengale, allejaes Sabone', are likely also to be in good demand. Send copies of their accounts, the originals of

---

[1] On the production of lead in the Kermān district see Lord Curzon's *Persia*, vol. ii. p. 518.

which went by the *Endeavour*. The arrival of Pitt is daily expected. *PS.*—Desire a small box of 'chirirgiry'; also a supply of sack and beer. *PPS.*—The yearly allowance of house provisions (rice, butter, oil, candles, 'doll' [pulse: Hind. *dāl*], &c., should be sent by the next ship. (*Copy.* 3¼ *pp.*)

PRESIDENT CARTWRIGHT AND COUNCIL AT BANTAM TO THE COMPANY, DECEMBER 23, 1645 (*O.C.* 1884[1]).

Out of the money received by the *William*, they sent upwards of 10,000*l.* to the Coast. They beg the Company not to fail in supplying those factories annually with means; and they promise on their own part to furnish the Coast with gold and other vendible commodities. 'Cogan connives att Yards estate for his owne ends.' . . . 'Difference betweene Hatch and Olton.' . . . (¼ *p.*)

CONSULTATION HELD 'ON SWALLY MARYNE' BY PRESIDENT BRETON AND MESSRS. MERRY, THURSTON, TASH, AND FITCH, DECEMBER 27, 1645 (*O.C.* 1965).

At a previous consultation held on October 11 [*missing*], it was decided that on the return of the *Falcon* from 'Scinda' and of the *Seahorse* from Tuticorin, they should be sent to the Red Sea to intercept the Malabars, 'our profest and invetterate enimies'. Now, however, intelligence has been received that 'the now Vice Roy[2], intending a suddaine warr against them, denieth his pass unto all Mallavars tradeing to the Redd Sea, prohibiting the granteing of them any securitie by any the Governors or Captaines of any his townes or forts on this coast'; and it is unlikely that in these circumstances any of the Malabars will venture upon such a voyage. Moreover, Broadbent, on being consulted, objected to the enterprise, 'by reason of the difficulties and hazzard hee saith there is in encountering them'. In view of all this, it is determined to abandon the project and find other employment for the two vessels. Although their expectation of good returns from Achin last year was disappointed, yet it is clear that considerable profits may be made

[1] These are notes only, made in London. No copy of the letter itself is extant.
[2] Filippe Mascarenhas, who had succeeded the Conde de Aveiras as Viceroy in September, 1644.

there by sales, and the *Falcon* is accordingly designated for that employment. She is to proceed thither at the end of the monsoon, by which time the baftas lately provided at 'Matchawara' will be ready to form part of her cargo. The *Seahorse*, after being overhauled in 'the river of Surratt', will be sent to Rājāpur, where some 'dungarees[1]' are already awaiting shipment, and it is expected that a large quantity of pepper will have been provided out of the money landed there from the *Hind* on her way back from Tuticorin. The *Seahorse* will then proceed to the Red Sea and sell her cargo. The differences between the Dutch and the Persians being now settled, it is resolved to notify the Surat merchants that freight goods will be accepted for Persia on the same terms as before. John Totty s appointed to command the *Seahorse*; and John Brown, master's mate of the *Hind*, is to succeed Broadbent as master of that vessel. Broadbent and Tindall are permitted to take passage in the *Eagle* for England. John Warner, coxswain of the *Hind*, who was maimed in a fight with the Malabars, is awarded 200 mahmūdīs to help him 'in this his misserie'. (2½ *pp.*)

THOMAS MERRY AT SWALLY MARINE TO THE COMPANY, DECEMBER 29, 1645 (*O.C.* 1966).

After a service of eight years he is now 'looking hoamewardes', and begs the Company to license his return to England at the same time as Breton. The accounts of the Fourth Joint Stock, made up to the end of September, are sent herewith. Urges that means be supplied for extinguishing the debt and thus freeing the factors from 'theis extortinge usurers'. (1 *p.*)

PRESIDENT BAKER AND COUNCIL AT BANTAM TO THE COMPANY, DECEMBER 29, 1645 (*O.C.* 1884[2]).

... The *Swan* has gone for Surat.... 'A minister needfull at Fort St. Georg, unto which place Mr. Isaackson from Surat was designed.'... (3 *lines*.)

[1] A coarse kind of cloth: Hind. *dungrī*.
[2] Notes only, made in London from a letter now missing. Cartwright had resigned the post of President to Aaron Baker a few days earlier and embarked for England in the *Mary*, with Robert Hatch as a fellow-passenger (*O.C.* 1969).

ANTHONY FENN'S[1] ACCOUNT OF THE VOYAGE OF THE *EAGLE* TO SURAT (*Marine Records*, vol. lxvii).

1645, *February* 11. Sailed from Blackwall, and anchored near Erith. *March* 15. Moved to Gravesend. *March* 24. Weighed anchor; 'in casteing our shipp', she fell foul of a vessel commanded by Captain Strong.[2] Anchored that evening in Margate Road. *March* 25. Got as far as the Downs. *April* 3. Sailed, accompanied by the *Lanneret*. *April* 4. Off Beachy Head they were overtaken by the *Falcon*. *April* 9. Passed the Start, in very thick weather. *April* 25. Saw Grand Canary. *May* 23. The *Lanneret* lost company. *May* 27. She joined again. The same day they crossed the Line. *June* 20. The weather being rough, the *Falcon* lost company. *June* 22. The *Lanneret* did the same. *July* 5. Saw land to the eastwards of the Cape. *July* 21. Anchored in St. Augustine's Bay [Madagascar]. 'Wee founde heere the *William*, belonging to Squier Curtene, Mr. Blakman comaunder, being come out of India and bound home for England but, haveing loste his munsone, wintered here. Likewise here was the *Jeames*, come out of Ingland, Mr. Weddall[3] comaunder, bounde for India.' *July* 22. 'Came in Mr. Spencer in the *Sunn*, from St. a Lucea, the French plantation uppon the backe side of St. Laurence' [*see* p. 200]. The same afternoon the *Falcon* and the *Lanneret* arrived. *July* 29. The fleet sailed. *August* 12. Anchored in Johanna Road, 'twharte off Brownes garden' [*see the preceding volume*, p. 170]. *August* 22. The ships sailed. *September* 23. Saw the coast of India. *September* 25. Anchored in Swally Hole, and found there a Dutch ship from Mokha. 'Your best rideing in Swallow Hoale is with the tody tree bearing of you S. and by E., and Swallow E.S.E., and the Divells tree E.N.E., and Bloody Poynte[4] N. and by E. ½ E.; and then you shall have 9½ fadoms att a hye watter and at a lowe watter some 6 fadoms.' *September* 28. The *Hester* came in from Goa and the *Swan* from Bantam. *October* 16. The *Hester* sailed for Goa.

---

[1] He was master's mate. The captain was Thomas Stevens.
[2] See *Court Minutes*, 1644-49, pp. 80, 84, 90.
[3] This was Jeremy Weddell, son of Captain John Weddell.
[4] The scene of the skirmish between the English and the Portuguese in 1630 (see the 1630-34 volume, p. x).

October 28. The *Falcon* departed for 'Sindey'. *November* 5. The *Endeavour*, under Bowen, and the *William*, under Stafford, arrived from Basrā. *November* 7. These two vessels went into the river to careen. *November* 28. The *William*, *Prosperous*, and *Christopher* came in from Surat River. *December* 1. The *Francis* went to Damān to fetch arrack. *December* 7. The *Falcon* returned from 'Sindey'. *December* 10. The *Francis* came in; also two Hollanders from Batavia. *December* 17. The *Lanneret* sailed for Persia. *December* 23. The *Hind*, under Broadbent, and the *Seahorse*, under Tindall, arrived from the [Malabar] Coast with pepper. *December* 24. The *Endeavour* came into the Hole from Surat River. *December* 31. The *Eagle* went over the bar, preparatory to sailing for England. (33 *pp.*)

INDEX

Abbāsīs, passim.
Abbās Qulī Beg, 297.
Abbot, Edward, 25.
Abdullah Qutb Shāh, Sultān. *See* Golconda, King of.
Āchār, 73 *n.*
Achin, Queen of, 128, 131; privileges granted to the English and Dutch at, 130, 212; native of, imprisoned by the Portuguese, 130, 212; Indian trade to, 92, 129, 130, 131, 281, 282; native merchants hinder Company's trade at, 128; trade between Arakan, Macassar, and, 131; Company's factory at, 130, 131; factors at, *see* Bowman, Dawes, Fitch, Scattergood; dispatch of ships from and for, 99, 128, 131, 139, 146, 148, 179, 212, 214, 231, 253, 272, 311; shipment of freight goods from and for, 131, 146; trade at and commodities from, 97, 128, 129, 139, 146, 148, 235, 253, 310, 311; goods provided for, 136, 161, 164 (3), 167, 204, 212; Courteen's trade to and factory at (*see also* Glascock, Kynaston), 29, 128, 129, 130, 148, 184, 217, 254; Courteen's debts at, 148, 217, 232; Dutch factory and ships at, 129, 130; Dutch chief at, *see* Willemszoon.
Ackersloot, the, 32, 272.
Acuerdo, 222.
Adams, Robert, 25.
Adams, Roger, 69, 81; death of, 234.
Aden, 19; Malabar junks trade to, 3, 139, 213.
Adhar Bhatt, 14.
Adler, Thomas, 26, 70, 83, 84, 98, 132, 135, 143, 148, 169, 172, 188, 218; letter from (*see also* Persia, *and* Surat), 189.
Advice, the, 35, 122, 146, 148, 294; master of, *see* Dowle *and* Pollen; voyage to Gombroon and back to Coromandel Coast, 31, 35, 40, 42, 56, 87; repairs to, 40, 43, 295; on Coromandel Coast, 33, 42, 56, 68, 69; voyage to Bengal and back to Masulipatam, 32, 43, 55, 67, 77, 101; sails to Narsapur and back to Madras, 77; at Madras, 71; voyage to Bantam, 41, 55, 70, 77, 78, 97, 101; dispatched on a voyage of discovery, 97, 118-119; again on Coromandel Coast, 116, 118, 140, 157, 159; returns to Bantam, 119;
120, 128, 164, 168; arrives at Coromandel Coast from Bantam, 293; sails to Tegnapatam and back to Madras, 281, 282; sails for Bantam, 281, 287 (2), 289, 292, 294.
Agra, xvi; factors at, *see* Blackwell, Bornford, Burnell, Davidge, Downs, Hammersley, Jesson, Knipe, Tash, Turner; letter from, 299; censure of factors at, 203; factory accounts and records, 16, 96, 97, 142, 232, 301; broker at, *see* Dhanjī; trouble with brokers at, 300; trade at, *passim*; customs duties on commodities from, 214; caravans from, 215, 300, 301, 302, 304; debts and want of money at, 302, 303, 304, 305; rate of interest on borrowed money at, 303, 304; failure of *sarrāfs* at, 303; debts due to Company at, 160, 301, 302; Anglo-Dutch agreement at, to reduce the price of indigo, 304; Shāh Jahān's army and treasure at, 59; designs of rebels on, 58, 59; presents for Shāh Jahān, etc., sent to, 160; Kotwāl of, *see* Sharafuddīn Husain; Jesuits at, 60, 63; Portuguese borrow money from Company at, 60; Courteen's trade to, 140; Dutch trade and merchants at (*see also* Van der Burgh), 98, 215, 227.
Ahmadābād, factors at, *see* Andrews, Cogan (Thomas), Heynes, Robinson, Smith (Anthony), Tash; factory accounts, 16, 236 *n.*; debts at, 5; money remitted to Sind from, 85; changing of money at, 144; supplies for, from Surat, 210; trade at, *passim*; manufacture and dyeing, etc., of cotton cloth at, 5, 7, 137, 164, 204; refining of saltpetre and borax at, 205, 233; customs duties on commodities from, 214; caravans from and for, 90, 163, 201, 210; Governor of, *see* Āzim Khān; Dutch trade at, 160, 164, 202; Dutch caravan for, 98.
Akbārīs. *See* Cotton goods.
Alamānī, 18.
Alamparai, Dutch factors and goods seized at, 280, 288.
Aleppo, dispatch of letters to and from England via, 27, 57, 59, 98, 122, 143, 169, 171, 299; cost of transmission of

INDEX

letters to, 59; trade between Basrā and, 58; Consul at, 59; depressed state of trade at, 294.
Aleppo Merchant, the, xix, 29; master of, *see* Millet; chartered for voyage to India, v, 28; Knipe (*q.v.*) to manage voyage of, 59; private trade aboard, 29 (2), 89, 123; outward voyage of, 57, 61, 83; voyage to Malabar Coast from Swally, 59–61, 69, 86, 106–109, 138; at Goa, 63 (2); passages for Portuguese on, 94; homeward voyage of, 95, 96, 98, 109, 110, 121, 122, 135, 201.
Alī Āghā, 284.
Alī Bāshā, 168, 186, 273, 274; presents for and from, 20, 23, 284; negotiations with, 27, 57; dispute with the Portuguese, 143.
Al-Katif, 100, 147.
Allah Bakhsh, 301, 302.
Allejas. *See* Cotton goods.
Allison, John, letter from, 1; commended, 15.
Almacen, 221, 225.
Almonds, 42, 73 *n.*
Almude, 217.
Aloes, 7, 124, 139 (2), 162, 205, 233, 252, 254.
Alum, 138, 167.
Amar Singh, 229 *n.*
Amber, 217, 233.
Ambergris, 120.
Amberties. *See* Cotton goods.
Amboina, the, 62.
Ameldee. *See* Emalde.
Amin, Mirzā, 253 *n.*
Amīr (pl. *umarā*), 229, 302.
'Andre Manfecks', 187.
'Andre Peela', 187.
Andrews, Thomas, 175, 231.
Ankleswar, 137.
Anthony, John, 236.
Appelton, William, 152.
Arabia, horses from, 38, 160, 284. *See also* Aden, Basrā, Mokha, etc.
Arab Khān, 297.
Arab, Mirzā, 23, 169.
Arakan, 131.
Archer, Anthony, 198 *n.*, 241.
Ardasse, 122.
Ardeas. *See* Cotton goods.
'Arlour'. *See* Vellore.
Armagon, Nāyak of, 52; complaint against, 53; death of, 80; attacked and captured by Srī Ranga Rāyalu, 44, 80; English ship wrecked at, 20; fort at, 47, 48; dismantling of fort at, 51, 52, 53; paintings from, 51; money due to and from Company at, 49, 52, 191; prices compared with those at Madras, 118, 157;

abandoned by the Company's factors, 305, 306.
Armenians, 18, 278, 303, 304.
Arrack, 7, 19, 61, 74, 103, 226, 234, 313.
Arras (*or* Arrash), 122.
Arrendt, the, 218.
Āsaf Khān, 109; death of, 25; his estate seized by Shāh Jahān, 25, 95.
Asālat Khān, Mīr Bakhshī to Shāh Jahān, 229 *n.*, 302; Boughton appointed surgeon to, 229; assists the Company's factors, 230, 232.
Āsā Vōra, 168.
Ascension Island, 241, 262, 264.
Assab, 99, 147.
Auditor, East India Company's. *See* Markham.
Aurangzīb, Viceroy of Gujarāt, 253 *n.*
Austin, Bartholomew, 256 *n.*
Ayappa Nāyak, forces King of Carnatic to release Damarla, 80 *n.*
Ayres, William, 237.
Āzim Khān, 5.

Bab-ul-Mandab, 19, 139, 213.
Baftas. *See* Cotton goods.
Baghdad, 58, 294.
Bairām Alī Beg Shaikhāvand, 297.
Baines, Rev. Andrew, 132, 152.
Baker, Aaron, letters to and from, *see* Bantam; resigns the Presidency at Bantam, 82; again becomes President, 311 *n.*
Balasore, factors at, *see* Bengal; letter from, 65; dispatch of ships for and from, 32, 65, 77, 101; trade at, in various commodities, 65, 66, 117; factors advise continuance of factory at, 65; price of provisions at, 72; private trade at, 72; debts at, 116; factory accounts, 126; accident to *Endeavour* at, 207; Persians at, 105. *See also* Bengal.
Bamboos, 276.
'Bamford' (*or* 'Bombard'), 104.
Banda, the, 260.
Bandar, 46, 170, 266, 269, 273. *See also* Masulipatam.
Bandar Abbāsī. *See* Gombroon.
Bandar Rig, 283.
Bandar Sūr. *See* Sūr.
Banksāl, 55.
Bantam, President at, *see* Baker *and* Cartwright; President and Council at: letters to and from, 33 (2), 38, 77, 82, 97, 113, 118 (2), 126, 133, 154, 293, 295, 310, 311; consultation by, 121; Coast accounts to be rendered to, 13, 45; Coast and Bay factories subordinate to, 45, 82, 127, 132, 140; disputes with and accusations against Surat Council, 11, 16, 33, 34, 85, 86, 172, 227; indebted to Surat

Council, 33, 34, 86, 99; money due to, from Coast factors, 39, 97; and the building of Fort St. George, 47; complaints against, 100, 140, 200; and the Manilla venture, 192, 193; factors at, *see* Collet, Jeffries, Winter (Thomas); dispatch of ships for and from, *passim*; commodities from, 6, 7, 16, 27, 35, 61, 70, 78, 80, 82, 86, 94, 97, 101, 121, 128, 134, 138, 139, 142, 165, 201, 211, 231; complaint of poor returns from, 20; goods vendible at, 5, 6, 137; supplies for, 21, 35, 40, 43, 55, 80, 100, 176, 194, 200, 201, 204; want of supplies and ships at, 34, 35, 36, 97, 128, 192, 193, 293; ship sent to, for service at, 147; debts at, 34; rate of interest for loans at, 34; state of Company's affairs at, 35; slaves for, 37, 81, 97, 120; trade between Surat and, 85, 142, 164, 172, 201, 231; suggested dispatch of ship to Bengal from, 293; Indian trade to, 294; Dutch and Portuguese given passages to, 80; Dutch at, 38; Danes at, 37, 40; their new factory at, 37, 38; Danish ship sails for, 36.

Banyans, 14, 18, 64, 108, 144, 204, 270, 283.

Barang-barang, 119.

Barbary, Courteen's Association trade to, 185; gold, 185.

Barker, Roger, 105, 111 *n*.

Baroda, dissolution of factory at, 164; factory accounts, 16; baftas and Guinea stuffs from, 6, 85, 123, 137, 164, 204; bleaching (*or* curing) of cotton goods at, 137, 204; manufacture of cots, etc., at, 295; customs duties on commodities from, 214; Dutch trade at, 6, 160.

Basrā, 57; letters from, 57, 186, 197, 273, 283, 298; Bāshā of, *see* Alī Bāshā; Shahbandar of (*see also* Mahmūd Āghā), 27, 168, 186, 273, 274; Governor of, *see* Hassan Beague; broker at, 168, 169; factors at, *see* Bowman, Buckeridge, Cogan (Thomas), Cranmer, Pearce, Rymell, Thurston, Walwyn, Weale; commodities vendible at, 5, 7, 136, 137, 202, 203, 284, 294; supplies for, 8, 20, 139, 143, 161, 163, 164, 204, 208, 268; establishment of residence at, 20, 143, 299; building of factory at, 27, 57; Company's agreement for trading to, 27; customhouse and customs duties, 27, 274, 275; factory accounts and expenses at, 58, 89, 226, 284; dispatch of ships for and from, *passim*; best time for dispatch of ships to, 284; transmission of letters to and from England via, 2, 82, 91, 98, 122, 135, 143, 169, 186, 200, 236, 273; sickness and mortality at, 276, 283; trade at, *passim*; horses from, 2, 19, 20, 147, 148, 284; Company in favour at, 58, 186, 273; Courteen's ships sail for and trade at, 277, 283, 284, 309; dispute between Courteen's and Company's factors at, 299; Indian trade to, 2, 21, 168, 186, 253, 274, 294; trade between Aleppo, Baghdad, etc., and, 58, 274; Dutch trade to and ships at, 274, 275, 283, 284, 294; destruction of Dutch ship at, xvii; Dutch chief at, *see* Sarcerius; Dutch demands refused and trade discouraged at, 274, 275, 283; Portuguese trade at, 274; Portuguese endeavour to spoil Company's trade at, 295.

Basrūr ('Bassalour'), English ships and trade at, 109.

Bassano, Henry, 101, 111 *n*.

Bassein, dispatch of ships for and from, 148, 160; Portuguese Captain of, 286 *n*.

Basting (Bastinck *or* Bastian) de Oude, Willem, 271, 272, 278.

Batavia (*or* Jakatra), Dutch ships for and from, 21, 22 (2), 32, 33 (2), 38, 68, 99, 129, 130, 150, 218, 313; trade in wine at, 145; commodities from, 22, 218; Courteen's sailors detained by Dutch at, 128; Dutch Governor-General at, 21; Portuguese negotiations with, 21, 148, 149; Persian mission to, 282; letter from Malaya to, 288, 292, 294.

Baticola, 20.

'Bayes', 18, 61, 91, 160, 170, 209.

Bayley, William, 2, 9, 39, 175, 183, 245, 259; letter from, 188.

Bāzār, 58.

Beads, 25, 124, 205, 210. *See also* Samisamy *and* Rango.

Beck, William, 103.

Bengal, Governor of, *see* Sultan Shujā; factors in, *see* Day, Gurney, Hatch (Robert), Netlam, Olton, Travell, Winter; factors recalled from, 13, 20; complaints against factors in, xxvii, 34, 72; want of factors, 66; trade in and commodities from, 55, 67, 72, 78, 137, 190, 207; price of provisions in, 72; dispatch of ships and supplies for and from, 13, 20, 32, 42, 67, 72, 125, 186, 190, 194, 206, 207, 253; shipment of passengers and freight goods for and from, 20, 67, 72, 77 (2), 186, 191; debts in, 13, 207; repairing of ships in, 36, 40; question of continuance of trade at and factory in, xxxv, 65, 66, 78, 134, 293; trade between Achin and, 130; value of Company's stock, etc., at, 191; small ships required for trade to, 229, 293; purchase of a junk in, *see* Endeavour; Dutch ship dispatched from, 42; Danes capture a junk of, 156. *See also* Balasore.

INDEX

Beni Dās, 57, 252.
Benzoin, 55, 139.
Betel-nuts, 74 (2), 75.
Bethills. *See* Cotton goods.
Bezoar, 178.
Bhatkal, Courteen's factors at, 109; Company invited to settle at, 109.
Bhikkū, 37.
Biāna, indigo, 5, 6, 84, 85, 122, 126, 201, 303, 304; complaint as to quality of, 202; Dutch and English trade at, 304.
Bījāpūr, King of, *see* Mahmūd Ādil Shāh. *See also* Dābhol, Kārwār, Vengurla, etc.
Billidge, Thomas, 236 *n.*
Bindlos, William, 95 *n.*
Blackman, Captain Jeremy, 148 (2), 168, 180, 254, 255, 312.
Blackwell, Joshua, 175, 231, 301.
Blessing (1), the, xix; destruction of, at Goa, 16.
Blessing (2), the, outward voyage to Bantam, 27, 87; at Bantam, 97, 100; homeward voyage of, 122; outward voyage of, 122, 177, 200.
Blocq, Klaas Korneliszoon, 255, 268, 269, 275; death of, 278, 279, 299.
Bloody Point, 312.|
Bombay, English ships at, 135, 147; supplies and reinforcements for Portuguese at, 217, 235.
Bona Speranza, the, master of, *see* Carter; outward voyage of, 26; on the Malabar Coast, 148; freighted for China by Portuguese, 148; captured by the Dutch, 128, 129, 130, 134, 148, 165, 168, 218.
Bonaventura, the. *See Henry Bonaventura.*
Bond, Captain, 144, 176, 231.
Borax ('tincal'), trade in and price of, 85, 124, 138, 147, 205, 254; refining and packing of, 138, 233; private trade in, forbidden, 124, 138.
Boreel, Pieter, 100, 149; death of, 149 *n.*
Bornford, Henry, 7, 18, 26, 69, 84, 89, 90, 98, 122, 173, 229.
Boughton, Gabriel, xxxv, xxxvi, 102 *n.*, 229.
Bowen, Adam, letter from, 258.
Bowen, Robert, 298, 313; letter from, 181, 185; complaint against, 277, 299.
Bowman, Maximilian, 95 *n.*, 131, 132, 146, 217; letters from, *see* Basrā.
Boyāo, 66.
Bradbent. *See* Broadbent.
Bradford (*or* Broadford), Geoffrey, 126, 158, 159, 194.
Bradgate, Martin, 193, 289.
Brahmans, 46, 280.
Brass, 220.
Breton, Francis, 29, 69, 96, 132, 216, 229, 310; nominated to succeed Fremlen as President at Surat, 29, 88, 96, 173; letters from, *see* Surat; endeavours to maintain friendly relations with Portuguese, 141; gifts from Shāh Jahān, etc., for, 230 *n.*; to return home, 311.
Breton, Thomas, 166, 167, 213, 218-226.
Brewster, Henry, 238-243.
Bridgeman, —, 293.
Brightwell, John, 28.
Brimstone, 63, 148; price of, 89.
Broach, factory accounts, 16; customs at, 24, 25; baftas from, 6, 85, 123, 137, 164, 204; bleaching of cotton goods at, 137, 204, 233; difficulties in transporting goods from, 137; dissolution of factory at, 164; broker at, *see* Deodāsī; Dutch trade at, 6, 160.
Broadbent, William, 16, 142, 212, 310, 311.
Broadcloth, trade in, *passim*; price of, 58, 60, 107, 230; for presents, 19, 91, 210.
Brookhaven, Captain, xxii.
Brown, John, 132, 193, 253, 311; letters from, *see* Madras.
Brown, William, 293.
Buckeridge, Nicholas, 168.
Buckingham, Thomas, 262.
Buckner, —, 301.
Bulsar, 3.
'Burgare', 28.
Burhānpur, 137, 140.
Burnell, John, 175, 177, 239, 245, 247, 249, 301, 305; letters from, 194, 198, 237.
Burnell, Thomas, 247.
Butter, 39, 114, 310.
Byars, Signor, 304.
Byrams. *See* Cotton goods.

Cabra (Cabritoll *or* Goat) Island, 219.
Caesar, the, 2, 49, 50.
Caldeira, João da Maya, 195, 249, 286, 298, 304, 305.
Calicoes. *See* Cotton goods.
Calicut, 7; dispatch of English ship for and from, 60, 108; natives given passage to, 107; trade at and commodities from, 60, 86, 108.
Calitore. *See* Kistnapatam.
Cambay, native trade to Mokha, Basrā, etc., from, 10, 186; trade at, in various commodities, 208; customs at, 24, 25.
Camboja, trade between Manilla and, 223.
Camels, 98.
Canary silk, 122; wine, 16, 173, 210.
Candahar, 18, 58, 83.
Candles, 226, 310.
Candy, 55, 81, 109, 191, 192, 212, 217.
Cannanore, King of, *see* Mammāli Koya; Courteen's ships at, 27; trade at, in various commodities, 109; junk of, destroyed by English ship, 179, 213, 236 *n.*

'Cannikeenes'. *See* Cotton goods.
Canton, 250.
Cape of Good Hope, 105; English ship at, 181, 185; Dutch ship wrecked at, *see* Mauritius Island.
Cape Verd Islands, 32.
Caphila (*qāfila*), 10, 23, 58, 90, 215, 270, 272, 304.
Capitāo Mōr, 44, 60.
Capuchins, 80.
Caravel, 217.
Cardamoms, 7, 8, 10, 60, 86, 99, 108, 109, 124, 138, 140, 147, 177, 205, 216, 233, 248, 267.
Caribbee Islands, 199 *n.*
Carnatic. *See* Vijayanagar.
Caron, François, xxiv.
Carpenters Bay, 153, 187. *See also* Mauritius.
Carpets, 60, 63, 64, 66, 73 *n.*
'Carracke', 186. *See also* Khargu Island.
Carter, John, 130.
Cartwright, Ralph, 36; letters from, *see* Bantam; becomes President at Bantam, 82; returns to England, 311 *n.*
Carvalho, Francisco, 14.
Cash, 42.
'Cassaes' (Cossas *or* Cassedees). *See* Cotton goods.
Castellano, 222.
'Catches'. *See* Cotton goods.
Catechu. *See Kattha*.
Catteife. *See* Al-Katif.
Cavitte, 219; Governor of entertains English factors, 219, 220; Company's trade at, 221.
Ceylon, Portuguese trade to, 10; Dutch ships at, 21, 100; Dutch expedition against the Portuguese in, xxiv, 128, 167, 255; Dutch forces defeated in, 114, 149, 167, 168; Dutch demand surrender of, by Portuguese, 151; monopoly of cinnamon trade in, 217, 218; cotton goods from, 248. *See also* Baticola, Colombo, Negombo, etc.
Chagos Islands, 185, 201.
Chaluva, 79.
Chandras. *See* Dammar.
Charles I, assists Courteen's Association, 3, 10; Courteen's ships carry Royal flag, 3.
Charles, the, xix.
Chaul, 65.
Chay, 79.
Cheloan, Captain William, 225, 251.
Chennappapatam, xxxiv.
Cherry, Robert, 169, 186 *n.*
Chhatarsāl. *See* Rao Rājā.
Chicacole, 206 *n.*
China, Dutch trade to and ships from, 22, 32, 99, 134, 150; gold and other commodities from, 66, 145, 165, 167, 221, 223, 250, 254; loss of Dutch ships in, 167; Portuguese trade to, 81, 134, 149, 150, 165; trade between Manilla and, 220, 223; attempt to establish Company's trade to, from Surat, 227, 228, 247; Courteen's ships and trade in, 232, 254; customs duties, etc., in, 254; Tsing Cheng, Emperor of, death of, 250. *See also* Macao.
Chinaware, 58, 66, 165, 167, 251, 254, 284.
'Chinder'. *See Khanjar.*
Chinnana Chetti. *See* Malaya.
Chintz. *See* Cotton goods.
Chit, 64.
Christianhaven, the, 156, 157.
Christopher, the, 313.
Chunam, 248.
Chungam, 306, 307.
Cinnamon, trade in, *passim*; price of, 89, 107, 124; trade in, prohibited, xxv, 60, 63, 205, 218; monopoly of trade in, 217, 218.
Citron preserves, 66.
Civil War and Company's trade, 139, 171, 172, 188.
Ckandara. *See* Kandiāro.
Clark, Richard, 132, 139, 174, 231, 234.
Clark, Richard, 238, 240, 243, 249, 258.
Clark, Thomas, 73, 94, 101, 103, 104, 105, 111 *n.*, 131; complaints against, 49, 56.
Clark, Walter, 138; letter from, 128; death of, 146; estate of, 142, 233, 234.
Clitherow, Anthony, 133.
Cloves, 16, 37, 86, 121, 131, 142, 218; freight rates on, 55.
Coals, 183. *See also* Collow.
Coaster, the, 2.
Cobb, William, 237.
Cochin, factors for, *see* Thurston *and* Pynn; ships at and dispatched from and for, 56, 59, 60, 61 (2), 86, 99, 100, 107, 128, 131, 138, 146, 147, 214; trade at, and commodities from, 60, 70, 92, 99, 107, 108, 109, 131, 138, 206, 211; shipment of freight from and for, 146, 147; Company advised against trading at, 231; Courteen's ships, factors and trade at, 62, 107, 146; Courteen's debts at, 146.
Cochin, Upper, Rājā of at war with the Portuguese, 138 (2).
Cochin China, Dutch encounter with native vessels of, 167.
'Cockenians', 276 *n.*
Coconuts, 2.
Cocos Keeling Island, 97, 118.
Codrington, Thomas, 132, 169, 266, 279; goes to Persia (*q.v.* for letters from), 70; his mission to new Shāh, 98; salary of, 84, 172.

INDEX

Coffee, 58, 59, 93, 114.
Cogan, Andrew, 49, 60, 74 (2), 117, 121, 131, 140, 190, 191, 228, 290; letters from, *see* Madras; and private trade, 11, 53; charges and complaints against, 35, 41, 45, 51, 310; and the founding of Fort St. George, 51-53, 127; desires to relinquish Coast Agency, 38, 41, 54, 55, 56, 68; his request opposed, 69, 70; his influence on the Coast, 70; agrees to remain as Agent, 79; desires to return to England, 112, 115; sails for Bantam and home, 116, 127, 189; salary of, 56.
Cogan, Thomas, 103, 132, 161, 253, 266, 299; letters from, *see* Basrā.
Coiba Islands, 199. *See also* Caribbee Islands.
Coins, complaint of supply of defective, etc., 17, 144, 145; values of various, 17, 18, 145, 209, 210; method of packing for shipment, 145; complaints of bad packing of, 295, 296; most in demand, 211.
Coir (cairo *or* bast), 167, 212, 283.
Cokayne, William, 276 *n.*
Colio, 179. *See also* Dewua.
Collet, Edward, 46, 79, 97, 114.
Collow (*or* coaldust), 183.
Colombo, Dutch designs on, 21; Dutch repulsed by Portuguese in attack on, xxiv, 167, 168; the *William* touches at, 254.
Comfort, the, 2, 131.
'Comitters'. *See* Cotton goods.
Comoro Islands (including Johanna, Mayotta, and Mohilla), 177; English ships at, 2, 32, 105, 135, 183, 185, 188, 189, 194, 200, 237, 239, 243, 260, 261, 263, 312; letters to English commanders calling at, 188, 189, 198; English garden (Browne's) at, 312; slaves from, 119; revolution at Mayotta in, 119; Queen of Johanna, 199.
Congo. *See* Kung.
Constant, Charles, 170, 266, 267, 269, 270, 271.
Cooper's Bay, 187.
Copper, 212, 218; sulphate of, *see* Mōrthuthu.
Copperas, 18.
Coral (including 'grezio', 'recaduti', and 'teraglia'), 9, 18, 22, 26, 29, 61, 64, 67, 68, 69, 70, 78, 86, 91, 99, 107, 108, 109, 120, 135 *n.*, 145, 157, 164, 174, 177, 178, 190, 193, 210, 211, 217, 226, 227, 230, 259; price of, 60, 190, 210; complaint as to quality of, 145, 231; beads, 210.
Corge, 137, 217, 300.
Coromandel Coast, Agents on, *see* Cogan, Day, and Ivy; factors on, Bradgate, Brown, Collet, Greenhill, Gurney, Hudson, Isaacson, Jermyn, Markham, Methwold, Minn, Netlam, Olton, Peniston, Perks, Robins, Styles, Travell, Winter (Edward), Winter (Thomas), Yardley; charges and complaints against factors on, 11, 12, 13, 31, 32, 36, 39, 45, 51, 53, 54, 72-77, 82, 113, 114, 117, 118, 126, 140, 154, 155, 173; factors complain of neglect by the Company, 155, 157, 287; factors at, lend money to the Portuguese, 60; chronicle of events on, 42-45; subordinate to Surat, 13, 33; factory accounts and expenses, 33, 54, 56, 82, 128, 133, 134, 155, 194, 293, 294; advantages of being under control of Surat Council, 54; factory accounts to be rendered to Bantam, 13, 45; made subordinate to Bantam, 82, 127, 140; want of supplies on, 38, 39, 45, 46, 54, 66, 79, 101, 117, 155, 281, 282, 287, 288, 289, 293, 310; supplies for, 11, 45, 87, 88, 190, 191, 193, 207; debts at, 17, 33, 39, 40, 41, 43, 49, 55, 65, 68, 79, 97, 112, 113, 115, 117, 120, 126, 127, 128, 155, 164, 191, 194, 228; borrowing of money at, 69, 70, 79, 101, 112, 280; value of Company's stock, etc., at, 190, 191, 194; trade at, *passim*; quarrel between Dutch and Malaya benefits Company's trade, 288; monopoly of trade on, offered to the Company, 288, 290; best time for trading at, 87; proposal to abandon trade on, 47; suggested increase of stock and shipping on, 133; native wars affect trade on, 65, 80; dispatch of ships from and for and ships at, *passim*; shipment of passengers and freight to and from, 20, 42, 55, 67, 72, 77, 191, 192, 268; want of ships on, 48, 117, 229, 282, 287, 288, 289, 293; best time for dispatching ships from, for Bantam, 287, 288; adjustment of charges against, 33, 34; debts due to Surat and Bantam from, 40, 97; Company exempt from customs duties at, 207, 208; trouble with natives at, 46; trade route to Persia from, 56; trade between Persia, Mokha, Achin and, 55, 67, 80, 81, 87, 125, 130, 207, 260, 268, 278, 281, 288; Persian merchants at, 87; oppression of Dutch at, 80; Dutch borrow money at, 79; oppression of Dutch at, 80; Dutch give presents to and assist the Sar-i-Khail, 80, 81; Dutch join in native intrigues on, 154; Dutch endeavour to monopolize trade on, 154, 155, 156, 191; Dutch in bad odour on, 281, 288; Company's factors trade in confiscated Dutch goods, 288, 289, 290, 291, 294; complaints against the Dutch on, 288; Dutch trade on, 13, 40, 45, 46, 68, 87, 117, 154, 164; Danes trade on, 40, 45, 113, 155; Danish President, 75; presents for Danes at, 74, 75; declining state of Portuguese affairs on,

THE ENGLISH FACTORIES

155; execution of a Portuguese at, see De Miranda. See also Madras, Masulipatam, Petapoli, Vīravāsaram, etc.
Correa, Duarte Fernandez, xv, 16, 25, 142, 159, 168, 171.
Cossumba. See Kusumbha.
Costus, 167 n.
Cots, 295.
Cotta. See Katthā.
Cotton goods and calicoes, trade in and references to, passim; akbarīs, 6, 123, 137, 203, 301; allejas, 87, 309; amberties, 302; ardeas, 7, 137; baftas, 6, 7, 85, 123 (2), 137, 138, 164, 200, 203, 204, 206, 223, 233, 274, 300, 304, 311; bethills (betteelas or calico lawns), 137 (3), 207, 287; byrams, 6, 137, 302; 'cannikeenes', 7, 137; cassaes (cossas or cassedees), 6, 65, 137, 207, 293; catches (or cattaketchies), 248, 252; chintz, 6, 85, 124, 137, 204, 233; comitters, 229; daryābāds, 6, 123, 137, 204, 233, 302; dungrī, 311; dutties, 7, 224; 'farradckaunes', 137; ginghams, 65, 190, 207, 293; guinea stuffs, 7, 85, 124, 138, 204, 233; guldars, 137 (2), 233; 'gurras', 65, 207 (2); 'guzzees', 7, 137 (2), 299, 300, 301; 'hummanees' (homoomies), 137, 207, 223; 'joories', 6, 85, 123, 163, 203 (2), 233; khairābāds, 6, 137, 300; longcloths, 207, 223, 224, 287; 'mercooles', 6, 123, 137, 203, 233; murrees (or moorees), 65, 190, 223; muslins, 137 n.; 'nicaneers', 124; red cloth, 287; 'salampores', 223, 292; salooes (or selaes), 6, 137 (2), 223, 233; sannoes (or sannas), 65, 207; sarasses (or Zarasses), 217, 223; semianoes, 85, 137, 204, 233; seryas (seriaes), 7, 218; sheerisadfs, 137; taffetas, 61; 'tappis' (or tapichindas), 79, 287; 'tapseels', 7, 85, 233; prices of, 203, 223, 300; dyeing and bleaching (or curing) of, 6, 7, 28, 79, 87, 123 (3), 137, 164, 204, 233, 251; thefts of, 3, 132, 172; discontinuance of investments in, 5, 82; dearness and scarcity of, 6, 137, 191; freight rates on, 55, 72; from various places compared, 84, 136, 192; distributed to General Voyage subscribers as dividends, 123; not in demand in England, 123, 124; complaint as to quality, etc., of, 126, 136; method of packing for shipment, 224, 293.
Cotton wool, 6, 26, 137; price of, 164.
Cotton yarn, 6, 25, 31 n., 85, 95, 136, 137, 205, 233, 248; price of, 124.
Courteen's Association, dispatch of ships and supplies to India for, 26, 27, 29, 56, 57, 61, 62, 89, 105, 106, 148, 176, 183, 200; wreck of ships of, see Henry Bonaventura and Little William; protection of Malabar pirates by, 3, 255; complaints against, 3, 276, 277, 283, 284, 286, 309, 312; Company's opposition to trade of, xxi, 8, 176; compete with and spoil Company's trade, v, 140, 247; Dutch competition with, 10; trade in various commodities, 10, 27, 97, 105, 107, 109; assisted by Charles I, 3, 10; ships of, wear King's colours, 198 n.; state of affairs of, 23, 148, 217, 231, 232, 247, 255; debts of, 217; ordered to withdraw factors, etc., from India, xx n., 29; quarrel between commanders of ships of, 89; and the attempted colonization of Madagascar, 144; carry freight for Portuguese, 148, 165; ship of, captured by the Dutch, see Bona Speranza; dispute with the Dutch, 148; money of, deposited with Company's factors, 184, 185; shipwrecked sailors of, rescued and employed by the Company, 185, 234; trade to Barbary, 185; Portuguese license trade to China of, 216; shipment of freight to Persia, etc., by, 217, 255, 276, 277; allegations of piracy against, 232, 237 n., 277, 286; complaints against Company's factors by, 236, 237, 276, 277, 299; deny complicity with Cobb and Ayres, 237; depredations by Malabars against settlements of, 236 n.; grant passages to Company's factors, 237; supply the John (q.v.) with stores, etc., 241; negotiations with the Portuguese, 254; grant passages to Portuguese, 286; Company's factors buy guns from, 295. See also Blackman, Cox, Hall, Woodman, etc., and Kārwār, Macao, Rājāpur, Rāybāg, etc.
Covado (or covett), 7, 58, 230, 300. See also Gaz.
Cowle. See Qaul.
Cowries, 224.
Cox, Thomas, 193; letters to and from, 182, 184 (4), 185 (2).
Crane, Sir Francis, 176, 232.
Cranmer, Robert, 23, 132, 161, 168, 253, 299; letters from, see Basrā.
Crispiana, the, xix, 89, 90; master of, see Bayley and Steevens; homeward voyage of, 2; at Comoro Islands, 2; outward voyage of, 28, 57, 61, 83, 105–106; voyage to Sind and back to Swally, 61; homeward voyage of, 89, 95, 96, 98, 109, 110, 121, 122, 135; men from employed as factors, 94; private trade aboard, 110, 123; outward voyage to Swally, 122, 125, 172, 175, 177, 188, 194, 195, 200, 228, 238, 239, 259, 260; disposal of, 125, 175; at Comoro Islands, 183, 188, 189; designed for England, 203, 205, 208, 209, 211, 215, 216; voyage to Sind and back to Swally, 211, 231, 234;

INDEX

homeward voyage of, 229, 231, 232, 234, 236, 242, 247, 260.
Croocq, Paulus, 161, 260.
Cross, Joseph, 143, 165, 252.
Cubebs, 201, 214.
Cubella. *See* Minicoy.
'Cuds Meirzaie', 309.
'Cuskus'. *See* Millet.
Cussumba. *See Kusumbha*.
Customs remitted to English and Dutch, 98, 130, 159, 160, 169, 207, 208, 214, 305, 307. *See also* Gombroon, Kung, Madras, etc.
Cutch. *See Kattha̅*.
Cuttan. *See Katana*.

Da Silva Tello de Meneses, João, Conde de Aveiras, Viceroy of Goa (*q.v.*), 66, 310 *n.*
Dabbah, 233.
Dābhol, the *Hopewell* at, 71, 74; shipment of freight goods for, 73, 74, 116; junks of, captured by the Portuguese, 272.
Dādū, 6.
Dāl, 310.
Damān, dispatch of ships for and from, 19, 313; commodities from, 19, 313; English ship at, 146, 234; Captain of, 66.
Damarla Venkatappa, Nayāk of Punamallee, 43, 47, 49, 53, 70, 80, 154, 290; complaint against, 11, 12; extent of his authority, 50, 306, 307; character of, 50, 51; superseded by Malaya, 154, 156.
Dammar (*chandras*), 35, 61, 66, 80, 86, 93, 205.
Danes, the, fortify their settlements, 12; state of affairs of, 23, 40; assist Company's ships, 36; seize native shipping to enforce restitution, 42; carry letters for the Company, 120; ship of, in the employ of the King of Spain, 156; wreck of ship of, 156; Company's factors lend money to, 157.
Dārā Shikoh, 160, 163, 214, 215, 230 *n.*
Darbēlo 'joorees', 123, 163, 203.
Darell, John, 236.
Daryābāds. *See* Cotton goods.
Daulatābād, 208.
Davidge, Richard, 175, 188 *n.*, 231, 301.
Dawes, William, 131.
Day, Francis, factor for First General Voyage, 33, 42, 55, 65, 67, 78, 134, 228; letter from (*see also* Madras), 116-118; and the founding of Fort St. George, 11, 12, 47, 52, 53, 126, 127; salary of, 56, 132; accusations by and against, 72-77, 102-105, 110, 112, 118; placed in command of the *Hopewell*, 74; sent to Bengal, 38; recommends continuance of trade there, 78; petition from, 111; proposed as Agent for Coromandel Coast, 41, 56,

69, 70, 112, 116; appointed Coast Agent, 117, 126, 127, 189; desires to relinquish the Agency and return home, 118, 121, 157; appeals for more power for Coast Agent, 117; suggests increase of shipping on Coromandel Coast, 133; sails for Bantam, 191.
De Aveiras, Conde. *See* Da Silva Tello de Meneses.
De Brito, Diego Mendez, 21 *n.*
De Brito, Joseph, 166, 219.
De Brito da Almeida, Francisco, 60, 206.
De Figueroa, Don Francisco, 220.
De Ladossa, Carolus, 115 *n.*
De Masters, Peeter, 276 *n.*, 299.
De Miranda, Antonio Pereira, execution of, 43, 44, 59, 60, 63, 106.
De Motta, Galvao, xxiv.
De Noronha, Miguel, Conde de Linhares, 30, 67, 173.
De São José, Frei Gonçalo, 21 *n.*
De Souza, Luiz de Carvalho, 129.
De Souza de Castro, Francisco, 37, 64, 65, 130.
De Vlaming (*or* Vlamingh) van Outshoorn, Arnold, 272.
Dearson. *See* Durson.
Deccan, the, trade in, in pepper and other commodities, 7, 10, 214, 233, 254, 255; Courteen's Association trade in, 89, 140; indebtedness of Courteen's Association in, 232, 255.
Delfshaven, the, 274 *n.*, 283 *n.*
Delft, the, 260.
Deodāsī, 204.
Deo Karan, 211.
Derham, John, death of, 144.
Derham, Thomas, 144, 146.
Dewcurn. *See* Deo Karan.
Dewua Bay, 181. *See also* Colio.
Dhairya Sāhū, 216.
Dhanji, 215.
Dholka *lungīs*, 58, 197.
Diamond, the, 144, 161; master of, *see* Whatmore; voyage to Sind and Gombroon, 20; thence to Masulipatam, 20; calls at Muskat, Baticola, and Fort St. George, 20; sails to Armagon, Masulipatam, etc., 20, 42; detained by Governor of Masulipatam, 42; voyage to Bay of Bengal, 13, 20, 42; designed for Bantam, 21; voyage to Bantam from Coromandel Coast, 33, 35 (2), 36, 40, 42, 68, 87, 100; repairs to, 36, 40; voyage to Jambi, 36, 38; voyage from Bantam to Swally, 37, 86.
Diamonds, 215, 230 *n.*
Diarbaker, 58.
Dieppe privateers, 8, 9, 176, 232.
Digart (*or* Digger), Captain David, 9.
Discovery, the, xix, 8, 9, 14, 138, 146, 172,

FOSTER VII

175, 200, 210, 213, 239, 247, 260; master of, *see* Allison *and* Minors; outward voyage from England, 2, 10, 19; voyage to Gombroon and Larak and back, 1, 4, 15, 16, 31, 91; designed for Mokha, 1, 23, 91, 92; voyage to Mokha, 8, 10, 15, 16, 61, 62, 70, 86, 91, 92; French pirates employed as sailors aboard, 9; private trade on, 25; pilfering aboard, 31; voyage to Gombroon, Mokha, Malabar Coast, and back to Swally, 98, 99, 100, 139, 144, 147; designed for England, 5, 6, 26, 88, 99, 101; homeward voyage of, 147, 153, 159, 187; Portuguese passengers aboard, 152; lost at sea, ix.
Diu, 10, 168.
Dofar, 237.
Dolfijn, the, 22 (2).
Dollars, 'cross', value of, 176, 209; 'rex', value of, 17, 145, 210.
Dolphin, the, xix, 150, 175, 210, 218, 231, 236 *n.*; master of, *see* Proud; outward voyage of, 121, 135, 146; letters from, 187, 189, 259; consultation aboard, 260 *n.*; voyage to Goa and back to Swally, 138, 151; Portuguese goods shipped on, 142; voyage to Malabar Coast and back, 147; homeward voyage of, 147, 153, 159, 187; makes for Mauritius in distress, 153; at Mauritius, 153, 183; forced to return to Swally, 188 (2), 189, 199, 200, 211, 214, 229, 239, 259, 260; designed again for England, 199; homeward voyage of, 234, 236, 242, 247, 259, 260.
Dominicans, 94.
Dongee. *See* Dhanjī.
Don John, Island of, (Macao), 180.
Dowle, Thomas, 56, 115, 140, 141; letters from, 71, 118.
Downs, Gregory, 236.
Downs, Matthew, 132.
Drake, John, 14.
Drugs, 136, 165, 171, 173, 252.
Ducatoons, 211; value of, 175, 209.
Ducats, 84 *n.*
Dungrī. *See* Cotton goods.
Durd [ ]. *See* Dādū.
Durson, Captain John, 29, 62, 176, 183, 231, 255, 276, 283, 284, 295, 299, 309.
Dutch, the, carry letters, goods and passengers for the Company, 1, 26, 36, 41, 52, 67, 100, 113, 139, 154, 215, 218, 236, 237, 238, 244, 257, 258, 293, 304; the Company carry passengers, letters, etc., for, 26, 38, 80, 116, 153; trade in various commodities, 6, 10, 21, 35, 80, 84, 85, 100, 122, 145, 150, 164, 171, 198, 201, 202, 217, 218, 227, 278, 303, 304; fortify their settlements, 12; complaints against, 16, 208, 215; complaints against the English, 63; hostilities with the Portuguese (*see also* Goa), 21 (2), 100, 114, 128, 151, 165; Portuguese peace negotiations with, 21, 99-100, 148, 149, 151, 218; hostilities treacherously recommenced by, 148; Portuguese prisoners in hands of, 129; ship of, captured by Portuguese, *see Pauw*; make peace with Portuguese, xxv, 228; threaten the Portuguese, 308; encounters between Malabars and, 22; state of affairs of, 22, 32, 40, 217, 255; insure Portuguese ships, 22; attack the *Reformation*, 37; stop and search the Company's ships, 93, 289, 290, 292; seizure of Courteen's ship by, *see Bona Speranza*; discoveries by, in the South Seas, etc., 134; ships built by, used by the Company, 141 *n.*; ship freight goods, 161; monopolize freight trade and passenger traffic, 142; superiority of ships of, 142; power of, at sea in the East, 225; obtain privileges from Shāh Jahān, 160; sailors employed by the Company, 226; ship wrecked at the Cape, *see Mauritius Island*; endeavour to control trade to Manilla, 251, 256; at war with natives, *see* Vijayanagar *and* Malaya; Company's factors trade in confiscated goods of, 280, 281, 288, 289, 290, 291, 292, 294; designs against native junks, 299. *See also* Batavia, Ceylon, Japan, Kishm, Macao, Ormuz, Pulicat, Rāybāg, etc.
Dutties. *See* Cotton goods.
Dyes *and* dyeing, 7, 79 *n.*, 203. *See also* Chay *and* Kusumbha.

Eagle (1), the, wreck of, 50.
Eagle (2), the, 259; master of, *see* Steevens; outward voyage of, 286, 312; homeward voyage of, 311, 313.
Earl, Captain William, 176; death of, 238, 244.
East India Company, the, letters to and from, *passim*; Secretary of (*see also* Swinglehurst), and private trade, 178; instructions to factors, 8, 30, 177; new style and title for ships' commanders, 15; interlopers damage the trade of, v, 27, 140, 172, 173, 247; endeavour to obtain protection from interlopers, 173; trade of, hampered by freight and private trade, 72, 77, 140, 202; disadvantages of employing chartered vessels, 89, 90; resolve to discontinue use of such ships, 173, 229; declining state of trade of, 90; monopoly on various commodities withdrawn, 94; Civil War affects trade of, v, 95, 125, 139, 171, 172, 188; dividends paid in kind, 123 (2); threat

INDEX

against private traders, 123; desired to supply better ships for East Indies, 141; practice of sending out wine for factors discontinued, 145; desire to maintain friendly relations with Portuguese, 230; disapprove of employment of sailors as factors, etc., 231; desire the return of only one ship a year, 231; Courteen's accusations against, 236, 237, 276, 277, 299. See also Joint Stock and Voyage, General.
Elchi Beg, 46.
Elder, Daniel, 132.
Elephant, the, 150.
Elephants, 81, 116.
Elephants' Teeth (ivory), 21, 146, 211, 217, 218.
Emalde, 71, 75, 156, 285, 287, 295.
Emeralds, 230 n.
Endeavour (1), the, 133, 234; voyage to Bengal and back to Coromandel Coast, 13, 20, 42, 77; at Madras, 70; designed for Persia, 66; found unfit for voyage, 70, 71, 78; destruction of, 113, 190.
Endeavour (2), the, 171, 229, 237 n., 293, 297, 310; master of, see Bowen; letters from, 181, 182, 185; outward voyage of, to Coromandel Coast, 121, 125, 173, 181, 182, 185, 189, 190, 200; survivors from Courteen's *William* aboard, 183, 185, 189, 193, 259; voyage to Bengal, 186, 190, 191, 206, 207; designed for Persia, 186, 191, 192; sails from Bengal to Coromandel Coast, 253; voyage to Gombroon, 253, 268, 278, 287; designed for Basrā, 214, 253; voyage to Swally from Gombroon, 268, 278; voyage to Basrā and Kung, 275, 276, 283, 284; accusations against the purser of, 295; voyage from Basrā to Gombroon and Swally, 298, 299, 313.
Engano, 36.
England's Forest. See Réunion.
Enkhuizen, the, 22, 32.
Escrivão, 267, 270.
Exchange, rate of, 207, 302.
Expedition, the, 2, 11, 147, 158, 159, 161, 172, 200; master of, see Gaidner; voyage to Sind, Gombroon and back to Swally, 19, 20; voyage to Bantam, from Swally, 19, 27; voyage to Macassar, 37, 97; goods missing from, 55; voyage to Swally from Bantam, 54, 97, 127, 138, 139, 142, 147; unfit for further service, 147.

Factors, lists of, 26, 289; want of, 26, 90, 142, 143, 247; salaries of, 26, 121, 132, 133, 175, 289; reduction in numbers of, 30; estates of deceased, 97; responsibility of, for unsaleable, etc., goods, 126,

206; detained after expiry of covenant, 133; commended, 143; entertainment of ships' officers as, 143, 174; desire supply of wine, 145; grants to, for sea voyages, 218, 234.
Falcon, the, outward voyage of, 286, 312; voyage to Sind and back to Swally, 285, 310, 313; designed for Achin, 310, 311.
Fanams, 42, 43, 108, 109, 116; value of, 213 n.
Fardles, 72, 203.
Farmāns, 4, 32, 84, 135, 160, 169, 214, 230, 257, 266, 278, 282, 285, 296 (2), 307.
Farren, John, 217, 236, 255.
Faulkner, Thomas, 131.
Faxardo, Don Diego, Governor of Manilla, negotiations with, 220-222; refuses presents from Company's factors, 224, 225; Company carry letters for, 226.
Fenn, Anthony, 312.
Fenn, Hugh, 175, 188 n., 231.
Ferdinand, Edouard. See Correa.
Fidalgo, 43.
Fisher, Richard, 17, 144.
Fitch, Richard, 17, 95 n., 132, 143, 310; letters from (see also Surat), 286.
Fitch, Thomas, 131, 146.
Flanner, Henry, death of, 244.
Flat Holme, 242 n.
Flying Hart, the, loss of, 167.
Formosa, 36, 99, 167; Dutch capture Portuguese fort at Kilung, 100.
Fort St. George. See Madras.
Francis, the, 14; master of, see Cherry and Gilson; voyage to Gombroon, Basrā, and back to Swally, 2, 19, 28, 31; encounter with Malabar pirates, 14, 27, 88, 89; voyage to Persia, Sind, and back, 19; voyage to Mokha, Gombroon, and back to Swally, 3, 19, 23, 59, 83, 93; voyage to Mokha and back to Swally, 100; designed again for Mokha, 139, 146; but goes to Basrā, 161, 168; thence to Gombroon and back to Basrā, 168, 169, 186, 197, 200, 208; returns to Swally via Gombroon and Sind, 169, 211, 234, 266; voyage from Sind to Swally, 248; designed for Basrā and thence for Mokha, Suakin, and Persia, 213, 214, 235, 252; voyage to Damān and back to Swally, 313.
Freight, rates for, 2, 55, 72, 131, 142, 146; alleged frauds in connection with shipment of, 35; shipment of, hampers Company's trade, 72; use of Company's ships for, deprecated, 31, 191, 192.
Fremlen, William, ix, x, 29, 69, 132, 153, 188, 218; appointed President at Surat, 15; letters from and to (see also

THE ENGLISH FACTORIES

Surat), 64, 66, 187, 189, 259; and private trade, xv, 15 *n*., 31 *n*., 64, 86, 298 *n*.; subscribes to General Voyage, 88; presents for, 138; goes home, 88, 90, 96, 141, 142, 147, 159, 173, 229; commendation of, 96, 141, 206; journal of, 146; death of, xv.
Frenchmen, given passages on English ships, 200, 259.
French pirates, 8–10, 15, 59, 141, 143 *n*., 144, 232. *See also* Dieppe.
Fruit, 211, 278.
Fuddle, Jacob, 116.
Fursman, William, 23, 26, 94; death of, 92.

Gadanki, 44.
Galen, Jan Dirksz., 21 *n*., 62, 63, 106.
Galle, 100; encounter between Dutch and Portuguese near, 114 *n*.
Gambling, 76.
Gandevi baftas, 233.
Gardenijs, —, 81 *n*.
Gardner, Gilbert, 147, 294.
Garry (*or* Gary), Henry, 175, 239, 245 *n*., 246 *n*.; letters from and to, 177, 194, 198, 258; accusations by and against, 238, 243–247, 258, 259, 261–263; imprisoned and ordered home, 249, 259.
Gaz, 300. *See also* Covado.
Gee, Thomas, letter from, 183.
Geldanke. *See* Gadanki.
Geleijnszoon, Wollebrant, 83, 114 *n*., 150, 271, 275, 299, 308.
Genoa, pepper, 227; velvet, 227 *n*.; swordblades, 18.
'Gentues', 45, 54, 67, 279, 288, 291; sailors, 282.
Gergelin. *See* Gingerly.
German swordblades, 18.
'Geru' (red earth), 38, 114.
Gilson, George, 14.
Gingelly oil, 248 *n*.
Ginger, 6, 85, 124, 139, 206.
Gingerly Coast, dispatch of ships for, 186, 206; attempt to establish a factory on, 206; trade at, 75, 253, 293; factor at, *see* Brown.
Ginghams. *See* Cotton goods.
Gingī, Nāyak of, 154 *n*., 194 *n*.
Girās, 299, 300.
Glascock, —, 131.
Goa, letters from, 226, 236; trade at, and commodities from, *passim*; commodities vendible at, 226, 227; Jesuits at, 14, 60, 64, 66; Jesuit College at, 16; dispatch of ships for and Company's ships at, 16, 34, 59, 60, 61 (2), 63, 64, 80, 86, 106, 138, 147, 167, 179, 181, 211, 212; Company's residence and factors at (*see also* Hill,

Oxenden, Pitt, Wylde), 8; debts due to the Company at, 8, 63, 64, 93 *n*.; factory accounts, 64; trade in cinnamon restricted at, 205; factors leave, 60, 64, 107, 138; dissolution of English factory at, 63; Portuguese soldiers attack an Englishman at, 64; presents for Portuguese at, 64; Courteen's ships and factors (*see also* Darell, Farren, Hunt) at, 8, 89, 138, 231, 236, 254, 255, 312; state of Courteen's affairs at, 148, 232; protest by Courteen's factors at, 255; Dutch ships off and blockade of, vii, 21 *n*., 38, 62, 63, 67 *n*., 93, 106, 107, 128, 151, 212; declaration by Dutch commanders at, 62, 63; Dutch complain of Company carrying relief to, 62, 63; Dutch molest Company's ships, 147; Dutch impede English trade to, 63 (2), 106, 107; peace negotiations between Dutch and Portuguese at, 100, 149, 218; Portuguese capture a Dutch ship at, 114, 116; dispatch of Dutch ships for, 150, 167, 218; supplies and reinforcements for Portuguese at, 151, 217; Achin native imprisoned at, 130, 212.
Goa, Viceroy of, 21, 22, 61; letter from, 66; negotiations between Company's factors and, 8, 60, 212; presents for and from, 60, 66, 138; assists and trades with the Company's factors, 8, 63, 138; Company carry letters and goods for, 30, 60, 63, 91, 173, 176, 195, 230; claim against the Company by, 249; endeavours to maintain peace with the English, 66, 91; and the execution of a Portuguese soldier on the Coast, 63; requests passages for priests on English ships, 94; grants licences to the Company and Courteen's Association for China trade, 165, 212, 216, 221. *See also* Da Silva Tello de Meneses, *and* Mascarenhas.
Godfrey, Thomas, 133, 185.
Godown, 129.
Goghā, 25.
Gokul, 300.
Golconda, Abdullah Qutb Shāh, King of, 44, 54, 207; present for, 39, 46; assists the Company's factors, 41, 46; grants privileges to the English and Dutch, 46; shipment of goods freight free for, to Persia, 55; designs on Vijayanagar, 70 *n*., 80; his ambassador to Persia, 73, 74, 116; Dutch present for, 80, 81; his forces attack Pulicat (*q.v.*), 193.
Golconda, Sar-i-Khail at, *see* Mīr Mahmūd Saiyid; dissolution of factory at, 46; debts due to the English at, 41, 46, 68; trade at and commodities from, 46, 208; 211, 233; factors at, *see* Collet *and* Rogers; Coast Agent desired to reside

INDEX

at, 48; borrowing of money from officials at, 69; Dutch trade at, 46; Dutch competition affects Company's trade in, 155, 156.
Gold, 21, 106, 145, 185, 223, 225, 226, 255; loaves of, 35, 254.
Golden Sun, the, 33, 36, 37, 40, 156.
Gombroon, Governor (Sultān) of, 1, 268, 269, 277, 309; death of, from injuries received in earthquake, 266, 267; Shāhbandar at, 32, 135, 170, 208, 265, 266, 267, 268, 269, 277, 278; factors at and letters to and from, *see* Persia; dispatch of ships, and shipment of passengers and freight goods for and from, *passim*; customhouse at, 1, 31, 98, 170, 172, 266, 267, 270, 296; dispute between the English and Persians at, 1, 31, 98; English share of customs at, 4, 28, 32, 84, 98, 135, 136, 169 (2), 171, 172, 207, 208, 227, 256, 257, 265, 266, 270, 271, 277; customs guard at, 1, 169; Company exempted from customs duties at, 169, 207; proposals for redressing grievances at, 84, 267; trade at, *passim*; trade between Coromandel Coast and, 56, 87, 88, 125, 207, 268, 278, 281; troubles at, affect trade, 283; broker at, 27, 296; money values at, 268; counterfeit coins at, 278; English house and house rent at, 4, 296; allowance of house provisions for, 310; factory accounts, 309; continuance of factory at, desirable, 268; English factory at, in ruins, 273; factors and merchants leave, during hot weather, 135, 268, 273; Indian native trade to, 32, 55, 67, 80, 87, 88, 172, 207, 208, 272, 309; trade route to, 73; private trade at, 73 (2); castle at, 271; earthquake at, 258, 266, 267; Dutch trade at, 266, 299; dispatch of Dutch ships from and for, 32, 98, 218, 283; quarrel between Dutch and English factors at, 105; Dutch forced to pay customs at, 170; Dutch extort customs at, 269; Dutch demand exemption from customs duties at, 268, 269, 282, 283, 307; and offer to defend the port for moiety of customs, 269; they are forbidden to trade at, and refused supplies, 269, 270; Dutch fleet off, 268, 269, 273; Dutch casualties at, 258, 267; Dutch hostilities against Persians at, 269, 270, 271, 273, 299; English factors protest against Dutch proceedings at, 257, 258, 269, 270, 272; and are warned not to assist the Persians, 272 n.; seizure of native junks by the Dutch at, 269, 299; rebuilding of Dutch house at, 275; Portuguese fleet anchors off, 272; Courteen's ship and trade at, 276, 277, 309; dispute between the Company and Courteen's Association at, 276, 277; customs duties remitted to Courteen's Association at, 277.
Goodyear, John, 132, 165, 252.
Gonī. See Gunny.
Gopaljī, 15.
Gorle (*or* Gourly), William, 129.
Gosnoll, George, 3.
Greenhill, Henry, 42, 74, 110, 132, 157, 159, 193, 289; letters from, *see* Madras; complaint against, 49, 76; private trade of, 72, 73, 75, 76; desires to go home, 157; goes on a mission to Srī Ranga Rāyalu, 290, 292, 305 n.
Grimstone, —, 49.
Guinea, trade to, xxii, 146.
Guinea stuffs. *See* Cotton goods.
Gujarāt, cotton goods from, 7; Viceroy of, *see* Aurangzīb *and* Āzim Khān.
Guldārīs, 85.
Gunny (*gonī*), 10, 78, 248.
Gunpowder, 39, 256, 264, 287; packing and shipment of, 78, 159; native, 141, 157, 158; price of, 141, 191.
Gurney, William, 132, 193, 289; letters from, *see* Masulipatam.
'Gurras' (Gurrahs). *See* Cotton goods.
'Guzzees'. *See* Cotton goods.

Haarlem, the, 260.
Hājī Zāhid Beg, 161, 257, 274, 294.
Hall, Captain Edward, 3.
Hall, Rev. Edward, 97.
Hall, William, 1, 70, 84, 90, 132, 143, 148, 172; letters from, *see* Persia.
Hammām, 266.
Hammersly, Francis, 7, 132.
Hampton Merchant, the, outward voyage of, xix, 26, 27.
Haraīk ('Herig'), 244.
Hariharpur, trade at, 65; English ship at, 77; factory accounts, etc., 96, 97, 126; dissolution of factory at, 126 n.
Harrison, Gilbert, 175, 231.
Harsfield, Richard, 111 n.
Hart, the, 126, 157; master of, *see* Godfrey; outward voyage of, to Coromandel Coast, 120 (2), 121, 127, 135, 189; disposal of, 120, 128; voyage to Bantam, 133; voyage to Swally from Bantam, 134, 185, 201; at Swally, 214; voyage to Rājāpur, 216; designed for Bantam, 229, 234; voyage to Sind and back to Swally, 234, 248; voyage to Bantam, 248.
'Hassan Beague', 284.
Hastas (*hāth*), 37.
Hatch, Robert, 65, 78, 132, 190, 207, 253, 294, 310, 311 n.
Hazel-nuts, 42.
Hemingway, Edward, 75, 111.

Hemskirk, the, 167.
Henriette Louise, the, 22, 32.
Henry Bonaventure, the, outward voyage of, xix, xx, 26; wreck of, on homeward voyage, 119, 148.
Herbert, Peter, 132, 197; sails for Mokha, 139, 161, 186; death of, 234, 266.
Hester, the, 28, 109, 176, 260; master of, *see* Hogg; homeward voyage from Cannanore, 10, 27; outward voyage of, 29, 105, 106; voyage to Kārwār from Rājāpur, 62; at Goa, 63, 89; at Cochin, 107; at Swally, 286, 298, 309, 312; sails for Goa, 312.
Heynes, Robert, 17, 132, 215, 302.
Heywood, Hercules, 193, 194, 289.
Hill, Stephen, 276 *n*.
Hill, Thomas, 7, 8, 132, 138; at Goa, 59; leaves Goa, 60, 64, 107; goes to Ahmadābād and Agra, 98; goes to Surat from Agra, 304.
Hill, Thomas, 193; letter from, 182.
Hill, William, 74, 103, 104.
Hind, the, 210, 249; master of, *see* Broadbent *and* Brown; outward voyage of, to Coromandel Coast, 121, 135; voyage to Bantam, 135; not suitable for Indian waters, 141; designed for Achin, 146; at Swally, 146; voyage to Sind and back to Swally, 147; voyage to Persia and back, 147, 159, 162, 168, 170, 186, 211; voyage from Swally to Macao, 165, 167, 179–181, 210, 212, 218, 249, 250; encounter with Malabar pirates, 179, 181, 235, 255; at Malacca, 235; designed for Persia and Bantam, 159, 214; voyage to Mokha, 252; voyage from Mokha to Tuticorin and then to Swally, 252, 275, 311, 312.
Hindaun, indigo from, 303, 304.
Hindoos. *See* Gentues.
Hinton, Thomas, 134.
Hogg, Robert, 62, 89, 206, 309.
Holmens, the. *See* Steep Holme *and* Flat Holme.
Honywood, Francis, 25.
Hope, the, 28; master of, *see* Brightwell; attacked by Malabar pirates, 88.
Hopewell, the, 11, 27, 33, 34, 55, 68, 97, 113, 114, 134, 147, 172, 232; master of, *see* Lock, Trumball, *and* Yates; outward voyage of, to Coromandel Coast, 26, 32, 33, 41, 42, 56, 65; accounts of voyages, etc., of, 71–77, 236 *n*.; designed for Persia, 55, 65, 66, 69; voyage to Bengal and back, 32, 43, 65, 67, 69, 77, 101; designed for England, 70, 78, 101, 128; voyage to Gombroon and back to the Coast, 70, 71, 77, 78, 88, 101, 116, 173; voyage to Tranquebar, etc., and back, 116; voyage to Bantam, 71, 110, 114, 126, 127, 133, 189; Day accused of inciting mutiny on, 74; Trumball superseded by Day in command of, 117; Trumball reinstated, 112, 116; petition from officers of, 111; Cogan sails for Bantam on, in place of Day, 115, 116, 189; homeward voyage of, from Bantam, 153, 189, 228, 234, 259; in distress, at Mauritius, 153, 187; at the Comoros, 188 *n*.; puts back to Swally, 183, 189, 200, 211, 234, 239, 260; bought by Joint Stock from General Voyage, 214; voyage to Malabar Coast and back, 214, 248; encounter with Malabar pirates, 248; voyage to Persia and back to Swally, 214; unfit for further service, 252, 256.
Horses, 68, 98, 114, 146, 160; price of, 76; shipment of, 78, 79. *See also* Basrā *and* Persia.
Howard, Bartholomew, 247, 261.
Hudson, Richard, 40, 49, 289; accusations against, 56, 294; letters from, *see* Masulipatam.
Hunt, Abraham, letter from, 236.
Hunt, Henry, 175, 177, 239, 245, 247, 252; letters from, 194, 198, 237.
Hurt, William, 17.
Husband, Richard, 25.

Ibrāhīm, 163.
Indigo, trade in, *passim*; complaint as to quality of, 4; frauds in connection with, 14, 122, 123, 173, 201; trade in, in Persia, 19, 309; packing of, 39; price of, 84, 94, 122, 123, 136, 163, 164, 191, 202, 203, 254, 304; improved method of preparing, 85; Company threaten to discontinue to trade in, 126; Anglo-Dutch combination to reduce prices of, 202, 304; sand mixed with, to preserve, 202; irregular purchase of, 229; high price prevents trade in, 303. *See also* Agra, Ahmadābād, Biāna, Lahore, Sarkhej, Sehwān, Sind, etc.
Ink, 18.
Insurance, marine, 22, 92, 161, 216.
Interlopers, 172, 173; suspected of piratical designs, 176. *See also* Courteen's Association.
Iron, 26, 65, 148, 219–222, 224, 225, 251, 256, 293.
Isaacson, Rev. William, 196, 244, 247, 249, 311.
Isaacson, William, 132; death of, 190.
Islām Khān Mashadī, the Wazir, 160.
Ispahān, the maidān at, 297; factors at and letters from, *see* Persia; necessity for retaining factory at, 4; trade at, 83, 169, 274, 277; factors and merchants retire to, during hot weather, 135, 268, 273; English factors go to the Court at, 257, 266, 276,

INDEX

277; the Dutch at, 270; ill-treatment of Dutch chief at, 170; the Shāh invites Dutch commissary to, 272; Dutch mission to Court at, 275, 278; the Dutch ordered to leave, 282.
Itimād-uddaula, the. *See* Taqi Mirzā *and* Khalīfa Sultān.
Ivy, Thomas, 49, 121, 193, 227, 228, 305; letters from, *see* Madras; and private trade, 11, 45; appointed to the Coast Agency, 126, 133, 134, 190, 289; becomes President at Bantam, 291.

Jaccal (*or* Jackal)-ground, 305.
Jacobsz, Jacob, 62.
Jagannāth. *See* Puri.
Jagat Singh, 18.
Jahānārā Begam, xxxv, 148.
Jahrum, Dutch caravan molested at, 272.
Jakatra. *See* Batavia.
Jākhau (*or* Jagatt), 216.
Jalālpur, 301.
Jambi, dispatch of ship to and from, 36, 134; trade at, 293; Queen of, 37, 38, 68.
James, the, xix, 176, 260, 312; master of, *see* Weddell (Jeremy).
Jam Qulī Beg, Mirzā, Governor of Surat, 3, 18, 23, 24, 98, 99, 144, 162; recalled to Court, 160.
Jānī Khān, the Qurchi Bāshī, 296, 297.
Janissaries, 58.
Japan, Dutch trade to and ship from, 21, 99; Dutch granted privileges by the Emperor of, 100; Portuguese debarred from trading to, 250; trade between Macao and, 250; silver, 100.
Jaques, James, 43.
Jast (*or* tutenague), 36, 55, 100, 218, 254.
Javanese embark on the *Reformation*, 36; and are slain in attack by the Dutch, 37.
Jeffries (*or* Jeffreys), John, 35; letters from, *see* Bantam; death of, 119, 120, 134.
Jelliah (*or* Gelliaes), 133, 157.
Jellowatt, 240.
Jenjerlee. *See* Gingerly.
Jentu. *See* Gentues.
Jermyn, Thomas, 289.
Jerreleene, 206. *See also* Gingerly.
Jesson, William, 17, 32, 301, 304; letter from, 299.
Jesuits, 8, 14, 36, 60, 63, 66; 149. *See also* Carvalho, Martyns, Xavier.
Jewel, the, 2, 97, 119.
Jewels, 153, 215, 230 *n*.
Jidda (Judda), 214; exactions by Governor of, 161, 162.
Jilaudār Bāshi, 297 *n*.
Johanna. *See* Comoro Islands.
John (1), the, wrecked at Armagon, 20.
John (2), the, 205, 206, 210, 213, 214, 216,
228, 230, 232, 234, 236; outward voyage of, 122, 125, 172, 175, 177, 178, 188, 189, 194, 200, 235, 238; seized by Mucknell for King Charles I, xiii, 194–197, 238–246, 249, 258, 259, 261–263; subsequent voyage of, 198, 199, 242, 262, 264; loss of, affects the Company's credit, 247, 249; Portuguese claim for money lost in, 240, 241, 263, 298, 305; obtains supplies from Courteen's *Thomas and John*, 264; members of crew, etc., ill-treated and left at St. Helena, 241, 260, 262, 264; ship's company rewarded by the King, 265; recovery of her cargo, xiv.
Joint Stock, Third, 62, 79; winding up of, 26, 41, 55, 83, 142, 172, 232; shipping and money of General Voyage used for, xxvii, 29, 30, 118, 214; debts of, 33, 96, 117; trade on behalf of, 77, 87, 97, 100; accounts of, 87, 88; remains of, transferred to Fourth Joint Stock, 142; Fourth, accounts of, 236, 311; Fourth, failure of, v.
Jonas, the, xix, 97, 119; loss of, 40, 86.
Jones, Daniel, 225.
Joories. *See* Cotton goods.
Joss sticks, 167 *n*.
Juan de Nova, 198.
Junkan. *See* Chungam.
Jussett (*Jast*), 218.

Kafīr, 81, 120.
Kajan, 267.
Kandahar. *See* Candahar.
Kandiāro, 163, 203, 233.
Kāngra, 18 *n*.
Kanjī, 251.
Karnāta (Carnatic). *See* Vijayanagar.
Karttika, 305.
Kārwār, Courteen's factory at, 29, 62; dispatch of Courteen's ships for and from, 62, 194, 237; depredations on Courteen's settlement at, by Malabar pirates, 236 *n*.
Kasbin, 98.
Kashān, 83.
Kāsim Alī, 193 *n*.
Katana, 241 *n*.
Katthā, 217.
Kavite. *See* Cavitte.
'Kedjans'. *See* Kajan.
Keeling Islands. *See* Cocos Keeling.
Kermān, 309.
Khairābād, Dutch resident at, 300.
Khairābāds. *See* Cotton goods.
Khairāt Khān, 207.
Khalifa Sultān, the Itimād-uddaula, 296.
Khanjar, 230 *n*.
Khargu Island, 186, 197, 273.
Ki-lung, 100 *n*.
King Road, 242, 264.

Kinnersley, Edward, 17.
Kishin, Company's and Courteen's ships at, 237, 244; King of, 286.
Kishm, Dutch design for fortifying, 255, 256, 257; their unsuccessful assault on the castle at, 275, 277, 278, 308; Dutch designs on, 299.
Kistappa Nāyak, 194 *n.*
Kistnapatam, 44.
Kit, the, 213, 214.
Klein Zutphen, the, 22, 32.
'Klings', 131.
Knipe, Edward, vii, 29, 66, 69, 91, 200, 228, 229, 300, 302, 304; salary of, 28, 175; letters from, 57, 62, 63, 64, 177, 178, 179, 194, 198, 237, 259, 299; letter-book of, 28 *n.*, 57; leaves Courteen's and re-enters Company's service, 57 *n.*; commission and instructions to, 59, 177; merchant for *Aleppo Merchant's* voyage, 57 *n.*, 59, 61, 86; commended, 89; diary of voyage of the *Aleppo Merchant,* 105–110; and private trade, 110; outward voyage to Malabar Coast, 172, 174, 175, 177; carries letters to Viceroy of Goa, 176; dispute with Ribeiro, 178; charges by and against, 194–197, 239, 240, 243–247, 249, 258, 259, 261, 262, 263, 298, 301, 304, 305; arrives at Surat in a Dutch ship, 237, 249; goes to Agra, 249, 259.
Knives, 193, 225; for presents, 145, 210.
Koil, 44 *n.*
Kolīs, 163.
Kōmati, 158.
Korīa, trade in indigo at, 303, 304.
Kos, 204.
Kotwāl, 302.
Kulī, 79.
Kung, Governor of, encourages Company's trade, 275, 276, 284; shipment of freight goods from, 186, 275, 276, 284; dispatch of ships for and Company's ships at, 273, 284; English factor at, *see* Walwyn; Portuguese demand customs at, 272.
Kusumbha, 136, 161, 167, 212.
Kynaston (*or* Keniston), Arthur, 128, 129, 131.

Lac, 7, 27, 55, 58, 85, 124, 139, 168, 186, 197, 205, 233.
Laccadives, the, 56 *n.*
Lahijan silk, 122.
Lahore, 18, 70, 173, 302; indigo from, 122, 126; Jesuits at, 60.
Lamberton, Thomas, 134.
Lanneret, the, 286, 308 *n.*, 312, 313.
Lar, Governor of, 267.
Larak, 1, 273, 309.
Lārībandar, 19, 20, 85, 234, 274.
Lārīs, 59, 226, 308, 309.

Lascars, 37 (2), 81, 216, 294.
Lashkar, 59.
Lawrence, Richard, 198 *n.*
Layton, John, 97.
Leachland, John, daughter of, 152.
Leachland, William, 152.
Lead, trade in, *passim*; price of, 60, 125, 309; bought for the Emperor, 211.
Leather, 73 *n.*
Lee, Adam, 135, 146, 147, 272.
Lee, ——, 284.
Leeuwerik, the, 99, 100.
Leigh, John, 102, 103.
Leno, Padre, 64.
Lewis, John, 175, 188 *n.*, 231.
Linhares, Conde de. *See* De Noronha.
Lioness, the, xxii; master of, *see* Brookhaven.
Little William, the, 182 (2), 185, 189, 193, 200, 216, 259; master of, *see* Cox.
Lock, Edward, 214.
Logwood, 223.
London, the, xix, 9, 14, 206, 250; master of, *see* Proud; outward voyage of, 2, 19, 68; dispatched to the Malabar Coast, 7, 16, 21, 61; homeward voyage of, 8, 10, 25, 31, 56; private trade on, 15, 25, 141; Portuguese goods on, 16.
Looking-glasses, 65, 115, 160, 193.
Lopez, Don João, 219.
Low, Richard, 239, 246.
Loyalty, 237 *n.*, 255, 299; master of, *see* Durson; outward voyage of, 29, 62, 106, 176, 183, 189, 194, 200, 231; at Goa, 89; voyage to Gombroon and Basrā, 217, 276, 283, 309.
Lucknow, 6, 96, 97, 204, 233, 301, 304.
Luipaard, the, 129.
Lungīs, 58, 197.

Maatzuiker, Jan, xxiv.
Macao, Dutch blockade of, 21, 22; Portuguese ship sails for, 36; Dutch, Portuguese, etc., trade to, 134, 212, 250; Portuguese license English trade to, 165, 212, 221; dispatch of English ships for, and trade at, 165, 167, 179, 180, 193, 210, 212, 217, 249, 250; further attempts to trade at, forbidden, xvii; factors for voyage to, *see* Oxenden *and* Thurston; Governor of, 180; East India Company's factors entertained at, 180; Courteen's Association trade to, 180, 216, 217; state of trade, etc., at, 250; Spanish envoy to, 224; excessive customs duties at, 250; trade between Japan, Manilla and, 250; Captain-General of, 254; letters from Portuguese at, 254.
Macassar, 166; commodities from, 37; trade at, in various commodities, 37, 51, 115

INDEX

192, 222, 293; dispatch of ships for, 97; Danes trade to, 75; trade between Achin, Manilla and, 131, 192, 222, 223.
Mace, 142, 218.
Māchhiwāra baftas, 204, 301, 304, 311.
Madagascar (St. Lawrence), 97, 119, 121, 177; French pirates at, 9; trade at, 25; provisioning of ships at, 119, 120, 135, 182, 183, 187; attempts to colonize and trade at, 144, 176, 260; French fort and settlement at, 200, 232, 259, 260, 312; beads used in barter at, 205. *See also* St. Augustine's Bay.
Madras, 32, 37; Nāyak of, *see* Damarla Venkatappa; letters from and to, 33, 38, 45, 61, 67, 68, 71, 77, 113, 120 (2), 154, 184 (4), 185, 189, 279, 285, 287, 292, 293; Agent and Council at: consultations by, 70, 74, 110, 112 (2), 120; petitions to, 111 (3); factors at, *see* Coromandel Coast; building of Fort St. George at, xxxii, xxxiii, 11, 12, 13, 40, 46, 47, 51, 53, 113, 126, 127 (2); sergeant of fort at, *see* Broadford; native accidentally killed at, 158, 159; salary and grant of clothing, etc., for sergeant at, 194; list of soldiers at, 126; manning of fort at, 282; advantages of fort at, 47, 48, 51, 127 (2), 191; ordnance for, 36, 39, 51, 70, 80; question of retention of fort at, 68; expense of fortifying and maintaining garrison, xxxii, xxxiii, 82, 190, 191; minister desired for, 294, 311; manufacture of salt at, 127; state of affairs at, 113, 115, 154, 287; bleaching, dyeing, etc., of cotton goods at, 79; Coromandel Coast head-quarters at, 49; factory accounts, 54, 126, 236 *n.*; debts cleared at, 189, 190, 207; advantages of, as a factory, 115, 118, 157; reasons for poor returns from, 157; customs duties at, 127; Courteen's distressed sailors at, 184, 185, 193; money saved from *Little William* deposited at, 184, 185, 189, 236 *n.*; affray between a Dane and Portuguese at, 63; Portuguese capture Dutch ship at, 115; Malaya endeavours to wrest privileges from the English at, 136; factors try to obtain confirmation of privileges at, 290; Dutch prisoner in Malaya's hands in care of Company's factors at, 279, 288; Company's factors at, purchase goods confiscated from the Dutch, 280; factors desired to assist Vijayanagar forces against the Dutch, 285; Srī Ranga Rāyalu's grant to the Company for, 305–307; Portuguese and Danish ships at, 33, 156.
Magdalen, the, 9.
Mahmūd Ādil Shāh, King of Bijāpur, 45; Portuguese treaty with, 22; Dutch excluded from his dominions, 22; encourages Company's trade, 108; allies himself with Vijayanagar, 115, 116.
Mahmūd Āghā, Governor of Basrā and afterwards Shāhbandar, 274, 275, 284.
Mahmūd Hussain, 162.
Mahmūd, Mirzā, 144.
Mahmūd Zamān, 162.
Mahmudī, the, 257.
Mahmudī, *passim;* value of, 17, 268.
Maidān, 297, 298 *n.*
Majlis, 296.
Malabar Coast, trade to and commodities from, 10, 69, 86, 94, 99, 124, 138, 140, 147, 148, 172, 177, 228, 231, 313; dispatch of Company's ships for and from, 21, 69, 86, 89, 106, 147, 172, 174, 177, 313; dispatch of Courteen's ships for and from, and trade to, 29, 89, 148; ships outward bound for Swally to trade on, 86; Company advised not to dispatch ships to, 231; dispatch of Dutch ship for, 150; Portuguese trade on, 230, 231. *See also* Calicut, Cannanore, Cochin, Kārwār, Rājāpur.
Malabar pirates, 32, 41, 59, 61, 73, 192; designs against, reprisals on and encounters with, 2, 3, 14, 20, 27, 28, 55, 88, 89, 93, 139, 140, 179, 181, 211, 212, 213, 218, 233, 234, 235, 248, 250, 255, 310; English forced to grant passes to, 3; trade to Aden, Mokha, and Achin, 3, 131, 139; protection by, by Courteen's Association and the Dutch, 3, 212; Dutch encounter with, 22; English ships forced to protect native shipping from, 90, 91, 92; English prisoners in hands of, 23, 25, 28; prisoners in hands of English, 37; exchange of prisoners with, 27; menace Company's and Portuguese ships, 141, 201, 213, 228, 253, 278; depredations on Courteen's settlements and ships, 236 *n.*
Malacca, 260; Dutch at, 225; Dutch Governor of, 180; Company's factors assisted by Governor of, 273; Courteen's sailors detained by Dutch at, 128; Dutch method of inducing trade to, 131; English ship at, 179, 181, 272; friendly reception of Company's ships at, by the Dutch, 179, 235; Company's ship taken to and searched by Dutch, 272, 273.
Malacca, Straits of, 218; Dutch control and molest shipping in, 129, 131, 166, 180, 218, 272, 293; Dutch capture Courteen's ship in, *see Bona Speranza;* Dutch enforce payment of customs from ships passing through, 131; Dutch ships in, 179.
Malaya (Chinnana Chetti), 50, 194, 280, 281;

honoured by Srī Ranga Rāyalu, 81; endeavours to wrest privileges from the English at Madras, 156; hinders Company's trade, 157; regains influence with the King of Vijayanagar and appointed his Treasurer, 154, 290; made Governor of Pulicat district, 154 *n.*; supersedes Damarla Venkatappa, 154; is deprived of his office and imprisoned, 154 *n.*; goods seized and family imprisoned at Pulicat, 288 *n.*; quarrel with the Dutch, 279, 280, 287, 288; proposal to purchase a junk from, 281; commands Vijayanagar troops against the Dutch, 285, 290, 291, 292; assistance of English factors desired by, 285; holds Dutch prisoners to ransom, 288; assists the Company, 290.
Maldives, the, 37, 56 *n.*
Malha, Shoals of, 109, 153, 187.
Mālpur, saltpetre from, 164, 205, 233.
Mammāli Koya, 236 *n.*
Manilla, Governor and Captain-General of, *see* Mendoso *and* Taxardo; letters carried for, 252; Spanish officials at, 220–224; bribery of officials at, 224; state of Spaniard's affairs at, 222–225; Spanish fleet at, 225; customs at, 221; Englishman and Dutchman employed by Spaniards at, *see* Jones *and* Cheloan; Dutch and Portuguese debarred from trading at, 22, 192, 220, 226, 250; attempts to establish English trade at, xvi, 192, 193, 212, 214, 218–228, 247, 250, 251; further attempts forbidden, xvii; dispatch of ship for, and Company's ship at, 180, 222, 228, 231, 253; factors for voyage to, *see* Breton, Mantell, Pearce; trade between Coromandel Coast, Macassar, China, etc., 192, 193, 220, 222, 223, 250; trade at, in various commodities, 192, 212, 223, 224, 226, 228, 232, 252, 293; allegations against English at, 221, 222; proposed further voyage to, 232, 251, 256; abandoned owing to Dutch threats, 293; iron, saltpetre, etc., required at, 219, 220, 221, 222, 224, 225, 251, 256; factors remain at, with Company's goods, 221, 222, 226; household expenses of Company's factors at, 226; Chinese at, 223; dyeing at, 223; envoy sent to Surat by Governor of, 225; unhealthiness of, 226. See also Cavitte.
Mantell, John, 94, 132, 133 *n.*, 166, 174, 231; letter from, 218.
Marguerite, the, 9 *n.* See also *Rose*.
Markham, Robert, death of, 68.
Markham, Thomas, 94; death of, 68, 144.
Markham, Valentine, 68.
Marmagao, xxiii, 150.

Martyns de Castello Branco, Father Gonsalvo, 60, 64.
Mary, the, xix, 241; outward voyage for Bantam, 121, 135; homeward voyage of, 127, 128, 134, 311 *n.*
Mascarenhas, Dom Filippe, Viceroy of Goa, 254, 310 *n.*; declares war on Malabars, 310.
Masulipatam, English ship detained by Governor of, 42, 48; letters to and from, 120 (2), 295; factors at, *see* Coromandel Coast; consultation at, 69; factory accounts and records, 16, 41, 42, 45, 126; English house at, 49; factory expenses at, 54; money due to factors at, 41; threatened seizure of junks, to enforce English rights at, 41; removal of Coast head-quarters from, 48; customs and customhouse at, 55; survivors from *Little William* at, 193; Dutch ships sail for, 42; Dutch use pinnaces for trade to, 48; Dutch competition affects Company's trade at, 154; Danes seize a junk of, 42 *n.*, 48; Danish ships sail for, 156.
Mataran, Sultan of, negotiations with, 36.
Matchawara. See Māchhīwāra.
Matthews, Richard, 179.
Maund, *passim*; Akbarī, 84; Surat, 95; value of, 72 (2), 86, 95 *n.*, 211.
Mauritius, 97; English ships at, 119, 153, 183, 187, 211, 234, 259; Dutch at, 119, 187; Dutch settlement at, 153; Dutch at, assist in repairing Company's distressed ships, 153 *n.*; provisioning of ships at, 119; wreck of Courteen's ship at, see *Bonaventura*.
Mauritius Island, the, wrecked at the Cape, 182, 185, 200, 260.
'Meanaes', 309.
Mecca, 36.
Melinda, Portuguese trade to, 149.
Mendoso, Don Sebastian Hurtatho Querquero, Governor of Manilla, 223; negotiations with, 219, 220; imprisoned for peculation, 226.
'Mercooles'. See Cotton Goods.
Merry, Thomas, 26, 29, 69, 132, 255, 286, 310, 311; letters from (*see also* Persia and Surat), 96, 237, 247, 311; recalled from Persia to Surat, 4, 28, 31, 88, 89; complaints by and against, 27, 237, 247; debts to the Company, etc., 96, 101, 140, 170, 176, 232; appointed second in Council and Accountant in Surat, 140, 173, 229.
Mestiço, 166, 223, 242.
Methwold, Thomas, 188 *n.*, 190, 236.
Methwold, William, 7, 16, 30, 179, 247.
Methwold, William (Junior), 132, 193, 289.

INDEX

Michael, the, 14, 28, 34, 37, 85, 86, 97, 228.
Millet, John, 28, 178; letter to, 59; private trade of, 28, 29; commended, 89.
Millet (cuskus), 92.
Mindoro, 180.
Minicoy, 56 *n.*, 71 *n.*
Ministers, 28, 294. See Baines, Isaacson, and Panton.
Minn, William, 132, 193; letters from, see Madras; salary, 289.
Minors, Captain William, 16.
Mīr Abdul Hādi, see Asālat Khān.
Mīr Mahmūd Saiyid, the Sar-i-Khail, 154, 207; the Danes seize a junk of, 42, 48; trades freight and custom free to Gombroon, 55, 207; his junk sails for Mokha, Persia, etc., 55, 67, 69, 80, 81, 88, 234; lends money to the Company, 69, 79; complaint against, 79; English and Dutch sailors for his junk, 69, 80, 81; oppresses the Dutch, 80.
Mīr Muhammad Amīn, 169.
'Mirta', 304.
Mirzā Amin. See (as also in similar cases) Amin, Mirzā.
Moerabath. See Murbāt.
'Mogulls', 303, 304.
Mohan Nārāyan, 168.
Mokha, Governor of, 143, 161, 162, 213; dispatch of ships for and from, and English trade at, *passim*; Indian trade to, vi *n.*, 10, 17, 19, 25, 62, 81, 144, 208, 234; factors at, see Cogan (Thomas), Cranmer, Cross, Goodyear, Herbert, Hunt, Oxenden, Rymell, Wylde (John); casualties among factors at, 94; English house at, 161; Shāh Jahān's junk sails for, 91, 92; customs at, 162; Company's goods shipped on native junk to, 215, 266; Arabs drive Turks from, 143; Dutch at, 150; Dutch trade to, 22, 100, 167, 216; dispatch of Dutch ships for and from, 61, 139, 150, 161, 167, 238, 312.
Montella, 163.
Morais, Manoel, 64.
Mōr-thuthu, 86, 124, 205.
Moss, John, 25, 28.
Mosul, 58.
Mozambique, dispatch of ships from and for, and English ships at, 57, 121, 135, 194, 195, 239, 243, 261; trade at, in various commodities, 105-106, 145, 177, 195, 239; gold from, 106; dispatch of Courteen's ship for, 194, 200; Portuguese at, 239, 249; Portuguese trade to, and ships at, 21, 57, 145, 149; Portuguese ship wrecked near, see São Bento; Portuguese Governor of, 195, 286; Portuguese take passages on Company's ship from, 195, 261, 263; King of Portugal's agent at, 195.
Mucknell, John, xii, xiii, xiv, 175, 237 *n.*; seizes Company's ship for Charles I, see John; his grievance against Parliament, 199 *n.*, 262; certain persons accused of abetting, 238; quarrel with Knipe, 239, 240, 243, 244-247, 259, 261-263, 298; accused of drunkenness, etc., 265; explores Ascension Island, 264.
Mughalkasarāī, 304.
Muizz-ul-Mulk, 2, 25; trades to Basrā, 2; assists the English, 3; superseded as Governor of Surat, 23, 24, 25; controls ports of Broach and Cambay, 24, 25.
Multan, customs at, 163.
Murād Bakhsh, 160.
Murbāt, 237 *n.*, 238.
Murrees (*or* Moorees). See Cotton goods.
Musk, 64, 233.
Muskat, English ship at, 20; letters sent to India overland via, 299; Portuguese at, 308.
Musters, 137, 209.
Myrando, Anthony. See De Miranda.
Myrrh, 7, 124, 139, 205, 233, 252, 254; *Habashī* (*or* Hobsee), 162.

Naqdī Khān, 297.
Nākhudā, 234.
Narayanavanam, 67 *n.*
Narsapur, 77.
Nasarpur, 'joories' of, 6, 85, 123, 203, 233; factory accounts, 236 *n.*
Nasir-bin-Murshid, 308 *n.*
Nassau, the, 218.
Nāyak, the Great. See Damarla.
Negapatam, 81; captured by the Dutch, xxiii.
Negombo, captured by the Dutch, xxiv, 151.
Netlam, William, 132, 134, 193, 207, 289, 293.
New Zealand, discovery of, 134.
'Nicaneers'. See Cotton goods.
Nicobars, the, 180.
Nishān, 215.
Nosārī, factory dissolved, 164; baftas, 6, 85, 123, 137, 164, 204, 233.
Nūri, 201.
Nutmegs, 142, 218.

Oil, 217, 302, 310.
Olibanum, 7, 85, 124, 139, 162, 205, 217, 233, 252, 254.
Olifant, the, 260.
Olton, Henry, 132, 190, 193, 289, 293, 294, 310; letter from, 181.
Opium, 61, 108, 138.
Oranges, 187.

Orangia, the, 260.
Orangkāya, 212.
Ormus, 73, 171, 258, 277 n.; agreement missing, 29, 90; red earth from, 38, 39; Dutch designs against, 255-258, 273, 295, 299.
Ouvidor, 224.
Overskay, the, 218.
Owen, Edward, 242.
Oxenden, George, 7, 23, 132, 139, 161, 212, 252.

Padres. *See* Jesuits, Dominicans, etc.
Pagodas (coins), *passim*; value of, 43, 109, 112, 191 n., 268; 'Dury' or Dhārwāri, 109.
Painters and 'paintings', 39, 46, 51, 53, 74, 75, 77, 79.
Palankeens, 54, 105.
Panton, Anthony, 28, 89.
Paradox, the, 14; outward voyage of, 10, 26.
Pardao. *See* Xerafin.
Parrots. *See* Nūri.
Parthiva, 305.
Passes, 3.
'Patolas', 37, 287.
Pattamars, 52.
Pauncefote, Samuel, 25.
Pauw, the, xxiii-xxv, 99, 150, 218.
Pearce, Edward, 14, 100, 132, 251; letters from (*see also* Basrā), 218; chief at Basrā, 143; factor for Manilla voyage, 166, 213, 218-226.
Pearce, John, 240, 243, 246.
Pearce, William, 236.
Pearl, the, 2.
Pearls, 25, 233, 283.
Pearson, John, 188 n., 234.
'Peaseing' (weighing), 241.
'Peculls' (weight), 192, 225, 254.
Pegu, 76, 130, 229.
Peniston, Thomas, 65, 68, 69, 121, 132, 157, 193, 253, 280, 289, 294; letters from, *see* Masulipatam; accused of private trade, etc., 72, 73, 76.
Pennington, Sir John, 242, 262, 264.
Pepper, trade in and references to, *passim*; price of, 10, 86, 108, 109, 124, 192, 214; loses weight in transit, 85; method of shipment, 231. *See also* Achin, Bantam, Deccan, Malabar, etc.
Perak, 35.
Pereira, Joseph Pinto, 14.
Perkins, John, 25; death of, 17.
Perks, Thomas, 193.
Perpetuanoes, 18, 61, 91, 227.
Persia, letters to and from, 31, 169, 257, 265, 276, 282, 296, 298 (2), 307; Agent in, *see* Adler, Honywood, Merry, Pitt; factors in, *see* Codrington, Hall, Herbert,

Wheeler, Willoughby, Wilton, Wylde (Philip); factors for, 169; disputes between Surat Council and factors in, 3; factors in, subordinate to Surat, 27; factors to correspond with the Company, 164; factors complain of unjust treatment, 227; trouble with broker in, 278; private trade in, 76; factory accounts, 101, 232, 278; trade in, in silk and other commodities, *passim*; horses from, 20, 37, 76, 81, 146, 211, 278, 298; supplies for, 19, 139, 207, 208; state of affairs in, 96, 98, 135, 136, 201, 208; merchants from, in Bengal and at Coromandel Coast, 87, 104, 105; complaint against Dutch chief (*see also* Constant *and* Gelijnszoon) in, 170, 171; Dutch trade to and ships for, 4, 32, 83, 150, 167, 170, 171, 201, 255, 268, 282, 308; Portuguese endeavour to exact customs duties in, 272; Queen-mother of, 296; *See also* Gombroon, Ispahān, etc.
Persia, Shāh Abbās I, 226; Shāh Safī of, vii, viii, 4; annual present for, 4; dispute with Shāh Jahān, 18, 58; ambassador to, from Golconda, 73, 74; death of, 83, 89; Shāh Abbās II becomes King of, viii, 83; English and Dutch missions to, 83, 84, 98; grants privileges to the English and Dutch, 83, 135, 271; presents for, 83, 84, 135, 170 (2), 208, 266; Dutch and English negotiations with, 136, 256, 257, 266, 268, 269, 271, 278; refuses to renew English privileges, 169, 170; the Dutch in disfavour with, 170, 266; favours the English, 171; ambassadors to Europe from, 171; controls the silk trade, 201, 271; Company's claim against, 227, 266, 279; Dutch contract with, 266; rumoured alliance of the Dutch and Portuguese against, 272; makes peace with and grants privileges to the Dutch, 275, 278, 279, 282, 283, 307, 308, 311; sends an agent to Batavia, 282; exactions on behalf of, 296; honours English and Dutch chiefs, 296; avenges Mirzā Taqī's murder, 296, 297.
Pessaert, Barent, 156.
Petapoli, 68, 71; factors at, *see* Coromandel Coast.
Pewter. *See* Jast.
Philippine Islands. *See* Manilla.
Pice (coins), 145, 147; (weight), 211.
Piece goods. *See* Cotton goods.
Pieter Butt's Bay (Mauritius), 153.
Pinson, Gerald, 49, 97.
Pinson, Humphrey, letter from, 181.
Pippli, xxxv.
Pirates. *See* French *and* Malabar.
Pishkash, 80, 81, 115, 306.

INDEX

Pistachios, 42, 73 *n.*
Pitt, William, 7, 8, 10, 59, 80, 133, 138, 257, 266, 309, 310; leaves Goa, 60, 64, 107; letters from (*see also* Persia), 169; his contract with the Portuguese, 107, 108; reported dangerously wounded, 60, 61; becomes Chief in Persia, 70, 84, 98; his mission to the Shāh, 256, 277, 279; desires to return to India, 279.
Planter, the, 146, 148.
Point de Galle, 180, 253; Dutch fort at, 180.
Pollen, John, 282.
Ponnāni, 107; trade at, in pepper, etc., 7, 60, 61; dispatch of ship for, 60, 61.
Porakād, Rāja of, 138; pepper from, 138, 147; ship at, 147.
Porbandar (*or* Por), 216 *n.*
Porcelain, 66.
Porto Novo, 281; Company's trade to, and ships for, 36, 42; Company's trade at, abandoned, 38; Dutch trade at, 38.
Portugal, John IV, King of, 22, 23, 67.
Portuguese, the, fortify their settlements, 12; goods, letters, and passengers on Company's and Courteen's ships, *passim*; hostilities with, and ships captured by, the Dutch, 21 (2), 38, 100, 114, 128, 308; Dutch ship captured by, *see* Pauw; peace negotiations with the Dutch, 21, 148, 149, 151, 218; debarred from trading to Manilla, 22, 192, 220, 250; ships of, insured by Dutch merchants, 22; treaty with the King of Bījāpur, 22; English treaty with, xxvi, 30, 67, 91, 114; borrowing of money from and by, 34, 60, 112; complaints by and against, 39, 44, 138; the Company endeavour to maintain friendly relations with, 50, 59, 80, 141, 151, 173, 174, 230; reinforcements and supplies for, 57, 151, 210; present for Srī Ranga Rāyalu from, 81; reported truce between the Dutch and, 99, 100; prisoners in the hands of the Dutch, 129; distracted state of affairs of, 145; the Dutch treacherously recommence hostilities against, 149; pilots, 167; Malabar pirates harass shipping of, 228; make peace with the Dutch, xxv, 228; claim against the Company, *see the John*; negotiations between Courteen's factors and, 254; supplied by the Company with guns, etc., 258; at war with Vijayanagar, 289; soldier executed by the Company's factors, *see* De Miranda; wreck of ship of, *see* São Bento. *See also* Basrā, Cochin, Goa, Macao, Persia, etc.
Poynter, William, 241.
'Prams', 1, 141 *n*. *See also Hind and Seaflower*.
Prāū (prow), 180.

Priaman, 130.
Privett, John, 256 *n.*
Prosperous, the, 69, 148; voyage to Malabar Coast, 21; voyage to Persia and back to Swally, 31; voyage to Basrā, Gombroon, and back, 21, 31, 59, 93; designed for the Red Sea, 213, 214; at Swally, 313.
Proud, John, 3, 9, 11, 17, 188; commended, 15, 142; account of the *Dolphin's* homeward voyage, 153; letters from, 187, 189, 259.
Puchok, 167 *n.* *See also Costus.*
Pulicat, Dutch Governor (*see also* Gardenijs) and Coast head-quarters at, 48, 81 *n.*, 193, 281, 288 *n.*; Company's factors threatened by Governor of, for trading in confiscated Dutch goods, 290, 291, 292, 294; Dutch ships at and dispatched for, 33 (2), 42; Dutch fort at, 47, 288; *Domine* of, *see* De Ladossa; Malaya appointed Governor of the district around, 154 *n.*; the Dutch at, besieged by King of Golconda, 184, 193; the siege raised by Vijayanagar troops, 194; the Dutch defeated near, 279; besieged by Vijayanagar army under Malaya, 285, 288, 289, 290; Malaya's goods seized and family imprisoned at, 288 *n.*
Pulo Condore, 180.
Pulo Jarak, 179.
Pulo Run, 134.
Pulo Tioman, 180.
Pulse. *See Dāl.*
Punamallee, 70 *n.*, 280, 306; Nāyak of, *see* Damarla Venkatappa; customs duties in, remitted to the Company, 306, 307.
Purakkātu (*or* 'Purcutt'). *See* Porakād.
Purchase (prize-taking), 176.
Purī (Jagannāth), 75 *n.*
Pym, Luke, 70, 94, 132, 143, 174.

Qāfila. *See* Caphila.
Qaul, 50, 156, 305, 306.
Quails, 264.
Quicksilver, 67, 78, 217, 234.
Quills, 18, 19.
Quilts (including 'Pintadoes'), 7, 85, 124, 126, 136, 138, 204, 229, 233.
Quintals, 63, 89, 107, 205.
Qūrchī Bāshī. *See* Jāni Khān.

Rāhdarī, 160.
Raisins, 42, 298.
Rāja Bāsū, 18.
Rājāpur, trade at, 147, 161, 205, 212, 216, 248, 255, 311; dispatch of ships for and from, 147, 161, 211, 216, 311; shipment of passengers and freight goods from, 276, 309; Courteen's ships and factory at and

trade to, 10, 29, 62, 140, 148, 168, 199, 217, 231, 255.
Ramsay, Anthony, 36.
Rānder, 202.
Rango, 182.
Rao Rājā Chhatarsāl, Rājā of Bundī, 159, 232, 301.
Rasa-mālā (storax), 61, 217.
Raya Elluru. *See* Vellore.
Rāyalavāru, 45 *n*.
Rāybāg, trade at, 138, 161, 205, 210, 230; Courteen's trade and affairs at, 10, 148, 255; Dutch and Portuguese trade to, 10, 210; English broker at (*see also* Benī Dās), 252.
Raylawar. *See* Srī Ranga Rāyalu.
Red-earth. *See* Geru.
Red Sea, pirates and interlopers in, 9, 141, 143 *n*., 144, 176; designs against and encounters with Malabar junks in, 3, 139, 179, 213, 234, 235, 311. *See also* Aden, Mokha, etc.
Reformation, the, xix, 11, 34; master of, *see* Bayley; at Comoro Islands, 2, 13; sails for Bantam, 13, 21, 36, 38, 39 (2); Dutch attack on, 37; at Madras, 49; homeward voyage of, 45, 56, 100, 109, 121.
Reshire, 258.
Resin. *See* Dammar.
Réunion, 97, 119 (2), 183.
Reynardson, Thomas, 133, 166.
Reynolds, Alexander, 111.
Reynolds, John, 102 *n*., 111.
Rhinoceros horns, 217.
Rhubarb, 26, 96, 176, 247.
Rials of eight, *passim*; value of, 17, 18, 28, 43, 107, 144, 145, 175, 191 *n*., 209; Mexico (Peru) and Seville, 209; chests of, 120, 206, 207; complaints as to quality, etc., of, 144, 145, 174, 209.
Ribeiro (*or* Soares) Lewis, 26, 64, 178, 205, 212, 213, 233, 235, 254, 255.
Rice, 276, 310.
Rice-water. *See Kanjī*.
Richards, John, 105, 111 *n*.
Richelieu, Cardinal, 9, 141 *n*.
Robins, Walter, 193, 289.
Robinson, Benjamin, 4, 5, 17, 29, 85, 206.
Rodriguez, 97, 118, 119.
Rogers, Thomas, 42, 68, 190; death of, 46, 68.
Roobacker, Cornelis, 274 *n*.
Root, Jeremy, 293.
Rose, the, 9.
Rosewater, 42, 73, 115, 146, 211, 278.
Rubies, 215, 230 *n*.
Rūnās, 73, 98.
Rupees, value of, 17, 95 *n*., 96, 209, 213 *n*.

Russell, Gervase, 29.
Rymell, John, 132, 168, 252.

Sack, 302, 310.
Sacrifice Rock, 180.
Sailors, 152, 153; ships' commanders styled masters, 15; Surat Council's authority over commanders, 95, 142; complaints against ships' commanders, 216, 236; Dutchmen and French pirates employed as, 9, 226; want of, 16, 236; and private trade, 18, 29, 124; ransomed from Malabars, 25; provisions and allowances for, 37, 226, 295; employed ashore as factors, etc., 94, 143, 174, 201, 231, 236; natives employed as (*see also* Lascars), 36, 49, 282; pilfer prize-money, 226.
St. Augustine's Bay, Company's and Courteen's ships at, 10, 32, 105, 119, 182, 183, 185, 187, 188, 200, 241, 259, 312; letters to commanders of ships touching at, 181, 182, 187; hostile attitude of natives at, 119; survivors from the *Little William* at, 182, 189; unhealthiness of, 183. *See also* Madagascar.
St. Christopher's Island, 199 *n*.
St. Helena, English ships at, 109, 121, 239, 241, 259, 260, 262; sailors and slaves left by Mucknell at, 242, 260, 264.
St. John's. *See* Sanjān.
St. Lawrence. *See* Madagascar.
St. Malo privateers, 8, 10.
Saker, —, death of, 153.
Salābat Khān, Mīr Bakhshī to Shāh Jahān, 229 *n*.
Salāmatī, the, 161, 168.
Salbet (Shiāl Bet), 93.
'Sallett' oil, 302.
Salt, 127.
Salter, Captain, 242.
Saltpetre, 6, 10, 27, 94, 124, 136, 139, 148, 164, 175, 203, 205, 219-222, 224, 232-234, 251, 255, 256.
Samāna, 137, 204, 233.
Sambah, 130 *n*.
Sambrooke, Jeremy, letter to, 237.
Samisamy, 182.
Sampson, Captain, 75.
Sandalwood, 81, 115, 218, 293.
Sanjān, 185, 238.
Sankar, 168, 253.
'Sannoes'. *See* Cotton goods.
San Salvador, 100 *n*.
Santa Lucia (Madagascar), 200.
San Thomé, 47; Portuguese at, 12, 49, 81, 112; Portuguese reinforcements for, 43, 60; under Nāyak of Tanjore, 47, 49; customs at, 49; disadvantages of as a factory site, 49; Dutch designs on, 43 *n*., 155; Dutch blockade of, 115.

INDEX

São Bento, the, 150, 151.
Sappanwood, 218, 228, 252.
Sarasses. See Cotton goods.
Sarcerius, Dirck, 275.
Sar-i-Khail. *See* Mīr Mahmūd Saiyid.
Sarkhej, indigo from, 5, 58, 85, 95, 122, 126, 136, 201, 202.
Sarrāfs (*or* Shroffs), 21, 61, 91, 144, 174, 209, 210, 252, 303.
Satins, 145, 160.
Saya de Malha Bank, 109, 153, 187.
Scattergood, Francis, 131, 146.
Schelvisch, the, 274 *n*.
Seaflower, the, 144, 147, 194, 293; master of, *see* Gardner *and* Lee; outward voyage of, to Swally, 121, 135, 145, 147; voyages to Persia and back, 139, 147, 159, 162, 168, 170, 186, 200; not suitable for service in Indian waters, 141; designed for Bantam, 142, 147, 159; voyage to Bantam, 200; voyage from Bantam to Coromandel Coast, 253, 254; voyage to Bantam from Coromandel Coast, 281, 287.
Seahorse, the, 14, 88, 101, 168, 213, 253, 295, 297; master of, *see* Lee, Tindall, *and* Totty; voyages to Gombroon and Basrā and back to Swally, 2, 19, 20, 21, 28, 31, 58, 59, 83, 89, 93; voyage to Diu, etc., vii, 93; again sails to Gombroon, Basrā, etc., and back, 89, 98, 100, 101, 139, 142, 147, 148, 170; voyage to Bassein and back, 148, 160; voyage to Rājāpur, 161, 167, 179, 211; designed for Sind and Basrā, 148, 161, 214; encounters with Malabar pirates, 27, 181, 211, 235, 255; voyage to Manilla and back, 165, 166, 167, 179, 180, 181, 212, 218–226, 249, 250; voyage to Gombroon and Basrā, 252, 272, 273, 276, 284; sails from Basrā to Tuticorin, 275, 283, 298, 310; voyage to Rājāpur, and then designed for Red Sea, 311; returns to Swally from Malabar Coast, 313.
Seer (weight), 202, 211, 303.
Sehwān, indigo and joories from, 85, 123, 136, 203. *See also* Sevestan.
Selaes. *See* Cotton goods.
Seleina, Andre, Vedor da Fazenda, 61, 64.
Semianoes. *See* Cotton goods.
Sequins (*or* Venetians), 17, 18, 64, 107, 145.
Serang, 81.
Serebafts, 85.
Seryas. *See* Cotton goods.
Seshadri Chetti, Nāyak, 81, 281, 285, 292, 294.
'Sevestan', 163, 203. *See also* Sehwān.
Seville money, 209.
Shāhbandar, 27, 169, 170.
Shāhīs, 42, 116, 227, 265, 267, 309; value of, 266 *n*., 268.

Shāh Jahān, the Emperor, junks of, 2, 10; Company's ships convoy junks for, 90, 91, 92; extent of his kingdom, 3; revolt and intrigues against, 18, 58, 59, 73 *n*.; dispute between Shāh of Persia and, 18, 58; tribute to, for Surat customs, etc., 23, 24; seizes Āsaf Khān's estate, 25, 95; treasure at Agra, 59; trade on behalf of, 69, 70, 95, 101, 147, 148, 211, 253; English and Dutch missions to, and presents for, 145, 159, 160, 162, 214; grants privileges to the Dutch and English, 160, 160 *n*., 214, 230; trouble with his *umarās*, 229, 302; honours Company's factors, 230; Company's factors appeal to, 232, 301, 302; his campaign against the Uzbeks, 302.
Shāh Walī, 282.
Sharafuddīn Husain, Kotwāl of Agra, afterwards Governor of Surat, 160, 302.
Sharīfs, 161.
Shashes, 87.
Shavelle (Shavallee *or* Shevallee), 282.
Shehr, 139, 213.
Shiāl Bet. *See* Salbet.
Shirāz, Khān of, 29; horses from, 278, 298.
Shīsham (or sīsū), 295.
Shujā, Sultān, 59.
Silk, trade in and references to, *passim*; price of, 83, 136, 201, 266, 271, 278, 279; Canary, Lahijan, and Arras, 122. *See also* China *and* Persia.
Silver, 65, 217, 226; value of, 176, 209; complaint as to quality of, 91; Japan, 100, 167.
Simoranees. *See Smaranī*.
Sims, John, 17.
Sind, factors in, *see* Elder, Fenn, Harrison, Spiller, Walwyn; trade in, *passim*; factory accounts, 16; Portuguese caphila from, 58; money remitted from Ahmadābād to, 85; goods shipped to, on native junks, 216; trade between Basrā and, 274; letter sent overland to Surat via, 299; Viceroy of, *see* Dārā Shikoh. *See also* Larībandar, Tatta, etc.
Singapore, Straits of, 180 (2). *See also* Malacca, Straits of.
Sironj, 137.
Skibbow, John, estate of, 15.
Skinner, Thomas, 96, 247.
Skins, 81, 233 *n*.
Skylark, the, 99. *See Leeuwerik*.
Slaves, 28, 37, 97, 241, 242, 263, 264; price of, 119, 120.
Smaranī, 170 *n*.
Smith, Anthony, 132, 144.
Snoek, the, 21, 22.
Soap, 37.

Soares, *see* Ribeiro.
Socotra, 19.
'Soerts', 73 *n.*
Sofala, 121.
Somajī Pārak, 161.
Souri, Pieter, 129, 130.
Spain, King of, 144; Company's negotiations with, 251, 252, 256.
Spaniards, English carry letters for, 226, 252; employ Danish ships, 156. *See also* Manilla.
Spanish money, enhancement in value of, 144, 145.
Spices, trade in and references to, 22, 80, 81, 205, 217.
Spiller, John, 132, 136, 144, 169, 203, 248.
Srī Ranga Rāyalu, King of Vijayanagar (*q.v.*), xxviii, 44, 67, 193, 194 *n.*; letters from, 285, 291, 293, 294; intrigues against, 70 *n.*, 80; presents for, 81, 115; Malaya in favour with, 154; Malaya again punished by, 154 *n.*; at war with Dutch, and confiscates their goods, etc., 279, 280, 285, 288, 292, 294; at war with Portuguese, 289; proposed English mission to, 285, 289, 290, 291, 292; confirms English privileges and encourages Company's trade, 115, 281; Malaya's influence with, 280, 290; offers monopoly of trade to the Company, 288, 290; his grant for Madras, 305-307.
Srī Ranga Rāyapatam, 305. *See also* Madras.
Stafford, 313.
Stallon, John, 95, 97.
Stammell (*or* Scarlet). *See* Broadcloth.
Stanford, John, 132, 165, 234.
Stanian, Edward, 239.
Steel, 26, 31 *n.*, 55.
Steep Holme, 242 *n.*
Steevens, Thomas, 28, 88, 286, 295, 312 *n.*
Storax. *See Rasa-mālā.*
Strong, Captain, 312.
Strong waters, 103, 104, 241, 302.
Styles, Edmund, 289, 295.
Suakin, Bāshā of, 213, 252; design for establishing trade at, 213, 214, 235, 252.
Sugar, trade in and references to, *passim*; freight rates on, 55, 72; price of, 308, 309; candy, 55.
Suhār, Portuguese at, 308 *n.*
Sumatra. *See* Achin, etc.
Sun, the, 176, 260, 312; master of, *see* Spencer.
Sunda, Straits of, 33, 222, 251, 256.
Supply, the, 14, 88, 213, 218, 248; master of, *see* Broadbent, Clark, Lee, *and* Stallon; forced to abandon voyage to Bantam, 16; voyage to Gombroon, Aden, and Red Sea, 3, 19; sails for Masulipatam, etc.,

19; voyage to Damān and back, 19; voyage to Persia and back, 19, 31, 91; again sails to Gombroon and back to Swally, 20, 31, 88, 92; voyage to Sind and back, 85, 92; designed for Persia and then for Achin, 92; further voyage to Gombroon and back, 98, 146; voyage to Cochin and Achin and back, 99, 128, 131, 138, 139, 146; designed for Red Sea, 139, 146; sails to Gombroon and back, 159, 162, 168, 170, 186, 267, 268; voyage to Achin and back, 179, 181, 212, 214, 231, 235; encounters with Malabar pirates, 181, 235, 255; designed for Persia and then to Manilla or Achin, 214, 236, 253; again sails to Persia, 248; voyage to Achin and back to Swally, 272; stopped and searched by Dutch, 273; pilfering of money aboard, 278.
Sūr (*or* Bandar Sūr), Portuguese expelled from and English trade invited to, 308 *n.*; Imām of, *see* Nāsir-bin-Murshid.
Surat, Governor of (*see also* Muizz-ul-Mulk, Jam Qulī Beg, Amīn, Sharafuddīn Husain): trades with the English, 94, 95, 211; places restrictions on shipment of freight goods, 91; presents for, 201, 210; Dīwān of, 23; Customer at (*see also* Arab, Mirzā), 144, 160, 169; President at (*see also* Breton *and* Fremlen): appointed for five years, 15; journal of, 17, 97; presents for, 20, 66, 91, 284; salary of, 29; President and Council: letters to and from, *passim*; consultations by, 69, 286, 310; commissions and instructions from, 59, 161, 168; complaints by, and against, 2, 34, 85, 86, 123, 202; disputes with Bantam and Persian factors, 3, 11, 16, 17, 34, 172, 201, 227, 228; and the founding of Fort St. George, 11, 12, 40, 51-53; authority over Coromandel Coast and Persia, 13, 27, 33, 45, 47, 54, 140; request small ships for coast trade, etc., 14, 88, 141, 173, 229, 247, 252; decline responsibility for factors' debts, 15; debts due to, 34, 86; advise the Company not to employ chartered vessels, 89, 90; authority over ships' commanders, 95, 142; disposal of shipping by, 125, 192, 231, 258; present for the Emperor, etc., from, 150; authority over factors in charge of special voyages, 177; endeavour to suppress private trade, 231; casualties among factors at, 94; want of factors at, 247; debts and want of money, etc., at, 5, 6, 8, 17, 26, 82, 84, 88, 94, 96, 100, 108, 139, 140, 172, 173, 228, 230, 236, 247, 249, 250, 311; borrowing of money at, 8, 30, 34, 87, 90, 152, 311; factory accounts, 16, 236 *n.*; bleaching at, 6; trade at, *passim*; supplies for, 17, 61,

INDEX

87, 88; money-changing and mint at, 17, 23, 209, 210; customs and customhouse at, 23, 24, 25, 99, 160, 165; customs remitted to the English and Dutch at, 160, 162, 214; tribute to Shāh Jahān for customs, etc., at, 23, 24; trade between Bantam, Manilla, Mokha, Persia, and, 10, 82, 84, 85, 142, 172, 192, 193, 231; shipment of freight goods for and from, 10, 19, 31, 62, 91, 101, 311; the *Discovery*'s delayed voyage causes trouble at, vi, 92, 144; effect of the loss of *John* on trade at, xvi, 247, 249; trouble with native brokers at, 300; Jesuits at, 64; Courteen's Association claim right to trade at, 286; junks of, molested by the Dutch and Portuguese, 269, 272; Dutch President at, 26, 38; Dutch trade at, 22, 35, 36, 100, 150.
Surgeons. See Anthony, Boughton, Hinton, Lee, Pearce, Reynolds, Tindall.
Surgical instruments, 173.
Swally, 183; best time for ships to arrive at, 14, 28; Shāh Jahān's junk at, 91; dispatch of ships for and from, *passim*; building and repairing of ships at, 148, 214, 248, 311, 313; Courteen's ships at, 286, 309, 312.
Swally Hole, 9, 100, 106, 109, 183, 185, 286, 312.
Swally Marine *and* Sands, 2, 15, 61, 82, 88, 96 (2), 98, 135, 142, 159, 162, 199, 247, 248, 256, 310, 311.
Swan, the, xix, 2, 33, 97, 147, 193; master of, *see* Yates; returns to Swally from Bantam, 6, 20; encounter with Malabar pirates, 20; voyage to Bantam and back, 8, 17, 20, 34, 35 (2), 36, 37, 62, 63, 106; voyage to Cochin and Bantam, 70, 80, 86, 93, 94, 99, 127, 138; stopped and searched by the Dutch, 93, 94; designed for Coromandel Coast on return from Jambi, 134; voyage from Bantam to the Coast, 189, 190, 191; returns to Bantam, 190, 191, 193, 207, 287; voyage to Manilla, postponed, 293; sails for Swally from Bantam, 311, 312.
Sweetbag, 160.
Swinglehurst, Richard, letter to, 178.
Swordblades, 18, 302.

Table (*or* Saldanha) Bay, 109, 182.
Taels, 128, 225, 226.
Taffetas. See Cotton goods.
Taiwan. See Formosa.
Tanga, value of, 18, 64, 107.
Tanjore, Nāyak of, 47, 49; besieges Negapatam, 81. See *also* San Thomé.
Tanni (*or Tannes*). See Thān.
Tapestry, 176, 232.
Tapī Dās Pārak, 15, 21, 61, 65.

Tappi, 79 n.; see *also* Cotton goods.
Tapseels. See Cotton goods.
Taqī, Mirzā, the Itimād-uddaula of Persia, 169, 170, 171, 256, 257, 266, 268, 277, 278, 279, 282, 296, 298 n.; murder of, 296, 297.
'Tartaria', 134.
Tartars, 302; see *also* Uzbeks.
Tash, George, 4, 85, 132, 140, 163, 215, 249, 254, 259, 286, 310; honoured by Shāh Jahān, 230.
Tasman, Abel, 134 n.
Tasūs (*or Tassooes*), 299, 300.
Tatta, 234; trade at, in various commodities, 7, 94, 137, 163, 205, 211, 227, 232; factory accounts, 97, 236 n.; dyeing at, 203; Dārā Shikoh grants privileges to the English at, 163, 215. See *also* Lārībandar *and* Sind.
Taurim, 286.
Tegnapatam, 281.
Tems, Nathaniel, 132.
Tenasserim, small ships required for trade to, 229.
Thān, 37.
Thomas and John, the, 176, 198, 199, 237, 238, 241, 244, 255, 264; master of, *see* Earle.
Thurston, William, 26, 70, 90, 92, 99, 131, 132, 138, 143, 165, 178, 180, 212, 228, 250, 286, 310; letters from, *see* Basrā *and* Surat.
Tiku, 130.
Timber, trade in, 276, 283.
Timberlake, Thomas, 94.
Tin, 35, 129, 131, 220; freight rates on, 55.
'Tincal'. See Borax.
Tindall, John, 236.
Tindall, Robert, 29, 90, 180, 295, 311.
Tirell (*or* Terrell), Henry. See Tyrrell.
Tobacco, 92, 148, 161, 216, 241.
Tolā, 209, 225, 252.
Tomblings, William, death of, 244.
Tomlins (*or* Tomplins), Thomas, 178, 286.
Tortoise shells, 35, 86, 165, 201, 211.
Totty, John, 311.
'Toyes', 29.
Trade, private, 4, 11, 15, 18, 25, 29, 31, 34, 45, 51, 64 n., 72-77, 85, 86, 89, 110, 123, 124, 138, 140, 141, 144, 174, 177, 178, 202, 209, 231, 234, 235, 247, 259, 274, 298 n.
'Tranka' (trankey), 273.
Tranquebar, trade at in various commodities, 74 (2), 75, 116, 157, 159; dispatch of ships for and from, and ships at, 36, 74, 75, 119, 157; Danish ships at, 36, 156; freedom of trade at, offered to Company, 156, 157; Danish President at, *see* Pessaert.

Travell, George, 65, 132, 193, 289; letters from, see Madras.
Trumball, Andrew, 32 n., 42, 286, 295; account of the *Hopewell*'s voyages, 71–77; accusations by and against, 72–77, 101–105, 110, 118; censured and removed from his command, 74, 116, 133; reinstated, 75, 110, 112, 113, 116; petitions against his reinstatement, 111, 112.
Tulsi Dās, 210.
Tūmāns, 2, 4, 32, 135, 136, 170, 227, 266, 268, 269, 299.
Turks, 143.
Turmeric, 7, 8, 25, 27, 85, 124, 126, 136, 139, 172, 206, 255.
Turner, John, 7, 84, 132, 160, 162, 215, 230, 253, 259; honoured by Shāh Jahān, 230.
Turtles, 119.
'Tusso'. See *Tasūs*.
Tutenague. See *Jast*.
Tuticorin, 56, 252, 275, 310, 311; commodities from, 252.
Twine, Marles, 97.
Tyrrell, Henry, 196 n., 238, 245, 249, 258.

'Udpotaes', 309.
Ulysses, the, 82, 109, 121, 122.
Umra, 92.
Unity, the, 29, 62, 106; master of, see Russell.
Upaleta (or Uploat), 167 n., 217; see also Costus.
Uzbeks, 302.

Valkenburg, the, 161, 167, 216, 237, 249.
'Vals', 209.
Van der Burgh, Nikolaas, 304.
Van Sanen, Cornelis, 62.
Van Thuijnen, Hendrik, 83 n.
Veal, Thomas, 94.
Vedor da Fazenda, at Goa, 91. See also Seleina.
Vellore, 285.
Velvets, 145, 160, 227.
Venetians. See Sequins.
Vengurla, Dutch forced to abandon factory at, 22; Dutch ships and trade at, 100, 161, 167.
Venice, dispatch of letters via, 159.
Venkatagiri, 44, 80 n.
Venkatapati, King of Vijayanagar (Carnatic), 45; death of, 67, 80.
Vermilion, 67, 78, 234.
Vijayanagar (Carnatic), 47 n., 50; Mussulman invasion of, 47, 67, 80, 193, 194; proposal to abandon trade in, 48; wars in, hinder communication between factories, 56; civil war in, 55, 65, 67, 70, 115, 154, 184, 194 n.; King of Bijāpur assists in

quelling rebels in, 115, 116; King of, see Srī Ranga Rāyalu *and* Venkatapati.
Vīravāsaram, factory records, 96, 97; factors at, see Coromandel Coast.
Vīrjī Vorā, 5, 7, 8, 18, 60, 86, 99, 107, 108, 138, 140, 145, 152, 164, 204, 210, 213, 249, 253.
Vitriol, Roman, 124, 126, 172, 177.
Vizagapatam, 76.
Vliegende Hert, the, 21, 22.
Voyage, First General, v, 27, 28, 41, 142, 169; the Joint Stock use and purchase shipping of, 29, 30, 214; trade on account of, 33, 77, 78, 97, 191; funds of, used for paying Joint Stock debts, xxvii, 55, 65, 96, 113, 117, 118; accounts of, 87, 88, 170, 216, 232; dividends paid in kind, 123 (2); winding up of, 176, 191.

Walwyn, Rivett, 132, 253, 284, 299; letter from, 273.
Warner, John, 311.
Washers, 37, 290, 292.
Waterhond, the, 167, 197, 218.
Wax, 223.
Weale, William, 253; letters, 273. See *also* Basrā.
Weddell, Captain John, 219, 254, 277 n., 312 n.
Weddell, Jeremy, 312.
Weedens, the, loss of, 167.
Weijland, Cornelis, 160 n.
Weston, Humphrey, 234.
Wezel, the, 218, 248, 258.
Whatmore, Thomas, 38; letter from, 272.
Wheat, 39, 226.
Wheatley, Henry, 196 n., 238, 249, 258.
Wheeler, Thomas, 1, 132, 148; letters from, see Persia; leaves Persia, 70, 84; returns to England, 90, 143, 172.
Willemszoon, Pieter, 129.
William (1), the, xix; outward voyage of, to Bantam, 13; homeward voyage of, 57, 105.
William (2), the, master of, see Gee; outward voyage of, to Bantam, 122, 183, 310.
William, the (Courteen's ship), 10, 14, 148, 168, 180, 216, 217, 232, 254, 255, 312; master of, see Blackman.
William, the (private pinnace), 31, 298 n., 313; master of, see Stafford.
Willoughby, John, 25, 170.
Wilton, Samuel, 269, 256; letters from, see Persia.
Wine, 56, 103, 173, 176, 177, 195, 210; Canary, 16, 29, 74, 90, 145; French, 145; Portuguese, 212, 217; Spanish, 232; Dutch monopoly in, 145.
Winter, Edward, 193, 289.

INDEX

Winter, Thomas, 66, 68, 69, 72, 73, 76, 79, 97, 114, 121, 128, 134, 190, 193, 289, 294, 295; letters from, see Bantam.
Woodman, Leonard, 8, 10, 14.
Woodward, John, death of, 131.
Woollen goods, 172.
'Wormeleiton', Daniel, 1 n.
Wright, Robert, 157.
'Writers'. See Factors.
Wyche, William, 132.
Wycherley, Robert, 111.
Wylde, John, 7, 17, 23, 26, 27, 70, 90, 92, 100, 132; letters from, see Surat; death of, 161; estate of, 142, 153, 234.
Wylde, Philip, 70, 84, 98, 132, 276, 279, 282; letters from, see Persia.

Xavier, Padre Andreas, 36.

Xerafins, 60, 64, 89, 107, 154 n., 178, 217.

Yacht, 129.
Yard, John, 20, 42, 113, 310; letter from, 199; complaints and claim against, 34, 38, 70, 71, 78, 133, 190, 199, 234; recalled from Bengal, 38, 65, 77; recommends continuance of trade in Bengal, 78; censured and recalled to England, 128, 133; commended, 134, 234.
Yardly, Christopher, 289.
Yarn, coarse, unsaleable in England, 124.
Yates, Michael, 93, 99, 106, 211; his journal of the *Hopewell*'s voyage, 183.

Zarasses. See Cotton goods.
Zealand, the, 21, 260.

CORRIGENDA.

Page 193, l. 23. William Hill *should be* Thomas Hill.
,, 237, l. 20. 1644 *should be* 1645.

OXFORD: HORACE HART M.A.
PRINTER TO THE UNIVERSITY

UNIVERSITY OF TORONTO LIBRARY

Do not remove the card from this Pocket.

Acme Library Card Pocket
Under Pat. "Ref. Index File."
Made by LIBRARY BUREAU